PRAISE FOR
THE BOYS OF '67

"Thoughtful and richly detailed, this outstanding account of the early phase of the War in Vietnam takes us into the forbidding Mekong River Delta with the men of Charlie Company, to witness their harrowing firefights and their fleeting victories, to appreciate the singular combat experience haunting their dreams and those of their country."
– Hugh Ambrose, author of *The Pacific*

"Compelling... A fine blend of military and social history, sympathetic, well-written but analytically rigorous."
– Professor Gary Sheffield, *BBC History Magazine*

"A powerful account of conflict, Andy Wiest's *The Boys of '67* provides what is all-too-rare, a 'face of battle' account that is at once scholarly and well-written, perceptive and engaging."
– Jeremy Black, author of *War since 1945*

"*The Boys of '67* is an exceptionally well researched and well told story of an exceptional US Army infantry company in Vietnam."
– Brigadier General H. R. McMaster, author of *Dereliction of Duty*

"Wiest's empathy and perception make the book as emotionally compelling as it is intellectually penetrating, impossible to read with a detached mind or dry eyes."
– Dennis Showalter, author of *Hitler's Panzers*

"A remarkable book written by a master storyteller and meticulous historian."
– James H. Willbanks, PhD, Vietnam veteran and author of *Abandoning Vietnam* and *The Battle of An Loc*

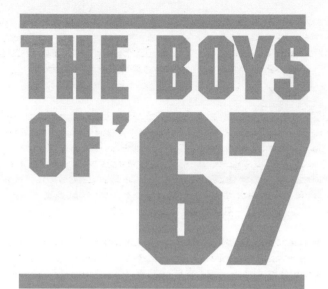

THE BOYS OF '67

OSPREY
PUBLISHING

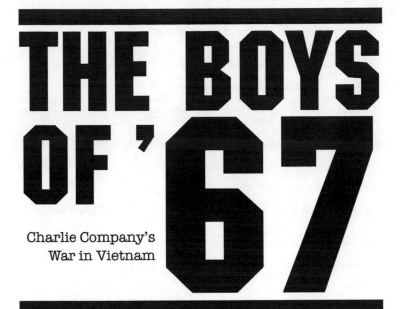

THE BOYS OF '67

Charlie Company's
War in Vietnam

Andrew Wiest

First published in Great Britain in 2012 by Osprey Publishing,
PO Box 883, Oxford, OX1 9PL, UK
1385 Broadway, 5th Floor, New York, NY 10018, USA
Email: info@ospreypublishing.com

Osprey Publishing is part of Bloomsbury Publishing Plc.

A CIP catalogue record for this book is available from the British Library

ISBN: 978 1 4728 0333 7
ePub ISBN: 978 1 78096 894 0
PDF ISBN: 978 1 78096 890 2

Index by Sharon Redmayne
Cartography by Peter Bull Art Studio
Typeset in American Typewriter, ITC Machine Std & ITC Stone Serif
Originated by PDQ Digital Media Solutions
Printed in China through World Print Ltd.

16 17 18 19   11 10 9 8 7 6 5 4 3

Osprey Publishing is supporting the Woodland Trust, the UK's leading woodland
conservation charity, by funding the dedication of trees.

www.ospreypublishing.com

EDITOR'S NOTE
The photographs included in this work are original photos taken by members of
Charlie Company. Many of the photos from Vietnam were taken early in the Charlie
Company tour before the move to the mud of the Rung Sat and the Mekong Delta.

CONTENTS

PREFACE:
MEETING CHARLIE

When I finished the book, a dog-eared copy of Ron Kovic's *Born on the Fourth of July*, I rolled over and placed it on the nightstand and turned off the light. Lying there in the combined afterglow of a good read and the dreamy feeling of the onset of slumber I knew exactly what I was going to do, but I had no idea that I had just made one of those snap decisions that changes your life forever. For those who have never been there, war is so hard to understand. So foreign. Over my years of leading classes on the history of war, I had done what I could to teach students about the realities of violent conflict, ranging from having veterans speak in class to wandering the battlefields of Europe. While standing with 25 students among the nearly endless crosses in the silent cemetery above Omaha Beach was intensely moving, the experience of war still remained elusive, somehow hovering just beyond our collective grasp. Kovic's eloquent prose, though, had forcefully reminded me that wars don't end at the cemetery. Veterans were out there, sometimes invisible in the crowd, still struggling with the painful remembrances of bygone days of battle and destruction. Before I drifted off to sleep I made up my mind to contact the local Veterans Affairs (VA) Health Care

Center to see if any of the veterans who remained under the care of the doctors there would mind sharing their experiences with the students from my class on the Vietnam War.

Once I got to work the next morning I called the main number for the VA and fumblingly tried to get my point across to a bemused operator. "How can I direct your call?" "Well, I'm not quite sure. I think I need to speak with a doctor." "Oh, are you a veteran with a health problem?" "No ma'am. I'm a history teacher, and I would like to speak with a doctor about having my class come and meet with some of the veterans there." A short pause followed as the operator tried to process the odd information. She finally responded, "I'll put you through." "Wait! Put me through to whom?" But it was too late. The phone was already ringing. The person who answered the phone identified herself as Dr Leslie Root, who was head of the post-traumatic stress disorder (PTSD) clinic. Her announcement left me in a bit of a panic. Post-traumatic stress disorder? What was that? Sure I had heard of it. Heck, I'd seen as many movies about Vietnam veterans as the next guy, but what was it really? What was I about to get myself into? At a loss regarding how to proceed, I told Dr Root about my plan. After a few minutes of conversation, during which she began my education into PTSD, Dr Root decided that some of her patients might benefit from, if not enjoy, talking about their experiences with a group of bright and interested college students. She would work to get the veterans ready; all I had to do was bring my class to the VA in two weeks' time.

Nobody quite knew what to expect that late spring day in 1997. My class and I had no real idea what PTSD was beyond the frightening, bastardized Hollywood depictions of unhinged Vietnam veterans. For the veterans who met with us, though, the situation was infinitely worse. They were about to share their most feared memories, things that had haunted them for decades – things they had not yet been able even to discuss with their closest loved ones. And they were going to share these closely guarded remembrances of horrors endured and friends lost with college students? College students had spat on them and jeered as they got off the freedom bird from Vietnam. Those college students? After everyone took their seats, there were a few tense moments before a shared realization descended upon the room.

We began to understand: these guys weren't crazy. They were just men who had seen things that were so terrible and heart-rending that they had never fully been able to forget. They began to understand: these college students weren't protestors waiting at the airport in San Francisco. They were young people who wanted to know about what had happened in Vietnam all those years ago – young people who really cared. After all these years, somebody cared about Vietnam.

The minute I walked into the room I noticed him sitting there at the table with three other veterans. He had long, graying hair that fell down beyond his shoulders, a craggy face – the kind that is etched by years of working in the sun – and wore an old military jacket bearing the roundel of the 9th Infantry Division. It was his eyes, though, that caught my attention. Gray, piercing eyes that betrayed his mistrust. The other veterans spoke movingly of their experiences in war, but this veteran held the group spellbound. The meeting was short, and the memories exchanged were by necessity fleeting snapshots of frozen moments from the jungles and rice paddies of Vietnam. Surges of death and destruction, moments of tenderness, nights of despair. As the river of memories eddied and swirled, something slowly dawned on me. He never spoke about himself, but instead about others, the boys of his unit who were boys no longer. Sometimes the verbal pictures were tragic; sometimes they were heroic – but the pictures were always of others. My notion was still vague and unformed, but I had a feeling that he was the steward of something special. After the meeting, the students and veterans shook hands and we made ready to depart. As I stood in the parking lot, the long-haired veteran walked up, fixed those eyes on me, and said that this was the first that he had ever heard of a class on Vietnam being taught at the college level. Then he asked if he could sit in the next time I taught. To this day I don't quite know why I said it, but I told him that he couldn't sit in, but if he wanted he could come and help me teach the class.

I next taught my Vietnam class the following spring semester. To be honest I was reasonably sure that this was going to be one of those nice promises that both sides mutually forget. In the intervening eight months the veteran with the haunting eyes would move on to other things, I would get lost in grading and writing and let his kind offer slip my mind, and the class would proceed as normal. But neither of us forgot, and on a cold January morning in 1998, he made the hour-long drive to meet with a fresh batch of students eager to learn about Vietnam. In those days I began my class with a movie, one made up mainly of action clips and reports from the time. After introducing the veteran to the class, I dimmed the lights and began the film. Settling back I watched as the story progressed from scenes of the Gulf of Tonkin and decision-makers in Washington, D.C. to graphic visions of firefights in the Mekong Delta. As I looked on, I noticed that my veteran visitor was holding on to his desk so tightly that his knuckles were turning white. Before I could even think that I ought to get up and stop the film, he jumped to his feet, violently kicking his desk to the side, and started yelling – screaming at the top of his lungs – and gesticulating wildly. I sat there frozen, thinking that this could not be happening as events crawled forward in slow motion. The students sat transfixed and shocked, with the sounds and flicker of the movie as mere backdrop. The veteran, wild-eyed and lost in his world of memories come to life, continued screaming – animalistic noises, unintelligible sounds. But then one phrase crystal in its clarity and meaning: "Get Down! Get Down!" He dove to the floor, gashing his forehead open on the hard concrete, and began to convulse uncontrollably.

Some students in the class, who were also Reserve Officers' Training Corps (ROTC) cadets, seized the moment and rushed to his side, elevating his feet, and making certain that he did not swallow his tongue. In the furor someone, perhaps me, called the ambulance and got in touch with Dr Root from the VA. Before the ambulance arrived, the students departed, each having to walk past the veteran still prone on the floor. His eyes, once so wild, were now still and open. Those eyes looked at each student as they walked past, but our veteran visitor was not there. He was not in those eyes. He was gone, lost in Vietnam. Outside the room, students gathered in their ones and twos, many weeping openly, as the paramedics loaded the veteran onto a gurney and took him away. I rode with him to the hospital – but I was alone. He was alone. I could only wonder at how horribly wrong it had all gone.

He just wanted to tell students about his war, about his friends, and now what was going to happen?

The veteran had been "awake" the whole time, but he came back to us in a hospital room a few hours later that day to find a doctor, me, and Dr Leslie Root all hovering nearby. It was Dr Root who told us all what had happened. He had experienced a total flashback to Vietnam, something that had never happened to him before, presumably brought on by a combination of the pressure-packed situation of coming to speak in front of a class for the first time and the battle scenes of the movie. After receiving assurances that I had done nothing wrong and that there was nothing more I could do to help, I went home. Needless to say, I didn't sleep well that night. On one hand, I couldn't stop thinking of what a horrible thing I had done – I had stepped into the world of PTSD without really even knowing what it was, much less what I was doing. I was certain that I had taken something fragile and crushed it due to my lack of care. On the other hand, I couldn't stop thinking about him. I had heard some of his story, tales of friends and violence, but I couldn't help wondering at what I had yet to hear. The stories he had yet to share. What could have happened so long ago – what events were so terribly powerful that they could reach across the decades and pull the man with the piercing eyes back into their awful embrace so thoroughly and so quickly? Part of me hoped that the veteran would have the good sense to save himself the heartache and never return to my class, but another part of me wanted nothing more than to see those haunting, haunted eyes again.

The door opened at the beginning of the next class, and there he was – complete with fresh stitches in his forehead – along with Dr Root. It took a lot of guts to walk through that door. He would much rather have faced an enemy machine gunner in Vietnam than to stand in front of a class of college students and have to explain his own human frailty – to explain how he has to live with PTSD. But he did it. He and Dr Root explained what had happened, how war had affected his very soul. The experience was powerful beyond words. From that day on the veteran came to every class, with me prattling on about facts – American troops splashed ashore outside Da Nang, air mobility a key tactic in the war – while he provided a texture and analysis that made the proceedings come alive. He could tell the students what it felt like to see a tripwire tighten around a friend's leg, how to burn leeches off with a lit cigarette, how it felt to watch someone you love die.

What began to emerge from that very first day was a Vietnam story like none I had ever before heard, a story I had somehow known was there from the very first moment I had met him. Once comfortable in a classroom setting, and sure of the fact that we meant his generation no historical harm, the veteran proved an impassioned educator, an eloquent speaker, and a fierce advocate of the men with whom he had served in Vietnam. Together we taught everywhere we could, to anyone willing to listen – in college classrooms, in church fellowship halls, and with study-abroad students in the steaming rice paddies of Vietnam. Along the way, I learned the extraordinary tale of the boys of Charlie Company, 4th Battalion of the 47th Infantry of the 9th Division in Vietnam during 1967. I heard their stories; I walked their battlefields in Vietnam; I met the boys themselves at their reunions and was welcomed with grace into their unit family. The more I heard, the more I knew that the stories were truly special, that Charlie Company occupied a unique position in the Vietnam War. There was something there that needed to be told.

In researching this project I consulted a wide variety of materials from archival sources that were especially rich given Charlie Company's place in the Mobile Riverine Force's joint army/navy command structure. Of special value were the battalion and divisional after action reports and command orders, which contained detailed descriptions of Charlie Company's every move on a day-to-day basis. The most important source for this work, though, is Charlie Company itself. Over a period of three years I was able to conduct extensive interviews with 71 officers and men who served with Charlie Company, including both of the company's commanders, one of the battalion chaplains, the company first sergeant, and two of the original four platoon leaders. To gain a fuller understanding of the reality of military life, and to learn the stories of those members of Charlie Company who did not survive Vietnam, I also conducted interviews with 21 family members of Charlie Company veterans, including wives, children, parents, and siblings. Several members of Charlie Company also generously sent me their personal papers, which included collections of letters, a diary, an abundance of newspaper clippings, training notebooks, field manuals, condolence letters, and photographs of every description. What emerged from the collection of sources was a vivid portrait of the life and times of Charlie Company; a portrait unprecedented in its completeness. Given that all of the views and details contained in this book are taken directly from interviews with the veterans and their families, footnotes will be kept to a minimum.

In the spring of 1966, while the war in Vietnam was still popular, the US military decided to reactivate the 9th Infantry Division as part of the military buildup. Across the nation, farm boys from the Midwest, surfers from California, city-slickers from Cleveland, and sharecroppers from the South opened their mail to find greetings from Uncle Sam. The newly shorn men in their ill-fitting uniforms got off the busses together at Fort Riley, Kansas, were hectored by drill instructors together in the time-honored rite of military passage, and trained together under the tutelage of officers and non-commissioned officers (NCOs) who would lead them into battle in Vietnam. Charlie Company was part of the 9th and was representative of the greater whole. Everyone was there in the newly raised company – the joker who roller skated into the company first sergeant's office wearing a dress, the nerdy guy with two left feet who would rather be off somewhere inventing computers, the gung-ho true believers bent on outshining everyone else, the everyman who just wanted to get through unnoticed, the guys who liked Motown, the guys who liked country music.

Most American soldiers of the Vietnam era trickled into the war zone as individual replacements for men who had become casualties or had rotated home, embarking on a wartime experience unparalleled in its individualism. Charlie Company, though, was different, part of the only division raised, drafted, and trained for service in the Vietnam War. During their training, the men of Charlie Company, a unit almost entirely composed of draftees, became a family without ever really knowing it. Its members entered Vietnam as brothers, sometimes squabbling, sometimes joking, sometimes missing their wives and children, but always brothers. Charlie Company was a throwback, part of an old breed. Charlie Company's experience of being drafted, thrown together, and trained for war hearkened back to the very heart of the American military tradition, a tradition that came to an end in Vietnam; a tradition that might never return, leaving Charlie Company historically the last of its kind.

The bonds of brotherhood made the Charlie Company that arrived in Vietnam in January 1967 a lethal military machine. Entering the conflict just as General William Westmoreland had finally gathered enough military force to translate his military plans into violent reality, Charlie Company faced a brutal year of relentless combat and constant loss. The 9th Infantry Division, Charlie Company's parent unit, formed the infantry component, the mailed fist, of the Mobile Riverine Force – a mix of river-borne naval power and infantry muscle designed to contest control of the populous Mekong Delta, the homeland of the Viet Cong (VC) in South Vietnam. Unlike many of their infantry brethren in Vietnam, Charlie Company usually went to work on converted landing craft instead of helicopters. Using the thousands of miles of rivers, canals, and streams that crisscross the delta, Charlie Company, along with the other units that made up the Mobile Riverine Force, searched for and sought to destroy enemy troop concentrations in the delta and wrest control of the population from the communists. The Viet Cong, though, had long dominated the region, had worked hard for years to prepare the battlefield, and were determined first to bloody and then drive off the new wave of invaders. The boys of Charlie Company entered an alien land of murderous heat, sucking mud, and unforgiving jungle. The Viet Cong had festooned the region with deadly mines and booby traps, dug defensive emplacements into thousands of rice paddy dikes – making each field a potential death trap – and hid away in the depths of steaming swamps where they could move like silent ghosts on familiar terrain while the Americans floundered in the chest-deep mud.

For a calendar year, the draftees of Charlie Company followed intelligence leads that usually proved to be stale and chased the VC across the watery landscape. On a few occasions, Charlie Company engaged with the Viet Cong, often at point-blank range, in great surges of battle, filled with death and killing. More often than not, though, Charlie Company's war took the form of endless marches through the sodden terrain in search of an elusive foe, marches that might seem only like a long walk in the hot sun at one moment but could split open into bloody violence at any turn. A sniper shot blowing open a buddy's head here, a mine ripping off a friend's legs there. War in Vietnam for the men in Charlie Company was unlike anything they could have dreamed – a war of stillness interrupted by sudden, terrible violence in which a friend was maimed or killed – an impersonal violence that all too often left the boys of Charlie Company with no targets for their rage. You can't shoot back at a booby trap.

While the continuing violence honed Charlie Company's fighting skills, the men dealt with their losses, the fear, and the killing as best they could. During their short spells of downtime, the boys of Charlie Company unburdened themselves in various manners, some of which were as old as war itself: writing letters home to loved ones, drinking, grousing about army life, sneaking out of the base to enjoy the "pleasures" of a local village, and praying. Nothing, though, could mask the truth. The inexorable crush of war, the sudden cataclysms of mass death, the broken bodies and shattered lives of comrades once so dear hardened the boys of Charlie Company. The carefree life of their youth was extinguished in a transition jarring in its suddenness. The draftees had become warriors in all of their time-honored guises – some became killers, others survivors. Some had their young souls stilled, while others turned to God.

The losses and wastage of war that so affected the men also had an indelible impact on Charlie Company itself, transforming the one-time family of brothers into a unit of near strangers that more typifies the dominant public perception of American units in Vietnam. In April 1967, just over two months after Charlie Company's arrival in Vietnam, one soldier wrote home to his parents that his platoon, which had numbered nearly 50 men when it had arrived in country, was down to only 24 originals. In September, another soldier told his parents that of the soldiers who had left Fort Riley in the entire company, which he estimated at 160 men, only 30 remained. Over time the Charlie Company that had trained together and had become true brothers-in-arms was whittled away, steadily eroded by a combination of death, crippling wounds, and a confusing system of intra-division transfers. To take the place of lost friends, brothers who had gone home in body bags or had been bundled – bleeding and broken – onto medevac choppers, came a flood of replacements. The new guys were good men faced with the unenviable task of trying to find a place in a tightly knit family. The Charlie Company originals worked well with the replacements; after all, their lives depended on it. Many were even lucky enough to find friendship. But it was a different kind of friendship, and Charlie Company was a different kind of unit. The band of brothers was gone. Those with the shared experience of training and war shrank to ever smaller groups at the core of the company. Their melody faded while the war of individual replacements came to be the dominant theme. By the end of its year in combat, Charlie Company, although still a lethal military formation, was no longer a brotherhood of draftees that hearkened back to America's military past. It had become a unit of replacements, a mixed group of veterans, draftees, new guys, and lifers. Charlie Company had come to typify an American unit in Vietnam.

In January 1968, on the eve of the Tet Offensive, the Charlie Company originals gathered in ones and twos to board the "freedom bird" for their flight back to "the world." After their unit had suffered 25 killed and 105 wounded during its year in combat, the lucky ones were going home again to reclaim their lives as postal workers, students, mechanics, farmers, husbands, sons, and Americans. But the boys of Charlie Company were returning to a country that many did not recognize. When they had received their draft notices, the nation was at peace, and support for their war was high. In 1968, though, the once nascent anti-war movement was nearing the apex of its tumultuous appeal and had begun to turn against the soldiers themselves. The returning veterans of Charlie Company were among the first to be greeted by crowds of jeering, cursing protesters. While in Vietnam, the boys of Charlie Company had heard of protests and marches, but they had never expected this: screams of "baby killer," spat curses, people throwing condoms full of urine. The members of Charlie Company, a unit so reminiscent of the American experience in World War II, were denied the victorious welcome home that their fathers and uncles had once enjoyed. There was no grateful nation waiting to absolve the boys of Charlie Company of the sins of war. The World War II experience was over; the Vietnam experience had begun.

After navigating the maze of protestors and saying their all-too-brief goodbyes to the closest friends of their lives, the boys of Charlie Company went home – some to joyous reunions, some to the hugs of children they had never before met, some to agonizing months of rehabilitation, some to prostheses and to the task of learning how to walk again. Some wives, parents, and toddlers never got the joy of a welcome home, only a flag-draped coffin. As Charlie Company shattered into its component pieces, the individual veterans and their families had to try to piece their old lives back together as best they could. For these men who had once held so much in common, reintegration into society was an intensely individual experience. There was no dominant veteran narrative of the war. Some of the members of Charlie Company locked the war away in dusty corners of their attics and got back to the business of living, working, and raising families. The war haunted others for the remainder of their days, dogging their every step with bloody memories and nights of unimaginable terror. Locked in worlds of fear, some lashed out at their loved ones, others tried to drown their feelings with a sea of alcohol, a few became homeless, and others simply went numb. Some never overcame their fear and remain consumed by a long-ago war, while others found solace and redemption in religion. Some members of Charlie Company refused to allow grievous wounds to get the best of them and learned to walk on false legs or to live life undaunted though they would never walk again. Some of the boys of Charlie Company became rich, others worked as artisans, and others were mired in poverty.

The only common thread that ties together the varied postwar experiences of the boys of Charlie Company is Vietnam. Their experience stands as unique in a war littered with military and cultural uniqueness. Plucked from society, trained and transformed into a band of brothers, the boys of Charlie Company were the last of something special in American history – the true citizen soldier at war. But the crucible of battle forged Charlie Company into something new, into a unit of replacements and individuals that came to typify the Vietnam War. That jarring transformation, along with the transformation of the country to which they returned, changed the lives of the boys of Charlie Company forever.

INTRODUCTION:
THE NEED FOR CHARLIE

Control of traffic on the inland waterways of the Mekong Delta is one of the key problems facing the Allied forces in South Vietnam. The Viet Cong presently have the freedom of movement required to support logistically all of their combat units in the Delta. Moreover, the present lack of waterways control allows them to use the Delta as a gigantic food supply depot and export foodstuffs and other material to units in other areas of the country. Freedom of movement over the waterways of the Delta also affords Viet Cong units lacking the strength of the better equipped and larger units in the Northern Corps areas, the mobility required to tie down large Government units and to exert their control over areas that would normally be beyond their influence. Viet Cong lines of communication are probably most vulnerable in the Delta.*

Order of Battle Study 66-44, VC Tactical Use of Inland Waterways in
South Vietnam, April 28, 1966

---

*   PLAF Tactics in Using Canals, Waterways, 1965. Headquarters US Military Assistance
Command, Vietnam. Office of Assistant Chief of Staff – J-2. Order of Battle Study
66-44, VC Tactical Use of Inland Waterways in South Vietnam, April 28, 1966.
Douglas Pike Collection, The Vietnam Archive, Texas Tech University

In much the same way that US forces in, for example, the Seminole War and the Civil War had used waterways to facilitate military operations, why could we not create special units equipped to utilize the extensive waterways of the Delta to get at the Viet Cong?*

General William Westmoreland

Beginning its life in a torrent of whitewater in the mountains of Tibet, the mighty Mekong River broadens and slows as it cuts through Laos and Cambodia before meandering to a near stop as it empties into the sea in southeastern Vietnam. Sometimes feared for its devastating floods, and on other occasions worshiped for the life-giving fertility of its alluvial soil deposits, the Mekong has long dominated the landscape, culture, and history of Southeast Asia. Nowhere, though, is the Mekong more important to the life of its dependent populace than where its flow slows to a crawl, allowing the river to spread out across the countryside. Fracturing and refracturing as it makes its way across its delta, the Mekong shatters into nine main channels as it nears the sea, giving the river its Vietnamese name of Cuu Long, or Nine Dragons. While nearly one-third of the delta's 15,500 square miles of wetlands consists of nonarable marsh or forest, including the fabled Plain of Reeds and the forbidding root-entangled depths of the Rung Sat mangrove swamps, the region is also one of the world's most fertile and productive for growing rice. Villages and hamlets, usually hugging the banks of their parent streams, dot the seemingly endless wet flatness of the delta, sending rice paddies large and small radiating out in all directions. In 1965 the Mekong Delta was home to an estimated 8 million inhabitants, over half of the population of the nation of South Vietnam, boasting a population density of more than 500 people per square mile.

Long ago the Vietnamese, and before them the Khmer, had learned to live in harmony with the twice-daily tidal surge and the yearly flooding of the Mekong to fuel the engine of wet rice agriculture. The ubiquitous paddies, with their countless miles of mud dikes constructed by the hands of untold generations of Vietnamese peasants acting to control and channel the Mekong's

---

* General William Westmoreland, *A Soldier Reports* (New York: Doubleday, 1976), p.208.

Map of Vietnam and Southeast Asia

bounty, are often broken by dense tree lines, which produce fruit, help control flooding, and provide shade from the usually oppressive heat. As early as ad 800, the delta population began to add further improvements to the natural drainage system by digging canals. As a result, by 1965 the delta's 1,500 miles of navigable natural waterways were supplemented by about 2,500 miles of canals. Apart from providing fertility to the land, the Mekong and its tributaries, both natural and man-made, formed the region's highway network. In vast flotillas of sampans, peasants and merchants plied the area's waters from the stilted homes of their local hamlets to join in the cacophony of waterborne traffic jams of floating markets in larger villages or cities, such as Can Tho, where farmers gathered from near and far to hawk their goods, buy needed supplies, and socialize. By the time the Americans arrived in Vietnam in great numbers in the 1960s, the delta had only one major hard-surface road – Route 4, which ran from Saigon southward to Ca Mau. While Americans were becoming even further addicted to their cars amid the hubbub of the 1960s, 90 percent of the traffic in the Mekong Delta was by boat.[*]

As the most valuable piece of real estate in South Vietnam, domination over the Mekong Delta was key to the success of both sides in the Vietnam War. For the communist insurgents the Mekong represented the most critical internal source of supplies, especially rice, and the most ready source of replacement troops for the VC. The maze of canals, rivers, and streams in the delta also provided the Viet Cong with a communication network that allowed for dispersal of supplies that had been carried down the fabled Ho Chi Minh Trail to units in the field across South Vietnam. For the United States and South Vietnam, control over the delta offered the best and quickest method by which to throttle the Viet Cong and transform the war from an insurgency to a more traditional conflict. Denying the VC access to the delta's rice harvest would effectively starve the insurgents and cause their military units to withdraw to Cambodia.

---

[*] Much of the information on the nature of the military operations in the Mekong Delta comes from Major General William B. Fulton, Vietnam Studies: *Riverine Operations, 1966–1969* (Washington, D.C.: Department of the Army, 1985), pp.17–30.

Allied supremacy in the delta would also deny the VC local recruits to make good their considerable battlefield losses. Success in the Mekong, then, held for the Allies the hope of altering the very nature of the Vietnam War.

While in some areas of South Vietnam, notably along the Demilitarized Zone, Allied forces squared off against a blend of Viet Cong insurgents and North Vietnamese Army (NVA) regulars, the war in the Mekong Delta was almost exclusively the purview of the Viet Cong. Furthest from the supplies and trained cadre of the North, the communist war in the delta formed the very heart of the insurgency. In 1966 the Viet Cong devoted a high percentage of its strength, an estimated 82,545 men, to military efforts in the delta. Of these, 19,270 were combat troops, 1,290 were support troops, 50,765 were part-time guerrillas, and 11,220 were members of the political cadre. Viet Cong penetration of the delta was often quite deep, with control over some villages and areas dating back to the early stages of the Viet Minh's war against the French. In some cases the VC presence was quite open, with major base areas in the Plain of Reeds, the U Minh Forest, and the Cam Son Secret Zone functioning as military supply depots and training sites of long standing. Often, though, VC control was covert, allowing the local apparatus of the South Vietnamese state to function while a VC shadow government levied taxes, gathered supplies, and recruited behind the scenes.

Born from the wreckage of French colonialism after Dien Bien Phu, South Vietnam had lurched from crisis to crisis, which had never allowed government institutions to penetrate the delta completely. By the early 1960s, though, the leadership in Saigon had worked hard to install its rule in the region, in part through the implementation of rural security schemes including the Strategic Hamlet Program. By 1962 much had been accomplished and the war in the delta stood at a point of stasis. However, 1963 proved to be a turning point, especially in the view of South Vietnam's American sponsors. Politically, the overthrow and assassination of South Vietnamese president Ngo Dinh Diem resulted in a period of chaos and governmental instability that had a serious impact on the fighting ability of the Army of the Republic of Vietnam (ARVN). Militarily, the outcome of two major battles in the delta caused the US to question South Vietnam's ability to survive. In January 1963 an ARVN force that enjoyed a 5:1 superiority in manpower cornered a VC unit of 300 near the village of Ap Bac. The VC, though, had fought well, downing five helicopters in the process, and survived to withdraw during the night. In December 1964 the Viet Cong 9th Division seized the village of Binh Gia. Reacting predictably to the affront, ARVN forces rushed to the scene only to be ambushed and virtually destroyed.

Judging that South Vietnam stood on the verge of defeat, the US sent its first combat forces ashore on the beaches outside Da Nang in March 1965. Initially US infantry units supported the bombing of North Vietnam, Operation *Rolling Thunder*, by guarding sensitive air bases and installations. By late 1965, though, the US mission had broadened considerably, allowing for offensive operations to find, fix, and finish the communists by locating and destroying their major troop concentrations. In considering profitable avenues of attack, the planners at Military Assistance Command, Vietnam (MACV) quickly turned their attention to the delta. Facing the Viet Cong in the region was an average of 40,000 ARVN forces, with the 7th Division at My Tho, the 9th Division at Sa Dec, and the 21st Division at Bac Lieu. Augmenting the regulars were units from the Regional Forces and the Popular Forces, undermanned and often poorly supplied local units tasked with protecting villages and districts. The success of the South Vietnamese government forces in the delta varied widely. While some areas (especially those containing Catholic villages) were considered "pacified," others were under nearly complete VC rule, with government forces in An Xuyen Province only controlling 4 percent of the countryside. In total the Viet Cong enjoyed open control of 24.6 percent of the delta, enough to choke off the critical flow of rice to the markets of Saigon. In 1963 rice arriving in Saigon had reached a high of about 4.5 million tons, but by 1966 that total had dropped to 3.3 million tons, making it necessary to rely on imports.

Although MACV did not believe that ARVN forces in the delta were on the verge of defeat, the resurgence of the Viet Cong in the area in July 1965 prompted Brigadier General William DePuy

– MACV assistant chief of staff for military operations – to direct a study on basing US troops in the delta. A unique difficulty, though, quickly came to light. Given the waterlogged nature of the terrain, coupled with its dense population, there was no uninhabited land area available large enough to house a sizeable US troop population. In addition, although the vast, flat expanses of the delta were conducive to helicopter operations, the lack of roads would make supplying and maneuvering a concentration of US forces nearly impossible. While the planning staff developed the innovative idea of *creating* a base by dredging silt from the bottom of the Mekong to form new land where none had existed, others focused on the past to find a solution for the riddle of operating in the delta.

The French, in operations later continued by the South Vietnamese, had utilized troops and firepower based aboard flotillas of modified World War II-era landing craft to combat the Viet Minh along the river networks of Vietnam. The flotillas, known as *Dinassauts*, had achieved considerable success both in supplying distant outposts and in providing tactical mobility. MACV planners took the concept one step further, contending that massive LSTs (landing ship, tank) could be converted into floating barracks, which, when grouped together, could form a mobile floating base from which entire American brigades could operate. The Mobile Afloat Force, as the idea was originally known, had the advantage that it could shift its location across the delta to hound the Viet Cong troops no matter where they fled. When briefed on the idea, Rear Admiral Norvell Ward agreed that the rather outlandish concept had merit.

In early December 1965, DePuy impressed Westmoreland with a briefing on his plans, which came to include both the construction of a land base and the formation of the Mobile Afloat Force. After assent to the scheme by Westmoreland's superiors at Headquarters, Pacific Command, the Joint Chiefs of Staff in Washington, D.C. tentatively approved an additional infantry division for use in the delta, initially designated "Z Division." The planning finally culminated on March 15 with a MACV study, "Mekong Delta Mobile Afloat Force Concept and Requirements," which laid out the detailed blueprint, ranging from logistic support to proposed dredging operations, for basing US infantry in the delta.

During final planning for the Mobile Afloat Force plan in Saigon, the Joint Chiefs gave the go ahead to reactivate the 9th Infantry Division at Fort Riley, Kansas, to serve as "Z Division" in the Mekong Delta. The choice to reactivate the 9th Division was no accident. Westmoreland himself had seen extensive service with the 9th in World War II, commanding the 60th Infantry and serving as chief of staff of the division in both France and Germany. The strategic decision arrived at in the halls of power in Washington had the effect of tossing a rock into the American national pond, causing ripples that reached into living rooms and dining rooms across the nation that changed many young lives forever.

PRELUDE:
LOSING THE BEST WE HAD

May 18

1 Year and 1 Day [since being drafted]

Dear Mom, Dad, and Fran,

I shouldn't tell you this, but you'll worry anyway, so I'll tell you. We ran into a battalion of 300 VC ... and they pinned us down... It started about 11 A.M. and we were still there at 6:30 that evening! I always thought I'd be scared to death in a situation like that, but you don't have time. When you hear a bullet go by (and you can hear it!) you just look around and say "you dirty son of a ____ " and fire back. You are so excited that you don't even think, you don't have to, you react. You're laying there, 40 guys, knowing that there is a hell of a lot of Charlies out there and all of a sudden the jets start bombing and strafing, artillery zeroes in, and the helicopter gunships start their destruction. And then you feel like you just won the Irish Sweepstakes! Your wife had a baby! Or the Cubs won the World Series! Probably all 3 rolled into one. Charlie started out with 300 guys that day, and left 150 lying in the field when he pulled out at nightfall. It is not good to kill, but it also is worse to be killed and I can't say that I have a guilty fiber in my body.

Love, Jim [Dennison]

On the evening of May 15, 1967, the bone-weary draftees of Charlie Company settled down into their night defensive positions, but few of the exhausted men could sleep. Some tossed and turned in the mud, while others gathered in small groups and discussed in hushed tones the adrenalized yet devastating events of the day.

It had been a day like any other, more notable for boredom and exhaustion than imminent death. With uniforms soaked to the skin in the 110-degree heat and unable to walk along the dikes, which were likely to be mined or booby trapped, the men had humped M16s, LAWs (Light Anti-Armor Weapons), M60 machine guns, spare ammo, spare barrels, and radios through the sucking, leech-infested paddy mud. Dug into invisible bunkers amid the dense foliage, a reinforced company of Viet Cong had waited until 1st Platoon had reached the middle of a wide paddy, where there was no cover, before springing a well-laid ambush, raking the Americans with small arms and automatic weapons fire. Amid the sudden fury a few GIs froze, one even lost control of his bowels, but the vast majority of the Charlie Company draftees reacted as their months of training had dictated. While the 2nd and 3rd platoons lay down a covering fire, the 1st and 3rd squads of 1st Platoon were able to scramble to cover behind nearby rice paddy dikes. The men of 2nd Squad, though, had been caught too far out in the open and fell where they had stood.

The battle had raged for most of the day; Charlie Company had attempted both to flank the well-concealed enemy positions and to rescue its fallen even as air and artillery strikes turned the tide against the Viet Cong. Finally, as evening neared, facing certain death at the hands of overwhelming American firepower, the surviving VC had burst into the open in a desperate bid to flee their crumbling bunkers. It had been a powerfully cathartic moment for the men of Charlie Company. After months of taking losses to unseen enemy snipers or booby traps and a day of battle against invisible foes in bunkers, there they were – live VC. Mud-spattered, black pajama-clad Victor Charles. Fire rang out from M16s, M60s, LAWs, and grenade launchers, and the killing was prodigious. With dead VC littering the landscape as night fell, by any accounts Charlie Company's battle had been a victory.

It was neither their victory nor the killing that were the main topics of quiet conversation that night. The firefight had been Charlie Company's first major engagement – its baptism of fire – and, amazingly, it had taken place exactly one year to the day after most of the men in the company had opened their mailboxes to find their draft notices. In the eerie calm that follows battle, and as the heat slowly dissipated in the tropic night, the men of Charlie Company spoke of loss – the abrupt and brutal loss of friends with whom they had trained, sweated, and toiled for a year of military life; the loss of their brothers.

Fourteen men had been wounded that day. While some of their wounds had been slight, others had been ghastly. Charlie Nelson, a Navajo Indian of whom the men of Charlie Company had become quite protective because of his diminutive stature, had been shot through the neck while attempting to help a buddy and had later received a second wound when a Viet Cong bullet sliced through his knee. Dave Jarczewski, who had stooped to help the fallen Nelson, had been shot through the shoulder. The bullet had exited through his back resulting in internal injuries that had left Jarczewski gasping for breath and turning blue as he hovered near death. Steve Huntsman had been hit in the arm, severing an artery that spewed a fountain of blood each time his heart beat. James "Smitty" Smith had hit the ground and held his arms in front of his head; the bullet that struck his forearm otherwise would have hit him square in the face. Tony Caliari had a bullet pass through his lower leg, shattering the bones and leaving his foot flopping uselessly. The explosion of a rifle grenade had left Don Trcka with wounds to his stomach and jaw, and he had also been shot through the arm. Worst, perhaps, was Carl Cortright, a recent replacement who was on one of his first operations with Charlie Company. Caught with those unlucky few who were furthest from cover, Cortright had been shot below the breastbone, and the bullet had exited through his spine, leaving him paralyzed. After lying helplessly for hours, Cortright had finally been rescued but had to be manhandled over the protective rice paddy dike, resulting in excruciating agony.

Emergency medevac helicopters had rushed to the scene to retrieve the most badly wounded. There had been no time for niceties, for speed was critical to saving lives. As the battle continued to rage, those who were still sound had wrestled the shattered bodies of their brothers onto the choppers, which had then sped them to hospitals at Dong Tam and Bien Hoa. For those who remained behind on the battlefield that night, dealing with the wounded had been jarring and unsettling. These men with whom they had trained, whose letters from home they had shared, were simply gone. One minute they were there like always, the next they were covered in their own blood, the tips of broken bones protruding from their wounds. Then they were simply and abruptly gone.

Whether silently wrapped in personal remembrance or in quiet commiseration with others, on the night of May 15 the thoughts of everyone in Charlie Company centered on the death of Don Peterson. "Pete," as he was known to many, had been a strapping kid from California. Good looking, and with an easy sense of humor, Peterson was respected and universally liked. In a group made up almost wholly of young men aged 19–21, Pete stood out from the crowd as one of the few who were married. While at Fort Riley, Pete and his wife Jacque had shared a cramped, off-base apartment with two of the other married couples from the unit, Don and Sue Deedrick and Steve and Karen Huntsman. Even the most convinced bachelors of Charlie Company felt an affinity for those few in their midst who had chosen to take on the responsibility of marriage amid the uncertainty of training for war and respected the difficulties the young couples faced. For Pete, though, the bonds of friendship with the men of Charlie Company had run even deeper. Just before his departure for Vietnam, Jacque had given birth to the couple's first child, Jimmy. Having spent only a few moments with his son before departing, Pete had carried a single picture of the child to Vietnam – a picture that everyone in Charlie Company knew well. Pete had never tired of showing that picture off – to audiences from sweaty base camps to muddy foxholes – always ready to talk about the future that he planned to share with his son. Although half a world away, through quiet conversations with a proud father amid the crucible of war, the men of Charlie Company had become Jimmy Peterson's surrogate uncles and cousins.

Pete had been hit in the chest by a burst of Viet Cong fire as he had tried to cover 2nd Squad's retreat from the kill zone, but it was near dusk before two members of 1st Platoon, Doug Wilson and John Bauler, had been able to retrieve Pete's body from the battlefield. Heavy enemy fire, the need to evacuate the badly wounded who still had a chance of survival, the rush to resupply dwindling ammo reserves, and the need to keep down during incoming friendly artillery fire and jet strikes – the symphonic chaos of battle – had all taken precedence. As darkness fell First Sergeant Lynn Crockett, a hard-bitten farm boy from Kentucky who had turned career soldier, knew the difficult truth. There would be no more evac flights; Pete would spend one more night with Charlie Company. Standing 6 feet 5 inches tall, features chiseled by a lifetime of hard work, Crockett was the looming figure who had met the bewildered Charlie Company recruits as they arrived at Fort Riley. While he had been a feared and respected presence during training, making liberal use of his booming voice and the colorful lexicon of a drill sergeant, over the past year Crockett had become quite close to his men and knew that the difficult night ahead was going to be a formative moment for the company. Their year of training and war had been invaluable in that it had given Charlie Company a sharp edge, but Crockett also knew that his men had become brothers in the process, brothers who now had to wrestle with the loss of one of their own.

Determined to do what he could to help, Crockett began to make the rounds to speak to his men. The first man Crockett met was Ben Acevedo. Of Hispanic descent, "Ace," as he was known to all in Charlie Company, was the son of rural farm laborers in the Yakima Valley, Washington, and had taken an instant liking to Don Peterson in training. Ace struggled to understand the value of Pete's sacrifice. In tears, Ace asked Crockett, "First Sergeant, what the hell are we doing over here?" With a pat on the shoulder Crockett replied, "Son, we are over here because our country sent us over here. We are here to do our job."

As Crockett walked further he came to a small knot of silent men gathered around Pete's body. In that group was John Young, a short, wiry Minnesotan. Unlike most of Charlie Company, Young was not a draftee but instead had actively sought service in

Vietnam. With a keen sense of duty, and afraid that the war would end before he could play his part, Young had dropped out of the University of Minnesota to enlist. A gung-ho true believer, Young found it jarring to deal with the loss of someone so close and with so much to live for, killed before his very eyes. When Crockett appeared, Young, through his tears, released a burden of regret that was common to the men of Charlie Company: "First Sergeant, we just couldn't find him out there; we just couldn't find him." Young had been part of a group of volunteers that had searched the battlefield under heavy enemy fire to retrieve the wounded – a group that had not been able to save Pete. Now Young and the others lived with that guilt – could they have saved him? Should they have saved him? Crockett did what he could to console the men. It had not been their fault. He stressed the brutal reality of combat; young men die – good young men, young men with everything to live for – and there was nothing that other young men, no matter how devoted and able, could do to change that.

All across their night defensive positions, the men of Charlie Company dealt with the losses of the day. Jim Dennison, a hardscrabble city kid whose father owned an Irish pub in Chicago, could not bring himself to look in the direction of Pete's body, feeling that if he didn't look it would not be real. But it was real, and had a transformative effect on the young Cubs fan. Before May 15, Dennison believed in the war, but after the loss of Peterson and the maiming of so many others he felt that his emotional spinal cord had been severed. As he sat there that night, the same refrain ran through his mind over and over: "The war ain't fuckin' worth it. It ain't fuckin' worth it." Even as he wrestled with the eternal question of the value of war against the price of losing friends, Dennison's mind shifted course – a course common for young men in combat that eventually exacted a heavy price of guilt. He had loved Pete, and grieved for his young family – but after the intensity of battle Dennison was still alive, his dreams intact. Even though Pete was his hero and he had so much to live for, Dennison couldn't help thinking, "Thank God it was him and not me."

James Nall had developed a special relationship with Don Peterson. A poor black kid from the streets of Fairfield, Alabama, Nall had grown up with the harsh reality of segregation. Only permitted to drink from "colored" water fountains, Nall had never even tasted "white water" until he arrived at Fort Riley. Initially Nall had been very unsure about what his relationship with white soldiers would be like – until he met Pete. The happy-go-lucky Californian had only limited interaction with blacks before joining the military, but his easy demeanor immediately impressed Nall, and the two had become fast friends, with Nall being one of the first to learn of the birth of Pete's son. Crouched in a foxhole within sight of Pete's body, Nall realized that his whole life had had been changed. It had taken a while for it to set in, but Pete was gone – this war was for keeps. Nall had lost a friend, one who had introduced him to a new way of looking at the world, but his thoughts that night ran deeper and were more visceral. Before May 15, Nall, with the sure invulnerability of youth, had believed that he could not die in Vietnam. But there was Pete, lying close by – a body beginning to smell after a day in the tropic sun – death had become real. Shaking both from the residual fear of the day and the onset of the relative cool of the night, Nall realized that anyone could die at any time in Vietnam. There was no such thing as invulnerability; there was only death.

Manning a defensive position in a nearby tree line, Doug Wilson, who had helped to carry Pete's body from the battlefield, had an eerie feeling as he heard quiet sobbing around him break the silence that night. Wilson was a kid from California, like Pete, who had been too interested in surfing to keep up his college grades, which had resulted in a surprise draft notice from Uncle Sam. Like everyone else, Wilson wept for Pete and for his wife and child, but as the night went on his thoughts drifted to the juxtaposition of the banality of war set alongside the human emotional shock of battle and loss. Pete was dead, and the wounded were struggling for their lives, but the war went on. Night defensive positions had to be dug and manned, supplies gathered, and tomorrow would be just another day of slogging through rice paddies looking for Viet Cong. The war didn't care about Pete, or Cortright, or Jarczewski, or the hundreds of enemy dead, or the strained nerves of the survivors – the war went on. To Wilson what had started as a job, or perhaps even a needed crusade, now seemed a slow march toward a distant goal. Reality became clear – it didn't matter how good or bad the next day was, the war was going to go on for another eight months or until the enemy got him too. And if he died, the men of Charlie Company would throw him onto a helicopter and continue their lives as their war marched on.

The next morning, as the men of Charlie Company gathered their gear and made ready to move out, a single helicopter arrived to take away the body of Don Peterson. The only other passenger on that chopper was Bill Reynolds, who was being sent to the rear to receive treatment for a painful cyst. Raised outside Los Angeles, Reynolds had been crazy about cars and loved the cruising and drag racing scene. Reynolds, like so many others, had looked up to Pete as a larger than life, heroic figure. As he squatted beside Pete and the chopper took off for the short ride back to the divisional base area at Dong Tam, the wash of the rotor blades blew the poncho off of Pete's body. For the remainder of the flight, Reynolds could not take his eyes off Pete. With tears running down his face, he thought, "Oh my God, if they can get Pete, we're all in big trouble."

1 WHO WAS CHARLIE?

Selective Service System
ORDER TO REPORT FOR INDUCTION

The President of the United States,	Local Board No. 67
To Timothy D.	Fischer Lake County
	Rm. 115, WACO Bldg
	25 East Earle Street
	Painesville, Ohio 44077

Greeting:

You are hereby ordered for induction into the Armed Forces of the United States, and to report at Painesville Post Office Lobby on May 18, 1966 at 6:45 AM DST for forwarding to an Armed Forces Induction Station.

M. J. Nolan
(Member or Clerk of Local Board)

A year prior to their trial by fire, Charlie Nelson, Doug Wilson, James Nall, Don Peterson, and all the rest were young men in the prime of their lives – racing cars in the California twilight, dancing to records in basements with their best girls, working in jobs, and trying to make a future. But decisions made by distant men in fine suits and immaculately pressed uniforms were about to change everything; decisions that would put an end to the carefree days of youth and begin a burst of blended violence and brotherhood that would dominate the lives of the boys of Charlie Company for the remainder of their days. In 1966 President Lyndon Johnson, on advice from Secretary of Defense Robert McNamara, General Westmoreland, and the Joint Chiefs of Staff, approved a massive troop buildup in Vietnam, resulting in a total draft call during 1966 of 382,010, the largest single yearly draft call of the Vietnam War. As part of the call-up of May 1966, telegrams went out from draft boards all over the United States to fill the ranks of the newly reactivated 9th Infantry Division, and Charlie Company was born.

The men of Charlie Company represent only a tiny slice of the vast Vietnam-era draft, and a breakdown of the unit's makeup cannot pretend to stand as representative of the demographic service experience of the war. Charlie was special in many ways. While draftees made up roughly only 33 percent of the total US military force sent to Vietnam during the conflict, Charlie Company was 99 percent draftee.* The experience of the men of Charlie Company was more reflective of their World War II-era fathers and uncles rather than of those who followed them into the rice paddies and jungles of Vietnam. Drafted before the war had become controversial, the conscripts of Charlie Company uniformly saw their service as a rite of passage – the duty of any American male during wartime.

While the boys of Charlie Company came from across the nation, a total of 36 percent of the unit's draftees hailed from the American West, with 26 percent of the company coming from California alone, especially the Los Angeles area. Stories about surfing, drag racing, and the ever-present music of the LA scene became a staple of Charlie Company base camps. Another 31 percent of Charlie Company came from the Midwest, with draftees from Cleveland accounting for 10 percent of the unit's

---

* Christian Appy, *Working-Class War: American Combat Soldiers and Vietnam* (Chapel Hill: University of North Carolina Press, 1993), p.28. Appy also points out that a further 33 percent of US military servicemen during Vietnam enlisted due to the pressure of the draft.

strength. Draftees from the South comprised 30 percent of Charlie's total, and included a concentration of 17 percent of the unit's men hailing from Texas and Louisiana.

Only 2 percent of the men of Charlie Company claimed a privileged or upper-class background, while 31 percent were members of the middle class – sons of businessmen, professionals, and skilled workers. A total of 25 percent of the unit identified themselves as of lower middle-class status, while 42 percent came from poor families. Members of these socio-economic groups included the sons of manual laborers, sharecroppers, farmers, and migrant workers. Strikingly, though, the class background of Charlie Company seems almost disconnected from the educational background of the unit's draftees. Only 4 percent of the unit's members were school dropouts, while 50 percent came to military service with a high school diploma and 46 percent of the men of Charlie Company entered service with some college experience, ranging from technical school to junior college to attendance at major universities. The generation of 1966 wanted something better than the lives that their depression-era parents had known.

The racial makeup of Charlie Company was representative of the American military of the 1960s – 68 percent of the unit was white, 15 percent black, and 13 percent Hispanic. (The remaining percentage was made up of Asian Americans and Native Americans, but these figures were very low.) While the Civil Rights Movement had passed its legislative peak by 1966, many of the members of Charlie Company came either from segregated communities or areas of little racial diversity. Training at Fort Riley served as the unit's melting pot, throwing whites, blacks, and Hispanics together for the first time. The racial breakdown of Charlie Company also closely reflects the unit's social geography. Approximately 23 percent of the members of Charlie Company hailed from urban environments, ranging from the mean streets to brownstone walkups. Another 42 percent of the draftees came from the country's societal "middle ground," the suburbs and mid-sized towns – the iconic America of the 1950s. A final 34 percent of the unit's members lived in rural areas, on independent farms or tiny villages, some of which still sported one-room schoolhouses.

Charlie Company was overwhelmingly young – with 90 percent of the draftees aged 22 or younger – and over 70 percent single, giving the unit the vibrancy of youth and the social hum of young men wanting to get the most out of life. The unit was indeed something of a boys' club – complete with the hi-jinks, excesses, and exuberance to be expected from a group of young men thrown together in time of war. However, there was a leavening of "older" men in the unit, who, while they were the same age, arguably had to mature more quickly due to family obligations, including the 18 percent of the men who had children either before they departed for the war or whose children were born during their tour in Vietnam.

Don Peterson was born in 1947 in Salinas, California. Following what work he could find as a house painter, Don's father, Pete, moved the family several times before settling in Arroyo Grande near Pismo Beach. With little money to spare, in part due to Pete's heavy drinking, Don and his brothers Bob and Rich had to work to help make ends meet. A strapping young man with piercing eyes, Don was bright, good looking, and popular, but he never believed that school was going to be very important since he was going to grow up to be a painter like his father. What interested Don the most was the sports scene. Both he and his brother Bob, only 14 months his senior, were high school football stars, Don at center blowing open running lanes for Bob at fullback.

One day, while walking along Pismo Beach, Don struck up a conversation with Jacque McMullen, a beautiful, dark-skinned girl with a vaguely French accent. Jacque was quite taken with Don, and asked him to the Sadie Hawkins dance. Don accepted, and the two began something of an on-again, off-again romance. As the two got to know each other better, Jacque found herself infatuated with this boy who always looked straight at her, was always interested in what she had to say, and was always cheerful. Don was just different than the other boys – somehow more serious and at the same time more playful. The young couple loved to stroll down the beach, she in her bikini and Don, muscular and tanned, shirtless and in Levis, talking about everything under the sun, until Don broke away to pull his favorite prank – running down the beach and working up enough speed to do a back flip into the surf. He would always land on his back with a thud amid a gale of laughter.

Life for the couple changed with Don's graduation in 1964. Jacque, two years Don's junior, remained in school, while Don went to work with his father and his older brother Bob, roaming up and down the California coast painting houses. Don saw Jacque less and less and even had to miss her junior prom to help his father, who had been evicted from his apartment. About to lose his girl, and forced to consider his future, Don Peterson decided that he wanted something different, something more than the life he was leading. In March 1966 Don, perhaps lacking a bit in the romantic category, phoned Jacque to ask for her hand in marriage, promising that they would leave California and begin a new life together. Two weeks later the couple, she 17 and he 19, was wed in a small ceremony in his grandparents' home. Although the newlyweds could only afford a spartan apartment, life together was wonderful, beyond what they could have hoped. Don worked hard, while Jacque learned to keep house. They were going to make something of themselves. By May Jacque suspected that she might be pregnant, and she went to the doctor for confirmation. After the test came back positive, Jacque drove home and, like any new mother-to-be, nervously wondered how her husband would take the news. When she opened the door she found Don standing there with a letter in his hand – it was his draft notice.

A deeply religious man who would serve, in part, as Charlie Company's conscience, Gary Maibach hailed from Sterling, Ohio, a town of about 300 people south of Cleveland. His great grandfather, who was a minister in the Apostolic Christian Church of America, had moved to the area to farm in 1899. Maibach's grandfather also remained active in the small, fundamentalist denomination, and founded a general store in Sterling, which, by the time of Gary's birth, was a bustling concern, employing his father Elmer, and there was never a doubt that Gary too would grow to play his part in the family business. Although his father was not involved in the church,

Gary's mother, Alma, was a staunch believer, and Gary attended services every Sunday, perched on the pew next to either his mother and grandfather. Upon graduation from high school in 1962, Gary enrolled in a small, religiously affiliated college in Cleveland to pursue a degree in business, which he hoped would benefit the family store. Even though he did well in his classes, Gary felt that his life was adrift and believed that he was headed in the wrong direction. After considerable soul-searching, he decided to return home and devote more time to his faith and to his family. Welcomed into the fold, Gary labored diligently on his life of faith, while also being groomed for positions of importance in the family business. Gary's young life seemed complete when he wed his sweetheart, Mary Ann, in 1965.

The Maibach family had a strong recent military tradition, with Gary's father and three uncles all serving in World War II – his father as part of the finance department of the Manhattan Project. Matters were complicated, though, by the family's religious beliefs. Founded by a Swiss seminary student in the 1820s, the Apostolic Christian Church had a long history of non-resistance. While most of the young men in the church believed that they could accept military service, they refused to carry or use weapons. Although there had been some problems with the conscientious objector (CO) status of members of the faith in World War I, by the time of Vietnam the CO status was a given, with the church becoming something of a traditional source of combat medics. Registered as a CO, Gary was ready to serve when his final draft notice arrived in early 1966. Newly pregnant with their first child, Mary Ann was initially somewhat shocked by the news, knowing that her husband was headed to war. But her faith was deep, and she realized that her husband would be saving, not taking, lives. As he boarded the bus to begin his service, though, Gary Maibach couldn't help but wonder what kind of reception he would get from his fellow draftees. How would they, who were preparing to become killers, accept a quiet, deeply religious CO in their midst?

One of Charlie Company's group of Hispanic soldiers, who would come to call themselves the "Santa Anna Brigade," Jimmie Salazar was born to a family that had long lived on the outskirts of Austin, Texas. One of seven children, Jimmie was raised as a migrant worker. Unable to read or write, or to speak much English, Jimmie's father worked following the crops around Texas, but eventually bought a small house in east Austin, in the "ghetto part of town." For half of the year, the family would be resident in Austin, where Jimmie was able to attend school. For the other half of the year, Jimmie and the other Salazar children followed their parents working in the fields of Texas. Living in the rough migrant camps, with little running water or amenities of any kind, the Salazars moved from field to field, picking cotton or vegetables, cutting sugar cane – a hard regimen of manual labor and a life of poverty.

After graduation from high school in 1965, Jimmie fell in love with a young woman named Aurora Gonzalez. Aurora was also from a poor family, one of nine children whose mother worked as a maid. At the tender age of 12, Aurora took a job as a waitress to help make ends meet. While visiting Austin one morning, she met Jimmie in a chance encounter on a street corner. After a whirlwind courtship, though Jimmie was 18 and she was merely 14, the young couple made plans to marry and move to the big city to seek their fortune. Aurora worked with her mother to plan a dream wedding scheduled for May 1966, and had their initial meeting with the Salazars to discuss details of the ceremony and the reception. The excitement was palpable, but as the meeting drew to a close the mail arrived, with Jimmie's draft notice.

Aurora was devastated; her dream wedding would have to wait, and her fiancé was off to war. Jimmie's reaction to the news, though, was more mixed. He desperately wanted to marry Aurora, and told her that they would wed after his basic training. But he also wanted to find a better life than the one of poverty he had known. Since he had been unable to secure a job at the post office, perhaps military service would provide him with another way forward. Even though he had heard of Vietnam, and knew that he might be headed there, Jimmie boarded the bus for San Antonio a happy man, looking forward to a bright future.

Part of both Charlie Company's sizeable African-American and southern contingents, Willie McTear was born in tiny Newellton, Louisiana, 22 miles southwest of the famous Civil War battlefield at Vicksburg, Mississippi. With father Willie working as an independent logger in the nearby forests and mother Mary bringing in money both as a seamstress and a hairdresser, Willie and his three siblings were poor, but their family support network was so strong that the children never realized the extent of their poverty.

With the Civil Rights Movement at its height, race relations in rural Louisiana were especially tense. During his youth, McTear witnessed several white beatings of local blacks, who were thrown in jail if they resisted and were only released when a local white farmer came in to vouch for their future good behavior. In 1955, the same year that Emmett Till was murdered in nearby Mississippi, Willie McTear was grabbed off the street by a group of local white citizens and hauled to the courthouse, where he was falsely accused of having made a harassing phone call to the wife of the local white sheriff. While one officer held Willie down across the desk, another began to beat him with a belt and told him to confess. One of Willie's cousins had witnessed his abduction and contacted his mother, who put out the call for the extended family to gather at the local calaboose where they began a protest to gain Willie's release. While the crowd grew, Willie's parents argued to the white authorities that their 12-year-old son was innocent and too young even to have considered harassing the sheriff's wife. Outside the jail local members of the Ku Klux Klan gathered to arrange a lynching party. Sensing that his town was about to erupt into a race war, the sheriff relented, releasing Willie into the custody of his family. Scarred by the ordeal, Willie McTear wondered if he would ever be able to trust whites again.

Neither of his parents had graduated from high school, and most of his friends wanted to grow up to be farmers. But Willie wanted much more. He hated working in the fields, and did not want to go into logging with his father; both avenues seemingly led only to a continued cycle of poverty. Willie decided instead to throw himself into his schoolwork. He wanted to go to college. He wanted to amount to something in a world that was trying to hold him down at every turn. His desire, though, caused conflict with his parents. Willie Senior valued hard work above all else, and had little time for folks who put on airs and went to college. He wanted his son to join him in the logging business – good, physical labor.

Mary, who had taken classes and earned her GED at 40, had more sympathy for her son's dreams. However, even Mary, with the family's precarious financial situation and the social odds stacked against a young black man, feared that her son's hopes would be dashed by bitter reality.

After high school Willie kept his dream alive by enrolling part time at Southern University. He still had to work to make ends meet, though, so Willie spent part of each year living with one of his older brothers in Las Vegas and working multiple jobs to pay for his college tuition. Although he had no social life because he spent all of his time either working at his two jobs or studying for class, Willie was happy and content. With little opportunity to read or reflect, Willie was oblivious to events unfolding a world away in Vietnam, and was unaware that his on-again off-again college schedule left him without a deferment and vulnerable to the draft. Finally classified as a junior after nearly four years, Willie was hard at work at his two Vegas jobs when he came home to his brother's apartment one day to find his draft notice. There were no thoughts of running away to Canada, no thoughts of any possible racial injustice at work. Willie had been called to do his duty and would go. He would go to war, but of more immediate concern, he was about to enter his first fully integrated institution and would have to interact with whites – the very people that the Jim Crow system had long portrayed as his betters. McTear couldn't help wondering what life with white people was going to be like.

Many of Charlie Company's draftees hailed from the Los Angeles area and had even known each other well in high school. Born in Los Angeles, Larry Lilley was the oldest of Barbara and Larry Lilley's three children. With the elder Larry working as a doorknob polisher for Kwikset Lock Company, the family struggled to make ends meet. Certain that there was something better out there, and fascinated with motorcycles, Larry's father eventually changed jobs and went to work for a local motorcycle dealership, taking his seven-year-old son with him to do odd jobs on the weekends. In between bouts of sweeping or emptying the garbage, young Larry got a chance to watch mechanics tinker with the machines. The smell of the oil, the roar of the engines, the entire motorcycle culture – well, it was all intoxicating to the young lad. His future was set, and it was motorcycles. With his eldest son constantly at his side, Larry Senior worked his way up through the ranks and by 1957 owned his own Triumph dealership in Lancaster – a town of 8,000 in the high desert.

Young Larry soaked up the motorcycle life, spending every spare moment away from his work and school tinkering on his own bikes and racing them in the California desert. Life was fun, albeit dirty and sweaty, and Larry immediately became something of a young sensation, defeating nearly all of his older peers. Throwing himself into the racing scene, Larry prospered and soon came to the attention of Honda, which became his sponsor – providing him with bikes and maintenance. All he had to do was show up at the racetrack with a suitcase full of leathers and a helmet. With Honda's support, Larry raced in and won events across California, and by 1961 – at the age of 15 – it seemed he was ready for the big time. Honda even sponsored its young prodigy in the 250cc class undercard to the main event at Florida's legendary Daytona Speedway, and he won. Larry returned home to a hero's welcome, heady stuff for a high school sophomore.

Once high school was complete, Larry took a step closer to adulthood by moving out of his parents' house and getting his own place, sharing an apartment with childhood friend Kenny Frakes. The two had grown up a block apart, and had been classmates since grade school. Kenny's father, Bob Taylor, owned a local Chevron gas station, which led the boys to bond while working on engines – with Kenny forever trying to whip his old beater into street shape. While Larry had been the local motorcycle hero, Kenny had been no slouch, starring on both the high school track and wrestling teams. Their other closest running buddy from high school, Tim Johnson, lived just a few blocks over. Tim was less athletically inclined and had instead been more of the joker of the crowd, a jovial free spirit, keeping the mood light no matter what the situation. The level-headed son of hard-working parents, Tim had gotten a job working for General Telephone right after graduation and hoped one day to save enough money to go to college and have his own business. After the shock of opening his own draft notice, Larry leafed further through the stack of mail only to find his roommate Kenny's draft notice as well. It seemed as if the two friends would remain together in life just a bit longer. Completing the surreal day was a phone call from Tim Johnson announcing that he, too, had been drafted.

Unable to believe the coincidence, Larry, Kenny, and Tim got together to discuss their future. There had been rumors that other draftees in the area had run away to Canada to avoid service. The thought ran through the conversation for a few minutes and then died away. Larry shook his head in thought and said, "I'd rather go to a foreign land and fight the war there than have the war come to knock on our own doorsteps." Frakes and Johnson nodded their heads in agreement. They knew that it was going to be a tough job, but somebody had to do it, and it might as well be them. On the day of their induction, Barbara Lilley picked the three boys up in her car, and they drove as a group – just like they had once gone to the movies together on the weekend. But the conversation was deadly serious. Kenny Frakes nervously fiddled with the door handle before saying, "I just can't shake the feeling that I'll never come back from Vietnam." Tim Johnson looked his buddy up and down and asked him what the hell he was thinking before adding, "I'm not sure I'll make it either." Larry Lilley couldn't believe what he was hearing. "You two can't get started with such negative feelings. I tell you what, I know I'm coming home from Vietnam, and you two are coming home too. And that's all there is to it."

Fred Kenney was born October 23, 1944, along with his twin sister Susan, to Mary and Elmer Kenney in Hollywood, California. Elmer worked as a hod carrier, hauling cement and mortar around construction sites, while Mary stayed at home working to raise a family that came to include eight children. Wanting to raise his children in a more rural atmosphere, Elmer moved the family north to a 5-acre orange grove in Chatsworth, just outside Canoga Park, in 1948.

In 1955, Elmer passed away after a short illness, and Fred became the man of the house. In part because he was now sidetracked by family duties, Fred was only an average student in school, but, handsome with wavy blond hair and a perpetual smile on his face, he was always one of the most popular kids around. Often visiting his grandparents in Hermosa Beach on the weekends, Fred became an avid and skilled surfer, developing a deep tan that only augmented his already good looks. But it was racing dirt bikes that was Fred's true passion. Fred and a few of his closest friends were seemingly perpetually covered in a mix of oil and dust, tinkering on bikes and zooming around the family orange grove.

During his late teen years, apart from school at Canoga High and racing, Fred loved hanging around with his sisters Mary Lou, Sandy, Susan, and Ruthie. Near each other in age, the siblings shared a large and close-knit group of friends, and enjoyed listening to records, chatting about life, and drinking a few beers. One night shortly after his graduation in 1963, Fred met Barbara Tobin at a family party. The two immediately hit it off and quickly became inseparable. Fred took a job as a carpenter on home construction sites and joined a union. Bringing in good money, after a whirlwind short romance Fred felt able to ask Barbara to marry him, and the couple wed on December 10, 1965. There was one minor hiccup on their wedding day, though, when the preacher asked Barbara if she took Elmer to be her wedded husband. At first she hesitated, wondering who Elmer was, because Fred never went by his given first name. After the minor gaffe, the rest of the ceremony went off without a hitch. The young couple enjoyed life together – renting an apartment and still racing and hanging out with their circle of family and friends. Everything seemed perfect, until May and the arrival of Fred's draft notice. It was a frightening moment for the young couple, but Fred did his best to convince Barbara that all would be well. The pay would be pretty good, he would save his money, and when he came back things would be even better than before.

After a family party, Fred made his way to the induction center where he was surprised to find Richard Rubio, one of his Canoga High classmates and surfing buddies. The two chatted for a few minutes about hot rods, life after high school – anything but Vietnam. At nearly the same time Kenney and Rubio spotted another old friend, Tim Johnson. Canoga was only a few miles from Lancaster down Highway 14, separated by the Angeles National Forest, and highschoolers from the two towns were often close, attending the same parties and enjoying something of a friendly sports rivalry. Johnson was hanging out with a couple of his classmates, including Bill Reed, Larry Lilley, and Kenny Frakes. The group immediately struck up a conversation, wondering how the draft had plucked so many from among their rather small group of friends.

After dropping Fred off at the induction center, Barbara was disconsolate. She wanted to follow Fred to wherever he underwent his training, but they couldn't afford it. All she knew was that she couldn't be alone. After a short stay with her mother, Marilyn, Barbara moved in with Fred's older sister Mary Lou. The two shared a close bond, which helped them both deal with the pain of Fred's absence. But, only a month later, everything changed when Barbara got the news: she was pregnant.

One of a small group of Chicagoans in Charlie Company, Bill Geier was born on May 1, 1946, the first of four children of Jack and Bernice Geier. The family lived in a small apartment behind a shoemaker's shop on the northwest side of Chicago, with Jack laboring in the press room of a printing company while Bernice raised the family and sometimes worked in a corner grocery store to help make ends meet. The neighborhood contained a comfortable mix of middle-class families, whose children walked in groups, navigating a maze of alleys to the local schools. The Geiers were a close-knit family, with Bill and his siblings Jackie, Bob, and Jim sometimes accompanying their father to work. As the oldest child, Bill also got to tag along with his father and grandfather to watch Ernie Banks and Ron Santo from the bleachers at Wrigley Field, and as a teen in 1965 to witness the magic of Gayle Sayer's rookie season with the Bears. The Geiers also loved the outdoors and took family vacations in the summer to Wisconsin, camping in old army tents and hiking around the nearby lakes with Bill only going to sleep at night after reading his favorite James Bond adventures by candlelight.

Bill was always a good student and hoped to become an architect. Jack and Bernice discovered Bill's ambition when they entered his room one day to find much of his floor taken up with an exact scale model of their house. The family moved to Maywood, a suburb just west of Chicago, where they bought their first house. While his younger siblings loved life in suburbia, life got a little more complicated for Bill. Pursuing his dream of becoming an architect, Bill enrolled in Triton College in the nearby suburb of River Grove. However, as a city kid, Bill had always been used to walking or using the elevated trains to get around, so he had never gotten a driver's license. It was up to mom to take him to and from school every day. The two used their time in transit to chat about Bill's future, often while eating Ju Ju Fruits that Bill had bought from his wages working part-time at Sears – a job he needed to help shoulder the burden of college tuition.

Unable to afford to go to school full-time, Bill's part-time status left him open to the draft, and a notice duly arrived in May 1966. Bill's parents took the news well; Jack remained rather quiet, having served as an MP during World War II, while Bernice did her best to hide the fears any mother would have for a son drafted in time of war. Jackie, Bob, and Jim looked up to their older brother, soon to be a soldier, in awe. As the family sat in the living room and discussed the coming change in Bill's life, Bernice smiled as Bill said, "Mom, I'm not sure if I can kill somebody. I'm just not sure if I can do it. I really think that what I want to be is a medic." Proud both of Bill's gentle nature and of his opportunity to serve his country, the Geiers looked to the future. Realizing that Bill's hitch would be up in 1968, the family made plans to welcome him home with the best camping adventure ever. During Bill's absence, the Geiers would secretly save their money so that they could trade in their tents, buy a camper, and surprise him with a camping trip among the mountains of Colorado. It was to be a family dream come true.

The lone Native American in Charlie Company, Charlie Nelson was born on the Navajo reservation near Winslow, Arizona, in his grandparents' hogan, a traditional one-room house made of logs and mud. Although spacious and divided into separate sections by blankets, the hogan got quite crowded over the years, housing Charlie's grandparents, parents, and five siblings. Charlie's father,

K.T. Nelson, tended the family flock of goats and sheep, while his mother cared for the home and made rugs that she took to the nearby trading post to swap for flour, sugar, and other essentials for cooking. As soon as he was old enough to be trusted out alone, Charlie began to pitch in and help with tending the sheep and goats, leaving the hogan early each morning in search of pasture, often not returning until after dark.

Wanting more for his family, K.T. applied to the Urban Indian Relocation Program, which was designed to move reservation dwellers to urban areas where better-paying jobs were more plentiful. While awaiting news, the family moved to Wickenburg, 60 miles northwest of Phoenix, where K.T. took a job working with the railroad. The move was hard on Charlie's grandparents, who were concerned that the family would be seduced by city life and lose touch with Navajo ways. In an effort to keep Charlie and his siblings well grounded, his grandmother and grandfather went to the extreme step of leaving the reservation for the first time in their lives to visit Wickenburg. Unable to speak English, or to decipher the intricacies of the rail system, the elderly couple simply went to the local train station wearing placards that read "K.T. Nelson." Eventually they found their way to Wickenburg, where a family friend spotted them and took them to the Nelson home.

As Charlie prepared to enter junior high school, the news came in that K.T. had landed a coveted job on an assembly line with Lockheed, and the family moved to Los Angeles. Unable to speak much English, dark-skinned and diminutive in stature, Charlie stood out in his new school, where, on one of his first days, a much larger Anglo boy called him a "dirty Indian" and spat in his face. Wiry and hardened by years of manual labor, Charlie quickly decked the larger lad with a wicked punch and then stood calmly and turned to the other Anglos and said, "So, do the rest of you have anything you want to say about Indians?" Nobody in the school ever questioned Charlie's background again.

Charlie's main goal in high school was simply to finish and become a machinist. He worked hard and mostly escaped notice, becoming one of the first in his family to receive a high school diploma in 1964. After graduation, Charlie went right to work in a factory and made ready to move out of his family's home, until, on

May 17, 1966, he received his draft notice. Both Charlie and his parents were proud of his chance to serve. He had long been taught that it was good to fight for your country – and the United States was *his* country. Whether "owned" by new groups or not, the land was eternal, and it was Indian land. He was privileged to fight for *his* land and *his* people. Before his service began in earnest, Charlie made a quick return trip to the reservation, where medicine men met in a communal hogan and performed a night-long ceremony designed to protect him from harm. The ceremony invoked the power of the warriors of his nation and of his family members who had passed before to protect Charlie in battle. Just prior to his departure, the Navajo elders presented Charlie with a medicine bag to wear around his neck, and then, like so many native warriors before him, Charlie went off to war.

Destined to become the smiling, good-natured heart of Charlie Company, Forrest Ramos was born on November 11, 1946, Veterans Day, to Narciso and Julia Ramos, part of a family that eventually included nine children, six boys and three girls. Narciso had emigrated to the United States from Mexico at age 13 and, after his marriage, made his way to Colorado to work in one of the state's many mines before moving on to Wapato, Washington, a small town outside Yakima in the southern part of the state. The Ramos family bought a house on the Yakima Indian Reservation, near the local farms on which Narciso found employment as a hop thrower – working in the large local industry dedicated to growing, harvesting, and baling the hops used in brewing. When Forrest was only six years old, his mother passed away, and, by the age of eight, he, along with his brothers, was following his father to work, toiling in whatever fields needed working at the time, including hops (for which they were paid by the hour), beets (for which they were paid by the acre), tomatoes (for which they were paid by the box), and apples (for which they were paid by the bushel).

Having to work most days after school, Forrest spent what time he could scrape together at the weekends boxing at the local Boys and Girls Club. Boxing was something of a tradition in the Ramos family. Two of Forrest's older brothers became professional boxers, with Paul Ramos only narrowly eliminated in his final bout of the trials of the US Olympic team for the Rome Olympics of 1960. After sweating in the gym, Forrest loved to get dressed up in his best slacks and shirt and go to community dances in Yakima, which was the preferred venue for the boys from Wapato to meet girls.

Forrest was not quite sure what he wanted to do after high school, but he knew where he wanted to do it. His older brother, Paul, who had also surfed professionally after his boxing career, had moved to Los Angeles. Forrest loved the stories that he had heard about the promised land of California and, after graduation in 1965, moved south to live with his brother. Soon after his arrival, Forrest landed a job working at a Packard Bell Electronics plant making televisions. In the evenings he often just hung out with Paul, talking about the future. Meanwhile, back home in Wapato, in May 1966 Narciso opened a letter addressed to Forrest from the government – it was his draft notice. Believing that when a man was called to serve his country he went, Forrest returned to Washington and prepared to report for duty in Spokane. As the family gathered to send him off, the normally stoic Narciso put a protective arm around Forrest's shoulder and, with tears glistening in the corner of his eyes, said, "Forrest, be safe and come back to us."

One of the many members of Charlie Company from a rural background, Elijah Taylor was born in Highbank, Texas, a tiny community 20 miles south of Waco where the cotton fields came right up to the door of the local two-room schoolhouse and cotton chopping and picking was a way of life. While Elijah's father, Jack, worked as a manual laborer for the railroad and was gone for weeks at a time, his mother, Lillie, worked in the cotton fields with her eight children in a constant battle to make enough money to keep food on the table. It was the local rhythm of life – the poor blacks of the area laboring on the land of affluent whites. At first the younger Taylor children helped their mother pick her two rows of cotton by hand. The work was tedious and hard, but their tiny hands quickly became expert at the task.

By age 13, Elijah got his own two rows of cotton to pick, often in tandem with one of his sisters, and also began to take part in the even more physical labor of chopping cotton, using hoes to hack weeds out of the soil and to thin out the growing crop. A regular day of labor in the fields for the children was ten hours, arriving at the fields when it was barely light and working all day with only short breaks for water and for lunch. Most of the work, especially the chopping, took place in the blazing heat of the Texas summers, but cotton picking, the most important chore of all, stretched well into the fall. While the local school year began in early September, Elijah and his siblings, and most of the other poor blacks of the area, could not afford to take time away from their labors. Only when it rained so heavily that work was impossible were the children able to rush into school for a few hours; otherwise they fell further and further behind.

In 1961, when Elijah was 15 years old, Jack and Lillie split up, and Jack moved the children to Dallas where he hoped that they would be able to work less and finish school. Moving from a small farming community to the middle of the urban sprawl of east Dallas was quite a shock for Elijah. There were more students in his school than there were people in Highbank There were fights at school, students talked back to teachers, and many of the kids were, in Taylor's view, "nothing but thugs." Elijah kept his head down, and treated school like a job – after all, studying was not nearly as hard as picking cotton – and quickly became an honor roll student.

After graduation in 1964, Elijah held down what work he could until he got his break in September 1965 – he was accepted to start work at the US Post Office. To celebrate, Elijah bought his first car, a 1959 Ford Fairlane. As he settled into what he hoped would be a long career, Elijah began to hear more about the draft and Vietnam. He tried to flunk the selective service examination to lower his draft status, but in May of 1966 the "greetings" letter came from Uncle Sam nonetheless. Having just turned 20, the prospect of serving in the military in time of war seemed more like an adventure than a danger. He would leave Texas for the first time; he would very likely get a chance to fly on an airplane for the first time. He would get to fire a weapon and defend his country. Leaving behind a proud father, Elijah departed for his adventure.

Charlie Company's sole enlistee, John Young was born on March 13, 1945 to Wilbur and Myrl Young, who eventually settled down in Saint Paul, Minnesota, where Wilbur worked at International Harvester. At first life in Saint Paul was rather claustrophobic, with the family, which now included John and two younger sisters, living in a small inner-city duplex. But Wilbur's salary continued to grow during the boom years of the 1950s, while Myrl brought in additional money through her own job as a waitress in a local restaurant. By 1957 the couple had saved enough money to buy a four-bedroom home in the suburbs. It was almost the perfect American middle-class existence.

As a high school sophomore, John, like so many of his generation, turned for inspiration to America's dashing new president, John F. Kennedy. Quite taken by JFK's charm, on January 20, 1961, Young sat spellbound while watching the pomp and circumstance of the presidential inauguration on television. One specific phrase from the speech immediately seized the youngster's imagination and became a centerpiece of his life – "Let every nation know, whether it wishes us well or ill, that we shall pay any price, bear any burden, meet any hardship, support any friend, oppose any foe, in order to assure the survival and the success of liberty." Kennedy had challenged the young generation in America to service and sacrifice in the name of a greater good. To John Young the words of the handsome young president were like a magnet. He would serve; the only question was how.

After graduation from high school in 1963, John enrolled at the University of Minnesota, commuting to campus in a brand-new VW Beetle that his father bought for $1,865. On a cold November day he and his friends were sitting in the crowded common room of the Newman Center chatting while the radio played in the background. Amid the daily din of college life, in the corner of his consciousness John picked up on some stray words that seemed unthinkable. He sprinted to the main counter and asked the receptionist to turn up the radio's volume. The next sentence of the news report brought all conversation in the Newman Center to a halt: John F. Kennedy had been shot. JFK's death affected the entire country, but the tragedy had a special meaning for John Young. He was determined to make good on his promise of service to honor Kennedy's memory.

Still seeking both direction and an opportunity to serve, John joined the ROTC and, during the summer, attended a shortened six-week version of basic training at Fort Knox. The physical and mental regimen helped Young to find focus, which developed into a deep admiration of his instructors – wise, hard-bitten combat veterans of Korea and World War II. These sure and strong men had what John lacked. Widely read and thoughtful, to John it seemed that these men were the "powerful" men of Walt Whitman's *Leaves of Grass*, and that in emulating them his own life would be changed.

Armed with a newfound sense of direction and purpose, Young began to pay more attention to developments in Vietnam than many of his college compatriots. It all seemed very simple. The North Vietnamese were encroaching on the freedom of the beleaguered nation of South Vietnam and even had the audacity to fire on American warships in the Gulf of Tonkin. The United States had responded to the provocation by once again sending its sons and daughters to war to defend liberty. In times of crisis, the Young family had always answered the call. The nation was once again at war, and John Young was determined to play his part. But the war in Vietnam was so small, and so distant, that John worried it would be over before his graduation and commissioning in 1968. Unwilling to wait, in May 1966 Young withdrew from classes at the University of Minnesota and went to an army recruiting office.

It was the kind of experience that made a recruiting sergeant's day. Confident and sure, Young asked to enlist in the army. The sergeant responded, "I can do that for you." Young then made it clear that he wanted to be in the infantry. The sergeant responded, "I can do that for you." Young finished by informing the sergeant that he did not want to go to Germany or some other cushy assignment; he wanted to go to Vietnam and fight. The sergeant responded, "Son, I guarantee I can do that for you."

With the deed done, John returned home and called the family together in the living room to tell them the news. His mother and two sisters burst into tears, while his father simply looked into his son's eyes and nodded in understanding. In an attempt to assuage the fears of his mother and sisters, John insisted that he would be fine, and told them of the deep meaning that lay behind his actions. For the first time in his life he felt like he was part of something, really part of something. Ready to do his part and soak up life, John departed for his induction determined to be a good soldier.

2 TRAINING

Company C
4th Battalion, 47th Infantry
Fort Riley, Kansas 66442

17 May 1966

Subject: Commander's Welcome

To: The "New Reliables" of Company C

1. I am Lt. Larson, Commander of Company C, 4th Battalion, 47th Infantry, and on behalf of the officers and non commissioned officers of this company I welcome you to Fort Riley, Kansas, home of the 9th Infantry Division. In due time I'm sure that you will learn to like Fort Riley and call it your second home.

2. The mission of the officers and NCO's here in the company is to convert each and every one of you into a fighting soldier. The world situation as we see it today makes it absolutely necessary for you, each and every one of you, to become a good fighting man...

3. The training which you will receive here will enable you to withstand the stress and strain that combat causes. During your instructions there may be something which you may have questions about. Don't hesitate to ask that question, chances are there is

someone else with the same question, but don't wait on the other fellow. Your attitude toward any and all of your training should be one of "I want the very best, my life may depend on it."

Dear Mom, Dad, and Fran,
Sunday has come again. And with it a degree of relaxation... I'd give anything to sleep till 8 like I did at home... Here it's 4:30 every day except Sunday and then it's 6:30. They give us from 4:30 to 5:30 to make our beds, shave, and clean up. Everything has to be perfect for inspection. Every day we have inspection and then they rank each platoon (there are four in our company). If we do poorly we catch hell; if we do good, they demand better. You just can't win. If our beds aren't made correctly, we have to drag them into the parking lot at 1800hrs (you figure it out) and make it for all to see. That's from the second floor, carrying your whole bed. Fortunately I haven't had to do it. I make a good bunk. Surprise!
    Love, Jim [Dennison]

Dear Mom, Dad, and Girls,
Got back from the field yesterday. What a really miserable week it was. Mud everywhere – on everything. It stuck to your boots and to your entrenching tool and anything else it touched. We went through a simulated POW camp and had to crawl up and down a muddy ditch on our bellies then our backs till we were thoroughly covered with sticky, black mud. Then they threw each one into a hole in the ground filled with mud and water. We spent 12 hours crawling in the mud and doing calisthenics, then had to escape and find our way back to base camp at night. Naturally it rained that night. But I came through everything pretty well... It's about time for chow, so I'll end here. I'll write a longer letter tomorrow.
    Love, John [Young]

While General Westmoreland and MACV put the finishing touches on the Mobile Afloat Force plan in Saigon, on February 1, 1966, the 9th Infantry Division was reactivated under the command of Major General George Eckhardt. The 9th, dubbed the "Old Reliables," was a storied unit that had seen hard fighting in North Africa, Sicily, Italy, and northern Europe during World War II. Chosen to serve as

"Z Division" to implement Westmoreland's offensive plan for the Mekong Delta, the 9th consisted of nine infantry battalions, a cavalry squadron, and the normal array of artillery and other supporting units. The military allotted a total of 24 weeks of training time to the division while at Fort Riley, including eight-week periods for both basic training and advanced individual training (AIT), and an additional eight weeks for both basic and advanced unit training. The 9th was on a strict schedule. It had to be ready to ship out to Vietnam by late December 1966 in order to coincide with the onset of the dry season in Vietnam, the time Westmoreland had chosen as the most favorable to introduce American troops into the volatile Mekong Delta.

Due to a shortage of men and equipment, the 9th was activated in bits and pieces. Division base elements, including divisional, brigade, and battalion headquarters, arrived at Fort Riley first, during January and February, with the new recruits for 1st, 2nd, and 3rd brigades scheduled to arrive in April, May, and June respectively. Apart from simple details of training regimen, creation of an entirely new divisional infrastructure in time of war posed critical challenges. A military already struggling to keep its ranks fully staffed had to cobble together several hundred officers and non-commissioned officers to form the professional leadership cadre of the 9th Infantry Division, gathering them from a number of sources, some reassigned from existing commands across the country and Europe, while others were fresh out of West Point or Officer Candidates School (OCS).

The eclectic leadership group, some of them hard-bitten veterans, others still wet behind the ears, gathered at Fort Riley during the first two months of 1966 and quickly realized that the training of the 9th Infantry would be quite different from the norm. Incoming draftees normally took their basic and advanced individual training under specialized training commands before being sent out individually to active units. In a scenario startling in its uniqueness, the leaders of the 9th Infantry were tasked with taking their charges through all levels of training, from basic individual to advanced unit training and then taking those same units into a year of battle in Vietnam. The officers of the 9th Infantry saw the task of forging a unit in training and then taking that same unit into battle, as a wonderful opportunity. It would be *their* unit. They would know the men intimately – understanding their strengths, weaknesses, and foibles. Not only would the experience weld those men into a cohesive group of soldiers but also it would form a strong bond between the units' officers, non-commissioned officers, and the ranks, forging a common brotherhood of war unique in the Vietnam era.

A major problem quickly came to light as the leadership groups began to sort out their difficult tasks. The military had not been able to gather together enough experienced non-commissioned officers to do the job, especially at the lowest level of command, that of the squad leader. Normally a squad leader was a staff sergeant (E-6), who might have six to eight years of military experience. A squad leader's task involved leading a ten-man squad, incorporating two fire teams each led by a sergeant (E-5), into battle – a task reputed to be one of the most difficult in the entire military. The squad was always at the sharp end of war, conducting assaults, clearing bunkers, manning defensive positions, and translating the orders of higher commands into violent reality; it was up to the squad leaders to make that violence happen and to make it effective. With no other alternative, the units of the 9th Division decided to identify the most qualified incoming trainees and to elevate many of the best among them to the position of squad leaders. Instead of years of training and experience, these civilians-turned-soldiers would have only a few months of training before being thrown into the crucible of battle. It was to be the new leading the new – putting the chosen young men who until recently had only been carefree surfers, schoolboys, and farm laborers into a position of almost unimaginable stress.

Captain Rollo Larson, an ex-enlisted man from Macon, Georgia who had graduated from OCS and had recently served in Korea, saw his chance to command a company in the 9th Division as a unique opportunity. He would be able to train a company and then take it into battle – something afforded very few officers. He had learned in his past postings that officers were best when they relied on their cadre of experienced NCOs, who were closer to the men and knew their needs and abilities better than anyone. After arriving at Fort Riley, Larson first reported to his superiors and then made his way to his own company orderly room. He immediately sent for Company First Sergeant Lynn Crockett. A few minutes later Crockett, who had joined the army to escape life in the cotton fields of Kentucky, entered the room – 6 feet 5 inches tall, muscular, and every inch a military man. Impressed at first sight, Larson introduced himself and said that his job as captain during training was to sign the morning reports, take the blame if anything went wrong, and to kick the butts that Crockett said needed kicking. It was Crockett's job to teach the young men who would soon be arriving for training. Crockett looked at Larson for a moment, and then replied in his Kentucky drawl, "Sir, you and me are gonna get along just fine."

Soon the young lieutenants who would serve as Charlie Company's platoon leaders began to arrive at Fort Riley. Jack Benedick was the hard-working son of blue-collar parents from Omaha, Nebraska. He had excelled in numerous sports in high school and went to college as a sociology major. After graduation and marriage to his college sweetheart Nancy, Benedick tried to join first the Marines and then the navy as a pilot, but was rejected due to poor eyesight. He finally bit the bullet and joined the army, going to OCS before reporting to his first command at Fort Riley. Lynn Hunt was from Miami, Florida, where his father worked as a carpenter. Hunt's prowess on his high school swim team netted two college scholarship offers, one from the University of Florida, the other from the United States Military Academy. At the time of his graduation from West Point in June 1966, Hunt and the rest of the senior cadets were herded into a vast auditorium where the yearly allocation of officers' slots in the army were on offer. Wanting to lead an infantry platoon in combat, when his name was called Hunt stepped forward and chose the 9th Infantry Division, which he knew was headed to Vietnam. To his right he saw that his classmate John Hoskins, who was renowned among the cadets both for his boxing skills and his poetry, had also chosen the 9th Infantry Division.

While married officers like Jack Benedick could live off post, single officers initially were housed in an old World War I-era barracks in Camp Funston, furnished with a pipe-frame cot, a dilapidated desk, and a chair. After finding their quarters, the young officers went to the company orderly room to receive their assignments, but had to wait, because Captain Larson was away attending a meeting at battalion headquarters. The group introduced themselves and talked while awaiting Larson's return, as Crockett went about his office work. When the captain returned, Crockett had simply had enough of the nattering and bellowed in his best parade ground voice, "Captain, will you get your goddamned lieutenants the hell out of my fucking office?" The startled newbie officers exited meekly, leaving the first sergeant and the captain to their business. Benedick, Hunt, and Hoskins realized that they did not know which end was up and went to Crockett for advice gleaned from the wisdom of years as an enlisted man. It was a command lesson that the young officers never forgot.

All across the country, from Fort Ord, California, to Fort Dix, New Jersey, young men called by the draft of May 1966 gathered to begin their military service. Representatives of the baby-boom generation, bushy-haired surfers, street-wise city toughs, muscle-bound factory laborers, and studious college boys assembled and traded their civilian clothes for often ill-fitting uniforms of olive drab. Given quick, and sometimes painful, haircuts that by design lessened their sense of individuality, the new recruits usually spent a few days getting yelled at by imposing NCOs and learning such military basics as standing at attention and the meaning of Kitchen Police (KP) duty.

Often wondering what on earth they had gotten themselves into, after only a few days the draftees gathered to receive their new, permanent assignments. The process, which for some was to mean life or death, was a moment of pure, bizarre randomness amid the system of military order. In some places the draftees were counted off by ones and twos, with all assigned the number one bound for Germany, while all twos were off to Fort Riley and eventually to Vietnam. In the case of Clarence Shires – who had been married but a divorce had affected his draft status – at Fort Jackson, South Carolina, things were done alphabetically. At Fort Benning, Georgia, they chose odd and even numbers, leaving John Bradfield, who had grown up on the tough east side of Cleveland, bound for the 9th Division. At Fort Polk, all of the draftees received random number assignments, with an NCO then reading off the numbers of those bound for Fort Riley. Henry Burleson, a very religious farm boy from Abilene, Texas who was number 35, was not quite sure what going to Fort Riley meant, but he was relieved to hear his number called. He was going somewhere, anywhere. After all, there was no way that Fort Riley could be worse than Fort Polk.

To many of the draftees, the trip to Fort Riley was their first time out of their home state and their first time to fly. Terry McBride kept a wary eye on the engine of his somewhat dilapidated military transport all the way to Kansas City, wondering if the oil leaking in a steady stream from around the engine cowling was important. Some of the newly minted soldiers, including Fred Kenney and Richard Rubio, were lucky enough to make the journey with lifetime neighbors and schoolmates, while others met for the first time aboard their aircraft. Drafted out of Las Vegas, Willie McTear had some trouble jamming his athletic frame into the tiny seat of the aircraft bound for Fort Riley, and was happy to find that his seatmate was a little fellow who did not take up much space. McTear wondered how on earth this little man with big glasses offsetting a tiny face and body was going to become a soldier. Interested not only by the man's diminutive size but also by the opportunity to have an extended conversation with a white person, McTear asked his name – Ronald Schworer.

Ron was the eldest of the four children of Frank and June Schworer. Frank was a hard driving salesman, and the couple had a rocky, on-again, off-again relationship full of arguments, separations, and family turmoil. The bickering and constant stress took a high toll on the Schworer children, often leaving Ron in charge of his younger siblings. Caught amidst the constant family drama, Ron became more and more self reliant, and spent more and more of his time engrossed in books, perhaps as an escape. By the age of 12 Ron Schworer was already exhibiting a level of brilliance that stunned his teachers; he was something special, something unlike anything they had ever seen. One outlet for his imagination was as leader of the Lancaster, California Rocket Club. Such clubs were quite common in the heyday of the

US space program, but Ron's was different. While other clubs produced rockets that often only sputtered a bit and fell over, Ron's efforts were so successful that they resulted in a visit by some very irate Air Force personnel. It seems Ron's rockets were buzzing past their jets in flight. While the Air Force representatives were impressed with the teenager's efforts, they brought his rocket club to a quick and unceremonious end.

His future in rocketry dashed, Ron threw himself into the world of mathematics, winning the coveted California High School Math League Championship two consecutive years and achieving a perfect score on the mathematics section of the SAT. As a junior in high school, Ron moved to be with his father in Las Vegas, where he became increasingly involved in something rather new to most Americans at the time – computers. In 1964 Ron graduated from Rancho High School early, and headed off to Mudd College in California – but the curriculum bored him, so he dropped out. Ron returned to Las Vegas and took a job teaching computer programming at a local junior college and then at the Nevada Test Site, home of much of the US atomic weapons program. To this day Ron Schworer's computer work at the Nevada Test Site remains top secret.

Ron left the Nevada Test Site in late 1965 to become an entrepreneur, founding a company called Comptex designed to offer computer programming services to major corporations. Ron was the brains behind the outfit – the programmer ready to solve customer's computer programming needs, while two of his friends worked to drum up business. Ron's was a vision of the future – a vision of a nation dominated by computers. But it was a costly vision, one that had left him open to the draft. Now he found himself aboard an aircraft bound for Fort Riley, Kansas sitting next to Willie McTear. The two men could not have been more different, but somehow before the aircraft had touched down in Kansas City, Schworer and McTear had become fast friends.

Usually arriving late at night, with their occupants weary from their travels, busses full of frightened new recruits began to pull into Fort Riley during late May to disgorge the newest members of Charlie Company. Mike Cramer was happy to hear that he was about to get off the bus at a place called Custer Hill; maybe Kansas would not be so different from his native San Fernando Valley,

California. Gathering his gear, Cramer emerged from the door only to face one of the most depressing moments of his life. Custer Hill was hardly a hill at all. In fact there were no hills to be seen, much less the beautiful mountains of home. Kansas seemed to be one big flat nothing. But Cramer was quickly shaken out of his moment of reflection, because the yelling had begun.

NCOs seemed to be everywhere, barking orders and trying to get the rookies into some semblance of a military formation. But one NCO in particular stood out. Bob French of Tampa, Florida, who had quit college to work at the post office only to find himself drafted a few weeks later, couldn't help thinking that the huge first sergeant, who loomed over them all in his starched fatigues, veins in his neck bulging as his voice boomed, looked like God barking orders. As the young men scrambled into place, the mountain of a sergeant bawled, in a voice that seemed too loud to be human, "My name is Company First Sergeant Lynn Crockett, and the first guy that calls me 'Davey' is going to get my size 18 boot up his ass!" Finally the anxious men stood at attention, and Captain Rollo Larson strode forward. His calm and quiet voice stood out sharply after all of the screaming, making his short announcement all the more ominous. "We are here to make you young men into soldiers, and if you don't learn your lessons, and learn them well, half of you are going to die." Henry Burleson swallowed heavily and offered a quick prayer, asking, "Lord, what have I gotten myself into?"

After Larson's departure, the military pandemonium began anew. Bellowing NCOs ordered the recruits to march and perform right- and left-face drills – tasks sadly beyond the limited martial experience of most of the men. Mercilessly the NCOs homed in on the fat and clumsy, ordering their hapless victims to drop onto the ground and do pushups. John Bradfield watched as the less fortunate of his new colleagues were driven to tears by their torment. Happy that it was them and not him, Bradfield made the mistake of cracking a smile. Almost immediately an NCO appeared and asked him what the hell he was smiling at, and ordered him to the ground for 50 pushups of his own. Big and athletic, Bradfield dropped and pounded out the pushups without difficulty before jumping back to his feet and smiling again. Enraged by the affront, the NCO shouted in semi-glee, "Oh, we have a smart one here! Drop and give me 50 more!"

TRAINING

Having gotten some of the worst of it that night due to his small size, Bill Geier dragged himself into the barracks where he met Idoluis Casares, a strapping, Hispanic draftee from Brownsville, Texas, who would be his bunkmate for the remainder of basic training. Although they were both dead tired, Geier and Casares were too excited to fall asleep quickly and stayed up chatting for a while, with Geier mentioning both his desire to become a medic and how much he already missed his family. For his part Casares could not believe that the baby-faced, diminutive Geier could be old enough to serve in the military. Casares rolled over and looked at Willie McTear, who was perched on a bunk nearby, motioned toward Geier, and said, "Can you believe that they are letting 16 year olds into the army?" McTear replied, "Goddamn the army," before trailing off into a stream of less audible cursing. A few feet away, Terry McBride, a rough and tumble young man from Greenfield, California, who was used to getting into scrapes and fights, couldn't help but smile as he got ready to go to sleep. As an aspiring boxer, he had been through much worse in his life, and as a product of Catholic schools, he was certain that these loudmouth NCOs could never match up with the verbal and physical torment meted out by the nuns of his youth.

The draftees of Charlie Company lived in a three-story barracks atop Custer Hill, to which they were confined for most of basic training, with company offices on the first floor and open bays for each platoon on the second and third floors, where the enlisted men slept in double-decked bunks, each man with his own foot and wall lockers. Most of the NCOs lived in a small suite of rooms located between the platoon bays in the middle of each floor. Before reveille each morning at 5am, each young soldier had to make certain that his own personal area was immaculate, with a properly made bunk, six pairs of socks folded neatly and lined up like babies in his footlocker, six t-shirts folded the exact same way (with the tab on the back showing), and boots spit shined (regardless of how muddy they had gotten the day before). The communal latrine, little more than a line of commodes perched on a tiled wall, had to shine, and the tile floors had to be so well polished that they reflected any incoming NCO's face like a mirror. Regardless of the care they had taken to do everything properly, the trainees soon discovered that the NCOs would find some fault, perhaps their reflection in the floor was hazy or there was a mote of dust on a commode, and pushups and other punishments were the result.

After inspection, it was off to physical training (PT), a burst of morning exercise that ended with a trip across a row of monkey bars that had to be navigated successfully before the trainee could have breakfast. For some the morning exercises were a cinch, but for the small or out of shape the monkey bars posed great difficulty. Barely able even to get onto the monkey bars, Ron Schworer only went forward a short way before hanging limply, unable to continue. Some of the guys began to hoot and jeer at the sight of Ron just hanging there, until Willie McTear, who had negotiated the bars with ease, came back and yelled, "Get off him! If you want him, you are going to have to come through me, and I guarantee I will put you on your asses boys!" With that, McTear began to cheer Schworer on, with many of the once-hostile crowd joining in support.

Bill Varskafsky was newly married and had been drafted out of Bremerton, Washington, where he had been attending junior college. Used to the cool climate of the Pacific northwest, Varskafsky had been stunned by the 95 degree heat and high humidity of a Kansas summer. One night early in training Varskafsky tumbled out of his bunk certain that there was a nuclear attack underway, only to find out that it was, instead, only a typical Kansas summer thunderstorm. The next morning, with the thought stuck in his mind that Kansas had to be the asshole of the universe, an instructor ran up screaming that Varskafsky's shirt was not tucked in correctly. Delighted to have found fresh quarry the instructor ordered Varskafsky, who was a bit out of shape at the time, to drop and pound out 50 pushups. Varskafsky thought, "50 pushups? Hell. I've never even done 20 pushups." But down he went to begin paying the price for his unkempt attire. Although there was considerable huffing and puffing near the end, Varskafsky completed his task. The instructor looked down at him quizzically, and said, "I'll be damned son. I didn't think you would make it to 50." Varskafsky replied, "Neither did I."

Punishment pushups were a staple of the pre-breakfast routine at Fort Riley, usually doled out by NCOs but also sometimes by officers. One morning Lieutenant Charles "Duffy" Black, the company executive officer, was on hand for the ritualized calisthenics. Hailing from Peoria, Illinois, Black had always been something of a daredevil, having run away from home at the age of 16 to join the merchant marines. After traveling the world, Black wanted another challenge and enlisted in the army in 1962, before going to OCS. Having been an enlisted man himself, Black felt a close affinity for these new trainees under his command, and he decided to work with them, perhaps more closely than an officer of his rank should – he knew that the lives of these young men depended on it. Black had a soft side to his personality and was a very religious man, but at the outset of morning calisthenics Black had to be hard-core military through and through. Walking up to the trainees, who stood at attention, Black challenged them by stating that he was stronger and better than they were, and would prove it if any of them wanted to take him on in a pushup competition. In the back of the ranks Tim Fischer, a tough young draftee from outside Cleveland, Ohio, began to laugh. Black called him to the front and the two went to the ground facing each other and began. After what seemed like an eternity, with the men cheering Fischer on, Black began to tire and turned red in the face. Eventually Black gave up, while Fischer threw in a few one-armed pushups for good measure. Fischer, who had worked as a hod carrier on construction sites for years, then jumped up, not knowing what to expect. Black stood back, complimented Fischer, and shook his hand, while informing the men that from now on Fischer got to go to the front of the chow line every meal.

Much of basic training centered on seemingly endless marches and physical exercise, ranging from long runs in full gear to low crawling across either brick-hard dirt or through knee-deep mud, all in the excessive heat of a Kansas summer. Many, including Idoluis Casares who was overweight and a smoker, found the physical regimen to be excruciatingly difficult. But he kept at it, getting into the best shape of his life, finding himself in the odd position of being cheered on by the puny – but physically-fit – Bill Geier. Others, like John Young or Tim Fischer, saw physical training and marching drill as something like a competition and were determined to stand out. Many of the young men competed with each other to get into the best shape, and Charlie Company as a whole developed an esprit de corps in part by trying to outdo the other companies of the 4th of the 47th.

Regardless of the effort, though, there remained screw-ups – both individual and group. Sometimes men would fall out, exhausted, somebody would trip, another would turn the wrong way on the command of "left face"; it always seemed to be something. Even when the men thought that they had done well, their demanding NCOs often found hidden reasons for fault. When disciplining the entire group, the NCOs would sometimes order the men on long marches carrying their footlockers or wearing their gas masks – stern punishments in 100-degree plus heat. In cases of individual infractions, the NCOs would tell the offender to fall out and do the "dead bug," which involved the trainee flopping to the ground on his back and flailing his arms and legs like a dying cockroach. Don Peterson, who, even though he was athletic, for some reason never could get the hang of marching, had to hit the dirt so many times that he became known throughout the company simply as "Bug."

James Nall, seventh of 11 children in a poor black family from a still-segregated Fairfield, Alabama, was somewhat unsure of his new surroundings and all too prone to laughter – an unfortunate trait if one is trying to go unnoticed in a formation of men. Once, after Nall had let out an involuntary laugh at another trainee's mistake, an NCO ran over shouting, "Jesus H. Christ on a popsicle stick, son! What the hell are you laughing at? Is there something funny going on here? Where is your mind? Have you lost it? Have you?" After calling the unit to a halt, the NCO bellowed "Nall, walk over to that tree and talk to it and see if it has your mind!" After a short arboreal conversation, the NCO ordered Nall back, warning him to be careful to carry his mind in his hands. Once back in formation, the NCO yelled, "Nall, get down on the ground [and] dig a hole and bury your mind in it. That way you won't ever lose it again. Dig, son, dig!" During the entire performance, other men in the formation could not help themselves and broke into laughter – meaning that they had to walk to their own trees and find their minds as well.

Sergeant Daniel Kerr, who had been abandoned by his father as a teenager and joined the army for survival, was often the most expressive with his punishments. Not only did he yell and liberally dole out dead bugs and pushups, but also he liked to take men who had fallen out of runs or marches and make the others watch as he handed the guilty party an entrenching tool and made him dig his own grave, yelling, "If you can't survive marching in basic training, how the hell are you going to survive Vietnam?" One of Kerr's least popular punishments, though, involved making those who had violated the rules sleep with their steel pot helmets on. Just for good measure, Kerr would sneak into the platoon barracks at night while the men were asleep and go down the row of bunks thwacking the men on their heads with a swagger stick. He could tell by whether the sound of his blow produced a "bonk" or a "bink" whether the men still had their helmets on and had followed his orders.

Bob Ehlert was born on a ranch in Montana, but had been raised in Minnesota. He always remained true to his rural roots, even selling his first car, a '56 Chevy, to raise money to buy feed for his horses. Drafted along with many of his high school classmates, Ehlert's hopes were high. He was going to war with his buddies at his side. Instead, though, the Minnesota draftees were parceled out across the military, and Ehlert found himself reporting to a unit that was full of guys from California and the South. However, he was tough and knew that he could handle it, the same as his father and uncle had in World War II. But then came that first day at Fort Riley, when Crockett had bellowed, "Forget everything you know! Your ass belongs to the US Army now boys!" A few days later, as the instructors had gotten their intimidation and cursing down to an art form, Ehlert developed a horrible toothache. He didn't want to, but he had to. He had to ask giant, imposing, frightening Company First Sergeant Crockett for permission to go on sick call. Crockett rose from behind his desk and, in a voice full of menace, said, "Son. I've heard that excuse before." Ehlert, though, stood his ground, and Crockett replied "I'll let you go, son, but you had better come back missing some teeth." The next day Ehlert returned to Crockett's office with a mouth full of bloody gauze, having lost two teeth. Crockett looked up from his papers, furrowed his brow at the sight, and nodded toward the door. He never said a word.

Without doubt, the obstacle and bayonet courses were the trainees' least favorite part of basic training. Both involved climbing, slithering through mud, running, and sometimes crossing rope bridges. Even before his men went on the obstacle course for the first time, Sergeant First Class Pedro Blas, a tough career soldier from Guam, informed the trainees that the course would "make you or break you." Jim Dennison, a trainee from the north side of Chicago whose father owned an Irish pub wrote home:

> I think I told you I was going through the bayonet course that day, and man did I go through it. Under barbed wire, over brick walls, jump into fox holes, cross a river with 2 wires twice, up a steep cliff and a final attack on a dummy. And all in 2 inches of mud (it just happened to rain that day). When we finally got through it we were beat to hell. But wait. The captain is not satisfied with our esprit d' corps. Do it a second time and scream more please. And away we went. I fell flat on my face in the mud toward the end of it and looked like a regular mud pie. I survived, though. That's one thing the army teaches you – you can do a hell of a lot more than you think you can.

When not hard at work training, the men were often confined to their barracks, time they spent readying for the next round of inspections or just bored as hell. Dennison wrote:

> Sunday has finally come again. And with it a degree of relaxation. The only trouble is that there isn't a hell of a lot to do. We're still restricted to the barracks for another week so we play 500 rummy or shoot the breeze. Fantastically exciting. It seems that we go from one end of the rope to the other here. During the week we have so much to do that we hardly have time to go to the john, and now we have so little to do that it's silly.

Even just milling around the barracks, though, could be fraught with danger for the trainees. Caught off guard one afternoon, Jace Johnston, who had grown up poor on the near north side of Chicago, and three of his fellows were ordered to wax the floor of the bay until it shined. But the NCO who gave the order made a point of locking the wax in his office. When he returned to find a scuffed floor, he went ballistic in affected anger. A few days later, the NCO tried the same stunt, but this time one of the trainees went out of the third-floor window, shimmied along a handy ledge until he reached the NCO's window, and liberated the wax. When the sergeant returned to find the floor shiny, he was maddened even further by the men's ingenuity, yelling at them until he went hoarse.

As had their soldier progenitors down through the ages, the boys of Charlie Company often spent large chunks of their down time writing letters home to families and girlfriends, but even that seemingly innocuous pastime was not without its share of dangers. Stan Cockerell was from Hollywood, California where his father worked as a roofer and his mother toiled as a riveter in an aircraft factory. Small, at only 5 feet 6 inches, Cockerell was immensely tough, standing out on his high school football team. After graduation Cockerell had gone to a local junior college, but had given up his deferment to volunteer for the draft. Cockerell had driven himself to the induction station and later had mailed his keys to his parents so they could retrieve his car. But Stan didn't like to write. In fact, he hated it. Weeks went by without another letter. Frantic about his fate, Cockerell's mother contacted her local congressman, who contacted the brass at Fort Riley, who contacted Company First Sergeant Crockett. Shocked by his misfortune, Cockerell was summoned to Crockett's office – a summons that trainees dreaded more than anything else. Crockett made a show of slamming his window shut before unloading on his terrified young guest. "What the hell were you thinking not writing to your mama? Each and every one of you needs to write to your mamas!" The tirade went on for what seemed like an eternity, complete with several asides about busybody congressmen. At the end of it all, Crockett informed Cockerell that he was to return to his office each and every week to write to his mama. Crockett was going to make damn sure that mama Cockerell was going to get her letters!

On one afternoon with nothing to do but nothing, Henry Burleson went outside for a smoke and made the cardinal sin of dropping his used cigarette butt on the ground – only to be seen by no less a personage than Lieutenant Black. Amazed by the affront to common decency, Black called Burleson to attention and gathered the men who happened to be around to witness the appropriate punishment. He ordered Burleson to prepare the body of the deceased cigarette for a decent burial. After cleaning the butt, Burleson then had to dig a hole and bury the cigarette with all due military honors. After completing his task, Black complimented Burleson and began to walk away, only to stop, turn around and ask if the cigarette was out when Burleson had buried it. Burleson answered that it was, but Black made him dig it up to double check. Sweating in the heat, Burleson confirmed that the cigarette was in fact dead before burying it again – at which point Larry Lukes, who had spent the last two years of his civilian life throwing hay bales in Nebraska, burst out in laughter. For his punishment he got a chance to help in the never-ending cigarette funeral. After turning to leave again, Black turned back around and asked the pair if the cigarette had been buried facing east-west or north-south. Not knowing, the pair had to dig up the cigarette again to confirm before mercifully committing the butt to its final rest.

Mario Lopez was from Calexico, California – a town with a population comprised mainly of farm workers. His mother died when he was very young, so Mario spent much of his time with his father and grandmother learning how to work the fields. At a young age Mario learned the importance of money – his grandmother keeping the family's monetary haul safely stashed away in a small pouch that was tied around her neck that she hid inside her bra. When he was a sophomore in high school Lopez told his father that he wanted to drop and go to work full time. His father smiled and replied, "if that's what you want mijo then that's fine with me." The next morning at 2am there was a tug at Mario's arm. Time to go to work. The following day was so brutal, unloading trucks full of watermelons in 100-degree heat, that Mario wound up puking, doubled over in pain. The next morning at 2am, when his father called him to work, Mario responded that had thought it over and had decided to stay in school. His father smiled and replied, "if that's what you want mijo then that's fine with me."

The migrant worker community provided prime draft fodder, and Mario Lopez was off to join the 9th Infantry Division in 1966. When he exited the bus at Fort Riley, Lopez was one of the very first to do pushups – because he had answered the bellowing sergeants in his native Spanish. Lopez quickly learned that every instructor had his favorite trick. Nearly everyone in Charlie Company smoked, and many rolled their own. One day, during a marching exercise, a sergeant called his charges to a halt and bellowed, "Smoke break!" Relieved and at ease some started smoking right away and others started rolling. As soon as everyone had taken a drag, though, the sergeant yelled, "Smoke break over!" Cigarettes everywhere were tamped out, and the sergeant flew into a feigned rage. Who were these men to be wasting all of this good tobacco? Time to drop for pushups! The next day when the sergeant called the march to a halt and yelled, "Smoke break!" Lopez and his buddies had wised up. There was not a lit cigarette to be seen. Once again the sergeant boiled over and started screaming, "Who the hell are you men? Are you too good to smoke during a perfectly good smoke break?" It was time to drop for pushups again. Lopez realized that he was in a no win situation.

In his good-natured way Lieutenant Black enjoyed ribbing Charlie Nelson, the Navajo Indian who was also the shortest man in the unit. Discovering Nelson's background, Black boasted that he had some Indian heritage as well. On one company maneuver, Nelson was marching near the back of the column when he heard Black shout, "Nelson. Front and center!" Nelson reported while Black stood with his hands folded behind his back. While Nelson stood at attention, Black suddenly took one of his hands out from behind his back and dangled a lizard in front of Nelson's face, presumably in an effort to startle him. Nelson calmly looked at the lizard and then back to Black and said, "Sir, can I see him?" Not knowing what to expect, Black handed Nelson the lizard. Nelson flipped the lizard onto its back, whispered some words into its ear while rubbing it on the stomach, and it fell asleep. Nelson then handed the dozing reptile back to Black and said, "You might be part Indian, but I'm a full-blooded Indian."

Sometimes just having so many young men living together in such confined circumstances presented difficulties. John Bradfield very much looked forward to chow time, seemingly perpetually hungry due to the exertions of basic. Once, though, he suddenly was knocked out of the chow line and across the room, only to look back and see the rather smallish Forrest Ramos standing there with his fist raised. Bradfield immediately went on the offensive, and a brawl developed that landed both Bradfield and Ramos a stint in KP peeling potatoes. While working, Bradfield turned to Ramos: "Why the hell did you hit me man?" Ramos replied that another guy in the line had bet him that he wouldn't do it. Ramos then said, "I sure wouldn't have hit you if I'd known you were going to fight back so damn hard." Bradfield smiled and replied, "Well, you are lucky someone broke it up, or I would have whipped your sorry ass." With the obligatory testosterone-laced posing complete, the two became fast friends, each respecting the other's toughness. Neither Bradfield, an African American, nor Ramos, a Hispanic, knew very much about the other's culture and were often found in deep conversation about their varied upbringings. Ramos was especially smitten by soul music. Bradfield was one of the few draftees who had managed to bring a record player to the barracks, and during periods of off time guys from all walks of life would gather around his bunk to hear him play songs like "My Girl" and "Since I Lost My Baby" by the Temptations. One of the favorites for the men, though, was Percy Sledge's "When a Man Loves a Woman," which invariably drew a crowd, including Greenfield, Illinois native Steve Hopper – who always requested an encore because the song reminded him of home.

Only a year after the passage of the Voting Rights Act, military training threw together, willy-nilly, young men from varied backgrounds into a potentially charged social situation. For many of the trainees, service in Charlie Company was the first time that they had meaningful and extended contact with people from other races. While there was, and would remain, a tendency for like to seek out like – blacks hanging out with blacks listening to soul music, Hispanics gathering with Hispanics where there were no language barriers – the men in the unit hung together remarkably well and did not tend to worry about whose skin was what color. After all, there were common enemies of much greater importance – first the screaming, taunting NCOs, then the Viet Cong. The shared difficulties and goals that would help weld the disparate elements of Charlie Company into one were an early focus point of the unit's training. Understanding that race and ethnic differences were a problem best attacked head-on, immediately after his arrival at Fort Riley, Lieutenant Benedick gathered his charges in 2nd Platoon and told them that he did not see, nor would he accept others seeing, black soldiers, Hispanic soldiers, or white soldiers. All he saw were soldiers trying to accomplish a life-or-death mission. He saw them all as equals and would treat them as such, and expected the same from them, stressing that their very lives depended on it.

While Charlie Company was largely free from racial strife, the young soldiers learned much about themselves and each other through their interactions. Elijah Taylor, who hailed from highly segregated communities in Texas, found himself at ease one afternoon after his platoon had finished its assigned training regimen early. Unwilling to let the trainees off, the NCO in charge gathered the men into a circle and had them remove their belts. He then had one trainee from the group walk behind the circle and drop his belt behind another man, who in turn snatched up the belt and beat him with it as the two ran around the circle – in a kind of militarily violent "Duck Duck Goose." Strong and fast, Taylor was sure that nobody would have the guts to challenge him – but then he heard the belt drop. Whirling around he snatched up the belt and within just a few steps caught up to the small white trainee who had dropped it and proceeded to "whoop him all the way around the field." After his unfortunate victim had returned to the circle, he turned and said, "Taylor, you didn't need to beat me like that." Elijah responded, "Yes I did. Because in Texas we can't beat white people," at which the circle erupted into laughter. For days after, Taylor asked the NCOs if they were going to play the game again, and they always responded, "No. Nobody wants to play with you."

Willie McTear's training was eye opening in many respects. A veteran of Civil Rights marches in his native South, McTear paid close attention to the rise of black activism, especially taken with the writings of H. Rap Brown of the Student Nonviolent Coordinating Committee. Having always heard from the dominant culture in his youth that blacks were inferior, McTear was quite unsure how his first sojourn among a large group of whites would unfold. Little by little, though, McTear became aware of something. These other trainees, whether white or black, were no better or smarter than him. He could outrun almost all of them, and performed better on tests than many as well. The tales of black inferiority had been just that, tales. He was no worse than any other man in the unit. The lesson gave McTear a critical boost to his self-esteem, but it carried even further. During training Ronald Schworer learned that his mother had died. After breaking the terrible news, Lieutenant Benedick had informed Schworer that his mother's passing meant that he could get out of the service due to family hardship. McTear thought that Schworer, who still had tremendous problems with the physical portion of the training regimen, would jump at the chance. Instead Schworer told Benedick that he was going to complete his training and his service, because Charlie Company was his family now. Touched by Schworer's dedication, McTear realized that his best friend was a white man – something he had never believed possible.

The mixing together of so many young men in such a stressful environment sometimes led to a letting off of steam in manners consistent with military prank-playing and buffoonery down through the ages. John Sclimenti, another of the California contingent who had been the popular vice-president of his high school class, was one of the many jokers of Charlie Company. His two favorite pranks were both nocturnal in nature. One involved himself and a co-conspirator sneaking into the platoon bay at night, removing a bunk and carrying both it and its somnolent passenger down to another platoon bay. The next morning the victim would arise bleary-eyed and rush to his footlocker to get ready for the day, only to find himself lost. Sclimenti's other favorite prank was a variation on the same theme, in which he and his partners in crime would pile footlockers three high in the latrine and then perch the bunk and its sleeping cargo atop the pile, leaving the soldier to awake at reveille the next morning only to find himself 8 feet in the air.

In a unit so full of jokesters that even Sclimenti's actions didn't raise many eyebrows, one joker stood out from the rest – so much so that his trainee compatriots whispered that he must be trying his best to get out of the army. Lamous Elliott was constantly in trouble for offenses as mundane as habitually sliding down the banisters of the barracks in full view of the NCOs to nearly dropping his rifle on the captain's feet during formation. Even when forced to do pushups as punishment, Elliott turned the scene to comedy by only pushing out one, and then (with arms and legs quivering in affected exhaustion) loudly stating in a put-on drawl, "Cap'n, I just can'ts takes no mo!" Elliott's many contrived gaffes, though, soon reached the level of military art form. After receiving a short leave to return to Chicago for the birth of his first child, Elliott returned to Fort Riley with a steamer trunk full of clothes. As he readied for his crowning performance, Elliott announced to a growing throng of interested onlookers that since they were going to war, he might never have time to do this again. Atop his military issue underwear Elliott donned a woman's silk night robe, an ensemble topped off with a pair of roller skates. To the amazement of everyone present, Elliott then burst into song and zoomed off down the hall where he disappeared into Company First Sergeant Crockett's office. The now muffled song was followed by the sounds of furniture moving and Crockett's voice bellowing, "What the hell are you doing?" As if by magic Elliott was no longer a member of Charlie Company.

After mastering the basics, including marching, physical fitness, and marksmanship, on August 8, 1966, the men of Charlie Company moved on to Advanced Individual Training (AIT) where they began to receive instruction in their individual areas of specialty and some rudimentary unit training. These men were not simply going to be soldiers; they were going to be riflemen, machine gunners, radio operators, and medics. The new level of importance dawned on Jace Johnston almost immediately when his NCO announced that he was now going to push them extra hard because his life was going to depend on how well they did their job in Vietnam as riflemen. After hearing the warning, John

Bradfield turned to Tim Fischer and asked him where Vietnam was. Fischer replied that it was a far away country where the US was involved in a war, a country to which they would soon be going, and that they could all die there. At that point the two men agreed that it was time to stop training to be soldiers and time to start training to go to war.

In one of the few deviations from the standard training regimen to prepare the men for work in the Mekong Delta, the 9th Division spent extra time in swimming instruction and river-crossing techniques. Standard practice called for one of the unit's stronger swimmers to cross the river first to tie off a rope on the far side. Others would cross using the rope as a guide, with the least capable swimmers using air mattresses, on which heavy equipment, such as machine guns, was floated across. Such crossings were always difficult for John Bradfield. The Cleveland native had never swum before and had an unnatural fear of water. On one occasion he lost his grip on the air mattress, panicked, and felt himself starting to drown. At that point a hand reached down and pulled him to safety – it was Richard Rubio. Another crossing method involved shuffling sideways across the river with the trainee grasping one taut rope in his hands while his feet were on another lower taut rope suspended 10 feet above the water. The exercise required the greatest concentration and delicate balance, resulting in many a splash down for the unfortunate. Making matters worse, Lieutenant Black delighted in appearing at the far side of the river where he would start shaking the bottom rope while asking the trainee who was suspended above the water, "Son, are you a true believer? You had better be a true believer!"

For many, the most memorable part of AIT was the simulated prisoner-of-war camp. Every trainee in Charlie Company served a stint in the POW camp, where conditions were as near as possible to what the soldiers could expect if they were captured in Vietnam. There were intense interrogation sessions, during which soldiers were shut into footlockers on which the NCOs proceeded to beat with baseball bats. Some were made to lie or sit in the mud, while others (who, the NCOs lied, were cooperating with their interrogators – a standard practice to sow dissension within the group) received much better treatment. The interrogations went on for hours, leaving Larry Lukes and Henry Burleson ready to make a change. Along with Butch Eakins, a country boy from Cape Girardeau, Missouri, the group waited until no NCO was looking and slithered through a hole in the concertina wire. After they had escaped from the enclosure, the threesome waited until a nearby lieutenant had his back turned, stole his jeep, and drove back to their barracks. Expecting the descent of the rough hand of military justice, Lukes, Burleson, and Eakins were surprised when they were complimented for their ingenuity. After all, it was the first duty of any POW to attempt an escape.

It was during AIT that the men of Charlie Company first began to act together in units, with platoons maneuvering around the open countryside in coordinated fashion. Having that many men, many of whom were smokers, traipsing about the bone-dry Kansas grasslands of late summer, though, was a recipe for disaster. After one particularly long march to the geographic center of the middle of nowhere, the NCO told his platoon to rest, adding the ubiquitous "smoke 'em if you got 'em." Doug Wilson, a Californian with two years of college to his credit, quickly took advantage of the opportunity and lit his smoke, tossing the used match over his shoulder. Almost immediately the grass all around his feet was aflame and men everywhere were grabbing their jackets and packs in an effort to beat out the spreading conflagration. Confounding the best efforts of his platoon, the fire spread until the entire battalion was brought in to beat the flames into submission. Through the smoke, Sergeant Crockett loomed, booming, "Wilson! Where is Wilson?" It was time for Doug Wilson to go and find his mind.

During late August Steve Moede sent a rather innocuous letter to his mother in California wondering in print whether or not training on the plains of Kansas was going to be all that useful in the jungles of Vietnam. Moede's mother wrote back that if he was concerned he ought to write a letter to complain, and amazingly Moede did so, writing a letter to no less a personage than President Lyndon Baines Johnson, a letter signed by many other members of his platoon. Since some young men can't keep a secret, the contents of the letter quickly became known within the battalion, and Bill Reynolds, a native of the Los Angeles area who was serving as one of the platoon's squad leaders, found himself called in to face both

Company First Sergeant Crockett and Captain Larson. With Larson taking something of a back seat in the meeting, Crockett boomed out a drill sergeant's profanity-laced exposition of the meaning of patriotism and the proper place of enlisted men in the army. Where the hell did a young private get off writing to the president? Their training was fine and their asses belonged to the military. After the dressing down of a lifetime, Reynolds returned to the platoon and suggested that the letter "go away." The remainder of the signers agreed and returned to their training, perhaps marking their final conversion from civilians to soldiers.

Much of AIT involved readying soldiers for performance in combat with their new weapons specialty. Most of Charlie Company trained with rifle squads, learning the basic art of infantry warfare. Each platoon, though, included an exception – the weapons squad, where soldiers now began to specialize as members of an M60 machine gun team or with a 90mm recoilless rifle. Within Charlie Company Sergeant Pedro Blas headed the training of one of the exceptions to the rule, the Mortar Platoon, where Richard Northcott, who used to love to race his hot rod on the streets of Encino, California, enjoyed the excitement of working with the 81mm mortar, a rifle company's standard light fire support. The Mortar Platoon usually trained separately, learning how to carry, assemble, and use its weapons to lay down a protective screen of fire for the surrounding infantry platoons. Those selected to be radiotelephone operators (RTOs), were another breed apart. These men, including Bob French, were going to be the indispensable link between the men in the field, their command element, and the sources of supporting fire from artillery and the air. Knowing that they were going to be prime enemy targets in battle, the RTOs received very specific training in the use of their PRC 25 radios and were usually separate from their trainee brethren – always at the shoulder of their NCO or officer during maneuvers as they would be in battle.

The most distinctive specialty of all, though, was that of the medics, who were taken from Fort Riley to Fort Sam Houston, Texas, where they underwent a ten-week course on military medicine at the US Army Medical Training Center. The select group included Robert Cara, Gary Maibach, the conscientious objector,

Bill Geier, who had always hoped for the assignment, and Elijah Taylor, who had no clue why he was chosen. At Fort Sam, the group sat down in a meeting room, and in walked a tough old NCO who announced: "Gentlemen, you are about to embark on a course of training at the US Army Medical Training Center. We will so well equip you to render service to your injured fellow servicemen that when in the future you come upon a field of battle and carnage in Vietnam you will be able to march up to any individual who may have suffered a traumatic amputation of both legs, arms, or even his head that when you present him with your certificate of accomplishment from the US Army Medical Training Center he will have no alternative but to recover."

The training received by Cara, Taylor, Geier, and Maibach, though, was somewhat less than what the impressive speech had implied. Not knowing whether the trainees were going to be hospital corpsmen or field medics, the course of study was rather chaotic. The instructors crammed in as much anatomy and physiology as they could before moving on to subjects as varied as triage, wound debridement, tourniquet use, and how to test for venereal disease. By the time the newly minted medics made their journey back to Fort Riley to join their units, Maibach thought that they had learned "just enough to be relatively dangerous." Elijah Taylor and Robert Cara had become especially close during their time at Fort Sam, spending much of their study time with records playing in the background. Taylor learned to tolerate Cara's favorites, including Paul Anka and Roy Orbison, but made damn sure that Cara got a chance to listen to the Temptations and Smokey Robinson and the Miracles.

Once back with Charlie Company, the medics found themselves assigned to company headquarters, from which they were parceled out to platoons as needed for maneuvers and eventually for service in Vietnam. Rather like the Mortar Platoon, the specialists who served with headquarters, both the RTOs and medics, were often separated from their fellow draftees in the company for long stretches of time. Since they now worked together, these specialists often formed their own set of friendships. While Bill Geier retained his close relationship with Idoluis Casares, whom he had affectionately dubbed "Bear," Geier also began to pal around with

RTO Bob French. Geier loved to talk about his sister Jackie, the light of his young life. She often sent him letters and care packages from home, which always wound up with Bill sharing her written exploits, and cookies, with Bob. In turn, French liked to hold forth on his own sister, Ginger. After seeing her picture, Geier was immediately smitten and, with Bob's permission and blessing, began to write to her. The correspondence went so well that Geier informed his parents of the budding relationship and that he could not wait to meet her in person, if he could only find a way to get to Florida.

During AIT, several of the young soldiers found themselves assigned the position of squad leader, an honor that conferred acting rank, but something meant for NCOs of much longer service. Some, like John Young, who was the battalion's outstanding trainee, seemed natural gung-ho fits for such a position. Bill Reynolds realized that someone would have to be assigned to such positions and felt that it might as well be him, so worked hard to be ready when called. Tim Fischer believed that his selection was due simply to the fact that he knew how to march and was kind of mean, two characteristics required of an NCO. Dave Jarczewski, son of a steel worker from a suburb of Buffalo and one of the few northeasterners in the unit, didn't much like the assignment, realizing that he was just a "pissbox" recruit like those who were going to be under his command. Why on earth would they listen to him? Although their new temporary rank came with some perks, with the Cleveland native son of Hungarian immigrants Frank Schwan noting that because of his exalted status he no longer had to do KP, the position of squad leader was one of great responsibility and authority. John Young described his new duties in a letter home to his parents:

I'm a squad leader of a rifle squad. I'm supposed to be a staff sergeant E-6, and I'll make that pay grade in country [Vietnam]. There's a total of ten men in a rifle squad. The squad is divided into two teams, Alfa and Bravo. Each team has a sergeant E-5 as its leader ... a grenadier, who carries an M-79 grenade launcher, which looks like a big-barreled sawed-off shotgun; an automatic rifleman, who carries an M16 rifle which is always set on automatic fire; this means that you don't have to pull the trigger once for each shot, you just hold the trigger down and it fires like a machinegun, the team is completed by a rifleman, also armed with an M16 set on semi-automatic (one shot per trigger pull). The Bravo team is the same, save the addition of a second rifleman. In Vietnam, it is standard procedure to have 2 of the squad's men armed with 12 gauge pump shotguns. I am responsible for everything my squad does and is. If they need ammo or toilet paper, mortar support or medical attention, I am supposed to get it.

Knowing that their tasks would be difficult, and that the lives of their men now depended on their skills, all the young squad leaders worked long and hard to get their jobs right. Tim Fischer was representative in that he kept a detailed diary of his squad's individual strengths and weaknesses:

> Caliari – obeys well, works with all the squad well, keeps going when it gets tough, helps others when they need help in something.
> McGowan – has fair attitude toward work, will do anything when asked to do it, works good with the other men in squad and gets in and gets squad's morale up.
> McBride – has very poor attitude toward work and military service, has to be helped in doing certain things, once he is on a job, though, he will do his best.
> Creagor – has to be helped with things quite often, works good but is very quiet and morale is very low, tries his best when doing something, I'm trying to get his morale up, the problem I think is that he has no friends and no one will lend him a hand when needed.

Fischer also kept a detailed list of "Dos and Don'ts" with which the squad leaders were supposed to keep their men up to speed:

> Do be prepared for the unexpected...
> Any stranger [can be] an enemy...
> Be alert for snipers in all places [including] haystacks and wells.
> When possible have villagers lead you into villages, rivers, etc...
> Don't discuss classified things over the telephone or radio.
> Don't drink water from unknown sources.

Don't trust children.

Don't shoot until you know you can kill.

Don't relax anytime, especially after a mission.

Cultural Relations – Avoid use of slang while talking.

Try and use Vietnamese language.

Always use rank or Mr. or Mrs.

When in doubt, be courteous.

As the squad leaders wrestled with their newfound responsibilities, AIT came to an end, and the components of the 9th Division readied for their basic and advanced unit training. It was at the end of AIT that the men of Charlie Company finally received their military occupation specialty (MOS), most designated 11 Bravo or light weapons infantry (riflemen), some designated 11 Charlie or indirect fire infantry (mortars), and a few designated 91 Bravo or medics. Now specialized cogs in the military machine, the soldiers gathered in what became their favorite event of the year. The entire battalion hunkered down and for a few mad minutes fired everything it had – M16s, mortars, machine guns, and artillery – at a small hill about half a mile distant. After the spectacle everyone in Charlie Company knew that their unit was a powerful killing machine.

Unit training involved the components of the entire 2nd Brigade learning to function on their own as squads, platoons, and companies navigating in maneuvers across the countryside, laying ambushes, mounting assaults, and defending against both infantry and armor attacks all while accurately calling in artillery and air support. Once the smaller units became proficient in their tasks, they were combined in battalion- and even brigade-sized operations. During much of the fall and early winter at Fort Riley the draftees were on nearly endless maneuvers out in the wilds of the Kansas countryside, often for a week at a time. Unlike basic and AIT, since the soldiers were gone for such long stretches from their barracks, they had to carry everything that they would need, just like it was going to be in Vietnam. John Young wrote home about this new experience:

The gear we're carrying on our backs is getting heavier and heavier. I'm now wearing and/or carrying 2 ammo pouches, a first aid pack, a canteen, a pack, a poncho, an entrenching tool (a small shovel), a mess kit, a flashlight, a pair of binoculars, a PRC 6 radio (walkie-talkie type), a compass, a protective (gas) mask, a bedroll (sleeping bag, tent half, tent poles, tent pins and tent rope), an extra set of fatigues, a winter work uniform, a change of socks and underwear, shaving gear, a flak jacket, and all this topped by that miserable steel helmet. All that stuff must weigh about 45–50 pounds, and I still have to find room for my rifle. Just walking with that load is fine, because you actually do get used to it, but running with all that is a different story entirely. About 50 yards running and you really do want to stop.

With many of the maneuvers involving an overnight stay under the stars, there were ample chances for mischief. Jimmie Salazar, who had at last finalized plans to marry his girlfriend Aurora, was adept at sneaking up beside men who were just ready to doze off after a hard day's march and launching into a very believable impression of a rattlesnake, which always led to the victim leaping up and stumbling around while tangled in his sleeping bag. Each night the units in the field had to set up defensive perimeters, which involved the men, exhausted after a day's march, digging foxholes and setting up a night watch rotation. Falling asleep on watch was a cardinal sin, but for tired young men, who were not overly worried about being attacked in Kansas, sleep was almost impossible to avoid. It was then that the "Phantom Shitter" would strike. Someone, perhaps multiple someones, would creep out of the unit perimeter on a regular basis and sneak around looking for those asleep while on guard duty. Once the phantom had located his snoozing quarry, he would leave a pile of freshly delivered human excrement on the lip of the victim's foxhole – a telltale and quite embarrassing sign of the soldier's failure.

As the training of all types progressed for the members of Charlie Company, real life continued. Most of the officers and senior NCOs were married and brought their wives and children to Fort Riley for the duration of their stay, wanting to spend every minute that they could with their loved ones before departing for the war zone. For some the strains of juggling home life with their military obligations placed an unbearable burden on their marriages. Although he hid it well from his men, Rollo Larson knew that his marriage was in trouble, with his wife unable to come to terms with the massive amount of time he had to devote to the training of his unit. The officers of Charlie Company had to be at Fort Riley from before sunup to after sundown every day, including most weekends. For others home life while at Fort Riley was cramped and busy, but workable. Jack Benedick and his wife Nancy rented a small apartment in Manhattan, Kansas, while Herb Lind, a Nebraska native, and his wife Becky were somewhat less fortunate and had to live in a trailer nearby. Both couples had only one car, meaning that the wives often found themselves stranded with no transportation while their husbands were on post. Only a few, including Daniel Kerr, who had gotten married during his last posting in Germany, lived on post. After a few weeks in Kansas, Kerr's wife, Karin, had come to join him from Germany. Everything was new to her in America, so she often kept to herself. It was her first time away from Germany and she was carrying the couple's first child. Kerr did the best he knew how to help but could not avoid his workload with the company. On the night of October 31, 1966, Kerr was in the company quarters when he received a frantic call from Karin. Something was wrong. Every few minutes children, dressed in outlandish costumes, came to the door demanding candy. What should she do? Kerr had forgotten to warn his startled bride about the American tradition of Halloween.

Chaplain Bernie Windmiller was a native of Gary, Indiana, who had been drafted in 1954 after the Korean armistice and served his stint in the military before going to Fuller Theological Seminary and becoming a minister in the Evangelical Covenant Church of America. Called to further service, Windmiller returned to the military as a chaplain and served with a unit outside of Chicago for only a month before reporting to duty as one of the chaplains of the 2nd Brigade of the 9th Infantry Division. After moving his wife Esther into their apartment, Windmiller made his first appearance among the trainees. As he walked up to the unit, some of the soldiers were lounging around having conversations in salty soldier-speak. A nearby NCO exploded, shouting, "You fucking guys shut your goddamn mouths! The chaplain's here!" Taking the military humor in his stride, Windmiller went about his duty of preparing the soldiers spiritually for what they would face in wartime, preparations that included everything from regular church services to personal counseling.

Immediately, Windmiller struck up a friendship with Duffy Black, who was both very religious and conscious of the danger the war would soon pose to those under his care. The two talked very nearly every evening about a wide range of subjects. One recurrent theme was love. Black very much admired the wonderful relationship shared by Windmiller and his wife Esther but worried that he might never find true love himself. Black knew that he would have difficulty letting go and trusting someone else so thoroughly. One day in early September, though, Black burst into Windmiller's office on Custer Hill and told the chaplain that he was in love, and "his face beamed like that of a child who has just placed the last piece into a puzzle." He had met and fallen in love with a beautiful girl named Ida, who happened to be the daughter of the postmaster of the 9th Infantry Division. Within weeks the young couple was coming to Windmiller for marriage counseling. The two were wed in the Custer Hill Chapel in late October 1966, with many of the men and officers of Charlie Company in attendance, and set up housekeeping on base, able to spend only a few months together before Duffy was scheduled to ship out to Vietnam.

After Don Peterson was drafted, his wife Jacque, who was newly pregnant, travelled to Biloxi, Mississippi to live with her mother and stepfather, a situation that their alcohol abuse made difficult. After basic training, Don received a short leave and met Jacque back in California, where the two decided that, regardless of the difficulty, they had to be together. After Don's return to Fort Riley for AIT, Jacque packed the couple's few things and made her way to Kansas. With little money to spare, Jacque and Don set up housekeeping in a three-bedroom home that they shared with two other married couples from Charlie Company, Don and Sue Deedrick and Steve and Karen Huntsman. Steve was from Saint George, Utah, and had worked on road crews in the desert heat before attending Brigham Young University. After falling in love with Karen, though, Steve dropped out of college and the couple married in December 1965, while Karen was still a 17-year-old high school senior. Now subject to the draft, Steve had to report to Fort Riley with all the others in Charlie Company, with Karen joining him there after a long train ride at the same time that Jacque Peterson arrived from California.

Even though the house was crowded, with the Deedricks and the Petersons sharing the sole upstairs bathroom, and their husbands gone for long stretches of training, the three young brides got along famously, "with stars in their eyes" as they worked the best they could to set up the perfect household. Often stranded in the house, since only the Petersons had a car and the boys usually used it to get to Fort Riley and back, the threesome chatted, drank coffee, and tried to have a hot meal waiting on the table when the fellas came home. Karen taught the group how to cook, specializing in Steve's favorites, macaroni and cheese and divinity fudge for dessert. One constant worry, though, was the water. It simply didn't taste right, so the girls mixed it with Goofy Grape for dinnertime drinks. During the days when the boys were away for longer periods, the girls often walked to do their shopping and got hooked on soap operas, especially *Days of Our Lives*.

In all it was great fun, and something of an adventure. Jacque took in ironing and hired out as a babysitter to make more money. When the boys were home, sometimes they would sit around drinking beer, which caused some conflict due to the Huntsmans' Mormon beliefs, but any problems soon faded amid the general atmosphere of milking each minute for all it was worth before the boys had to ship out. As AIT gave way to unit training the mood in the house began to darken. Karen noticed that Steve was growing more and more silent, but, so new to the everyday rituals of being married, did not know what to do. After wondering for days if she had done something wrong, Karen finally got to the truth of the matter – Steve was petrified of going to Vietnam. The two talked, as did the other couples, about the war, but there was little that the wives could do to help other than offer their unflagging support. Usually, though, the couples tucked Vietnam away in their marital attics, not wanting to waste their precious time together talking of things they could not change. But as Christmas neared and it became clear that the unit would be shipping out soon, the war cast an ever-larger shadow over their lives. Each wife knew that there was a chance that her husband would never return. Each husband knew that he could leave his young wife a grieving widow.

For some of the boys of Charlie Company, going through training and preparing to depart for a war zone was just the motivation they needed to pop the question. Tom Conroy, the son of a meat packer who had been drafted along with several of his friends from Lancaster, California, had met his sweetheart, Vivian, at a high school football game. The couple had dated for five years, and had often spoken of their future together, but had never quite made it to the altar. They were young, Vivian being only 18 at the time, and had an entire future to think of such matters. Tom's draft notice had changed all of that. Who knew what their future held, and Vivian certainly did not want to wind up "an old maid." So the couple got married after Tom completed basic training, and Vivian made her way to Fort Riley. Bill Reed, himself from a middle class Lancaster, California family, had also taken the plunge and gotten married during the very same leave period. Surprised that they now shared so much in common, the Reeds and the Conroys decided to share an apartment with a third married couple from the unit. The place was so cramped that one unlucky couple had to sleep in the pantry.

Gene Harvey was another of the California contingent of draftees, son of a Lockheed mechanic from Hollywood. Attending junior college and working on cars with his father in his spare time, Harvey had fallen for a girl named Deana. The two had dated and were quite serious, but the arrival of Gene's draft notice had almost split them up. A few weeks at Fort Riley reminded the couple of what they had together and how quickly they could lose each other. Perhaps, too, Harvey had been affected by the example of Lieutenant Black. The day before Black's wedding Harvey had asked him why he had decided to settle down. Black had replied simply, "Because I'm in love." He hadn't needed any other reason. Following Black's example, Gene and Deana married in November 1966, and soon invited John Sclimenti, the noted unit jokester, and his girlfriend over for a Thanksgiving dinner with all of the trimmings. As the date of their departure for Vietnam drew nearer, Harvey and Conroy were very aware that they were preparing to leave behind new wives – women they had sworn to love and honor. Now, after so little time together, the brides would have to put their new lives on hold while their husbands risked their lives in foreign fields far from home. Harvey and Conroy knew that fighting in Vietnam would be difficult, but they both feared that their wives would have it worse.

Fred Kenney had been in the crowded platoon bay one afternoon after drills toward the end of basic training when he opened a letter from his wife Barbara that he had thought was just going to be full of the normal, mundane news and gossip that were staples of a long-distance relationship. Instead he leapt for joy when he learned that he was going to be a father, after which he went around poking the letter into the faces of whoever happened to be around, clapping them on the shoulder, and announcing his impending papahood. The news, though, was bittersweet because, unlike his other married friends, Fred could not afford to have Barbara move to be with him at Fort Riley. Instead she had to stay behind in California, where she first bunked in with her mother before moving in with Fred's sister Mary Lou. It was difficult on the young couple, being apart at such an important time. While Fred felt somewhat jealous of his more fortunate married buddies, he never let it show. Instead he put his efforts into planning the couple's future as parents, dreaming about where they might live, what they might do, and what kind of parents they would be when the war finally allowed them to live together. Back in California, Barbara pored over every word that Fred wrote, usually sharing the letters with the Kenney family. In Freddie's absence, the old mixed group of friends and family became even closer, with Barbara a nearly constant fixture at the Kenney household. Together the friends plotted to throw Freddie the best party ever when he came home on leave before he left for Vietnam.

Although he did not have his wife close at hand, Fred continued to take solace in being in a unit with so many of his friends. Fred, Richard Rubio, Tim Johnson, Larry Lilley, and Kenny Frakes formed a tight-knit sub-unit of the California contingent in Charlie Company. Having heard stories about the five Sullivan brothers who had been killed in World War II aboard the USS *Juneau*, the Canoga and Lancaster High graduates were amazed when they had been allowed to serve together. The group also came to include

Forrest Ramos, whom they had met on the train to Fort Riley and with whom they shared an interest because of Ramos' time spent living in Los Angeles. The group was close in many ways, often passing around letters from home. Forrest Ramos particularly liked the letters from Richard Rubio's cousin Patricia. She seemed quite nice, and to hear Rubio tell it, she was beautiful. Forrest asked his pal if it would be OK to write to her, and Rubio gave his assent, figuring, "What the heck. Nothing will come of it."

The friends often plotted what kind of mischief they could get up to when they once again rejoined the civilian world and worked to cheer Fred on through the difficult times. Through it all, Fred remained especially close with Richard Rubio. The two did everything together, from helping each other through physical training to slopping through the brutal experience of the mock prisoner-of-war camp. Both were in awe of their young platoon leader, Lieutenant John Hoskins. A tough, true believer in the cause of Vietnam, Hoskins had immediately become close friends with his officer colleagues in Charlie Company and had taken a deep interest in both the training and lives of his men. Like Lieutenant Black before him, Hoskins had introduced himself to his trainees by issuing a challenge to a pushup contest. It was the small, but immensely strong Rubio who had taken the challenge, leaving Hoskins wondering how he had been beaten so easily. After the performance, Hoskins, who wrote poetry instead of frequenting the officers' club during his off hours, took both Rubio and Kenney under his wing. Feeling an affinity for the young friends, Hoskins made Rubio his first RTO and always seemed to have Fred close by his side on maneuvers. For Fred Kenney the seemingly constant work, tempered by friendship and mentoring, made the prospect of leaving a wife and young child behind while fighting in a war zone somehow less daunting.

Although the work level remained high, as AIT gave way to unit training, the men of Charlie Company finally began to receive a bit more free time, and were even allowed to visit the surrounding towns of Manhattan and Junction City. Without much money, and often without transport, many of the men, as is so often the case in the military, just hung around the barracks listening to music, writing letters home, reading, or catching up on their labors. Fort Riley itself offered a few recreational options, including a ratty pool table located in the battalion area, movies, and an enlisted men's beer garden. Beer was cheap and the yarns spun around the tables were usually good, making the beer garden especially popular. Tacoma, Washington, native Ron Vidovic, still smarting from a recent divorce and the resulting separation from his two children, was one of the top pool players in the unit, and often held forth against all comers while making small, usually successful, bets on the outcome. If an officer came by, though, all bets would suddenly cease, and Vidovic's billiards talent would vanish as the interloper was allowed to win. Once the officer had lost interest and departed, Vidovic would return to business as usual. It was not as if the officers and NCOs had an aversion to gambling, though, since they could often be found during what little spare time they had on the weekends in their own group poker games. In part as an effort at information gathering for the other men, Jace Johnston often sat in on the NCOs' poker games as a runner. Amid the smoke and conversation, Johnston picked up what he could before being sent away to acquire whatever the members of the group needed, from smokes to drinks. Nobody's fool, Johnston would buy the goods from wherever he could find them, and then sell them to the thirsty officers at a profit.

On occasion drinking took place clandestinely in the barracks. After a short visit home, Willie McTear managed to smuggle a bottle of down-home moonshine into the platoon bay. Upon learning of their booze windfall, the other members of the platoon who happened to be present gathered around to gaze longingly at McTear's liquid gold. Ready to share his good fortune with his pals, McTear, a seasoned alcohol veteran, first turned to Stan Cockerell, who had been keeping up a steady stream of letters home under Company First Sergeant Crockett's tutelage. McTear knew that, as the youngest guy in Charlie Company, Cockerell was a drinking novice who was unprepared for the near lethal effects of real, homemade shine. The next morning found McTear and his buddies gloriously hung over, but Cockerell was exceptional in his distress. Pale, sweating profusely, and nearly incomprehensible, Cockerell had to be supported by his partners in crime to make it through morning inspection. A passing NCO, though, noticed Cockerell's sorry condition, informed the group that they were an affront to the entire army, and placed everyone on KP until further notice.

For the soldiers of Charlie Company, though, the number one favorite pastime was going into the surrounding towns in search of girls. For Doug Wilson, Manhattan was the place to be, since, as a college town, it offered potential access to coeds. He and the other California guys, sure that their charms would be irresistible to the locals, went to the bars and dancehalls around Kansas State University, where they often sighted the quarry, but rarely had any luck – a sad state of affairs that the soldiers blamed on their nearly bald heads. They knew in their hearts that if they only had the bushy locks of their surfer days everything would have been different.

The more adventurous members of Charlie Company eventually found their way to 9th Street in Junction City. Known as the "Harlem of Kansas" the vibrant community around 9th Street boasted a strip of black-owned bars, pool halls, and the odd house of ill repute. Most of the white soldiers, ill at ease entering this side of a still-segregated Junction City on their own, usually first visited 9th Street with one of their African-American compatriots. Alan Richards, a country boy from rural Wisconsin, first went to 9th Street with a group of his buddies from the mortar platoon. Parched as they were after the rigors of basic training, the group huddled into a bar crowded with other soldiers. Eager to drink their fill as quickly as possible, Richards and his friends elbowed their way to the bar, but the pushing and shoving quickly led to a fully fledged barroom brawl. Amid flying punches and a rain of chairs, the platoon hung together in its first-ever combat, forming a wedge and making its way to the relative safety of the girls' bathroom. When the front door burst open and the first MPs appeared, Richards and his friends, along with a scantily-clad female "performer," made a hurried exit from the establishment through the bathroom window. Once outside they looked back as the building seemed to have sprung a leak, with frantic GIs flowing freely from all of the bar's windows and doors. On another occasion, in the darkened upstairs rooms of a similar establishment, one soldier from Charlie Company successfully negotiated the price for an end to his virginity. With others who did not want to go to Vietnam and war as sexual innocents impatiently waiting their turn, the business transaction began. Within minutes, though, the whole affair came to an abrupt halt as an agitated, gun-wielding pimp entered the room, resulting in another hurried window exit before the MPs arrived.

By the time training had come to an end and the men of Charlie Company were making ready to spend two weeks at home before the unit shipped out to Vietnam, civilians had been transformed into soldiers. After the first live-fire event of basic training, Jim Dennison had gone off to be by himself, wondering if he would ever have the guts to kill somebody. By December, though, he realized that he had gone from being a Christian doubter of the morality of war to being a trained killer. Regardless of the moral implications of his discovery, he took solace in the knowledge that he would be able to get the job done in battle and not let his friends down.

The men had become much more than trained soldiers; along the way they had become brothers. The bonds of camaraderie were especially apparent to the older, more experienced officers and NCOs. Company First Sergeant Crockett looked upon Charlie Company with great pride, knowing that his boys would no doubt bitch and complain, in the best army fashion, about everything in Vietnam from the heat to the mosquitoes. But he also knew that the unit was ready. The men would do their jobs and could count on each other as the officers and NCOs could count on them. Lost in the moment, the men were in the main unaware of the closeness of the bonds that they had developed with one another. They all had a vague sense of accomplishment, with Richard Rubio speaking for all in stating that the training had "made us better than we knew we could be." The true depth of their camaraderie, though, would only become apparent when the boys of Charlie Company lost the first of their brothers to combat.

In mid-December 1966, the soldiers of Charlie Company fanned back out across the nation for two weeks of leave with their families and sweethearts. For most it was great just to be home again. Certainly they were different, having grown and put on more muscle during their training. After modeling their uniforms for their curious siblings, the young men soaked up what they could of civilian life, going to movies, going on dates, and drinking too much beer. But just below the surface there was a mounting tension. Nobody really wanted to talk about it, but in a few short days the boys of Charlie Company would be off to Vietnam: many would never return. Mothers cried silently in their rooms at night, siblings sat more closely together, and stone-faced fathers grappled with unfamiliar emotions, even though their soldier sons had told them that everything would be fine. With the invulnerability of youth, these men were convinced that it would not be them who died in Vietnam. Each of the sons and brothers of Charlie Company dealt with the difficulties presented by imminent departure for Vietnam in his own way. Ron Vidovic told his grandmother the truth, but, fearing it would break her heart, he did not tell his mother that he was headed to Vietnam; instead he lied that he was going to receive a stateside assignment. Henry Burleson gratefully accepted a New Testament from his weeping mother, as his father patted him on the back and told him how proud he was that he was going to do his duty for his country. Burleson promised to read the Bible each day and to stay safe. Back at his home in Encino, Richard Northcott did his best to ignore his mother's tendency to shake slightly in the few moments that they had alone together during his leave. In Calexico, California Mario Lopez knew by the tears in his father's eyes that he was saying goodbye to a new man – a respectful and proud soldier. That look of pride Mario never forgot.

For some in the unit, leaving for Vietnam brought out other emotions. Things got a bit heated during Terry McBride's visit home when two of his World War II veteran relatives told him that they had better not hear him whining about that little war that he was off to. McBride lashed out, promising to survive the fighting just to come back and show them what was what. Ronnie Gann returned home to Los Angeles only to discover that his father, who evidently did not believe that Ronnie was going to return from Vietnam, had sold his car. When Bill Varskafsky returned to Washington for his leave, he discovered that his pregnant wife had horrified his mother by trotting out all of the paperwork for his military life insurance forms to demonstrate how well off she would be if Bill did not make it home.

For some families the occasion of having their soldier boy back home for a short period called for a party, partly in an effort to keep the blues of his imminent departure at bay. In Canoga Park, Barbara and the Kenneys threw an epic bash for Fred's return home, involving a visit to the beach and, of course, motorcycle riding. During his short stay Fred was able to pamper his wife just a bit and marveled at the opportunity to place his hand on her abdomen and feel the baby kick. He was thrilled with the idea of being a father, and the two spent time picking out baby names and making plans for life together upon his return. In Maywood, Illinois, the Geiers put out the red carpet for Bill's leave. His mother, Bernice, was so pleased that he had indeed become a medic that she nearly burst with pride. The night before his departure, the family held a big neighborhood party in the basement, playing all of Bill's favorite 45s, ending up in a group Conga line that went on until folks nearly passed out from exhaustion. As the festivities drew to a close, at the urging of his siblings, Bill donned his Class A uniform and posed for a picture in front of the adoring crowd.

Many within Charlie Company saw their leave as the perfect time to make a major life change. Bob French had already set the standard by getting married to his sweetheart between basic training and AIT, a sweetheart he now had to drive back to Tampa, Florida, with her crying on and off the whole way. He didn't know she was pregnant. Larry Lukes, who had led the escape from the POW camp, had fallen in love with a girl from Nebraska during training, and the couple wed during his leave in December, in part to allow her to collect his life insurance if he died in Vietnam. Jimmie Salazar finally gave Aurora the big wedding she wanted, not knowing that he was leaving her pregnant as he departed for Vietnam.

At the conclusion of training, Don Peterson boarded a train in Fort Riley bound for Montgomery, Alabama, to take Jacque to live with her mother and stepfather while he was in Vietnam. In order to board, Jacque had to lie and say that she was only seven months pregnant, since the train conductor evidently wanted no part of helping to deliver a baby on the journey south. After two grueling days of travel, the couple got off in Montgomery, where Jacque's parents met them, and a few days later she went into labor. The delivery was long and difficult, eventually resulting in 9-pound baby James being delivered by C-section. In those days hospitals, especially air force hospitals like the one in which James was born, did not allow fathers and babies into the same room. The dad could only gaze at the child through the glass of the big nursery room window. Don was able to visit Jacque, but whenever the nurse brought James into the room, he had to leave. Suffering from postpartum depression, and wanting to have both her husband and baby in the room at the same time, by the third day of the regimen Jacque had had enough. She began crying hysterically while holding James, and a nurse rushed in and asked how she could be of help. Jacque replied, "Go and get my husband." The nurse went to take the crib away, but Jacque held on, still crying, and said again, "Go get my husband." Finally the elderly nurse just shook her head, left the crib and its occupant behind and summoned Don to the room. For an hour and a half, Don got to hold and play with James, and even got the opportunity to change a diaper. With both of them together, Jacque was able to notice that James was the spitting image of his father, who bragged about how well this big baby was going to be able to play football one day. He would take him out in the backyard of the house that they were going to buy together and teach him how to throw and catch. All too soon, though, the nurse returned, and Don had to leave to get ready to return to Fort Riley the next day.

The following morning, Don and Jacque's stepfather Deloy returned to the hospital to say goodbye. The two were amazed to find Jacque up and dressed. Don had to say goodbye to James in the hospital, but she was determined to accompany her husband to the train depot for his send-off. With Deloy hovering in the background, Don and Jacque spent an hour together talking on the platform while waiting for the train to arrive. Jacque had never once laid down the law to Don, but she did now, saying through her tears, "Don't run out and be any kind of hero. Keep your head down. We need you." As the train pulled into the station, Deloy slipped Don a bottle of booze to help dull the pain of the trip back to Fort Riley, and Don held Jacque in a long embrace promising in a whisper that he would be good before jumping onto the train car at the very last minute. As the train pulled away, Jacque was overwhelmed by it all – alone with a new baby as her husband went to war. She just sat there on the platform and sobbed. Deloy, a crusty old air force NCO, didn't quite know how to react, so he just sat beside his stepdaughter, who buried her head into his chest and cried for half an hour. Deloy promised his stepdaughter that he would put in for a transfer to Vietnam to try to keep close to Don. On the train, Don looked up through his own tears and was surprised to see James Nall, who was returning to Fort Riley from his own leave. The two quickly worked their way through the bottle of booze while Don showed off his only picture of James and bragged about the exploits that he and his son would have in future days.

The men returned to Fort Riley to find a massive train backed into a vast open area in Camp Funston, ready for its human cargo. On January 7, 1967, as if by some script, the men boarded the westbound train in a snowstorm. Tim Fischer thought that it was a wonderful irony: here they were headed to one of the hottest places in the world, "and here it's as cold as a well-digger's ass." Standing next to Fischer was Bobby Jindra; the two had become close during training after Fischer had learned that Jindra had gone to a rival high school in Wickliffe near Cleveland. The two often hung around with Ken Idle, who was drafted from Wickliffe along with Jindra, but had wound up in Bravo Company. For his part, Jindra had planned to go to college and major in electrical engineering but instead had fallen in love and gotten married to his sweetheart, Dolly, who, along with their young daughter Jacque, had lived with him during training at Fort Riley. The young family had often invited Fischer over for dinner. Hanging in each other's arms, with little Jacque clutched between them as the snow came pelting down, through tears Bobby wondered aloud if he would ever see them again. The normally gruff and rough Fischer patted Bobby on the back and assured him that he would come home safe and sound to play with little Jacque. He continued to comfort his friend as the two went to find their seats.

Becky Lind finally found her husband Herb, who was overloaded with his duties as commander of the departure, since many of the other officers and NCOs had left earlier on an aircraft as part of an advance party to ready the division infrastructure for the arrival of the men in Vietnam. The two shared a quick embrace; as a military wife Becky was used to seeing her husband leave, just not to war. Then she returned to her car, only to find that the engine had died even as the snow began to pile higher. Aboard the train Larry Lukes sat disconsolate; his new family had been scheduled to see him off but had not turned up. Just as the train began to pull away, and the music of the Salvation Army Band began to pick up in tempo, he caught sight of them running through the snow. He waved, but they never saw him as the train departed.

The emotions of the men of Charlie Company ran the gamut from talkative excitement, to mute depression, to tearful agony as the train picked up speed. Doug Wilson, who had decided to keep a diary of his Vietnam experiences, simply wrote, "Well here I am on a train on my way to California. We finally are on our way. We left about 1500 to the music of the Salvation Army Band. We leave behind only a blizzard and head ourselves toward the waters of the Pacific." As Wilson scribbled in his diary, a few cars away Lynn Hunt sat among the officers, thinking. He knew that this was a good unit, and that the officers and men were dependable. But he couldn't help wonder how Charlie Company would react in battle. Then it struck him. In the entire battalion, only its commander, Lieutenant Colonel Guy Tutwiler, who was a veteran of both World War II and Korea, had ever been shot at before.

3 TO VIETNAM AND INTO THE RUNG SAT

Rung Sat Special Zone
FPO, San Francisco, California, 96621

KIN

CONFIDENTIAL

Rung Sat Special Zone Intelligence Study

The Rung Sat Special Zone, which lies about 20 miles SSE of Saigon ... is a large, poorly drained tidal swamp covered primarily in Mangrove and Nipa Palm... The soil composition, with very few exceptions, consists of perpetually wet sticky mud... The only mode of transportation which can be utilized is boat or helicopter. Due to constant dampness (wet feet and clothing) troops operating in this terrain for a period in excess of 48 hours will frequently have "immersion foot."

The VC felt that the Rung Sat Special Zone was of great importance and thus, in April 1966, made the decision to establish a special MR (Military Region) and called it T-10 ... [which] was given three general missions...

a. Interdict shipping on the Long Tau River [the main shipping channel to the port of Saigon].

b. Hold three Allied battalions in the Rung Sat Special Zone at all times.

c. Make the Rung Sat Special Zone a "safe" area for all VC.

All Viet Cong in the Rung Sat ... are vulnerable to concentrated search and destroy operations when confined to small areas which have river boundaries.[*]

Dear Mom, Dad, and Fran,

Things are pretty confused around here right now, because we're trying to organize our base camp and get used to the heat, we dug all day yesterday and all day today in about 110 degree heat and you know that hurts! But you do it because if the trenches aren't dug there's nothing to dive into if mortars hit, and if the sand bags aren't piled around the tents there's no protection any way, and you do it, but it feels good because each guy is working harder than ever for the same reason and I guess you get the first feeling of being a man.

Charlie is around, but he doesn't bother us at night. This is the time he operates and during the day he hides. Now that I'm here he doesn't scare me anymore and I want to go out and move him out of Vietnam. This is because I saw the poverty and I smelled the stench, and saw the fear in the eyes of the Vietnamese. You could find no slum in America more pitiful or poor than the best village here! The kids have no clothes and we saw them taking baths in mud holes! It's bad. It's almost 10 p.m. so I have to retire. I'll tell you more tomorrow, but there's so much to say you can't think it all out at once. I'll keep you informed. Good night for now.

Love, Jim [Dennison]

P.S. 29" of snow? Oh Dear!

In October 1966 as the training of the 9th Division progressed, the 2nd Brigade commander, Colonel William B. Fulton, made a trip to Vietnam both to survey the local terrain in which his troops would operate and to investigate basing options for the division. He soon discovered that things had fallen well behind the ambitious schedule for readying the local infrastructure to receive such a massive infusion of new troops. He learned from naval officials that

---

[*]   Rung Sat Special Zone Intelligence Study, No date, Folder 05, Box 01, Carl Nelson Collection, The Vietnam Archive, Texas Tech University.

the concentration of ships needed to accommodate an entire infantry brigade afloat would not be ready until late spring 1967 at the earliest. A bigger problem, though, was that the division also needed a land base, complete with an anchorage for use by its naval elements. However, in the land-starved delta, dry, riverfront property was at a premium, and no such site existed that was not already occupied by sizeable numbers of Vietnamese civilians. In consultation with General Cao Van Vien, Chairman of the Joint General Staff of the Republic of Vietnam, General Westmoreland had struck on the novel idea of dredging silt from the My Tho River to create a vast, muddy expanse, a new alluvial plain, 4 miles west of the city of My Tho in the Dinh Tuong Province that would serve as the 9th Division's base camp. Once completed, the new base, located some 50 miles southwest of Saigon and dubbed "Dong Tam" (United Hearts and Minds), would enable the units of what now was to be called the Mobile Riverine Force (MRF) to strike far and wide across the Mekong Delta. But the creation of a new land area was a laborious process, and even with the *Jamaica Bay*, the fourth-largest dredge in the world, spewing out mud and sand at a near record pace, Fulton learned that Dong Tam would not be ready until March 1967. Bedeviled by these logistic difficulties, Fulton decided to extemporize and base the incoming units of the 9th Division at Bear Cat, a site already in use as a brigade base camp for the 1st Infantry Division 10 miles south of Long Binh, while the finishing touches were put on both the afloat base and Dong Tam. Fulton planned to use the time at Bear Cat well and developed a phased program of in-country unit and riverine training to round the 9th Division into final combat readiness.

As planning progressed to project US power into the populous Mekong Delta, allied military attention began to shift toward a very unlikely target, the Rung Sat Special Zone. The vast mangrove swamp, nearly unpopulated and impassable to vehicular traffic, seemed an odd place for military operations, but the remoteness of the region made it a haven for the Viet Cong, who used the area to regroup and train. By 1966 US intelligence suggested that the Rung Sat had become home for upwards of 1,000 Viet Cong, including elite sapper units tasked with attacking merchant vessels on the Long Tau River, the critical shipping channel that connected the port of Saigon to the outside world. Severance of the artery had to be avoided at all costs, but US planners were not certain that American forces could even operate effectively in the forbidding environment of the Rung Sat, much less destroy the Viet Cong forces located there. On March 26, 1966, though, the US Navy and elements of the 1st Battalion of the 5th Regiment of the United States Marine Corps launched Operation *Jackstay*, a ten-day amphibious foray into the Rung Sat. Although the going was quite difficult, the Marines, moving by boats and helicopters, caught the Viet Cong by surprise, killing 63 and seizing substantial caches of equipment and supplies. Although it would never be possible to base US troops in the Rung Sat on a permanent basis, Operation *Jackstay* proved that operations in the swamp were feasible.

On January 9, 1967, the troop train carrying the men of the 9th Infantry Division pulled into Oakland, California, where the soldiers of Charlie Company made their way to the USS *General John Pope*, a World War II-era troopship that, when fully loaded, shoehorned in a total of 5,500 men and nearly 500 civilian crew. The remainder of the afternoon and evening were spent storing equipment and finding berthing assignments for the journey. The officers of Charlie Company had it relatively good, occupying state rooms on the upper decks of the ship, each of which contained 12 individual bunks – a bit crowded but acceptable. The men, though, were housed in cavernous bays with a narrow gangway running down the middle, flanked by row upon row of pipe-frame cots stacked five high. The cots, with canvas strung between the pipes and a rudimentary sort of mattress, were hung so closely together that the men could not sit up and had to slither into their berth while jostling the occupants of the bunks above and below. With so many men crammed into such a small area, the overheated and poorly ventilated troop bays quickly took on an almost overwhelming odor of unwashed feet and sweat – a smell that everyone quickly realized would only worsen on the three-week voyage to Vietnam.

The next day, at 2pm, the *John Pope* steamed out of the harbor, and most of the men gathered on the top deck to watch as the

Golden Gate Bridge receded into the distance, their last sight of the United States. Once beyond the sheltered waters of the San Francisco Bay, though, the ship began to pitch and toss in the open ocean, and the men of Charlie Company, most of whom had never before been to sea, began to get sick. Thousands of men rushed to the railings and began to vomit over the side. Some, like Jace Johnston, were immune to the effects of rolling decks and took great pleasure in taunting their less fortunate brethren. Johnston would look around for the nearest person who seemed to be turning a sickly shade of green and casually discuss how the ship was going up and down, up and down and ask him if the motion made him want to puke. Also not seasick, John Bradfield thought the performance quite amusing and followed one of Johnston's victims to the railing to laugh. Perhaps fittingly, though, Bradfield made the mistake of standing downwind from his upchucking brother in arms, only to find himself coated in warm vomit, resulting in his own surrender to barfing.

While some slowly got used to ocean travel, developed "sea legs," and got over their illness, for others sea sickness was a constant companion for their entire journey to Vietnam. Captain Herb Lind was not exceptional in losing nearly 20 pounds while on board because he couldn't keep his food down. The situation was worst in the crowded troop bays, each of which contained a 55-gallon vomit barrel. However, when the urge hit often there was too little time for the victim to wriggle free of his bunk, leaving the unfortunate people lying below to suffer the consequences. Since the barrels were changed only rarely, the bays took on an ever greater stench, leaving enterprising soldiers like Frank Schwan to go and seek refuge by sleeping in the cargo compartment with the duffel bags, while Terry McBride made a habit of sleeping hidden and alone aboard one of the many lifeboats.

Worst, though, were the many, overcrowded latrines aboard ship, which were designed in an open, horse-trough configuration. At the very best of times, the latrines stank atrociously and even light wave action forced occupants to hold on to whatever fixtures were to hand to maintain their balance. Much to his chagrin, Jim Dennison discovered that at the worst of times large waves could force the ship to lurch, resulting in the malodorous contents of the open latrines splashing out of the toilet holes to drench the unwary.

Although at first many men could not dream of eating, forcing something down was advised to ward off the worst seasickness, and even the most prone to illness had to eat something in the next three weeks. One by one, the men gathered for breakfast the first morning, only to find that the *John Pope* was singularly ill equipped to feed so many people at one time. For those unlucky enough to find themselves stranded at the end, waiting in line to get fed in the galley could take hours, leaving them little time to eat before joining the line once again for lunch. Once the soldiers finally reached the front of the line, they found a poor bill of fare: sickly green powdered eggs, unidentifiable hunks of meat, and stale bread. Shocked that his long wait had resulted only in a nearly inedible meal, Kirby Spain, a country boy from a farm in Arkansas, lamented to a nearby friend that "this is the sorriest damn food I have ever eaten in my life. Our hogs on the farm have a higher quality of slop to eat." Having procured their delicacies, the men had to stand at metal tables to eat; the risk posed by the ever-pitching deck was too great to allow for chairs. Regardless of precautions, though, at nearly every meal food flew in all directions, and drinks constantly sloshed over as the ship rolled with the swells. As in the troop bays, there were 55-gallon drums located at strategic areas throughout the galley for those who could not avoid illness. Often, though, nausea would set in too quickly, resulting in a soldier puking directly into his lunch, which usually had the effect of setting off a chain reaction of sympathy barfs at the unfortunate's table.

Even with all the illness, it was sheer boredom that quickly became enemy number one aboard the *John Pope*. By the end of the first day of the journey, Lieutenant Lynn Hunt became quite concerned that there was not enough to do on board to keep his men occupied and out of trouble. Sure there was waiting in line, the occasional bad movie, and a ship's library – but the men had far too much time on their hands. Hunt and the other officers tried to intervene by scheduling physical training every day, but workouts on a rolling ship were fraught with danger. If the deck heaved at the wrong moment, a jumping jack might loft a man up to 7 feet in the air, leaving him to crash down onto the deck. The officers also assigned their men cleaning duties, but swabbing puke off of the deck lost its luster after a few repetitions. Jim Dennison expressed the feelings of many when he wrote home:

> We've been gone almost 2 weeks now and this is the first time that I've touched paper since I got aboard. The days are so repetitive that there really isn't much to write about.
>
> What I wouldn't give for some of that home cooking, mom. The slop aboard this tub is even worse than C-Rations. Most of us survive on lots and lots of candy bars [from the Post Exchange or PX].
>
> You wouldn't have believed this boat on the second day out of port. That was the first time that we hit rough water, and seasickness attacked like the plague. I was sick for only a few hours, but some guys were sick for 4 days...
>
> It's about 75 degrees aboard but that doesn't do us very much good. We have to stand on deck until 10:30 every day until inspection is over with. And that's about all there is to do until we can go below. They supplied us with a lot of books to read, but that gets very boring after a while. There's always cards to be played and that's what we usually do. It makes the time go faster than it normally would.
>
> When I first saw the ocean, I was really overwhelmed. But after a few days of nothing but water, its grandeur faded decidedly. In all the time we've been out here, we've only seen one island and that was nothing but a shadow. Water, water everywhere and not a beer to drink.

The men of Charlie Company fought off the boredom as best they could. There always seemed to be games of gin rummy or pinochle going on somewhere, or for the truly adventurous there was Mess Sergeant Robert "Smitty" Smith's perpetual high stakes poker game. Many spent time reading or writing letters home, while a couple of the Hispanic soldiers who had brought guitars on board especially liked to spend evenings on deck playing songs, singing, and even giving guitar lessons. Bob Ehlert, Bill Varskafsky, and Stan Cockerell of 2nd Platoon located a quiet spot under a stairwell and played Monopoly for hours on end, only taking breaks to clear their hidey hole of accumulated cigarette butts and candy wrappers. The prize for being the most enterprising with his free time went to Doug Wilson, who had gotten a Polaroid Instant Camera and five rolls of film for Christmas while at home in California on leave. It seemed that nearly everyone wanted a picture of themselves on the *John Pope*, and were willing to pay 50 cents for the privilege. Since the PX on the ship carried additional film, Wilson went into the photography business, but there was a production bottleneck because he could only buy three rolls of film at a time and the line at the PX often required a wait of hours. Wilson took on two employees, one paid perpetually to stand in line to buy film and the other to line up clients. By the time the *John Pope* reached Vietnam, Wilson had bought up all the film on the ship and everyone, including officers and NCOs, seemed to owe him money.

While at Fort Riley, 1st Platoon had adopted a stray kitten, dubbed "Charlie the Cat," that the platoon sergeant, William Lerquin, had found in an abandoned farmhouse. The men had pitched in and bought a small cage for Charlie and fed him from the mess hall. Clarence Shires succeeded in smuggling Charlie aboard first the troop train and then the John Pope. Lodged in his cage hidden beneath Shires' bottom bunk in the troop bay, Charlie began his trip to Vietnam. The adoptive parents of 1st Platoon all pitched in to sneak food for Charlie from the galley, until an announcement appeared in the ship's newspaper that the officers were aware of Charlie's presence and that it was safe to bring him on deck. From then on Charlie pretty much had the run of the ship, and photographs of soldiers posing with Charlie quickly became one of Wilson's best sellers.

Much of the downtime was simply spent in talking, showing pictures from home, and clowning around – further cementing the bonds of friendship that had been established in training. Forrest Ramos, the tough boxer from Wapato who often worked in comedy tandem with John Bradfield and Richard Rubio, quickly got the reputation of being one of the leading jokesters of the company. From short-sheeting to the obligatory placing of shaving cream on a sleeping man's hand and then tickling his nose, Ramos developed quite a repertoire. His favorite joke, though, was to shout, "Sharks!," which inevitably caused several men, who were desperate to see anything other than water, to rush to the railings of the ship. Since leaning over the railings was dangerous, Ramos' actions would send the sailors tasked with the soldiers' well-being into fits of apoplexy and Ramos into gales of laughter. The railings, it seems, were reserved for puking.

Jose Sauceda fit right in with 3rd Platoon's elite prankster shock troops. From Mercedes, Texas, a hardscrabble town hard on the Mexican border, Sauceda was the son of Mexican immigrants and had grown up as a migrant farm worker. If it could be picked, the Saucedas picked it – cotton, cabbage, strawberries, peaches – work that took them all over the country from Texas, to California, to Michigan; following the growing seasons and the work from place to place. It was a tough life, one that didn't allow for much in the way of leisure activities, and Jose had grown up strong and lean. One summer Jose had landed a plum job as an assistant lifeguard at the local pool in Mercedes to augment his family's earnings. Almost immediately he noticed a beautiful young swimmer named Noemi, called MiMi by her friends. The two quickly became a couple and dated all through high school. Noemi even waited patiently as Jose went off to Michigan to work at a General Motors plant after high school. She also waited patiently after Jose received his draft notice and departed for Fort Riley. During training Sauceda became a well-known figure in 3rd Platoon; he was the only one brave enough to wake up Terry McBride. A sound sleeper with a legendary temper, McBride had made many a trooper pay for having the temerity to rouse him from his slumbers. But Sauceda was from a tough neighborhood and took on the task of serving as the mercurial McBride's personal alarm clock.

When not involved in pulling or planning for pranks Ramos, Sauceda, Jim Cusanelli, and their pals would often pile into an available lifeboat to play gin rummy and eat sandwiches and fruit away from the smell of puke that pervaded most of the rest of the *John Pope*. For Sauceda it was a welcome escape from thoughts that were focused elsewhere. Increasingly Sauceda had sought out the company of Fred Kenney, because the two had something very much in common. On leave after basic training Sauceda had returned to Mercedes, Texas, and had married his beloved Noemi. On board the *John Pope* Sauceda, like Kenney, was soon expecting the birth of his first child. Pranks, camaraderie, cards – nothing could take Sauceda's mind far from the reality of what he faced. Back home Noemi was going through the last stages of pregnancy, but with every day that passed he got nearer and nearer to Vietnam. He couldn't help but wonder if he would ever make it home to see his baby.

For the married men, and especially the fathers in the group, the journey on the *John Pope* was an especially lonesome time. Don Peterson, who like so many of his friends had started to grow a mustache on the trip, never tired of showing off his only picture of little Jimmy, telling everyone who would listen how he was going to grow up to be a football star. Peterson often went on to spin yarns about where he and Jacque would wind up living, what their house would be like, and how many more children they were going to have. It was plain that Don missed his little family deeply, but he was determined to do his duty.

Nearly two weeks into the voyage, one of the civilians who manned the *John Pope* wandered into the 3rd Platoon bay in search of Elmer Kenney. At first the men did not know whom the man wanted. There was no "Elmer" in their midst. They did have a Fred, but hardly anyone even knew that name. Like so many in the military, Fred was universally known by a nickname. He had been dubbed "Cool Wig" because of his wavy, blond hair. Once the identity problem had been sorted out, one of the platoon went off to find Fred, who returned to find an emergency Red Cross telegram. Barbara had given birth to a boy – his son – Frederick. Risking injury on the pitching and rolling ship, Fred jumped for joy, waving the telegram and clapping everyone on the back. He was a papa and couldn't really even begin to believe it. For the remainder of the trip, Fred didn't stop talking about his son. What was he like? Was he big or little? He was bound to be cute, right? All babies are cute. More than any other soldier on board, Fred Kenney was in a hurry to reach Vietnam. There he hoped to find a picture of his son waiting, and there the calendar would begin to tick off the days to when he would be able to go home and see his baby in person.

During the trip to Vietnam, the medics, including Robert Cara, Bill Geier, Elijah Taylor, and Gary Maibach, were occupied in offering first aid classes and in giving lectures on the perils of venereal disease. For Geier and Taylor especially, just being on a ship of such size lost in the immensity of the Pacific Ocean was a subject of great wonder and reflection. In the background, though, both men realized that each passing day brought them closer to Vietnam and their test. Men would soon be maimed in battle and would scream for their help. While the others were doing their best to stay out of harm's way, it was going to be their duty to rush *into* the fire to save their buddies. As they sat there giving classes to the men of their unit they wondered if they would be able to get up and do their jobs when the time came. What if they cracked under the pressure? Their men trusted them implicitly, and never asked the tough questions. But they delighted in asking Geier and Taylor what they would do if a soldier under their care had the misfortune of being bitten on the pecker by a snake. Relieved by the levity of the question, both answered, "If you get bit on the pecker by a snake, then I will leave you. You'll be on your own."

As a conscientious objector, Gary Maibach was something of a curiosity. The soldiers of Charlie Company knew well enough that Maibach would do his job, but they delighted in pushing the envelope. Again and again they pressed him: "Hey doc. Let's say the whole platoon is down. You come in and save the day and stabilize us. What happens if the VC come then to finish us off? You would pick up one of our weapons and defend us then, right?" Maibach would always answer the same way saying, "I don't think that is a scenario that would ever play out. But if it did; no. I would not take up a weapon and fire it at someone else." Following Maibach's explanation with protests of, "aww, man, that ain't right," the soldiers would warn him that while they were kind and understanding enough to let him off, he had better watch out for John Young, the gung-ho enlistee from Minnesota. Sure enough, when Young first met the conscientious objector, Young tested Maibach by looking him square in the eyes and saying, "You aren't going to like me. I'm going to enjoy killing people in Vietnam." Unwilling to take the bait, Maibach simply replied, "Sergeant Young, you do what you feel you have to do, and so will I, and call me when

Jacque Peterson's high school graduation photograph, 1966.

Elijah Taylor playing baseball in the summer of 1965.

Fred and Barbara Kenney on their wedding day.

Top left
Forrest and Jesse Ramos at home in Wapato, Washington.

Top right
Duffy Black and Ida at the company Christmas party at Fort Riley.

Bottom left
Bill Geier and his mother Bernice posing at home in 1966 after the completion of training.

Right
Jimmie Salazar posing with an M60 machine gun at Fort Riley.

Top
Charlie Company officers at ease at Fort Riley. Left to right, battalion commander Lieutenant Colonel Guy Tutwiler and his wife Elaine, Lieutenant Jack Benedick and his wife Nancy, Ida Black, and Captain Rollo Larson and his wife.

Middle
Aboard the John Pope – *clockwise from left to right, Idoluis Casares, Ray Layman, Mario Lopez, Jimmie Salazar, and Bill Reynolds.*

Bottom
At Camp Bear Cat, left to right, Benny Bridges, Jim Dennison, and Don Peterson.

James Nall on patrol outside Bear Cat with his grenade launcher.

John Sclimenti on a smoke break outside Bear Cat.

Bill Reynolds navigating the sodden terrain of the Rung Sat.

John Young during operations early in 1967.

Charlie Company troopers being hosed off on an ammi barge after a mission in the Rung Sat.

Left, Ted Searcy; right Duffy Black. This is the last photograph taken of Lieutenant Black.

Jack Benedick (standing on the left) during 2nd Platoon operations outside Bear Cat.

Lynn Hunt (in rear operating engine) and Charlie Company soldiers aboard a Plastic Assault Boat (PAB).

you need me." Plain spoken and truthful in their disagreement, both men instantly decided that they liked the other.

In an oddity of shipboard room assignments, Company First Sergeant Lynn Crockett and Company Executive Officer Lieutenant Duffy Black found themselves assigned to a double room, while most of the other officers and NCOs had to share more crowded quarters. With the two working so closely on matters of company administration, the pairing seemed natural. Having been an enlisted man himself, Black allowed the imaginary line between officer and NCO to blur, resulting in Crockett becoming his close friend. While the men wrote letters home and many of the other officers and NCOs tried to beat Mess Sergeant Smith at poker, Black and Crockett spent much of their downtime in conversation. Crockett sympathized with Black's heartache at leaving his new bride behind, and offered what advice he could from his own years of experience of military-induced periods of separation from his wife Norma. Crockett assured Black that his feelings were a natural part of military life, and that, while things would never be easy, he would eventually get used to being away. Black then went further and surprised Crockett by confiding, "Top, I've got a funny feeling. I don't think I will make it back from Vietnam." Crockett replied, "Lieutenant, put that out of your mind. You will get home to take care of that young wife of yours." Black let the matter drop and moved on to another subject, but it seemed to Crockett that a shadow still lay over the young officer.

On January 24, 1967, the *John Pope* arrived in Naha, Okinawa for a refueling stop, and, after some deliberation, the division brass decided to grant the soldiers a few hours of shore leave. While the officers counseled discretion, many of the young men of Charlie Company made up their minds to have as much fun as they could as quickly as they could. After all, they were headed to war. How badly could the military punish them? The luckless, and there were many, surrounded the few on board ship who were known to have money, including Mess Sergeant Smith and Doug Wilson, to arrange loans so that they could have money to procure "goods and services" while ashore. As the men stormed off the ship, they passed a table that the local military authorities had set up to find blood donors. Medic Gary Maibach stopped to do his part, but he was fairly certain that he was the only one who did.

There were busses waiting nearby to take the soldiers to Fort Buckner, where they could while away the hours drinking beers in the enlisted men's club. But the men of Charlie Company were one step ahead; they knew that the action was in a rather seedy strip of clubs that "catered to military men" in the Koza area outside of Kadena Air Base. As the bus he was on made its way through Koza toward the more sedate pleasures of Fort Buckner, Terry McBride asked the driver to pull over, but the driver replied that he had orders to keep going. McBride then calmly told the driver that this was the last stop for him and his buddies before they went to Vietnam and that if he didn't pull over they would kill him. The driver suddenly remembered that he was indeed supposed to make a scheduled stop in Koza, and the group departed.

Seven hours later the men dutifully returned to the *John Pope* after their bacchanalia. Lieutenant Lynn Hunt, who was in charge of making sure the men of Charlie Company got back aboard the ship in good order, saw "a scene beyond comprehension in its confusion and mayhem." Taxi drivers came whizzing up to the docks with men piled in the back of their small vehicles like cordwood. Rickshaws poured in from all directions with swaying human cargo. One enterprising crew returned in a stolen garbage truck with its trash compartment packed full of drunken soldiers engaged in a lusty sing-along. Many of the men returned with booze, hoping to bring it on the *John Pope*, only to be rebuffed. While some griped, Bill Riley, a kid from an Indiana family with a strong military tradition, became an entrepreneur. Berthed next to the *John Pope* was a ship full of Marines, who were angry that they were not going to get a shore leave during their refueling stop. What military man in his right mind wanted a group of drunk Marines to mix with the already drunk men of the 9th Infantry Division while ashore in Okinawa on their way to war? The fighting would have been legendary. So the Marines remained cooped up and dry on their transport. With two fifths of useless bourbon in his hands, Riley negotiated a price of $10 per bottle with the thirsty Marines, who tossed him the money, and he tossed them the bottles. With some time to spare before having to board, Riley made two more trips to a nearby liquor store and repeated the process, pocketing a tidy profit.

At 1am, as the *John Pope* steamed toward Vietnam and the weary men rested from their shore leave exertions, all the lights snapped on followed by an announcement that everybody needed to report to the main deck for a head count. Bleary-eyed and tired, Charlie Company gathered, wondering what the hell was going on, and the story quickly went around in hushed whispers among the confused men that a man from another company had been involved in a scuffle in the ship's mess hall and had been hauled off to the brig. The soldier, though, had broken away from his captors and in desperation had vaulted over a railing – the outside railing of the ship – and had plunged into the ocean. After the head count hundreds of men crowded the railing of the *John Pope* scanning the waters for the unfortunate drunk. The ship, joined in its search by other vessels that happened to be in the area, circled for 24 hours, and several members of Charlie Company thought that they caught glimpses of a body in the water, and some even tossed life preservers out, but the body was never recovered. The 9th Infantry Division had suffered its first fatality, and had not even reached Vietnam.

As the ship neared Vietnam, and the weather grew warmer and the water shifted from deep blue to a dark brown, tension and anticipation among the men began to rise. On Sunday, January 29, after 20 days at sea, the *John Pope* reached Vung Tau harbor where it rode at anchor for a day unloading equipment and stores, while the men of Charlie Company collected their gear, cleaned their weapons, and made ready to disembark. As the sun set that evening, the men watched as a battle raged in the distance – red tracer rounds burning through the darkening sky, helicopter gunships wheeling overhead before returning to the battlefield with guns blazing, and artillery bursts lighting the horizon. The show went on all night, leaving its enraptured audience wondering what their own fate would be. Echoing the fears of most of the others, Richard Northcott, the mortarman from California, thought to himself, "What the hell are we getting into here? Tomorrow is going to be rough; we will be fighting as soon as we hit the ground."

The next day the men moved from the John Pope to landing craft that took them ashore at Vung Tau. A wave of apprehension washed over the group as the bow ramp first started to shudder and then began to fall. Stifling in the heat, Dave Jarczewski, from a steel-working family in the suburbs of Buffalo, New York, was surprised that, instead of being greeted by Viet Cong, his first sight in Vietnam was an American military band getting ready to play the "Star Spangled Banner." There wasn't a battle, and the men simply marched out and formed up to hear a few obligatory "welcome to Vietnam" speeches by divisional brass. Jace Johnston knew that there had to be more to it than that, and looked around for a source of information. He spotted a couple of enlisted men nearby leaning up against the hood of a deuce-and-a-half truck drinking soda pop and asked them, "Hey, buddy, where is the war?" One replied, "Man, we've been waiting on you guys. Don't worry, we'll take you to the war."

Stan Cockerell couldn't help but be amused that the small ceremony ended with the band playing Wilbert Harrison's hit song *Kansas City*. If the band had chosen that tune to make the men feel at home, it didn't work. The Kansas they had left had been well below freezing with snow blanketing the ground. In Vietnam it was over 100 degrees in the shade as the men from the *John Pope* sorted themselves out into smaller groups for transport by truck convoy to their new base at Bear Cat. Some felt a bit naked, because they had been given their weapons but no ammunition. What if they got ambushed? But it turned out that the convoy was heavily guarded, in part by troops from Australia. Bill Riley struck up a conversation with one of the Aussies and asked him why the truck was loaded with so many sandbags. In a thick down-under accent the man answered, "Yank, those bags are for sitting on, so if the truck hits a mine you won't lose the family jewels."

It was while the trucks careened down the dusty roads that the men of Charlie Company got their first real introduction to

Vietnam. While zooming through the open countryside, Mario Lopez watched as women, accompanied by their children, tended their rice paddies. It reminded him of home, of working the onion and carrot fields with his father and grandmother. People were the same everywhere. Suddenly one of the men remarked that things had "begun to smell like shit," which heralded the convoy's arrival in a village. As the convoy slowed amid the hubbub of pedestrians and bicycles that thronged the thoroughfare, Jace Johnston saw cages of dogs stacked ten high, and slanted boards that carried a load of rats impaled on nails. To his amazement Vietnamese women arrived to poke the rats and dogs with sticks, shopping for the night's dinner. Holding back the urge to retch, Johnston vowed to stick to American food. Even if he had to subsist only on the dreaded lima bean variety of C Rations, Johnston swore to avoid Vietnamese cuisine for the entire year. In another truck, Bill Reynolds was entranced by seeing his first Vietnamese civilian up close. A woman had emerged from her small shop and looked up at the soldier from a foreign land. She didn't say anything, but just gave him a wry grin, pulled down her baggy slacks and proceeded to pee on the side of the road. After the performance, the woman simply walked away. Shaking his head free from the vision, Reynolds looked off to the side, only to see two naked Vietnamese children bathing in a mud puddle.

After their crash course on Vietnamese culture, the men of Charlie Company arrived at their new home – Bear Cat. But there were no buildings, no mess halls, no PX – no nothing. John Bradfield looked at Forrest Ramos, his partner in pranks, and said, "This can't be right. The trucks must have got lost. This is just a big ass open field!" But the convoy had not gotten lost. When Charlie Company arrived, Bear Cat was nothing more than a freshly bulldozed square mile in the middle of the jungle surrounded by an 8-foot-tall berm. As the men piled out of their trucks in the 100-degree heat, up strode Sergeant Crockett who informed them in his best parade ground voice, "This is your new home, and if anything is going to be here, you are going to have to build it!"

At Bear Cat, Charlie Company met up with its advance element, made up of officers and senior NCOs who had flown to Vietnam ahead of the main body of troops. A week prior, Rollo Larson had been among the first of the officers to reach Bear Cat, and, seeing the camp's primitive state, had decided that he would rather not sleep under the stars. So Larson had turned to company supply sergeant Cerveny, who some referred to as the "mad Hungarian," and told him to take two trucks and get whatever he thought that they needed. Cerveny was, like so many other supply sergeants, a master scrounger and negotiator. Having left with nothing, Cerveny magically returned a few hours later with several generators and tent kits – the only such supplies at Bear Cat. Shortly thereafter the battalion commander, Lieutenant Colonel Tutwiler, had happened by. He had looked down at the pile of building supplies then back up at Larson and had said, "Larson, I don't know where you got all this shit from, and I'm not going to ask. Just make sure that I have a tent and electricity too." Moments later the mail finally caught up to Charlie Company, including a letter to Bill Varskafsky from his wife; she had given birth to their first child – a daughter. Fumbling with both the paper and his emotions, Varskafsky looked at the enclosed picture. What a cute little girl, but she was bald. Was she supposed to be bald? He figured that he had better go and ask Fred Kenney about babies now that he was a father himself.

The men of Charlie Company went to work, constructing their own tents, platoon-sized affairs with wooden frames, canvas roofs, screen walls, and raised wooden floors, and smaller tents for the officers and NCOs, all laid out in military order. Over the following weeks they also constructed raised latrines, with 55-gallon drums to serve as receptacles, a mess hall, and a PX as, over time, a real military base began to take shape. But the hardest part was the digging. Each tent had to have a sandbagged bunker, well over 8 feet in depth and large enough to hold an entire platoon, in which the men could take refuge during a mortar attack. It was miserable work in the oppressive heat, and, since there was no rain at the height of the dry season, the constant foot traffic and the comings and goings of trucks and helicopters kicked up fine clouds of choking dust from the freshly bulldozed fields, forcing many of the men to work with bandannas tied around their noses and mouths.

While some men worked to build the camp, others had to man the berm and keep an eye out for the Viet Cong. As the day gave way to night, the men on the berm strained to see into the opposite tree line. Did that tree move? Had that lump on the ground always been there? Should I fire? In one bunker, Clarence Shires thought that it was his ears that were being fooled. He could have sworn that he had just heard someone, very faintly, say "fuck you." He strained to listen harder, and there it was again, more distinct this time: "fuck you." Shires turned to his bunker mates saying, "Listen, someone is hollering at us." They listened but heard nothing. A few moments later, though, they all heard it: "fuck you." The VC were out there! But where the hell were they? Were they going to attack? Drenched in sweat with eyes straining into the blackness the group listened all night as the VC taunted them. Only later did they discover that the sounds had emanated from a type of giant Tokay gecko, which GIs across Vietnam simply came to know as the "fuck you lizard." But the dangers were not all imaginary. A few hundred yards away a Viet Cong sniper shot a man from another company dead off the berm, hitting him square between the eyes.

On February 7, Charlie Company left Bear Cat for its first mission in the field. Before leaving, though, Lieutenant Black had given Charlie Nelson some bad news. Since he was so short, and dark skinned, Black and Captain Larson feared that he could easily be mistaken for a Viet Cong. Charlie would have to stay behind and be the company mailman. For the young Indian who had hoped to make his mark as a warrior, the news came as a difficult blow, and he decided that he would pester Black every day to be allowed to accompany his buddies into the field. With Nelson left behind, the company departed on a ten-day mission to search a set of villages outside the berm for Viet Cong. As the Americans lumbered along, hacking their way through the undergrowth with machetes, it dawned on Larry Lilley that even a half-baked Viet Cong would be able to hear them coming. With little to show for the day's efforts except a particularly noticeable trail snaking behind them through the jungle, Charlie Company halted prior to the onset of nightfall and dug in. As darkness gathered, Gary Maibach was stunned by the lack of light discipline; men were smoking and even using their flashlights. Any Viet Cong within miles would be able to see them.

As the night wore on, officers and NCOs made their rounds and discovered another problem. The men were dog-tired after a long day of slogging through the heat, and they all had gone to sleep – even those who were supposed to be on guard. Charlie Company still had a lot to learn.

After having been read the riot act by their officers and NCOs, the company moved with more silence and agility on the next day of the operation, and as night fell there were no lights to be seen. Lynn Hunt, though, remained very worried about the problem of men sleeping on duty and decided to sneak out to check on the perimeter foxholes. When he reached the first position, he found all of its occupants awake. He asked the men how they were, and one answered a bit too quickly, "Good sir. Very good sir." Hunt sensed tension in the man's voice, but since he could not see him in the darkness he only asked him if he had seen any movement outside the perimeter, and he replied that he had not. Writing off the tenseness as a case of nerves, Hunt went on to the next position. There he also found everyone awake, and they too gave terse and tense answers to his questions. Getting a bit worried, Hunt proceeded to the third foxhole. Its occupants were also awake, but in response to his question of how it was going, one of the men answered, "Not too well. The sergeant was here just before you and caught us asleep. He woke me up and gave me this to hold." Hunt looked down and saw that the man was holding a grenade. The man looked up and said, "The sergeant pulled the pin on the grenade, told me to hold it and not go to sleep." After that night the company had very few problems with soldiers nodding off while on guard duty.

For the next few days Charlie Company maneuvered through the countryside, finding its operational legs. Although the men didn't know it, the unit was something of a shakedown cruise in a relatively safe area. Americans had been operating in and around Bear Cat for some time, and the Viet Cong had, in the main, enough sense to have fled or gone into hiding. To the boys of Charlie Company, though, it seemed that the Viet Cong could be lurking anywhere. Jace Johnston and a few of his mates from 3rd Platoon split off from the main group to collect some water from a nearby stream. As he paused to place iodine tablets in the water to

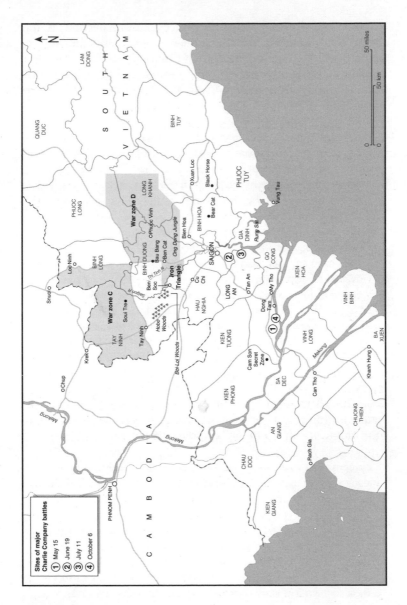

Map of the Mekong Delta

make it safe to drink, Johnston peered at the reflection in the stream. Something was moving in the treetops behind him. Sniper! As he whirled to fire Johnston found himself face to face with a monkey. Just a damn monkey! Like to scared him shitless, and just a damn monkey! During the mission, Jim Dennison wrote home to his parents:

> I [have been] in the field for ten days and haven't even smelled a Cong... Today ... we moved our base camp again and naturally had to set up another one at our destination. That means digging fox holes and chopping down the jungle in front of your position so you can see what is in front of you. Well it was my job to cut this crap down with a machete... During this time we pulled patrols out into the jungle to keep Charlie on his toes. I went on a night ambush and two day patrols and all we saw was jungle.
>
> My company still hasn't seen any VC out there. They just must be scared to death of us... After having been on my first mission, Vietnam is not so scary or threatening. After the first day or so you relax into a wary watchfulness rather than being in a state of shock! It becomes a strange situation after a while. You feel as if you're still training in the hills of Kansas and that Charlie just doesn't exist... I've seen more fighting in Chicago than I have in Vietnam. That's OK with me, though.

Even though the Viet Cong did not yet pose much of a threat, simply learning to live and work in the tropics proved a challenge. John Young attempted to explain to his parents:

> I suppose that when I say that we walked, you picture us just loping along a road or trail. Well, it's not at all like that. We can't often use the trails or roads, because Charlie mines or booby traps them. We have to use machetes to chop our way through. I had seen bamboo before I came here, but I didn't know that it had long thorn-covered creepers splayed all over. The bamboo thorns are bad because they are curved, almost barbed. They rip your fatigues to pieces. They cut your arms and hands and legs and neck. They stab into your knees when you kneel on them. The black palms are bad, too. They look quite innocent, but they have hundreds of very thin thorns on the leaves and stems,

with a kind of pain-causing sap, which will make you feel like you have sprained a joint when you get one stuck into your knuckle or wrist. There's a kind of vine, which you can never see in time to avoid, with hooked spines that stay in your skin when you hit it. There is another plant that has thousands of slivers, like the slivers you get from fiberglass, that get all over you and sting while they're stuck in you. There is a bush with thorns about 2 inches long that you often brush against, and there are any number of other thorny vines. There is one that is particularly loathsome; it has hooked thorns, and for some reason, the red ants like it. The thorns pull your helmet off, and the ants jump on your head. These red ants are really evil. They have a bite like a bee sting. They like to get on you on the back of your neck, but they'll sometimes get down your shirt and trousers. Ants come in all colors and sizes, from almost invisible to 1 inch long. When you sleep in the jungle they'll crawl all over you at night. And when you do stop to sit down or sleep you have to check the area closely for tarantulas and scorpions ... and there are always ticks. It's pretty miserable, hard work moving any distance in the jungle.

Although the entire jungle seemed to be out to get the boys of Charlie Company, it was the red ants in particular that were the bane of their Vietnam existence. The ants lived in bushes and trees, and formed hive-like structures by weaving leaves together into a ball. Against the never-ending backdrop of green, the nests, which sometimes housed thousands of ants, were nearly invisible. On their own, single red ants were unnaturally aggressive in defending their territory. The men swore that the ants would jump on them as they walked by just to sting them. But in their thousands, the ants were unbearable. An unlucky swipe with a machete meant getting covered with a writhing, biting mass that would search for any way into a soldiers' clothing. A worst case scenario, which happened on an all-too regular basis, involved a soldier in front of the file pushing back a tree branch and then letting it go, only to hit the soldier next in line in the face with an exploding nest of maddened ants. Whenever an attack took place, whether in the dead of night or in the heat of battle, the only remedy for the stricken soldier was to strip off, while slapping at his mass of tormentors, and then jump into any nearby water.

After a few days of continuous operations outside Bear Cat, Charlie Company set up a perimeter alongside a small creek. Without access to showers or clean clothes, the men had developed a bit of an odor. Ready to take advantage of a singular opportunity, Sergeant Crockett joined many of the other men in disrobing and bathing in the creek, laying his clothes on the bank nearby. Refreshed and rejuvenated, Crockett put his clothes back on and walked through the surrounding men toward the company headquarters. A few paces into the journey, though, it became painfully aware to Sergeant Crockett that he had placed his clothes on a nest of red ants while he had been bathing. As thousands of tiny tormentors attacked, Crockett cursed in the finest drill sergeant vernacular, danced around, and began to disrobe at a frantic pace. At first the men watched the spectacle wide-eyed and silent. Then the applause began, as the man who had assigned them all so many pushups back at Fort Riley threw his clothes in all directions and performed an ungraceful bellyflop back into the creek. Jose Sauceda, so often involved in pranks alongside his buddy Forrest Ramos, normally would have laughed himself silly at the spectacle. But, instead, he only looked up from a letter he was reading and smiled. His wife, Noemi, had given birth to the couple's first child, Belinda. He was a father. He knew that war was dangerous, and he knew that this war was going to get worse. But he also knew that, with the help of his 3rd Platoon buddies – Ramos, Cusanelli, McBride, and the rest – he would get home and have a chance to meet Belinda in person.

As the operation continued, the men of Charlie Company hoped for a little more action when they learned that they were headed to the Binh Son rubber plantation to provide security against a suspected Viet Cong attack. The entire 4th of the 47th made its way to the area and dug in around the village of Binh Son, studding their defensive works with lethal Claymore mines. As the seemingly endless digging and preparation of defensive positions progressed, the men figured this finally had to be the real deal. The VC had to be coming. But nothing happened. The officers knew what an important time it was for their men – green squad leaders planning and executing patrols in and among the Vietnamese, the mortar platoon functioning for the first time as a rifle platoon since its organic firepower was not yet needed, young officers learning how to call in accurate artillery marking rounds, all engaged in dead reckoning navigation through difficult jungle terrain. These were all lessons that, when learned well, would mean the difference between life and death when the stakes were raised. The command element quickly realized what was going on. The French owners of the rubber plantation had bought off the Viet Cong. There would be no attacks; maybe just a few booby traps. But for the men the lack of action was wearing. Doug Wilson jotted in his diary: "This really seems to be a joke. It is hard to imagine that this is a war... It seems more like bivouac during training." Making matters worse, the officers and NCOs had to instruct the men *not* to fire their weapons in and around the rubber trees. If the trees were damaged, the army would have to pay for them. Even in his noncombatant position as a medic, Bill Geier wondered at the wisdom of the decision, turning to Idoluis Casares and saying, "Bear, this doesn't make any sense. The Cong can shoot at us, but we can't fire back? What kind of war is this anyway?"

Within a day of Charlie Company's arrival, the local Vietnamese peasants from the village of Binh Son began to approach the American bunkers in ones and twos. Somehow they had magically procured items of all types to sell, especially soft drinks and the ubiquitous Ba Muoi Ba beer. Brewed in Saigon, the GIs universally detested Ba Muoi Ba (Vietnamese for 33, the number that adorned the label of the can or bottle). It was almost always warm, was quite bitter, and was rumored to contain everything from formaldehyde to bamboo shoots. But even warm Ba Muoi Ba was better than nothing, and the Vietnamese entrepreneurs began a thriving trade. Some girls turned up near the American perimeter, set up a table, and started offering haircuts, and within days a house of ill repute began operation in the village and provided service to a steady stream of clandestine customers.

On February 20 the battalion returned to Bear Cat, allowing the men their first change of clothes in nearly three weeks. While they were gone a shower rig had been constructed, and even though it was only a hose that spewed pond water, getting at least a bit cleaner seemed like heaven. For the next month Charlie Company fell into a rhythm of working in construction on the base for a few days and then moving out, often as single platoons, in local search and destroy operations around Bear Cat. The routine was not without its dangers. Mines injured a few men in the battalion, and an entire mortar crew was badly mauled when one of its own shells detonated prematurely. Most tragically, on March 18, Sergeant Benito Alaniz, who had loved to pal around and sing with the "Santa Anna Brigade" of Hispanic soldiers, somehow got separated from his unit while on patrol and was shot and killed by his own men.

For most, though, the time spent at Bear Cat mainly was one of acclimatization, which meant hard work, endless patrols, and boredom. Things at the camp had taken on more of an air of permanence. There was now a PX and even rudimentary officers', NCOs', and enlisted men's clubs, where the men could enjoy beer other than Ba Muoi Ba and the officers could have their mixed drinks and flirt with the division's nurses. Much of what little leisure time the men had was spent writing letters and opening packages from home, which everyone shared. Alan Richards was always popular in the mortar platoon, because his family often sent two very valuable items – Jiffy Pop Popcorn and Kool-Aid, which made the horrible-tasting local water a bit more palatable. He had also received a pile of letters from a Wisconsin grade school that the other members of his platoon took great joy in answering. There were always card games of every variety going on, and it was rumored that Sergeant Smith had already made a $10,000 profit in his perpetual poker game. Some thought that he had to be cheating, but nobody ever caught him. Elijah Taylor got together with the West Point graduate and poet Lieutenant Hoskins to organize a series of football games, which immediately attracted the attention of Forrest Ramos, the boxer and company jokester from Wapato. Ramos also kept up his soul music education by hanging around with John Bradfield, who had managed to bring his record player and a load of 45s to Vietnam.

For those more adventurous in their search for recreation, the local Vietnamese sold nearly everything. Finding the local trade to be of deep interest, Jim Dennison wrote to his parents:

All the Vietnamese prostitutes come down to the fox holes at night to peddle their wares! Only about ½ the guys will touch them and there are a few who have already paid the price. One guy I know came in to see the doctor and found out he had 4 different types of V.D.! **4** The docs told him it would be impossible to cure him because they've never seen anything like the 4 types he's got. Incurable. They're going to send him back to the states to see if anything can be done there, but they doubt it. He's a very unhappy and sorrowful boy right now. It sounds kind of funny, but if they can't cure all 4, he signed his death warrant.

Some of the most adventurous liked to sneak out beyond the Bear Cat perimeter at night to visit the local village hot spots – something that was strictly forbidden and quite dangerous. One night Alan Richards, who had himself been chased out of the local villages by MPs, was manning one of the perimeter bunkers. While on lookout, he heard sounds in the surrounding bush and knew full well that it was some of his buddies returning from one of their nocturnal sojourns. But at that very moment an officer came by on an inspection, and he, too, heard the commotion. The officer insisted that Richards shoot off a flare, which, when it exploded, illuminated three forms in the distance. The lieutenant cocked the 50-caliber machine gun, which made quite a loud and ominous CLICK CLICK, before shouting, "Who's out there?" At that point, still illuminated by the hissing flare, the three men stood up with their arms raised, resulting in the trousers of one falling down around his ankles. Happy to have avoided being shot, the returnees were assigned KP for their transgressions.

There were also cheap drugs of all types available in Vietnam. Raised by an abusive and drunk stepfather, Ted Searcy had turned to a life of alcohol and drugs. After a youthful run-in with the law, Searcy had been given a choice by a local Tennessee judge – either go to jail or join the military. Although Searcy enlisted in the army in 1959 and quickly rose through the ranks, his abuse of alcohol and drugs never let up. In 1966 Searcy had been assigned to the 2nd Platoon of Charlie Company, where he prided himself on being one of the meanest NCOs at Fort Riley. In Vietnam, Searcy remained a stern taskmaster, but he also crossed a line. Dope was easy to find and cheap; a carton of the finest marijuana cigarettes cost only $2. He and a few of the men began to smoke during some of their off time in Bear Cat. It was common knowledge among the men that there were smokers in their midst, and a great many tried a puff or two when it was offered. However, the number of committed pot smokers always remained low, and dope was only smoked during downtime. The smokers would not risk their own lives by using it before or during an operation, nor would they risk the lives of their buddies.

While at Bear Cat Don Peterson wrote to Jacque and James very nearly every day. After Don's departure for Vietnam, Jacque had returned to California and had gotten an apartment that was only two blocks from the home of Don's beloved grandparents, who helped Jacque as best they could in taking care of young James. Don's letters were all happy – things in Vietnam were good. The people were nice, the surroundings were fascinating, and the boys in the company always said hello. In the letters Don mused that maybe Chicago would be a good place to move to after he came home; after all if Jim Dennison and Bill Geier liked the place so well, it had to be good. For her part, Jacque kept Don constantly updated on what James was doing, hoping that writing about the baby would help keep Don from missing him so much. She, and the rest of the Peterson family, also sent several care packages full of cookies, which were always a big hit among the boys of 1st Platoon.

After Fred's departure for Vietnam, Barbara Kenney had moved in with her mother to prepare for the birth of their son Frederick. It was very hard on Barbara to go through the birth process alone, but she knew that Fred loved her. One of the very first letters that Fred received at Bear Cat contained several pictures of little Freddie, pictures that got endlessly passed around 3rd Platoon and even resulted in someone producing obligatory cigars for the proud papa. Unable to see them in person, Fred had to express his love and happiness to his young family in letters, in which he launched into wonderful dreams about the life he, Barbara, and little Freddie would embark upon when he returned home – the kind of house they would buy, the kind of sports Freddie would play, even the number of grandkids they would have one day. Fred loved to write about the good things and about the goings on of his many California friends, especially Forrest Ramos. Some pages in the letters were entirely taken up with a recounting of Forrest's most recent pranks. He also sent home several pictures of the group of friends clowning around together. Kenney added one tidbit of company gossip; it seemed that tough little Ramos had fallen hard for Richard Rubio's cousin Patricia. When Ramos had first written to her on a whim back at Fort Riley, Patricia had asked her cousin Richard how to respond. Rubio informed her that it would be OK to write to him, because Forrest was an all right kind of guy who sometimes felt left out because he rarely received letters of his own. Flattered by the attention, Ramos cherished Patricia's letters, remarking that they even seemed to smell good, and loved the cakes and cookies that she often sent. Forrest wrote to Patricia at least once a week, beginning an official long-distance relationship. Although Fred had written about everything else, from the places they would live to Forrest's budding romance with Rubio's cousin, Barbara was able to pick up on the subtle clues; Fred was having great difficulty being away at war and missing out on life with little Freddie.

Bill Geier, who had several conversations with Don Peterson about how much he liked living in Chicago, kept up a steady stream of letters to his parents, to his sister Jackie, and more and more to Bob French's sister Ginger. The letters home covered some of his exploits as a medic, including having to treat a soldier who had suffered a severe allergic reaction when he was attacked by red ants, but mainly Geier asked about how the family was doing and tried to keep up with the local sports teams. He and his father celebrated the fact that their beloved Blackhawks were coming off their best regular season in history and seemed to be primed for the playoffs. Led by stars like Bobby Hull and Stan Mikita, the Hawks were a lock to win it all, and Geier wondered if there was a chance that he and his father would celebrate a new Stanley Cup victory while Bill was away in Vietnam.

Having persevered through training, Ron Schworer had become something of a favorite in 2nd Platoon. While the other guys were out drinking and carousing, Ron would always read or keep himself busy by jotting lines in a mysterious, spiral-bound notebook. Finally his buddy Willie McTear asked Ron what the hell he kept writing about in that little book. It just didn't make any sense, because it was all numbers. Ron replied that it was all about his passion, computers. He and two of his civilian friends from Las Vegas had founded a small computer company, and he was writing code for use in something called software. Code that would make the computers do things. Computers? Code? It all sounded like Greek to McTear. Schworer's ability with numbers was already legendary in the unit. On operations Lieutenant Benedick often kept Ron by his side, and after they had been on the move for a while would ask, "Schworer, how many steps we been?" Without hesitation Ron would reply, "2,397 sir." Benedick would then ask, "And how many meters is that, son?" For which Ron always had a ready and exact answer. If the lieutenant trusted his ability with numbers that much, who was McTear to question what Schworer said about computers? Maybe he would have to buy himself a piece of the action on this company when they all made it home.

By March 20 the other companies of the 4th of the 47th had redeployed to the Mekong Delta, but Charlie stayed behind as perimeter security for Bear Cat. Plans quickly changed, though. In February, a Viet Cong attack on shipping in the Long Tau River prompted brigade commander Colonel Fulton to order Charlie Company's sister unit, the 3rd Battalion, 47th Infantry, into the Rung Sat to destroy the Viet Cong base areas there and to protect the shipping channel. Operation *River Raider I* lasted from February 16 through March 20, and achieved marked success. By the end of the operation, Colonel Lucien Bolduc's 3rd of the 47th was worn out and in need of respite, while Fulton believed that the pressure needed to be maintained to keep the Viet Cong in the Rung Sat at bay.[*] The task would fall to Tutwiler's 4th of the 47th, and on March 31 the choppers arrived at Bear Cat to transport Charlie Company into the fray in the Rung Sat.

The Rung Sat is a vast expanse of saltwater tidal marsh, crisscrossed by thousands of large and small streams, located between Saigon and the South China Sea. With an average variance of 11 feet, when the tide is out the rivers of the region run as

---

[*]   Major General William B. Fulton, Vietnam Studies: *Riverine Operations, 1966–1969* (Washington, D.C.: Department of the Army, 1985), pp.60, 67.

steep-banked, brown trickles, and the ground is a vast expanse of knee-deep, sticky mud. At high tide rivers are nearly impassable, and the ground disappears under an ankle- to chest-deep flood. Mangroves are the most common form of vegetation in the Rung Sat – stout trees supported by an inverted umbrella of roots often standing around 1 to 3 yards in height and supporting a trunk and tree as much as 6½ yards in height. The network of interwoven mangrove roots form an almost impenetrable barrier to ground movement, making the Rung Sat a perfect hideout for the Viet Cong in their shallow-draft sampans.

The soldiers of Charlie Company could not believe that they were going to operate in such a place, and had a great deal of difficulty in describing the conditions to their loved ones. One soldier wrote:

> At high tide only the mangrove foliage remains above the water, leaves and branches dragging in the current, like a huge flooded forest during a natural disaster. To be on foot in the swamp during the rising tide is to know a singular helplessness. Dead brown water licks its way over the mud, to knee-level, hip-level, waist-level, and there is no way to escape from it because there is no land, there is only the mud, and soon the water covers it all.
>
> Low tide is the time of mud. At low tide even the big channels are shallow, with long, grey-brown mud banks, and the small streams are empty, steep-sided ditches. Now the mangrove sits exposed atop thousands of piles of mud. The mud is slippery, foul from the eons-worth of dead things rotted and rotting there. The stink is thick under the heavy sun, and there is no breeze to take it away. The mud is everywhere, inescapable, filthy, too thick to wade, too thin for foothold; there is no end to it and no bottom to it. At low tide the world is mud, and a man in it is a panting, straining, futile animal, trapped and useless...
>
> When the tide was in, patrolling meant deep water, weapon and ammunition held overhead on bone-aching arms, tripping over submerged roots, wading through opaque salt water made viscous by the fear of coming under fire while in it. Miserable, agonizing hours of slow-motion movement, when lighting a cigarette or eating a C-Ration meal was a balancing act performed in chest-deep water.

Hours of small frights as one foot would slip toward deeper water; sometimes stepping unexpectedly into it. The trick was to turn around underwater and climb back up the bank using your hands and feet. Don't panic, and don't lose your weapon. It worked, when there was no strong current.

But at low tide every step went knee-deep or more into the mud. Each step meant a groaning strain to pull up the trail foot, hands gripping the mangrove, fighting the suction at your boots, knee and ankle joints stretching, thigh muscles going rubbery; falling sometimes, and needing a rope thrown by the men in front to get unstuck. Then take another step and start it all over again. Crossing the empty stream beds always called for the ropes. In an hour a platoon could move 300 feet, and be reduced to gasping, blubbering, spent men, whimpering in a world of endless mud.

For the shorter guys in the unit, operating in the Rung Sat was a nightmare of constantly slipping over their heads into unexpected deep spots in the water. For non-swimmers, though, it was even worse. In the course of a day's operation in the Rung Sat the platoons of Charlie Company might have to cross 15 or 20 rivers. Accidents were frequent – air mattresses were slippery, and ropes sometimes went slack. Many of the men in the unit could relate to Elijah Taylor's experience. As a non-swimmer he usually crossed rivers on an air mattress, but on one occasion he decided to cross one of the smaller streams using only the rope. In mid-stream the rope went slack and Taylor went under. Weighted down by his gear and heavy boots, Taylor began to panic and drown; he "saw heaven down there" and knew that his time had come. But soon he felt a strong arm on his shoulder as Lieutenant Hoskins had plunged into the water to pull him out. In the Rung Sat Charlie Company had to function as a team, with each of this band of brothers looking out for all of his comrades, because you never knew when it might be your turn to slip into the deep water or become enmeshed in the nearly bottomless mud.

Operations for Charlie Company in the Rung Sat generally lasted for three days, which meant that the men had to find some way to sleep in a place where they might start the night in mud only to find themselves in chest-deep water six hours later. As evening closed in, units worked to find the highest ground possible in hopes of a real sleep, but that was a rarity. Most often men were forced to sleep standing up, maybe leaning against a tree. Many carried hammocks into the field and strung them above the water in the mangroves; in times of danger, when climbing around in trees to hang hammocks was ill advised, men would simply wedge themselves into the branches and hope not to fall when they dozed off. Others blew up their air mattresses and lay down, hoping to rise in comfort with the tide. On the first such occasion, though, the sleepers had forgotten that tides involved strong currents, and they floated off during the night to find themselves alone. After finding their way back to their unit, the night travelers had a good laugh – but from then on they remembered to lash their air mattresses to the trees during the night.

The mangrove swamp was also full of interesting wildlife, some beautiful and some maddening. At low tide thousands of blue crabs, each with one enlarged claw, covered the landscape, battling over their own patches of muddy real estate. Mudskippers, ugly brown fish capable of breathing oxygen and walking on stubby fin-legs, waddled and splashed all over at both high and low tide. Nearly invisible against the backdrop of mud, the mudskippers were not dangerous, but often gave the men terrible frights. The most hated of the water-based worries, though, was the leeches. The men would wear long sleeves and tuck their trousers into their boots, but still the leeches found a way in. Some swore that they could see the leeches chasing them through the water. Their bites did not particularly hurt, and they were easy enough to remove – holding a lit cigarette to their body usually forced them to let go. But still leeches just gave many of the men the "heebie-jeebies." Clarence Shires remembers that after coming back from an operation, the water in the showers would run red from the blood of leech bites. Sometimes men would take their clothes off to get ready for their shower, only to find a little brown football come tumbling out – a leech that had eaten its fill and let go.

The Rung Sat contained what seemed to be an infinite variety of snakes, ranging from tiny, but highly poisonous, vipers to large constrictors. Snakes seemed to be everywhere in the depths of the swamp, dangling from trees, swimming through the water, slithering across soldiers' legs at night. They were simply a part of Rung Sat existence. In early April, Marty Renert, who had been a student at UCLA but had volunteered for the draft, was walking in 1st Platoon's file behind Platoon Sergeant Buford Hoover when a snake launched itself from a tree branch, seemingly intent on biting Hoover square on the neck. Hoover, though, caught the movement out of the corner of his eye and lashed out with his machete, cutting the snake in half. Renert was amazed to see that the half of the snake with the head still managed to slither over and bite Hoover's boot. Luckily the fangs didn't penetrate the tough leather, and, as the snake writhed from side to side while still stuck into Hoover's boot, Renert wondered aloud whether it was poisonous. Hoover bent over, cut the snake's head off, and replied, "Ain't poisonous now. Let's move out!"

Worst of all, though, were the mosquitoes: vast clouds of mosquitoes that Sergeant Crockett swore grew to the size of turkeys. Sure the army distributed bug juice to ward them off, but the men usually chose not to use it. Some swore that the mosquitoes licked it off before they bit them, and others believed the VC could smell bug juice from a mile away. Larry Lilley had a much more practical reason to avoid the stuff. After an initial orientation on the use of bug juice, Lilley had done as he was told and slathered his exposed skin. A few minutes later nature called, and thinking nothing of it Lilley unbuttoned his fly and urinated and found that he "nearly set his dick on fire." After dancing around in agony, Lilley swore never to touch bug juice again. During the day most of the members of Charlie Company simply wore their long sleeves fully extended and slapped constantly at their tormentors. Night was the worst. Some tried special sleeping bags with attached mosquito netting. Others, like Jimmie Salazar, huddled under ponchos, amazed that they could hear the buzzing mass of mosquitoes slamming into the fabric of the poncho in an effort to get to their skin. But when waiting in ambush, with absolute silence and vigilance a must, the men were totally unprotected. They could not huddle under anything, and they could not even slap. They just had to sit there and let the mosquitoes have their feast. But nothing could really bother Salazar at that moment, not even ravenous mosquitoes. He had just learned that Aurora was pregnant with their first child. Now life was really going to change.

Charlie Company normally entered the Rung Sat by landing craft or helicopter and operated for three days on the ground, with each platoon usually working separately while searching a prescribed area for the Viet Cong. Any operation lasting longer than three days risked disabling the company through foot casualties, such as immersion foot, much like the trench foot seen in World War I. The company headquarters group would accompany one of the platoons on a rotational basis. Maneuvering through the swamp was slow and dangerous, and there was always the possibility of wandering off course in the morass. Some days the platoons struggled to move forward only 200 yards, but on they trudged. Charlie's primary mission was to find and destroy enemy base camps, usually just small hills of mud piled up just above the high-water mark with a few bunkers and shanties for comfort. Although the company found several such encampments, some with food still sizzling above the fire and with laundry strung on lines, the noise of hacking through the mangrove roots and slopping through the mud usually alerted the Viet Cong to the Americans' approach, giving them ample time to slip away.

Whenever possible, Lieutenant Benedick had his men of 2nd Platoon wade in the streams, which produced much less noise than hacking through the mangrove. One morning in early April, after a fitful night of battling mud and mosquitoes, Bill Geier could have sworn that he smelled fish cooking and reported the find to Benedick. Thinking the olfactory intelligence worth pursuing, Benedick ordered Sergeant George Smith's squad to wade up the stream and check it out. Sure enough, after a few yards Smith and his men caught sight of a small mud island with a cooking fire – a Viet Cong base camp. Believing that the VC had heard their approach, Smith sent three of his men forward, certain that the Viet Cong had fled – another missed chance. Walking point for the tiny group, Idoluis Casares was the first to reach the small berm surrounding the camp. When he looked over the side, he found himself staring into the eyes of a Viet Cong who had popped his head up at the exact same time. No more than 5 feet apart the two stared at each other, wide-eyed – not knowing what to do. Suddenly the VC came to his senses, let out a yelp and galloped off into the undergrowth. Only then did Casares seem to remember that he was carrying a rifle, but it was too late. Casares returned to his friends with a story that they would tell and retell for months – a story that he would never quite live down. Good naturedly, Geier loved to remind Bear of the time the VC had gotten away.

Charlie Company always had to be on the lookout for booby traps, usually small grenades of Chinese manufacture attached to a tripwire of fishing line that hung slack in the water. The grenades themselves were usually tucked away unseen in the dense foliage, often waist high. Booby traps could be anywhere, but were especially thick around Viet Cong camps. In such areas the VC often dug small holes designed to make the unwary stumble into the tripwire of a nearby booby trap. Late one afternoon in early April, as 3rd Platoon searched a tiny base camp, Larry Lukes, perhaps lost in a daydream about his young wife back in Nebraska, got his foot hung up in a hole and fell. On the way to the ground he felt the tug of a tripwire and glanced to the right in time to see the wire, in slow motion, pull the pin from a grenade. Standing next to Lukes, Terry McBride, the tough kid from California, also caught a glimpse of the grenade, lodged a few feet from his waist, but did not have time to react. Lukes thought to himself, "Aw shit! This is it!" But the grenade only fizzled a bit – it was a dud. Lying there in the mud, with McBride shaking in relieved laughter, Lukes was assaulted by a series of quick, difficult questions. Why had the grenade not gone off? Why was he saved? He was just a country boy, he didn't yet have a family; didn't have a college education. Why him? The questions always hovered nearby for the rest of Lukes' tour – questions that became more insistent as others in the unit, his brothers, with families and so much more to live for, began to die.

For months Duffy Black had been asking Captain Larson for a chance to take command of Charlie Company in the field. As company executive officer, Black always had to remain behind, taking care of logistical chores and endless piles of paperwork while

Larson led the men on patrols and ambushes. Having had such a role in their training, though, Black ached to be in the thick of the action with the men he had come to love so dearly. He felt useless back on the base and wanted to be out there. He wanted to matter. Even while he pressed for a chance to enter the fray, Black continued to confide his fears to Company First Sergeant Crockett that he would never leave Vietnam alive. Crockett always responded by saying that Black shouldn't worry; he would return home to his new bride, and Black always seemed to agree. When the company returned from its first mission into the Rung Sat, for a short break to clean weapons and dry out feet and gear, Black once again visited Larson to ask to be allowed to go out with the unit. His timing was finally right, because Larson had come down with a bad case of stomach flu. Larson gave in to Duffy Black's request. He could lead the company on its second mission into the Rung Sat, but Larson gave Black strict orders to stay close to one of the platoon commanders. These men – Benedick, Hunt, and Hoskins – knew what they were doing out there and would keep Black safe. Black agreed to abide by Larson's wishes and went to his tent to get prepared for his first combat command. Before the night was over, Black paid a visit to company supply sergeant Cerveny, the master scrounger. Black gave Cerveny his duffel bag, packed with all of his possessions, and strict orders to have it sent to his wife Ida if he did not make it back.

On April 8, with Black accompanying 1st Platoon, Charlie Company re-entered the Rung Sat. During the first day's slog, although he never saw any movement, Lieutenant Benedick got the strong feeling that the Viet Cong were shadowing the movements of his 2nd Platoon. Benedick called his unit to a halt and ordered the men to hide on both sides of a small stream to await events. Within minutes, and while Benedick's machine gunner Frank Schwan was still crossing the tiny stream, a sampan carrying three Viet Cong slipped into view. For a few seconds Schwan and the VC who stood at the rear of the sampan just stared at each other, until, breaking free from the trance, Schwan yelled "Halt!" The three VC suddenly burst into motion, diving from the sampan in an effort to get away from the killing zone. But, as Idoluis Casares realized, the VC "didn't stand a chance." Twenty rifles and Schwan's machine gun opened fire and riddled the VC until the water ran red. Casares and the others searched the sampan as the bodies of the VC bobbed nearby, and collected what weapons and intelligence they could find. It was Charlie Company's first up-close kill. There had been firing before, and even a few blood trails, but this was different. There were bodies to search, bodies that the men had seen explode in fire. Somehow, though, it all seemed more mechanical than anyone had expected. They had done their job, reported their kills, gathered intelligence and weapons, and moved on. It was the army way.

During his 1st Platoon's operations on April 8, Lieutenant Hunt believed that he was close to finding the Viet Cong, and he warned Black and the headquarters group to be on alert, but nothing happened. The next morning, the platoon had just moved out when the point man for the day, Kirby Spain, a country boy from Arkansas, reported back that he saw something that might be a Viet Cong camp. Hunt ordered two squads of the platoon to spread out and move toward the camp with caution and told Black to stick by his side. When Spain made his way across the berm, he reported the disheartening news that everyone expected. The camp was recently deserted, and the VC had gotten away. Approaching the middle of the tiny base, Spain peered into the cooking pot and noticed that it contained rice that was still boiling and thought to himself, "Christ, we spent the night 50 yards away from the VC!" Hunt then ordered the platoon to surround the small 40-foot-wide camp and to conduct a thorough search of the area as he informed battalion headquarters of the situation. It seemed to be a very routine find, just a couple of ramshackle cots and a cooking fire. Nothing new, nothing special. His men all knew how to handle it. Still Hunt yelled out a reminder, "Be on the lookout for booby traps. They could be anywhere!"

After about 30 minutes of futile searching, Hunt was ready to call for the platoon to pick up and move out when there was a muffled THUMP about 40 yards away – the telltale report of a booby trap. Hunt blurted out, "Holy God, what was that?" He quickly formed up his platoon to get a head count. Everyone was there. What the hell could it have been; it was so close. Could it be the VC coming back for a fight? Not knowing what he would find, Hunt grabbed five of his men and slipped out into the thick of the mangrove to investigate. As they closed in on the source of the explosion, Hunt caught sight of movement in the undergrowth and heard a man moaning. That explained it. A Viet Cong had made his way back to the 1st Platoon perimeter and had been planting a booby trap when it had gone off. Realizing that the VC might have planted more than one mine, Hunt warned his men to watch for more booby traps. Hunt then looked to his right just in time to see a tripwire tighten around the leg of Danny Bailey. In surrealistic slow motion Hunt watched in amazement as the grenade went off, hitting him first with an intense blast of sulfuric heat before peppering his left leg with red-hot fragments.

Danny Bailey was a country boy from Hot Springs, Arkansas, who had never before been far from his rural home. Gangly and "not much on book learning," Danny had often been a step behind his peers during training, something that had made him the butt of many jokes and pranks. Soon it had become clear to the men of Charlie Company, though, that Danny was the most genuinely good guy in the whole unit. He was always cheerful, wearing a perpetual bemused grin, and, though he often took his time, was the hardest worker of the bunch. And once he finished his task, he would go straight into helping others finish theirs. Once he had shaken off the cobwebs and realized that his injured leg could take his weight, Hunt hobbled over to check on the wounded. He first came across Kirby Spain, who had taken fragments in his arm and back, perilously close to his spine. Spain assured Hunt that he was OK and could walk. Hunt then made his way over to Bailey. The blast had laid Danny's left leg open to the bone from the thigh nearly to the ankle, a wound so ghastly that Hunt couldn't help staring for a few moments. When he looked closer, Hunt noticed that Bailey's steel helmet, which was dangling from his pistol belt, was riddled with shrapnel holes; it had taken much of the blow. Had Danny not decided to strap his helmet to his belt that day, in strictly un-regulation fashion, the grenade would have blown his groin to bits and likely killed him. Hunt leaned close to ask the boy how he was, and Danny, seemingly oblivious to the pain, responded in a normal voice, "I'm sure sorry, sir. I heard what you said about booby traps, but right then I felt something tug. I looked down and it went off. You know, it damn near blowed my ass off."

As the dust and smoke from the blast settled, Hunt joined up with Clarence Shires and Marty Renert, and the three made their way toward the source of the moaning. As they parted the foliage, Hunt was initially stopped short at what he saw. "Jesus Christ, it's Duffy Black!" Somehow during the confusion created by the platoon's search of the enemy base camp, Black had wandered off into the mangrove alone. There he lay, with fragment wounds in his extremities and a gaping hole at the base of his neck. Given the nature of the wound pattern, Hunt thought to himself, "Oh no. Duffy found a booby trap and tried to disarm it himself, and the damn thing went off in his hands." Field veterans could disarm these rudimentary booby traps with ease, but this was Black's first time out with the unit. Shires knelt by Black's side. He was still breathing, and making horrible gurgling sounds. Shires told Black to hang in there; help was coming. For a few moments Black seized up, and Shires gave him mouth-to-mouth resuscitation until Doc Maibach arrived on the scene.

Maibach did what he could to make Black comfortable, and applied dressings to the worst of his many wounds, but his training had taught him that Black had little hope. The shrapnel that had torn the hole in his neck had travelled upward into his brain. After checking the wounds of Hunt and Spain, Maibach then went to work on Danny Bailey. He just had to save that leg. As Maibach worked, Shires and Renert sat with Lieutenant Black. For Renert, Black had always been a kind of hero. He had been there all through training, urging him on. He had been a constant presence in Vietnam, always sure of their purpose. Black looked up into Renert's eyes and asked, "Am I going to die?" Renert didn't know how to respond. This was his leader, his hero, his friend. He replied, "Sir, you are gonna make it. The medevac is coming, the docs are going to sew you up, and you are gonna be fine." As Black closed his eyes and struggled for breath, Renert fought back his tears and had to look away.

Wounded, but still in command of the situation, Hunt ordered that a Landing Zone (LZ) be cut into the swamp and called for an emergency dustoff. Men flew into a frenzy of chopping with their machetes to cut a hole in the undergrowth big enough for a helicopter to land. With the going difficult, an engineer wrapped detcord, a flexible cord filled with explosive, around the base of several small trees, the explosion creating an LZ just big enough for the purpose. The chopper thundered in, spewing water and mud in every direction.

The clearing in the mangrove was so tiny, though, that the chopper couldn't land. Instead it hovered nearly 4 feet above the ground. Jim Stephens, a Charlie Company original drafted out of a poor family from Morro Bay, California, worked with several other 1st Platoon troopers to get Lieutenant Black aboard the medevac. As the men, mired in knee-deep mud, lifted Black onto the deck of the chopper, Stephens could feel Black's slick, warm blood coating his arms and hands; it even got into his eyes and obscured his vision. As he strained with Black's weight, Stephens wondered if the officer he admired so much from training was going to make it. Then the job was done; Black was aboard, followed by Danny Bailey. Hunt and Spain were able to climb aboard under their own power. The helicopter slowly rose out of sight, and just like that, the wounded were gone.

A few thousand yards away, just near enough for the explosions to be barely audible, 2nd Platoon under Jack Benedick continued its search pattern. Their morning had been much less eventful, with no Viet Cong in sight and no hints of traffic to be found anywhere. For 2nd Platoon April 9 was just another dreary day of slogging through the endless mud. In mid-afternoon the platoon reached another of the Rung Sat's limitless supply of small, nondescript rivers. In what had settled into a normal routine, Benedick swam across the 30-foot-wide stream and tied a rope to a mangrove tree on the far side. While Benedick was in the water, the other men busied themselves with blowing up air mattresses and getting their gear ready, while some stopped for a much-needed smoke. As usual, Willie McTear and Ron Schworer stood near the back of the group talking while they blew up their air mattresses. They would cross in the middle of the pack, flanked by some of the better swimmers, and pull themselves across hand-over-hand along the rope while floating on their air mattresses.

When about half of the unit had reached the far bank, it came time for McTear and Schworer to enter the water. There was nothing to it. McTear led the way, with Schworer behind and Benedick swimming alongside to make sure that nothing went wrong. Suddenly Benedick heard a roar off to his right, and looked in horror to see a US helicopter gunship skimming about 4 feet above the stream beginning an attack run on his men. Before Benedick could scream a warning, the chopper opened up with its machine guns. All of those still in the river made a mad scramble for the nearest shore. Frank Schwan watched in almost detached amazement as machine gun bullets cracked and hissed past him, and left trails of bubbles as they zoomed by in the water. Idoluis Casares and the youngest man of Charlie Company, Stan Cockerell, were on the bank of the stream waving madly at the pilot, whom they could see clearly – even his eyes – he was so close. But the chopper zipped by too fast to notice. Amazingly nobody was hurt. As McTear clambered off of his air mattress, Benedick emerged from the water and sprinted to his RTO. Furiously Benedick ordered Schwan to ready his machine gun and fire on the helicopter if it came back for another pass. Benedick then screamed into the radio, "You had better get that goddamn helicopter the hell out of here, or we are going to shoot it down. I mean I will shoot those sons of bitches down! Do you get me? They had better get their asses out of here!" The men of 2nd Platoon could not see through the thick canopy, but they knew that the helicopter was still there, and they listened helplessly as it wheeled back to its original attack position. Within a few minutes Casares and Cockerell saw the chopper reappear above the stream and yelled at Benedick that it was getting ready for another run. Benedick screamed at Schwan to be ready as he furiously repeated his radio message to have the helicopter call off its attack. Just as the chopper started forward, instead of leveling off for another attack run, it climbed vertically into the sky and flew away above the trees. Somehow the message had gotten through.

As the commotion died down, and the men of 2nd Platoon marveled at the fact that they were still alive, Benedick looked out into the river. Schworer's air mattress was still floating there undamaged, but Ron was gone. Frantically Benedick dove into the water to search. In all of the commotion nobody had noticed Ron fall off of his air mattress – nobody had gone to his rescue. The stronger swimmers all joined Benedick in the effort to find Ron –

but there was nothing to find. The tide was on its way out and the strong current must have dragged his body away. As Benedick dove into the water again and again, Willie McTear just couldn't believe what he was seeing. Ron, his buddy Ron, had been right behind him. How did he lose him? Where was he? He couldn't have drowned – not like that. Not such a senseless death so far from home. Not Ron; he was the genius who was going to get rich by putting a computer into every home. Not Ron. Willie knew that soldiers weren't supposed to cry, but as the unit sat there for hours while Benedick searched under every log and in every deep hole, Willie just couldn't help it. He just sat there and wept. His best friend was gone.

While Benedick dove into the murky water in search of Ron Schworer, the dustoff carrying the wounded of 1st Platoon touched down at the 24th Evacuation Hospital at Long Binh. Lynn Hunt needed surgery that would keep him out of action for several weeks. Danny Bailey required extensive treatment on his mangled leg, but refused a trip to the hospital in Japan. He wanted to stay in Vietnam with his buddies. The surgeons were a bit worried when they saw the X-rays of Kirby Spain, which seemed to indicate that he had fragments in his stomach. Spain tried to tell them that they were wrong; he had been wounded in the back, not the stomach. He informed the surgeons that the X-ray must be picking up what he had for breakfast that morning, "beefsteak, taters, and gravy." Still, to be on the safe side, the doctors performed exploratory surgery, leaving Spain feeling much worse than he had before. After he came out from under the anesthesia the doctors informed Spain that he had been right. They had found no shrapnel, only "taters." Spain then informed the surgeon that "taters are tasty when you cook 'em over C-4."

Worst by far, though, was Duffy Black. Placed on the bed next to Hunt, Black mumbled incoherently, and was plainly in bad shape. Rollo Larson visited his young friend in the hospital and was crushed by what he found. He blamed himself, a deep blame that would never leave him for the rest of his days. He kept telling himself that he should have never let Duffy go out with the company. If he had been there, none of this would have happened. When he had heard about the tragedy, Chaplain Bernie Windmiller, Black's confidant and close friend from Fort Riley, also hurried to his side. Shortly after Windmiller arrived on the scene, the doctors rushed Black off into surgery, and Windmiller went off to the chapel to pray. Windmiller wrote of what happened next to his wife:

After surgery the doctor said that his condition was grave and that he could offer us no hope of recovery. Said he had done all he could and it was now out of his hands. They've operated 3 times on Duffy and the Doc said they could operate again and save his life but it would mean a vegetable life for Duffy – and he couldn't do that. Duffy's father-in-law [who was also in Vietnam with the 9th Division and who had also arrived at the hospital] took this report very hard, so we both walked outside. We stood in the silence of the night, trying to find some answer – trying to find some cohesion to our confused thoughts. I walked over to Sgt. Acevedo [from 1st Platoon] and put my arm on his shoulder – and said nothing for a few minutes. What can one say? Then I assured him that I had prayed earnestly and that we had to prepare ourselves to give him up. I assured him that God understood our confusion and was acting in accordance with what He allows, even though we don't understand. Sgt Acevedo is a real great man, of few words, but of depth. He put his arm on my shoulder – said nothing, but we felt and understood each other's feelings perfectly. I felt the need of prayer, so I walked the short distance to the chapel and knelt at the altar. I found myself arguing with God for Duffy's life – I was struggling, not willing to accept the end... Duffy was like a spiritual son to me – there is something of me in Duffy and I didn't want to let go of it... When I submitted to what God might want and what I wanted, peace came over me – a relief of soul. At that point I felt someone beside me – it was Duffy's father-in-law kneeling in prayer also...

Sgt. Acevedo and I slept about 2 hours ... and at 0400 the neurosurgeon woke us and said that he had abandoned all hope and death could come at any time. His pupils (Duffy's) were dilated and fixed and there were no voluntary responses. Poor Duffy, he just lay there, a hunk of flesh breathing.

Somehow Duffy Black held on for several hours more, lingering between death and life. But on April 11 he finally passed away, leaving Windmiller with the difficult task of writing to his widow, Ida.

Dear Ida,

You have been in my thoughts and prayers so very much during these past few weeks. Duffy's death has brought you more sorrow and grief than you have ever known in your life. No one else grieves his death more than you; no one's heart breaks like yours. Yet you are not alone in your sufferings.

Duffy was popular with his men. He himself had been among their enlisted ranks and knew their needs, their problems. He understood them. He worked hard for their welfare, nothing was too good for Charlie Company... So you understand why you weren't alone in sorrowing your husband's death. In a sense, he was married to Charlie Company; his death was their death...

Now you are alone. A young woman approaching her twenties; you have loved a man for 3 months and now you are a widow. Duffy is dead; these facts you cannot reverse. But you have not loved and lost. True love never loses. When we give ourselves to another the way you did to your husband, it cannot be evaluated as a defeat. In the brief life you had together you gave Duffy more love than he had ever known. You brought him more joy and happiness than he imagined possible from one woman... Yes, you, more than anyone else, must know that in a little span of history you gave your husband a life-time.

You are young, Ida, you have a life before you. God has blessed you with beauty, personality, and charm. Time will heal the heartache... In God's own time and way He will again bring to life within you the gifts you need to live and love.

In Christian Love,
Bernard Windmiller
Chaplain USA

For the men of Charlie Company there was no time to mourn. Military deaths are different from civilian deaths. In the civilian world people often die in hospitals with their family around them, and there is nearly always a period of cathartic mourning. But the boys in Charlie Company had just learned how different things were during war. One minute Black and Schworer were there, and the next minute they were gone. One never to be found and the other whisked away on a helicopter to a distant hospital. Maybe there was a moment to cry, and later Chaplain Windmiller memorialized both men in a service, but out in the field the beat went on. The boys of Charlie Company had to put the past behind them immediately and go about their business. Any slip up, any blubbering, might cause more men to die. It was a difficult lesson to learn, a lesson that was the first step in hardening the hearts of the young soldiers who were so far away from home and the civilian life they had once known.

As Charlie Company's time in the Rung Sat dragged on, losses to mines and booby traps continued to impose a slow wastage on the unit, leaving the men feeling helpless. The Viet Cong seemed like ghosts – you never saw them and were never able to fight back, but you kept getting hurt. On April 18, though, 1st Platoon bumped into the Viet Cong for the first time. Jim Dennison was walking along with the point squad when he heard a shot ring out. He thought to himself, "What dumb fuck fired his weapon?" when he heard a whistle blow "and the whole world exploded." The men of 1st Platoon hit the dirt, searched for cover, and returned fire at the unseen attackers. Marty Renert hunkered down behind a small tree and fired his M16 in short bursts. His Fort Riley training kicked in immediately – he dug his heels into the dirt (to minimize the chance of getting shot in the feet) and searched for the tell tale muzzle flashes that would give away the enemy position. But, even though bullets kept cracking past, he couldn't make out exactly where they were coming from, so the best he could do was fire in the general direction. Time seemed to slow to a crawl as a flurry of thoughts flashed through Renert's mind. He didn't want to die thousands of miles from home and so far from the family that that he loved. He swore never to forget that moment – the fear, the threat, the danger. He wanted to remember it, and hold it dear, so that he would remember never again to let trivial things worry him. Life is what mattered.

Dennison's squad mate Doug Wilson recorded the events in his diary:

> Today I got my first actual taste of combat. It had been raining all day long and everybody was wet and muddy and generally miserable. At about 1500 we ran across some footprints along a river and started following them. Charlie was waiting for us and we walked right into an ambush. It all happened so fast. The fire fight lasted maybe a minute but a whole lot of rounds were exchanged. They had ARs [Automatic Rifles] and grenade launchers. About 5 seconds after the fight started Stancil was hit. He was lying almost on top of me when he got it and it almost made me sick. Rounds were coming in so close to me that I could hardly return the fire. As soon as it started it was over and at the sound of a whistle he retreated leaving us with one casualty. That makes the second man in ten days from my squad to be going back to the states.

Wayne Stancil was from a poor family from rural eastern North Carolina. A rich military tradition suffused the family, with uncles and cousins gathering from miles around to break out a jug of "shine" on Saturday nights to tell their war stories and relive the glorious days of their past. After high school Stancil got married and went to work for a local refrigerated truck body company where he was offered a work deferment from the draft. It didn't seem right to Stancil, though, that others should go to Vietnam while he remained safely at home, so he refused the offer – the only employee of the company to do so. Six months later Stancil's draft notice arrived, and he was off to Fort Bragg, North Carolina for basic training. In March 1967, Stancil arrived at Cam Ranh Bay and received his assignment to the 9th Infantry Division. As one of the first replacements in the 1st Platoon of Charlie Company, Stancil naturally gravitated toward some of the guys who were also from rural areas, including Danny Bailey, Clarence Shires, and Kirby Spain.

It had been gently raining that morning when 1st Platoon had picked up some tracks and started following them up a small stream. Then came the sudden whistle blast and the deafening burst of enemy fire. Along with the other members of 1st Platoon

Stancil hit the ground and opened up with his M16. After squeezing off only a few rounds Stancil's eyes widened in horror as he looked down at his weapon. It had jammed, leaving him defenseless. Almost at that precise moment the Viet Cong round slammed home, entering Stancil's hand and exiting from his elbow. Wayne Stancil had a "million dollar wound"; his stint as a member of Charlie Company had come to a quick and violent end – a sad reality that was becoming all-too common.

During the brief hail of fire, Gary Maibach heard Stancil yell "Medic!" Without hesitation Maibach jumped up amid the wild shooting and sprinted to Stancil's side to bandage his wounds. Calmly amid the rain of bullets Maibach went about his work. John Young, who had been so sure that he and the conscientious objector would never be able to get along, was amazed that a man who would not carry a gun and "has never been heard to say anything stronger than 'doggone' or 'cotton-picking'" could be so thoroughly brave. Everyone in the 1st Platoon realized that they were in good hands with Doc Maibach. After the firing was over, the men of 1st Platoon gathered their wits. They had taken losses to booby traps and mines. They had killed a few VC in ambushes, but this was different. Even though it had been short, this had been 1st Platoon's baptism of fire, and they had survived. Amid the joy of being alive, Jim Dennison finally became aware of a warm sensation between his legs. At first he was afraid it was blood, but then, after some investigation, he realized what it was. He had shit himself during the firefight. He was not the only one.

One Viet Cong soldier had been shot in the short engagement, and, as 1st Platoon went back about its business, each soldier in the file had to walk by the dying man. When John Young reached the scene of the encounter, the file came to a halt to clear a booby trap, leaving him to stand and light a cigarette as he looked down on his fallen foe. Lying there in his sandals and black pajamas beside the trail, the Vietnamese, who could not have been more than 17 years old, had four bullet holes in his chest. He was plainly beyond hope but still alive, gazing at the sky in confusion. As his lung wounds bubbled air mixed with blood, the young Vietnamese made gulping sounds as if he were trying to eat the air that his lungs could no longer reach. Young had never before seen anyone die, and watched spellbound. Here he was, a Vietnamese peasant, younger even than his American adversaries. No doubt he lay dying no more than a few minutes' walk from his home, from his parents and family. Yet in his final moments of life there was nobody there who knew him, to hold his hand, and offer comfort. Instead he died with a foreign soldier standing over him. Somehow it all seemed so tragic. Young couldn't help thinking, "Man this is some serious shit we are involved in." Then the call came to saddle up and move out, and 1st Platoon went back to work.

After the Viet Cong had escaped, Charlie Company attempted a pursuit, which necessitated a longer than usual stay in the Rung Sat. Guessing where the enemy had gone, the platoons of Charlie Company fanned out in an effort to run down their prey. Each of the platoon leaders used extra caution, though, realizing that the fleeing Viet Cong would leave behind mines and booby traps to cover their retreat. Just as Charlie Company was about to give up its pursuit on April 23, Marty Renert felt a tug at his boot and heard a roar before he lost consciousness. All hell had broken loose once again with 1st Platoon at its center. Doug Wilson wrote:

> At about 1400 the column was stopped and somebody yelled they had found a booby trap. About a minute later I heard the explosion and then the screams. I was the last man in the column. Four men got hit, Renert, Parkinson, Roy, and Cardia who had a piece in the stomach, the doc said it was serious. Five more booby traps were found in the area. After the dustoff, which only took about 15 minutes, the word came back to me to back out of the area the way we came in. We were going to go around it. I turned around and walked out carefully. All of a sudden another explosion and then those horrible screams again. This time it was Davidson and Stein, who I guess almost had his leg blown off. Again the dustoff and again I am point. I hate to say it, but I was so scared I could hardly walk. We finally got to the LZ after crossing a big river where I had one hell of a time getting everyone across because of the current. We got back to the ship around 2200. THANK GOD.
>
> Well in the past 2 weeks our platoon has had 12 combat casualties, the most in the battalion. We started in Vietnam with 50 men; now we have 24 left. Pretty bad.

The Viet Cong seemed to be everywhere that day. Even as 1st Platoon tried to extricate itself from the minefield, Jack Benedick's 2nd Platoon was operating nearby with Bob Ehlert walking point alongside his buddy Curtis Irvin when sniper fire cracked past. Everyone hit the ground, and Ehlert squeezed off a quick round from his grenade launcher. Cracking a half smile, Ehlert turned to Irvin and said, "You know, a guy could get killed around here." His eyes wide with the fright of the moment, Irvin could only respond to his friend's attempt at humor, "You asshole!" Silence quickly returned to the Rung Sat; the sniper had fled, but everyone knew that the VC were out there – lurking, watching, and waiting. Benedick and his men continued their sweep conscious that the were being hunted.

That night 2nd Platoon set up an ambush position at the junction of two streams; everyone was on alert behind a defensive array of claymore mines. The wait as the time slowly crawled past was excruciating. Staring into the dark but seeing nothing but afraid to blink; straining to hear the slightest sound; unable to move while under assault from a relentless cloud of mosquitoes. Ehlert had just passed the controls of a claymore to Irvin when at once the night was lit up as bright as day. In the wake of the massive explosion, 2nd Platoon responded with everything it had. Automatic fire cut through the night as an array of tracers lit the sky. A few minutes later Benedick's voice somehow cut through the din – "Cease fire! Cease fire!" Stillness returned to the Rung Sat with startling rapidity, leaving the men with ears ringing as they tried to readjust to the silence. The only sound was a quiet moan from Ray Layman. Shrapnel from the explosion had ripped through the Charlie Company original and Cleveland native's foot and also, somewhat embarrassingly, hit him in the butt. Bill Geier quickly dressed Layman's wounds, and the long night continued.

The next morning 2nd Platoon troopers fanned out to clear the area, discovering a Viet Cong claymore mine mounted on the far side of the nearest stream. As Benedick had suspected, the VC had been shadowing his platoon's movements for the previous day and had struck in the dead of night. The cat and mouse struggle in the Rung Sat was heating up, and the hunter could become the hunted at any time. As troopers from his platoon began to hack an LZ into the swamp for Layman's helicopter evacuation Benedick wiped away the sweat from his forehead. Ray Layman, a fine young trooper was gone and likely wouldn't return. Benedick knew that bleeding of Charlie Company had begun in earnest and that the war was about to heat up in a major way. As he looked around at his men of 2nd Platoon he knew that his men and the men of Charlie Company were ready.

It was during the quiet times after operations, when the men of Charlie Company were able to see the empty bunks of those who had been lost, that the magnitude of what was happening became clear. Vietnam was a lethal place. All innocent thoughts that this was somehow "not a real war" had long since been banished. With a shocking randomness war was taking its toll. There was no rhyme or reason about who would get hurt or how or when. Violence would suddenly descend upon the boys of Charlie Company and one of their buddies would be thrown into a chopper, gone maybe for good. The guys could not help but notice that Willie McTear almost constantly gazed at the empty bunk next to him, the bunk that had been Ron Schworer's. When they had patrolled the fields around Bear Cat, strong and confident in their immortality, the boys of Charlie Company had loudly asked for more action. They had gotten their wish. War had come, and it was becoming more and more obvious that the boys of Charlie Company "were not going to get out of this thing without getting hurt."

As the men of his platoon took more and more losses, Lieutenant Hunt grew more and more frustrated. He was able to walk, but the doctors had ordered him not to get his wounds and sutures wet – something impossible in the Rung Sat. So Hunt languished on light duty in the rear, while his platoon fell under the temporary command of Lieutenant Sam Thompson.[*] From the get go, Hunt had not liked Thompson. It seemed that the young lieutenant was out to prove something. He was arrogant and brash. Although new to the field, Thompson refused to listen to his experienced NCOs, and Hunt kept catching rumors that Thompson took needless risks with the lives of his men. Specifically, Hunt heard the complaint that Thompson was falling into the lethal habit of sending reconnaissance elements out too far in advance of the unit. The

---

[*]   Fictitious name.

news worried Hunt greatly. When patrolling broken terrain, reconnaissance elements of a few men, sometimes as few as three, would scout ahead of the main body of troops to reconnoiter the next tree line for the enemy. It was dangerous work, but it was better than having an entire squad or platoon caught in the open to fight against a dug-in enemy force. Reconnaissance was a dangerous job at the best of times. If Viet Cong were in that tree line, there would be hell to pay, with the recon element suffering the most. If the recon element were sent out too far, without the remainder of the platoon close at hand to offer fire support, it was a potential suicide mission.

As April turned to May, and Hunt still had not returned to combat, Platoon Sergeant Buford Hoover, Hunt's right-hand man, came to visit him in his quarters. It was an extraordinary moment. NCOs could bitch and moan among themselves, but they never complained to officers about other officers. That was a good way to end a career. But Hoover calmly sat down and said, "Sir, we need to talk." Sensing that Hoover was deadly serious about something, Hunt sat down and said, "Sure. What do you need?" Hoover went on. "Sir, this new lieutenant is an asshole. He thinks that he is great, but he is not very bright. He takes risks with the lives of the men, and they hate him. Sir, you need to get back to the platoon quickly before somebody gets killed."

Hunt was horrified. He had to get back to his boys before it was too late.

4 INTO BATTLE

Doug Wilson; Friday May 5, 1967 [diary entry]
We have another new lieutenant... I don't like the way our new platoon leader operates already. He sends out small squad recon patrols too far from the main element. And at night he only uses 1 squad for ambush while the rest set up 200 meters away.

Dear Mom, Dad, and Girls,
Tomorrow we are moving down to the Delta, to a place called Dong Tam. We're going to fly down there. We have a battalion mission on the 14th or 15th. It's supposed to be a pretty hot area. But the terrain is dry ground, and we'll feel so good to be out of the mud that I don't think we'll have much trouble. I feel pretty good about it...

I guess that's about all the news for now. Don't worry about me, because I'm eating pretty well. I feel very good and the time is going fast. Hope everybody is ok.

Love, John [Young]

At the beginning of May, as the men of Charlie Company neared the one year mark of their military service, the units of the 4th of the 47th continued working in the Rung Sat, with only occasional forays into the drier areas of the Mekong Delta. The now familiar missions produced continued losses to mines and booby traps and several discoveries of Viet Cong base camps, but very little in the way of meaningful contact. On May 10, though, as Charlie Company wended its way through a somewhat more habitable part of the Rung Sat, Jimmie Salazar, who was walking point for 2nd Platoon, caught some movement out of the corner of his eye as he neared the remnants of an enemy camp. Like a scene from a combat movie, a Viet Cong jumped to his feet from behind a log in a nearby stream and leveled his rifle at the surprised GI. With water pouring from his clothes and weapon, the VC pulled the trigger. As Salazar winced in anticipation of the end, he heard only a loud CLICK, CLICK, CLICK; the Viet Cong's weapon had misfired. As the young Vietnamese soldier looked down in horror at his useless rifle, Salazar, with his heart threatening to pound out of his chest, lowered his M16 and emptied his entire magazine. The VC's body lurched and bobbed in rhythm with the impacting bullets before hitting the ground only a few feet away. Two more VC jumped up and sprinted away, and 2nd Platoon responded with a hail of fire. Realizing that his elusive quarry was escaping, Lieutenant Benedick called for his men to cease fire. Working quickly, Benedick called in an artillery strike hoping to confuse the fleeing VC and drive them back toward his men, who he had take cover behind a small dike. Soon the artillery whistled overhead and exploded among the mangrove, throwing bits and pieces of trees in all directions. Jimmy Salazar, Bill Reynolds, Mike Cramer, Bill Varskasfky and the rest of 2nd Platoon couldn't believe their eyes. Benedick's idea had worked. There came a lone VC walking down the trail with his rifle slung over his shoulder – like he didn't have a care in the world. The entire platoon opened up, and the Viet Cong soldier didn't stand a chance. His body seemed to dance as the bullets struck home. After searching the dead VC, 2nd Platoon troopers tossed his body in the river, and the war went on. After a few obligatory messages confirming the contact to battalion headquarters, 2nd Platoon resumed its march. It had already been a hectic day.

Salazar, though, could only think of how close he had come to dying before his baby was born.

During operations in the Rung Sat, the 4th of the 47th moved from Bear Cat to its new accommodations aboard ship. After more than a year of planning and organization, the naval element of the Mobile Riverine Force (MRF) had come on line. Task Force 117 controlled what became known as the River Assault Force, consisting of two River Assault Squadrons, which carried out offensive operations, and one River Support Squadron, which served as the Mobile Riverine Base (MRB). The troops lived aboard the barracks ships of the MRB, the *Colleton*, the *Benewah*, and the *APL-26* (universally known as the "green apple"), World War II-vintage landing craft that had undergone recent upgrades in the Philadelphia Naval Yard. Initially the ships of the MRB were anchored off Vung Tau, but later they served as mobile staging areas for the troops of the MRF. To provide docking facilities for the barracks ships, two 30-by-90-foot pontoons, called "ammi barges," moored alongside each anchored ship. The barges served as storage facilities and allowed the men of the MRF to get from their barracks ships to their assault craft without having to use embarkation nets.

The Armored Troop Carrier (ATC) was the workhorse of the MRF. Known by the troops as "Tango Boats," the ATCs carried the men of the MRF from the base ships into battle. Each platoon had its own Tango Boat, a converted World War II landing craft, which was 56 feet in length and had a top speed of 6 knots. Armed with one 20mm cannon, two 50-caliber machine guns, and two grenade launchers, the ATCs would pick up their men from the ammi barges alongside the barracks ships and then steam to the site of operations, a journey that often took the slow craft several hours. Accompanied by monitor gunboats and command vessels, the ATCs, usually in groups of four, would proceed to their designated target and then beach simultaneously. Their bow doors would drop open and the men would charge out to undertake the ground element of their mission. Often the ATCs would remain close at hand during the operation, to act as supply vessels and to ferry men across larger water obstacles as well as to provide needed organic firepower.*

The men of Charlie Company could hardly believe their good fortune when they first came out of the Rung Sat and boarded their new barracks ships. After trying to sleep in the mud or in trees they now had real, comfortable bunks with clean linen. There were showers with hot water, toilets, hot chow, and even air conditioning. It seemed like heaven, so much so that the men did not mind that they were held to a higher code of spit and polish than they had experienced at Bear Cat. They didn't even mind getting blasted by fire hoses on board the ammi barges. Seems that the navy didn't want all of that unseemly Rung Sat mud on their nice clean boats. After this first step in the cleaning process the men then went on board and took showers, with their weapons and all, before collecting freshly laundered uniforms. Their next stop was always the galley, where Mess Sergeant Smith could always be heard bellowing, "My boys are back, and they're hungry!" When Charlie Company was returning from a mission, Smith always had some delicacy ready and waiting and would run navy personnel out of the galley by whacking them with a large wooden spoon if they did not give way to his men. Jim Dennison wrote home regarding his new accommodations in glee:

> We moved to a … boat today … the food is really good. There's piped in music all day long, which gives us a big lift. This may not sound like much to you, but over here you feel like you're in heaven when you have an ice cream bar and a coke. It's ecstasy. This place at least has taught me how to appreciate life to its fullest measure. You'll never have to call me twice once I get home mom, because each new day will be pure joy.

The officers had it especially good, living in single accommodations with linens changed daily. Where the men had good food in a communal galley setting, the officers messed with their navy brethren in the ward room of the ship, with starched linen tablecloths and fine silver settings, while being served by Filipino

---

*   Thomas Cutler, *Brown Water, Black Berets: Coastal and Riverine Warfare in Vietnam* (Annapolis: United States Naval Institute Press, 1988), pp.240–250.

waiters. Somehow all the air-conditioned comfort seemed a bit jarring, though, leaving Lynn Hunt to wonder how his men would be able to adapt. Here they could be civilized – clean water, real soap, fresh uniforms. But hanging over their heads every moment was the thought that they would soon have to leave this civilization and re-enter "the war world," slogging through the mud and facing death. Would the transition be too difficult?

Usually Charlie Company remained aboard the barracks ships for one or two days, and the men were instructed to wear only shower shoes to allow their feet to dry in an attempt to avoid losses due to immersion foot. While the men spent much of the "downtime" cleaning weapons and resting from their exertions, the boys of Charlie Company, ever resourceful, found ways to enjoy themselves in their new home. On occasion the company brass would make the search for recreation easier by holding a beer bash and ice cream party on the ammi barge. Although the men would have preferred Pabst or Schlitz, they were at least happy that the beer of choice, San Miguel, was not the dreaded Ba Muoi Ba local brew that had been the bane of their existence at Bear Cat. By June someone in the company had located a tucked-away compartment where he and his compatriots stored several mattresses and a record player. On days off, after a hard mission, a few men would gather to smoke a little pot and listen to the Beatles. One enterprising sailor even ran a small business by showing porn movies to the soldiers for a nominal fee.

In general, though, the men of Charlie Company whiled away their off hours by writing letters home and engaging in conversation. Several of the men tried to console Willie McTear over the loss of Ron Schworer by talking and sharing letters. Forrest Ramos even took McTear into his elite group of pranksters, who were afforded ample opportunity for honing their craft by the cramped quarters and close proximity of shipboard life. A rash of short sheetings and "kick me" signs seemed to do McTear some good. Bill Geier wrote home in disbelief that his beloved Blackhawks had folded in the semi-finals of the NHL playoffs, beaten by the Toronto Maple Leafs. How did the Golden Jet and his boys lose? It's not like they were the Cubs after all – the Hawks had won the Stanley Cup as recently as 1961. Oh well, Geier and his father still held out hope that this would be the year for the Cubbies, breaking a World Series drought that had reached 59 years. Many of the members of 3rd Platoon, which included Forrest Ramos' elite group of pranksters, had bonded even further by vicariously sharing in the experiences of the two new fathers in their midst – Jose Sauceda and Fred Kenney. The two now spent a good deal of their time showing pictures around the group and wondering what they were missing. Both men spent much of their down time writing to their wives assuring them that all was well, even sending home pictures of the guys, which always seemed to include snaps of them hanging out with Forrest Ramos or Terry McBride. In turn Noemi and Barbara responded with new photos of Belinda and Freddie and updates on all the milestones of their lives. Little Freddie was holding his head up on his own. Could Belinda be that far behind?

Charlie Nelson spent much of his time pestering anybody who would listen. He wanted to get into the field with his buddies. He had trained for war, and this mailman job was a crock of shit. Crockett, Larson, Hunt – he pressed his case to whoever happened to be handy. By April they relented. No matter how small his stature or what he looked like, letting him go out had to be better than putting up with his constant hectoring. Some of the on-board conversations, though, were of an increasingly serious and disturbing nature. The men of 1st Platoon were convinced that Lieutenant Thompson was not up to the task of leading them in combat. Enlisted men always bitch and grouse about their officers and NCOs, but this was different. Thompson's shortcomings were a risk to their lives. Two of the men even took the extraordinary step of taking their fears directly to Captain Larson. He assured them that the situation was temporary and that Lieutenant Hunt was about to return to duty. They just had to be patient a little while longer.

It also became obvious aboard ship that Charlie Company had begun a slow and relentless cycle of change. Faces were different. Although it began as just a trickle, replacements were arriving in the company to take the place of the dead and badly wounded; replacements who had not trained with the unit; people who were taking the place of lost brothers. These new men had to be treated well and welcomed, but their faces were bitter reminders of friends who were gone. Like it or not, the replacements were always the odd men out.

Carl Cortright was the youngest of three children of Aubrey and Dorothy Cortright, who, in 1956, moved their family from Michigan to Mission Hills, California. After high school graduation Carl had hoped to go to college to get into broadcasting, but his father did not support the idea, wanting Carl to be a machinist like him instead. Taking a part-time job, Carl spent what little money he had on a white 1958 Chevy Impala, complete with a V-8 engine and a leather interior. He tinkered on the car from time to time, enjoyed the local cruising scene, and hoped to get it ready to race. But his plans were interrupted in May 1966 when he received his draft notice. Like so many others from the San Fernando Valley, Carl Cortright made his way to the induction center, where he stood alone in line behind Fred Kenney, Richard Rubio, and their friends from Canoga Park who were destined for Charlie Company. While the others passed their physicals and made their way to Fort Riley, though, Carl ran into a problem. His blood pressure was too high. Relieved by his unexpected good fortune, Carl returned home to his job and car, eventually getting into a couple of races. Things were picking up, and Carl was even considering the idea of broaching the subject of a broadcasting career to his father once again, when in October 1966 he received another draft notice, and this time he passed his physical.

Cortright went through basic training at Fort Ord, California, surviving the standard regimen of pushups and yelling. Then, like most Vietnam-era soldiers, he went with another group of men to AIT at Fort Polk, Louisiana, where he was trained as a mortarman. Although Carl made friends in both basic and AIT, he knew that he was not destined to serve with those men. He was headed to Vietnam as a single replacement for a unit that had lost a mortarman who had been killed, wounded, or had reached the end of his tour. In April 1967, even though Carl boarded an aircraft packed with soldiers, he was going to Vietnam alone. Grabbing his duffel bag after the long flight, Cortright made his way to the replacement depot to receive his assignment. A harried lieutenant sat puffing a cigarette behind a small table checking the men off on a list and directing them to their new military homes. When Cortright got to the front of the line the lieutenant asked him his name and his military occupation specialty (MOS). Carl replied that he was a mortarman. The lieutenant glanced up, and after a long drag on his cigarette, informed Cortright, "We don't need any more goddamn mortarmen; we need riflemen. Son, you are now officially a goddamn rifleman. You got a problem with that?" Cortright then boarded a truck bound for Bear Cat, where he was to report to Charlie Company, 4th of the 47th, where he was going to replace a man in 1st Platoon who had been lost to a mine. After arriving at the camp, Carl and five other replacements were hustled onto a waiting helicopter, which flew them out over the ocean and then made ready to land on a large ship riding at anchor. Carl thought to himself, "This has to be a mistake; I'm in the army, not the navy."

Charlie Company was out on patrol, so Cortright and the others found their berths and got settled in to wait. Two days later, on April 28, he made his way to the ammi barge to watch his new unit return from its operation. The men looked old and weary as they climbed off the ATC covered in layers of thick mud, while they talked easily about a brief firefight they had fought on the operation. As the sailors hosed the soldiers down, Cortright thought, "Holy shit. These guys have really been to war." Cortright discovered that several men from the company were from the San Fernando Valley, and, although they were in different platoons, quickly made friends with Fred Kenney, from nearby Chatsworth, who immediately pulled out and showed off several tattered pictures of his son Freddie. Carl also met Kenney's friends from 3rd Platoon, including the larger-than-life Terry McBride, perhaps the most boisterous and self-assured man in the whole unit. The machine gunner was a great friend to have, in part because you sure as hell did not want to have him as an enemy. Kenney also got to know Steve Hopper, the middle child of a family of ten from a farm outside Greenfield, Illinois. Having grown up strong baling hay on the farm, Hopper had been a football star in high school, even dating one of the prettiest cheerleaders. Hopper had hoped to go to college, but had lacked the means, and had instead wound up working for Caterpillar in Peoria, Illinois, making crankshafts before being drafted. Hopper struck Cortright as a straight-shooter and a good soldier. Even though he was in a different platoon, Hopper warned Cortright to steer clear of his squad leader, Sergeant David West,* who was something of a hard ass who liked to pick on new guys. Cortright was also introduced to Don Trcka, of League City, Texas, near Galveston. Stoutly built, Trcka had been the only student at Clear Creek High School to letter in all four major sports each year of high school. A standout on a championship football team, Trcka had received a scholarship to play at Southwest Texas State University. It was a dream come true, but Trcka had become a bit sidetracked by a combination of practice and the university's social scene, and his grades soon tumbled, which had left him eligible for the draft.

After introductions and a few formalities, Lieutenant Thompson assigned Cortright to 2nd Squad of 1st Platoon, under Sergeant Dave Jarczewski. Ski, as he was universally known to the men, was from Depew, New York, a hardscrabble suburb of Buffalo. His father, Valentine, was a life-long employee of Bethlehem Steel, where he worked on the production line. Valentine had served as a soldier in the Pacific during World War II and impressed upon his son that he had two basic choices once he had graduated from high school. He could come to work in the steel mill like almost everyone else in the area, or he could join the army. Although part of him wished that he could have gone to college, Ski joined the other 22,000 employees at the Lackawanna, New York, plant of Bethlehem Steel. He rode to work with his father each day, until his draft notice arrived in May of 1966. Ski welcomed Cortright warmly and introduced him around the squad, with Cortright being particularly impressed with Charlie Nelson. The diminutive Navajo Indian seemed especially eager, and told Cortright that he had better be ready, because they were gonna go mix it up with Charlie out there in the Rung Sat right quick. Ski then introduced Cortright to his team leader, the man who would show him the ropes and lead him in battle, Don Peterson.

Obviously tired, but easy going and friendly, Peterson welcomed Cortright to the unit and took him aside to give him a crash course on how not to die and how not to get others killed in Vietnam. As

---

*   Fictitious name.

he sat there and listened to a guy he considered to be a grizzled veteran, little did Cortright know that if he had passed his first physical back in May of 1966, he would have been serving with Peterson, Kenney, and the rest of Charlie Company all along. The information came at him fast and furious. This was Vietnam, not some stateside training facility. He had to learn and learn quickly so that he would not be much of a danger to himself or others. It was a lot to take in – how to spot tripwires, how to tell a fresh trail from a cold one, how he had to keep 10 feet between himself and the next man in the unit to avoid more than one person being blown up by a mine. Two days later, Cortright went out on his first operation with the unit, and learned firsthand the difficulties of life in Vietnam. Just in attempting to move forward, slogging through the Rung Sat, he felt like a burden, constantly tripping and nearly drowning in the platoon's first river crossing. Cortright looked in awe at his new friends who navigated the terrain with such ease. They were real, hard-bitten soldiers. He also noticed that they were a club, a family. They treated each other with the easy camaraderie typical of soldiers who have trained and suffered together – joking, arguing, sharing letters, and sharing hopes and dreams. Although the men of Charlie Company treated him well and were always helpful, it was plain that Carl was not yet a member of the family. He would have to prove himself over time.

Don Peterson hid it from everyone, especially his wife, but he was getting worried. He had always thought that he would not be hurt in Vietnam; he was lucky. He was going to get home to teach young James how to play football as he grew up. Although Peterson maintained his jovial exterior around his buddies and wrote letters home that were full of hope for the future, the events in the Rung Sat had changed him. Death could come from any direction at any time. Death didn't seem to care if you were a good soldier or a bad one; death made its own choices. More and more Don Peterson got the feeling that he would not make it home to see James again. He was going to die in Vietnam. Back in their apartment at Fort Riley, Don had discussed with Jacque the possibility that Vietnam might become too difficult. They had decided that he would use code and write and ask her what she wanted for Christmas. That would be the signal that he had had enough. She would then write back demanding a divorce, which they hoped would cause him to receive a hardship leave. Once home, they could run off to Canada together. But on May 10, 1967, Jacque read a letter from Don that brought her up short. There was no code; in desperation he did not hold back. He simply wrote, "Please honey, get me the fuck out of here. I'm going to die." Don had never written anything like that before. He had to be serious, and there was no time to waste with fake divorces. Frantic, Jacque called her air force NCO stepfather who promised to try to reach Don in Vietnam to see what he could do.

Back in Vietnam, the soldiers of Charlie Company received word to get ready. They were headed out for their first major operation in the Mekong Delta – the assignment for which they had been preparing ever since the first day at Fort Riley. There was a sense of excitement in the enlisted men's quarters on the ship. They were going to chase Charlie through rice paddies, not slop around in the endless mud of the Rung Sat. Maybe there would be a real battle, and not just hit-or-miss contact with guerrillas and booby traps in the swamps. Even as Charlie Company made ready for a new type of operation, life for the unit went on. Ralph Wilson arrived in the unit as part of a fresh batch of replacements to make good losses suffered in the Rung Sat. Born into a poor family in Andover Township, New Jersey, Wilson had been forced to grow up early when, at only nine years of age, he lost his father in a mining accident. A wrestling standout in high school, Wilson dreamed on opening his own bait and tackle shop but had dropped out of high school, worked on construction sites, and gotten married instead. Only three days after his wedding, Ralph's draft notice arrived, and he was off to Fort Dix and Fort Jackson for training before arriving with Charlie Company as it made ready to move out into the Mekong Delta. Amazed by all of the hubbub of preparing for war, Wilson made his way to his assignment in 1st Platoon and realized that he had a lot to learn and very little time to learn it.

As they prepared their weapons and gear for action, the men of Charlie Company talked in twos and threes about what was to come. Jim Dennison, the pub owner's son from the north side of Chicago, decided to get in a quick shave. He stood next to Don

Peterson who was shaving off his mustache. Most of the men of Charlie Company had grown mustaches on their trip to Vietnam aboard the *John Pope* – scraggly affairs that most had shaved off once they had reached Bear Cat. Peterson's mustache, though, had grown in well – a thick, handlebar mustache of which he was very proud. But there he stood, shaving it off. Dennison asked, "Pete, what the hell are you doing shaving off your mustache?" The answer he received stopped him short. "Dennison, my wife never liked my mustache. I know that I'm gonna die tomorrow, and I don't want her to have to see me this way in my coffin."

In the predawn hours of May 15, 1967, elements of two battalions of the MRF made their way toward their first operation in the Cam Son Secret Zone, one of the main bases of operation for the Viet Cong in Dinh Tuong Province in the Mekong Delta south of Saigon. Intelligence indicated that the Viet Cong 514th Provincial Battalion had retreated to recover its strength after a recent sharp battle with the 3rd of the 47th to the area between where the Rach Ba Rai and the Rach Tra Tan streams branch off from the My Tho River. The brigade commander, Colonel Fulton, hoped that an advance from three directions would catch the 514th in a pincer, destroying the Viet Cong unit for good. The battalion established a forward command post near Cai Be and brought in supporting artillery on barges 3 miles southeast of the site of the coming operation. The strike force consisted of 22 ATCs, two heavily armed monitor gunboats, and two command boats that landed Bravo and Charlie companies of the 4th of the 47th on the north bank of the My Tho, between the Rach Ba Rai and the Rach Tra Tan, while Alpha Company choppered into the south to act as a blocking force. Further to the west, the 3rd of the 47th searched the area at the mouth of the Rach Ba Rai.[*]

At 8:30am the bow ramps of the ATCs dropped and Charlie Company hit the beach on the north bank of the My Tho River. An artillery barrage had preceded their arrival, and the men exited the landing craft into an interlocking and still smoking series of shell holes and fallen trees that initially made the going quite difficult.

---

[*] Major General William B. Fulton, Vietnam Studies: *Riverine Operations, 1966–1969* (Washington, D.C.: Department of the Army, 1985), pp.80–81.

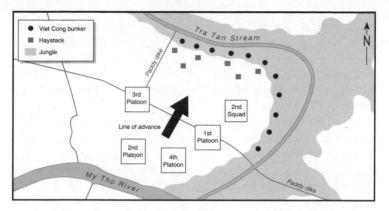

Battle of May 15

Terry McBride felt something hit his neck, and slapped at it. When he pulled his hand back he found a dead red ant. He looked around to see ants falling from the sky like rain all around. The artillery barrage had destroyed the ants' nests and blown their occupants high into the sky. After floating to the ground the enraged insects took their vengeance on anything in sight, especially the soldiers of Charlie Company.

Emerging from the blizzard of red ants, Charlie Company entered the dominant terrain of the Mekong Delta, a checkerboard of small rice paddies bounded by tree lines flanking the numerous large and small watercourses used to irrigate the fields. Within minutes, the company reached a large, open expanse of paddies almost two football fields in size. Across the open paddy was a densely grown tree line, dotted here and there with haystacks, which extended around to the right flank, forming a kind of horseshoe. There was a hesitation as the 1st Platoon edged up on the open area, with 3rd Platoon trailing just behind and to the left, while 2nd and 4th platoons brought up the rear. Charlie Nelson had seen enough cowboy and Indian movies to know that this was a perfect place for an ambush. No doubt the company would hold up here to wait and see what would happen. He wasn't surprised at all when the first few sniper rounds buzzed past.

Lieutenant Thompson then gave the order to move out. While it was common military practice to move toward light and sporadic fire, there was over 300 yards of open ground to cover and nobody knew how large the enemy force was on the other side. Even a replacement like Carl Cortright wondered to himself, "Why is he sending us out into the open like this?" But, true to their training, 1st Platoon moved on – all but Lance Morgan* from New York who froze in his tracks with his eyes fixed forward and not saying a word. As the other men in Jarczewski's 2nd Squad turned to watch, Lieutenant Thompson pulled out his pistol, placed it at Morgan's temple, and ordered him forward. Shocked back to reality Morgan stumbled forward, and the men of Ski's squad followed while muttering threats under their breaths.

With Ski's 2nd Squad in the lead and on the right flank, headed toward the bend of the horseshoe, 1st Platoon inched out into the open as the sniper fire picked up in intensity. Don Peterson turned to Carl Cortright and wondered aloud if they were walking into a trap. Trailing behind and to the left, 1st and 3rd squads got the word from their RTOs that Thompson had decided that the fire was too heavy and had given the order to fall back to a rice paddy dike about 35 yards to their rear to take cover. As more and more enemy bullets cracked past, some kicking up puffs of dirt from the dry rice paddy, John Young of 1st Squad noticed something peculiar. Edward Hoffman,† Dave Jarczewski's RTO, was with him. What the hell was he doing here? He was supposed to be with 2nd Squad. Without Hoffman, Ski would have no idea about the order to fall back. He would be cut off and helpless. Young realized what had happened. Hoffman had received the order to fall back, and in his fear had retreated without telling Ski. As he reached the safety of the rice paddy dike, Young turned and yelled at Ski and his men, who were nearly 100 yards away and still advancing through open terrain toward the enemy position. But Ski could not hear him over the sound of the fire. A knot of fear welled up in Young's stomach. Ski and his men were on their own.

As the fire grew in intensity, Ski looked around and realized that Hoffman wasn't there. After wondering for a second or two where

---

*   Fictitious name.

†   Fictitious name.

he could have gone, Ski looked to his left and realized that his squad was alone, thinking, "Christ, where did everybody go?" He shouted to Peterson and Cortright, who were even further ahead of him, to stop while he tried to figure out what the hell was going on. Glancing around, Ski couldn't locate Lance Morgan, who had last been seen off to his left with Enoch Scott, a big, athletic guy from Texas. Glancing around, it was Charlie Nelson who first spotted Morgan curled up in a fetal position in the tall rice. Sprinting off to the left Nelson quickly reached Morgan's side to ask him where he had been hit. But Morgan had not been hit and could only whimper, "Mama, mama." With bullets whipping all around, Nelson stooped to grab Morgan by the neck and shook him, all the while cussing his mama and all of his family members. "Fuck your mother you idiot, you had better get the hell up and run! You hear me you son-of-a-bitch?" At that moment Nelson was struck by a bullet in his chin, and tumbled to the ground screaming, "You motherfuckers! You shot me!" The bullet had passed through the fold of skin beneath the bone of his lower jaw. It wasn't all that bad a wound, but Nelson was surprised that his fingers could touch each other through the entry and exit holes. The shock of the moment forced Morgan out of his trance, and he started yelling for the medic. Nelson replied, "Fuck the medic. He's too far back," and applied his own pressure bandage to the wound. He and Morgan then ran back to Ski and the others, the whole incident taking only a few seconds.

Kneeling to get what little cover they could from the tall rice, the little knot of men were in real trouble. Without orders and without any information regarding what was going on around him, Ski was at a loss. Staying put seemed to be nothing but a death trap – but moving without knowledge of the location of friendly forces could get them all caught in crossfire. As he tried to figure out the best course of action, Ski was surprised to see Morgan running back in the direction he had just come from. Morgan had noticed that Charlie Nelson had lost his helmet when he had gotten hit in the chin – the helmet that contained his medicine bag. Without prompting, Morgan ran back to where he had fallen, zigzagging to avoid incoming fire, and returned with the helmet. Nelson thanked him, pulled the medicine bag out of his helmet liner and began praying. With fire now blazing in from the entire tree line to their front, and from the haystacks, Ski made the decision. No matter what the risk, it was fall back or die. He shouted the order, and Don Peterson, who was at the point of the tiny formation said, "You guys run like hell, and I'll cover you!"

Peterson popped up and shot from the hip with his M16 on full automatic as the other men began their dash, but he had fired for only a few seconds before yelling "My chest! My chest!" and tumbling backward into the rice. Enoch Scott fell almost simultaneously, shot through the arm. Carl Cortright took only a few steps before a thought ran through his head: "Maybe I ought to get down and crawl?" Just then he heard someone shout, "Pete's dead!" and next he felt a sledgehammer strike him in the back and toss him violently to the ground. The pain was excruciating, especially in his legs, which he noticed with an almost detached amazement he could no longer move. Even though they blazed in agonizing pain, try as he might Cortright could not move his legs at all. He was paralyzed. He looked up to see a form next to him, maybe it was Ski, and shouted, "Shoot me man! Just shoot me! I can't go on like this!" Whoever it was looked down quickly and said, "It'll be all right man, you got yourself a million dollar wound!"

Charlie Nelson was hit again in the leg almost as soon as he had begun to run toward the rear. With the bullet entering from the back of his leg and blowing his kneecap off as it passed through, Nelson wasn't going anywhere. Unwilling to leave without him, Ski jumped down by his side to see what he could do, and wound up with his head facing toward the enemy fire. Nelson yelled at Ski, "Get away from me man, they are going to be shooting at me again. Get the hell out of here!" At that moment Ski's body lurched and his whole insides felt like they were on fire. The bullet had entered through his shoulder and had cut down through his midsection, breaking five ribs and puncturing a lung, before exiting through his back. The impact of the blow had spun Ski around just far enough that he was able to see that there was a Viet Cong machine gun in one of the haystacks shooting at them. Ski thought to himself, "That's where those assholes are," and he tried to motion toward the haystack with his good arm. But there was nobody remaining in his squad to see the motion. They were all down. As bullets from the machine gun traversed the concealing rice, Ski thought, "This is it. The party is over. It's all done." Then he felt a pain that he had not felt before, a pain that came from everywhere all at once. Moving his neck just a little to try to catch a glimpse of the source of his agony, Ski realized that he had fallen on a nest of red ants. He could only think, "Holy fuck!" before he passed out.

As 2nd Squad was cut to pieces in mere minutes, 1st and 3rd squads sprinted to the cover of the rice paddy dike. Larry Lilley, the California motorcycle champion, felt his body jerk twice in the hail of fire, but amazingly felt no pain. As he hurdled the paddy dike and hit the ground, he keyed his radio handset to send a message about the deteriorating situation, but nothing happened. Ripping the radio around to see what the problem was, Lilley noticed two large bullet holes. Wearing the radio had saved his life. Lilley looked back toward Ski's squad and saw James Nall, who had once been asked to go and find his mind back at Fort Riley, running for all he was worth for the cover of the dike, with bullets kicking up puffs of dirt around his feet. As Nall finally belly flopped down by Lilley's side, Viet Cong machine gun fire began to chew the dike to bits.

Frustration and an impotent rage set in among the men of 1st and 3rd squads. Their buddies were out there somewhere getting shot to pieces. It was torture for Gary Maibach. He knew that men were down out there in the rice. He had seen two fall and had heard their screams. But when he had grabbed up his medical kit to go and tend to the wounded, he had felt Lieutenant Thompson's hand on his shoulder. He looked up at the lieutenant, who informed him that he couldn't go out there; it was suicide. The best that the men behind the dike could do was to send out fire toward enemy positions in an effort to force the Viet Cong to keep their heads down. As Maibach looked on, hoping for his chance, they all fired everything they had – M16s, machine guns, and grenade launchers, burning through ammunition quite literally like there was no tomorrow. John Young was directing his squad to put out as much firepower downrange as possible when he saw that Bob Eisenbaugh, a replacement drafted out of Shamokin, Pennsylvania, was just sitting there looking toward the Viet Cong positions with a blank stare on his face. Young shouted, "Eisenbaugh! Fire your goddamn grenade launcher at that tree line!" Eisenbaugh looked at him quizzically and replied, "But Sergeant Young, I don't see anything to shoot at." Young responded, "I don't care what you can see and what you can't see. Just fire that grenade launcher at the tree line!" After Eisenbaugh had been shaken from his fog and begun firing, Gene Harvey, who had married his sweetheart Deana in November just before the unit departed for Vietnam, saw that the grenade launcher wasn't making a dent in the enemy bunkers. He grabbed a nearby shoulder-fired Light Anti-Armor Weapon (LAW) and sent an armor-piercing rocket toward the enemy positions. A direct hit. But after the smoke cleared it became apparent that the Viet Cong positions were so well concealed and heavily fortified that they were impervious to everything but a strike by heavy ordnance. There was nothing that 1st and 3rd squads could do to help their friends.

On the left flank of Charlie Company's advance, 3rd Platoon had also fallen under fire while caught in the open paddy. The platoon's point man, John Howell, who grew up near Don Peterson, had seen movement ahead and had hit the ground just before the firing began. Howell fired back until his M16 jammed. Vulnerable and exposed, Howell crawled back to the platoon's lines and relative safety. Jose Sauceda, the new father from Mercedes, Texas, and Jim Cusanelli were also marooned far out in advance of 3rd Platoon's main positions when the firing erupted. Both men took cover 5 feet apart in a small, muddy stream and did their best to return fire. Amid the din and frantic activity, Sauceda couldn't help but think that it was like for real cowboys and Indians – just like the movies. All thought fled, though, when a nearby Viet Cong popped his head up and fired off a rocket propelled grenade right at the duo. As both Sauceda and Cusanelli covered up, expecting the worst, the grenade slammed into the brown, gravy-like mud of the stream bank. It didn't explode. Eyes wide with a mixture of sheer terror and relief at their unbelievable good fortune, Cusanelli shouted, "Goddamn it! Let's get the hell out of here!"

As the fire exploded into their midst, most of 3rd Platoon hit the deck amid the high rice and began to maneuver toward the cover of a small canal to their front. The buoyant and ever aggressive poet-platoon leader, Lieutenant Hoskins, yelled above the fire for his men to "get the fucking lead out" and to hustle to his position in the canal. With good cover, and with most of the enemy fire directed toward Ski's downed squad, Hoskins was sure that he could get his men forward to hit the enemy positions in the flank. As he began his move toward the canal, Steve Hopper noticed that his squad leader, Sergeant West – who had been such a spit-and-polish hard ass – was cowering on the ground unable to move. Shaking his head in disgust, Hopper dragged West forward with him to the protection of the canal and took command of the squad himself.

After gathering as many men as he could in the cover of the canal, Hoskins ordered the move toward the flank of the Viet Cong positions. One by one the men of 3rd Platoon crawled forward, with Terry McBride laying down covering fire with his machine gun. The enemy fire, though, was still far too heavy. Within seconds McBride's assistant gunner, Jerald Scott, took a bullet through his helmet, laying his scalp open to the bone. Tony Caliari, an Italian from the suburbs of Pittsburgh, had moved only a few feet before a bullet blew through his ankle, shattering the bones and leaving his foot dangling at an odd angle. In his own move forward Don Trcka had somehow found himself alone. In a panic he stood up to try to catch sight of Hoskins and the rest, just as a Viet Cong rifle grenade detonated nearby. The force of the explosion threw Trcka back across the canal, where he landed with a thud. He opened his eyes and found himself looking at the picture of his girlfriend, which he had taped to his rifle stock. With his chest a blaze of pain, Trcka was somehow gladdened by the thought that her picture was going to be the last thing he ever saw. In the hail of fire, James "Smitty" Smith, an African American from outside Cleveland who loved to hang around with Fred Kenney and Richard Rubio, had hit the ground with his arms wrapped around his head. Within seconds a bullet struck him in the upper arm and exited through his elbow. The force of the blow had spun Smitty around to face the safety of the canal. Both Caliari and Smith began to make their way back toward cover, crawling in agonizing pain. As he made his first difficult movement, though, Smith came face to face with a snake. He didn't know what kind it was – to Smitty all snakes were poisonous – and in terror he leapt to his feet and ran back through the fire to the canal, hurdling over Caliari on the way.

With so many voices yelling "medic," Elijah Taylor didn't know where to start. He had always wondered how he was going to react when the company finally got into a real battle and he heard his name called when the bullets were flying. All thoughts of how he might react just evaporated. Taylor grabbed his gear and set to work tending to the wounded. He applied field dressings to Scott, Caliari, and Smitty and got them stabilized, but Trcka was another matter. The fragment wounds to his chest were so severe that Taylor thought he might not make it. He bent down over Trcka, assured him that he had a "million dollar wound," gave him a curette of morphine, and then informed the nearest RTO that they needed a medevac quickly or Trcka might not make it. Taylor then noticed another wounded man huddled at the bottom of the canal and went to see what he could do. Placing his hand on the man's shoulder Taylor asked him where he was hit. Sergeant West replied weakly that he hadn't been hit and added, "Doc, I just can't take it." Not quite knowing how to react, Taylor told West to make his way to the rear where the medevacs would be arriving soon.

The 2nd and 4th platoons had been trailing the advance and were not as heavily engaged but had to be constantly on watch for high rounds that flew over the company's forward elements. Also harried by Viet Cong snipers perched in nearby trees, 2nd and 4th platoons helped to lay down covering fire, hauled supplies forward, and readied an LZ for incoming resupply choppers and medevacs. The relative inaction was difficult for Bill Geier to bear. The forward units were taking losses, and no doubt needed medics. He begged his 2nd Platoon leader, Lieutenant Benedick, to be allowed to go up to the front lines to help, but Benedick told him that he had to stay to help with the medevacs and in case 2nd Platoon suffered any casualties. Seeing the helpless look in Geier's eyes, Benedick patted him on the shoulder and assured him that he would have his chance.

Located with 2nd Platoon, Captain Larson watched events unfold through his binoculars. He knew what he needed to do; he had to maneuver his units to flank the enemy positions and drive the Viet Cong out of their bunkers, but the enemy fire was too heavy. Larson realized that he first had to call in artillery and air support to lessen the volume of enemy fire, but he had a unit out there cut off near the Viet Cong lines. Unable to communicate with Ski's squad, Larson had no way of knowing where they were or how many of them had survived. Without knowing the location of 2nd Squad, Larson could not take the risk of calling in the heavy ordnance that he needed. He could kill his own men.

As afternoon approached the men of 1st Platoon were getting desperate; Ski's squad had been down in the paddy for two hours and the badly wounded were no doubt nearing death. Gene Harvey had already taken matters into his own hands and crawled over the paddy dike into the fire zone to see what he could do to help the fallen. Although the fire had not slackened much, Lieutenant Thompson, still unwilling to let Doc Maibach go forward, shortly thereafter asked for volunteers to go out and get those boys back. Jim Stephenson, a farm boy from rural Missouri, Ben Acevedo, a Hispanic farm laborer from Washington's Yakima Valley, and Gene Harvey all shot their hands up. They had trained and worked with most of the guys from 2nd Squad for almost exactly a year now and could not imagine just leaving them to their fate. John Sclimenti, the popular high school vice president, and John Young, the enlistee from Minnesota, also volunteered for the desperate mission. The men only carried their M16s and one magazine of ammunition – they had to travel light and get into and out of the killing zone fast if they were to have a chance. With Acevedo letting out a war cry the group jumped over the protective dike and ran low and fast out into the rice, hoping to find someone alive. With bullets cracking by overhead, Acevedo and Sclimenti located Nelson and Ski lying almost side by side. Nelson yelled, "You guys had better get down or we had all better get the fuck out of here!" Ski, who had passed out, was already turning blue and appeared to be drowning in his own blood. Sclimenti wrestled Nelson onto his back and carried him back to the protective dike piggy-back style, while Acevedo laboriously dragged Ski back to safety through the rice. Amazingly none of the men were hit.

After running full out with his head down for a short time, John Young caught sight of a prone form from the corner of his eye. Crashing down behind the GI, Young noticed that there was a hole right in the middle of his back, surrounded by a large bloodstain and thought, "Jesus, this is going to be bad." Carl Cortright had lain there for two hours wondering how he was going to die. Facing the Viet Cong positions and unable to move, partly concealed by the tall rice, he had watched the muzzle blasts of the weapons that were trying to search him out. Sooner or later they were bound to find their mark. But then when all hope had passed, an American came up behind him and said the impossible, "I'm here to take you back." When he found out that Cortright couldn't walk, Young was at a momentary loss. As one of the smaller men in the unit, there was no way that Young could carry Cortright back all that way without them both being shot. Thinking frantically, Young lay down flat on the ground and instructed Cortright to crawl up onto his back. With great difficulty, Cortright wrestled himself onto Young and latched his arms around the sergeant's neck. Young then raised up on all fours and began to crawl back toward the paddy dike. After a few yards, though, Young began to breathe heavily and asked Cortright if it would be OK to rest. A few minutes later, Young resumed his crawl, noticing that Cortright, instead of complaining about his agonizing wound, was now using his own arms and doing his best to help Young crawl forward. Only a few seconds had passed before Young heard Cortright say, "Sergeant, you had better stop again." Young replied that he was OK to go further, but Cortright said, "No, you had better stop; they are shooting at us again." Sure enough the slow and steady movement in the rice had caught the Viet Cong's attention, and Young noticed that bullets were hitting all around them and kicking up puffs of dirt. After the fire slackened, Young resumed his journey. When he had struggled his way to within a few yards of the American positions, Young yelled out that he was coming in. Seeing what was going on, Sclimenti vaulted the dike and rushed out to help Young the rest of the way. With Young and Sclimenti each taking one arm the duo dragged Cortright back, with his injured back bouncing through the rice, and manhandled him over the dike. As Doc Maibach quickly got to work, Young noticed something. After lying out there for hours and enduring a journey that must have resulted in continuous and excruciating pain, only once they were over the dike and in relative safety did Carl Cortright begin to cry.

Gene Harvey initially had run out the furthest and came skidding to a halt beside Don Peterson. A quick check confirmed what he feared; Peterson had no pulse. Realizing that there was nothing he could do, Harvey moved on to try to find the others in Peterson's squad. Shortly thereafter Jim Stephenson crashed down beside Peterson, hoping to save his buddy. But he, too, was crushed to discover that Pete was dead. Stephenson marked the spot by popping a smoke grenade and hustled back to the cover of the paddy dike. Stephenson reported to Lieutenant Thompson that he was convinced by what he had seen in the paddy that Peterson's body marked the furthest penetration of 2nd Squad, news that Thompson passed on immediately to Captain Larson. It was what the captain had been waiting for; he could now call in artillery and air strikes beyond the smoke marker without fear of friendly casualties.

Before the artillery and aircraft began to hit their targets, Lieutenant Thompson ordered the nine men of 1st Squad, under John Young, to gather their gear and assault the tree line on the platoon's right flank. But the order didn't seem to make good sense. There was no fire coming from that direction. What were they supposed to do over there? After firing so much that day, the men were all low on ammunition, some down to as few as ten rounds. Worst, standing up would only make the men vulnerable to the lethal Viet Cong fire coming from the bunker line to their front; the same bunkers that had shot up Ski's squad. It all just seemed wrong, and after watching the events of the day unfold, several of the men of 1st Squad wondered if Thompson had just lost it. In receipt of a direct order, though, there was little recourse for Young and his men, so they did as they were told and made ready for the assault. After the men got to their feet, they walked forward, firing as they went. Within seconds one man was shot down by enemy fire, Acevedo had his radio literally blown off of his back,

Eisenbaugh and two other men had their M16s jam, and another two ran out of ammunition. Now out of radio contact, and sure that he could not complete the mission, Young turned to Acevedo and gave his order for the men to keep firing as they fell back to their original position behind the dike. Out of the corner of his eye, Eisenbaugh caught sight of a man running toward their position with boxes of ammunition, but before he could reach them his arm jumped away from his body, struck by rifle fire. Having accomplished nothing, while losing two men, 1st Squad made its way back to the platoon perimeter, now more sure than ever of Lieutenant Thompson's incompetence.

There was no time to dwell on anger, though, because artillery rounds had started to explode among the Viet Cong positions and soon bombers began their first runs. The tide of the battle had turned, and the men of Charlie Company watched as hell was unleashed upon the VC. Explosions showered the GIs with mud, followed by waves of heat after napalm strikes. Jim Dennison couldn't take his eyes off the spectacle. As he watched he could not help but be amazed as he saw one lone Viet Cong, sitting in a tree, taking shot after shot at the American jets as they thundered past. This guy was not panicking, he was not running; he was calmly taking aim and shooting at his tormentors. The bravery of that lone Viet Cong struck Dennison deeply. "Who are these guys we are fighting? Damn it, is this fucking worth it?" Steve Huntsman, who had lived with Don Peterson during their training at Fort Riley, was also engrossed by the sight – until a direct hit vaporized the tree and its occupant. Huntsman flew backward about 3 feet, struck in the arm by a shell fragment. He thought, "My God, I've been hit," and then noticed that blood spurted in a fountain from the jagged wound every time his heart beat. His artery had been severed, a wound that without immediate treatment meant certain death.

Huntsman tied off the wound as best he could before making his way to Doc Maibach, who applied a tourniquet. Maibach then took Huntsman to the rear where, since the artillery fire and air strikes had silenced some of the Viet Cong fire, the first medevacs were on their way in. Company First Sergeant Crockett had been working feverishly both to get an LZ cleared and to coordinate with the choppers, which were going to come in under enemy fire. Doc Taylor, Terry McBride, and Richard Rubio brought in the wounded from 3rd Platoon and loaded them on board. Barely able to catch his breath through the pain radiating through his chest, Don Trcka looked around to see Tony Caliari and Smitty close by his side, but he wondered what the hell Sergeant West was doing sitting there on the chopper. He seemed just fine. The whole group was stunned by the sight of Dave Jarczewski, lying there without a shirt on covered in blood with a large, ugly exit wound in his back that bubbled air every time he drew a shallow breath. Knowing that there was little that he could do, Doc Maibach helped load Ski aboard, and wondered if it was going to be the last time that he ever saw him alive. Worst, though, was Carl Cortright. Since the bullet had entered from the front, Doc Maibach had not been able to give him morphine – afraid that the bullet might have blown open his stomach on its way through his body. Running through the diminishing fire, four men of the 1st Platoon had grabbed Cortright by the loose ends of his shirt and trousers and carried him back to the LZ at a trot – each step jarring and grinding Cortright's severed spine. The men loaded Cortright aboard the helicopter as easily as they could, but even that involved pushing and dragging, resulting in pain that nearly made Cortright pass out. As the chopper took off, somebody had the decency to jam a lit cigarette between Cortright's lips and he took a few puffs as the aircraft rose into the sky. While Cortright looked at the other shattered bodies all around, he realized that he did not recognize most of the faces. It was only his second operation with Charlie Company, and he was still the new guy. He never had the opportunity to become part of the family. As the chopper finally rose above the level of the Viet Cong fire, Cortright breathed a sigh of relief and thought, "Oh well. Just get me the hell out of here."

Back on the ground everything had begun to go wrong for the Viet Cong. Even as their hardened bunkers began to cave in under artillery fire and air strikes, Colonel Fulton, who was circling above the battlefield in a chopper of his own, had directed Alpha and Bravo companies of the 4th of the 47th to close in on the enemy positions from the north and west respectively. In danger of being surrounded and summarily destroyed, the Viet Cong began to abandon their positions and flee the field of battle, many trying to escape by floating down the Rach Tra Tan. While Alpha Company blazed away at the Viet Cong who fled to the north, and helicopter gunships mopped up the unfortunates in the river, Charlie Company got its revenge. Everywhere the Viet Cong were popping up out of their holes and running away for all they were worth, and up and down the line Charlie Company soldiers struck back with everything they had. Doug Wilson, who had once sold pictures aboard the *John Pope*, picked up a nearby LAW and fired at a VC bunker, the impact resulting in a shower of mud and body parts. Gene Harvey, who was still wrestling with the impact of the loss of Don Peterson, saw his chance to exact a measure of revenge. As 1st Platoon looked on, three Viet Cong dove into one of the haystacks near their bunkers. Harvey picked up a LAW, stood up and took careful aim, even pausing to ask if he was looking at the right haystack. Although the enemy fire had diminished, there were still bullets cracking and popping through the air, and the men admonished Harvey to hurry up and fire. They all watched as the rocket sped downrange and struck the base of the haystack, the explosion sending Viet Cong bodies flying through the air like a scene out of some cartoon. A wild cheer went up from the men as Harvey sat back down with a smirk on his face.

In ones and twos VC kept popping up, some from spider holes in advance of the enemy bunker line, and zigzagged away. Perhaps inspired by Wilson's shot, Gary Gronseth, a quiet GI who had been with the unit since Fort Riley, stood up and unlimbered his M79 grenade launcher, known among the troops as a "blooper" because of the noise it made when it was shot. He carefully took aim at a single fleeing VC at 200 yards, a nearly impossible shot for the slow-moving shell. When he pulled the trigger, the men watched as the grenade arced into the sky and then fell toward its target. To everyone's amazement the grenade struck the VC square on top of the head, killing him instantly. It was a miracle shot that brought a second storm of cheers from the weary troops.

On Charlie Company's left flank, Lieutenant Hoskins, who had seen the previous advance of his 3rd Platoon halted in its tracks, shouted, "Charge, boys! We've got them on the run now!" and ran forward to the attack. Fred Kenney and Richard Rubio, fast friends and unit jokesters, were close on Hoskins' heels. As the lieutenant and a small knot of men peeled off to the left, Kenney and Rubio, followed by Steve Hopper and John Howell, skirted the first of the many haystacks in the area. As the group rounded the haystack they came face-to-face with a Viet Cong machine gunner. Kenney, Howell, and Rubio skidded to a halt and quickly backpedalled, with someone yelling "Granny Goose! Get down!" Surprised by their sudden approach and with eyes wide in fear, the VC machine gunner froze, allowing Kenney and Rubio to slip out of sight behind the haystack. With their hearts hammering, Kenney and Rubio linked up with Hopper and Howell and tossed grenades over the haystack into the machine gun position and a nearby bunker of which they had caught a fleeting glimpse. After hearing multiple detonations, and a few muffled screams, the trio carefully made its way back around the haystack to see what had happened. Hopper simply muttered "Jesus" under his breath as he first saw a sight that would stick with him forever. The VC must have jumped out of their bunker to run just as the grenades exploded. Body parts and shorn muscles lay everywhere. One Viet Cong was missing the entire top of his head. Kenney, Rubio, and Hopper agreed that they had only done what they had to. "It was them or us," Hopper said. "Somebody had to die. It was their bad day and our lucky day." Nearby Jose Sauceda and Jim Cusanelli had finally made their way back from their exposed position and nearly fatal brush with a rocket propelled grenade. As Kenney, Rubio, and Hopper were rounding the haystack, Sauceda and Cusanelli stumbled across what appeared to be a Viet Cong aid station. The group of enemy soldiers, including doctors, vainly scattered in all directions. Sauceda and Cusanelli had them dead to rights and cut them down.

As men across the front picked off the last of the fleeing VC, Doug Wilson and John Bauler of 1st Platoon went out into the open rice paddy to Don Peterson's body. Although he had two large bullet holes in his chest, somehow he looked more asleep than dead. The two spread out a poncho and rolled Pete into it, and then carried him back to the dike that 1st Platoon had sheltered behind for most of the day. From all around, the men of Charlie

Company froze in place as the sad procession passed by. Pete had been larger than life, everyone's favorite. He had the most of anyone to live for – a beautiful wife, a new child who everyone knew was going to be a football star one day. And he was gone. Since night was already falling after the day-long battle, it was too dangerous to bring in a helicopter for a dead man. Don Peterson would remain with his brothers of Charlie Company for one more night. Doc Maibach gave Pete a quick inspection, and then affixed a killed-in-action (KIA) tag to his young friend. It was his duty. He didn't want some doctor in some faraway hospital or morgue to be the one who did it. Pete deserved a friend at his last moment with the unit.

The battle, Charlie Company's baptism by fire, was over. By any accounts it had been a victory. Charlie Company had suffered 14 wounded seriously enough to need evacuation and one fatality, while it was estimated that the joint actions of the American forces that day had resulted in over 100 enemy KIA. The Viet Cong had been driven from the field in disarray, and it would be a long time before the 514th Provincial Battalion made good its losses. For the men of Charlie Company, the fight of May 15, a battle so small that it was never even graced with a real name, was many things. For the men of 1st Platoon, the men who knew Pete best, May 15 was a terrible shock. As they gazed at Pete's body that night, some of the men of 1st Platoon wrestled with guilt: if they would have only gotten to him earlier maybe they could have saved him. Some fought with another guilt – of being relieved that it was he who had died and not them. Others dealt with rage: if Thompson had not ordered them out when even they knew it was a trap; if Hoffman had warned Ski instead of fleeing his post, Pete would still be alive. John Howell, Peterson's hometown friend, vowed to make the VC pay for what they had done. Some wondered if this crappy, smelly country of Vietnam was worth such a price. Many wondered that if Pete could die, could they be next? Although loss was a central feature of that long night, May 15 carried several other meanings. Even the men who had been closest to all those who had been lost – Pete, Trcka, Ski, and the rest – had to admit that the day had been full of adrenaline: somehow they had never felt so alive as they had that day when death hovered nearby. Battle had come, full-blown battle, and they had not been found wanting. A few had crumbled, but most had stood tall – fighting, yelling, reacting – as the bullets had flown. After the battle Bob Eisenbaugh reached for his C Rations and froze. He, like many others in Charlie Company, carried his favorite C Rations tucked away in socks tied across his back. The C Rations and the socks were gone – shot away in battle. It suddenly dawned on Bob that he had been less than an inch from death. John Bradfield, who had blazed away with his machine gun that day during 3rd Platoon's advance, felt good about himself. That evening he sat with Forrest Ramos, who had been his bunkmate since Fort Riley when Bradfield had first introduced Ramos to soul music, and the two spoke of how they really felt like warriors. Richard Rubio spent the night of May 15 with Fred Kenney talking about how lucky they had been when they had run smack into the Viet Cong machine gunner who had been too surprised to fire. "Can you believe that dude didn't off us?" "Naw, man. Did you see the look in his eyes? They were as big as saucers!" Somehow that day everything had gone their way, and in the excitement that followed, the two felt invincible.

After spending the following day policing the battlefield, collecting weapons, and making a body count, Charlie Company returned to its barracks ship. Remaining in the field, though it brought on a never-ending feeling to operations, had at least kept the men busy and occupied – away from their thoughts. Back on ship, though, the men had more time to realize how many bunks were empty – a feeling heightened when replacements arrived to take the place of dear friends. Doug Wilson spoke for many when he wrote in his diary, "Today our platoon got 9 new replacements. I don't really care for them too much. I guess it's just because our platoon just isn't the same anymore. We don't even have half the original platoon left." Charlie Company was changing, becoming something new. The ones who had been there since Fort Riley were now tested warriors and knew that they could trust one another. Their bonds of friendship were tied more tightly than ever, bonds that replacements would find harder and harder to penetrate.

After a day of being back on board ship, an army re-enlistment NCO turned up and went around the ranks of Charlie Company with an offer: if the men re-enlisted for another three-year hitch, he could get them out of the infantry. For some men who had just been through their first battle, the pull was irresistible – more time in the army in return for a safe, rear-echelon job. The re-enlistment NCO visited Steve Huntsman at a particularly vulnerable time, when he was in the hospital recuperating from the shell fragment wound that had severed an artery in his arm. Huntsman had already come to the conclusion that he was not too keen on being shot at, but he had also received a disturbing letter from his wife Karen's brother back in the States. The letter had gone into great detail about the rising tide of anti-war protest on the homefront, and his brother-in-law wondered along with the protestors whether or not the war was worth all of the sacrifice. The letter closed with an admonition: Steve had a loving wife back home who missed him terribly. He needed to do whatever he could to get back to her safely; dying in this war was not worth it. Huntsman was one of more than 20 in Charlie Company who took the re-enlistment NCO up on his offer. Although the deal was tempting, most of the men of Charlie Company chose to remain with their own unit. At some level they were all scared – but still they chose to stay. Doug Wilson recorded his thoughts in his diary: "I even went and talked to the re-enlistment NCO today. I am not kidding the thought of staying down here in the infantry really scares me. But the thought of three more years in the army scares me worse. So I told the guy no thanks."

For some, dealing with the aftermath of May 15 was intensely personal. Charlie Nelson woke up tied down in a hospital bed in Long Binh. With no memory of events since his wounding, Nelson asked the doctor why he had been restrained, and the doctor replied that, in a drug-induced haze, Nelson had first tried to get up out of bed to return to the battlefield, "to get those little bastards." Things had only gotten worse when Nelson had received his first visitor, Lance Morgan, who was there to apologize for having frozen up on the battlefield. Still in a fog, Nelson had gone after Morgan, yelling, "You got me all shot up because you were scared! If you are gonna die, you are gonna die. There ain't no reason to be scared!" Nelson was then sent to Japan, along with Don Trcka and Enoch

Scott. In the hospital, Nelson and Scott became a team – wounded badly in the arms, Scott would do anything that required walking, while Nelson in his wheelchair served as Scott's hands. After surgery in Japan to repair his battered leg, Nelson went on to Letterman Army Medical Center in San Francisco, where he learned that his leg would be crippled forever. After giving him the news, the staff offered Nelson whatever he wanted to eat as a welcome home. After a bit of thought, Nelson requested fried bread and mutton stew, some of his favorites from the reservation. After a few quizzical looks, the staff informed Charlie that they could not fulfil his culinary request, so he decided to settle for pizza instead.

Dave Jarczewski awoke in the 24th Evacuation Hospital to the sight of a priest hovering over him offering the last rites. After informing the priest that he had no intention of dying, Ski passed out. When he awoke again, three days later, he discovered that the doctors had placed aluminum sutures in his chest, shoulder, and back. He was in the hospital in Vietnam for another week, during which time he received a visit from Ann Landers, before being sent to the military hospital in Camp Zama, Japan, for recuperation. While in Japan, the doctors and nurses gave Ski therapy and gave him the bad news: while his injuries were serious, they weren't serious enough, and he was probably headed back to Vietnam after a couple of months' recuperation. Lying there in his bed, facing Vietnam again, Ski could not shake the idea that it was he who had ordered Pete into that rice paddy, and he could not forgive himself for not finding a way to get to Pete before it had been too late. Blame that would never fully dissipate. In June, Ski wrote a letter to Company First Sergeant Crockett. He didn't want to go to some other unit in Vietnam; he wanted to return to the unit with which he had trained. He wanted to come back home to Charlie Company. Ski had only one request – Hoffman, the RTO who had failed him in battle, had better be gone by the time he got back, or there would be hell to pay.

Don Trcka awoke on his hospital bed in Saigon to find two purple hearts pinned to his pillow. He quickly took inventory of his body parts and discovered that the doctors had left a large wound in his arm open to drain, and that he had a huge gauze patch on his stomach, where he had taken the worst of the wounds from the grenade fragments. The doctor sat down next to him and explained that his wounds had necessitated a colostomy, which meant that he could not defecate on his own and instead had to collect the feces in a small pouch; a situation that might be, in time, reversible. Trcka also had eight aluminum sutures in his stomach. Although, as was the case with the other wounded soldiers, Trcka realized that the army had informed his next of kin that he had been injured, it took Trcka several days before he contacted his parents. He just didn't know how to inform them about what had happened. How do you explain a colostomy to your father? Trcka finally called his parents from Camp Zama, and informed them only that he would be all right. After a 30-day stay in Japan, Trcka flew to California lying on a bunk strapped into a cargo aircraft with an IV for the pain dangling from his arm. After the plane touched down, Trcka refused the proffered wheelchair. He was going to walk back onto American soil, no matter the pain. From California, Trcka made his way to the San Antonio Military Medical Center, where he was met by his parents. After the tearful reunion, Trcka went with his father into the restroom and showed him what had happened. His father looked at the wound for a moment or two, and then helped his son change his dressing, after which he took Don into a close embrace and said simply, "Son, you did good. I'm proud of you."

When he arrived at his first hospital stop in Vietnam, Carl Cortright finally received a shot of morphine, which was pure bliss, and news that he was going to be relocated to a hospital where there were specialists in spinal injuries. From then Cortright remembers little until he woke up face down in a bed wondering where he was. Suddenly it hit him, "Oh, shit. I really was injured." The first thing that he wanted was a drink of water, which the nurses informed him he could not have for another two days, and news about whether he would walk again. He was crushed to hear the surgeon reply, "It does not look very good son." Carl Cortright had only been in Vietnam for a month and had only seen one real battle, and now, at age 21, he had to face the terrible reality. He would never walk again.

Jacque Peterson was enjoying a late Mother's Day celebration with her sister-in-law, drinking A&W root beer floats and playing with young Jimmy, when a friend burst in and told Jacque that she had better get home in a hurry. When Jacque reached her small apartment, she was surprised to find three military men taking up her entire couch. The men all stood in unison as she entered the room. Jacque was a little mad that these strangers did not have the decency to allow her to sit with her baby, so she just asked them what on earth they wanted. One stepped forward and said, "Mrs. Peterson, I am sorry to inform you that your husband has been killed in action in Vietnam." She was incensed. "Why are you bothering me with this? Can't you see that you have the wrong Don Peterson? There was another Don Peterson drafted from this area. This message was meant for his wife. My Don Peterson is fine." The man in uniform then informed Jacque, "Lady, we don't make those kind of mistakes. Your husband is dead. We have to go because we have other stops to make." At that point she glanced down to see Jimmy on the floor. She didn't remember putting him down, but she must have. The men left, informing her that they would come back tomorrow. She told them in a fury that someone could come tomorrow, but it had better not be them, and that tomorrow she would get a letter from Don telling her that it was all a crazy mix up.

Jacque had to talk to someone, anyone. Even though she refused to believe that her husband was dead, she had to pass on the news. With no phone in her apartment, Jacque went to her landlady's and called her mother in Montgomery, Alabama. When there was no answer, they called the Montgomery Police Department, who had to break down the door because Jacque's mother was passed out drunk. Jacque then called Don's father, Pete, who, when he heard the quaver in Jacque's voice, responded, "My son's dead, isn't he?" Pete said that he would be there as quickly as he could, and the two agreed not to let Don's grandparents know anything until he had arrived. The news would crush them, and they would both need to be there to help them cope. Hanging up, Jacque returned to her apartment and clung to little Jimmy, feeling desperately alone. She knew it had to be a mistake. They had the wrong Peterson. Maybe her husband was MIA or wounded or something, but he would turn up soon.

A few days later, Jacque received a call from the mortuary; would she come down and identify Don Peterson's body? She dropped

Jimmy off with a friend and went in alone, shaking uncontrollably. The director of the funeral home asked her what she wanted to do, and she replied that she wasn't sure. Seeing her obvious distress, the director told her that he would open the casket and leave the room to allow her time alone. After the funeral home director left, Jacque cautiously inched toward the casket, and there he was. It was her Don Peterson. He looked so calm, so beautiful. He didn't seem to be hurt at all. Somehow she couldn't cry; she just sat there with the casket and talked to Don, talked to him about everything – their son, the house they would have, everything – talked to Don for four hours straight. Worried that she had not returned, the friend with whom Jacque had left Jimmy finally came and opened the door and told her that she needed to come out Jimmy needed his mother. Jacque was only barely able to make herself leave Don's side, turning to say, "I'll be right back" as she left.

It then fell to Jacque to arrange the funeral, as relatives and friends began to gather. Several friends brought over outfits for Jacque to try on. None of her clothes fit anymore because she had hardly eaten since she had received the tragic news. Three days later, Don Peterson was laid to rest in Arroyo Grande with full military honors. Don was the first from the area to die in Vietnam, so the ceremony attracted great interest, complete with local television coverage, while school flags were flown at half-mast for 50 miles around. The military guard informed Jacque that she was to sit in the place of honor with Don's family during the ceremony and that she was to remain seated to receive the folded flag and to await the 21-gun salute. Jacque nodded her head in understanding, but everything was such a blur. Everything was so wrong. On the way to the funeral, Jacque rode in the lead vehicle with Richard, Don's younger brother, who was disconsolate. He could not believe that Don, his idol and best friend, was really gone. The two were hand in hand for most of the ceremony. After Don's casket was lowered into the grave the crowd let out a gasp as Jacque stood at her tallest to receive the flag. She shook the guard's hand and with tears streaming down her face simply said, "He is my husband." Jacque then turned and gave the flag to Don's mother before resuming her seat. At the ceremony's conclusion Jacque was in a haze of despair. She knew that everyone meant well, but she had to be alone. Leaving Don's parents to the job of receiving the condolences from Don's many friends, Jacque took Richard, who was still sobbing deeply, by the hand and walked through the crowd to the limousine. Having had all she could take, she told the driver "just take us home." After picking up Jimmy from the babysitter, Jacque took him to their tiny apartment where she held him close as she cried for hours. What were they going to do now?

5 THE DAY EVERYTHING CHANGED

June 23, 1967

Hi Ma, Dad, and Suzy,

Well by the time you get this letter you probably already know that I have been shot. Well I was lucky and guess I will be all right in a few months. I got hit Monday around noon. And I got to a hospital in Saigon a couple of hours later.

We didn't make any contact Monday morning out in the rice fields, so we moved to a different area. About fifteen minutes we landed in the new rice field area. We were hit hard. I didn't have any cover to hide behind near me so I had to hit the ground right where I was at. But I prayed and the bullets just kept coming over my head. A guy ahead of me got hit; he was about 30 to 50 yards away. So I made up my mind I would try to get up to him so I would have some cover. But as soon as I started to crawl, I got about half way, then I got hit.

The bullet went through my left hand into my chest bone by my right chest and came out above my right hip. So that stopped me right then and there. They cut a twelve inch cut on my belly to fix up my insides, which I guess I was real lucky. I have to go into the operating room Monday again to have my bullet holes fixed up. They had to let a drain out for the infection.

Today is the first time I had anything to eat or drink in five days. I was eating through the vein and a tube down my nose in my stomach, and I had tubes just all over the place. I guess from here I will be going to Japan and if I am real lucky, maybe I can come back to the states. Anyway I sure hope I can.

So you don't have to worry anymore. I am going to be all right. It will just take time. I never went through so much pain in my whole life as I have here.

Well I will write again when I feel up to it again. So don't worry.

Love, Jim [Rademacher]

P.S. I also got a medal, a Purple Heart

Upon returning from the field after the battle of May 15, Charlie Company made its way to its new home at Dong Tam. John Bradfield, the tough Cleveland draftee, could not shake a feeling of déjà vu when he looked around the base and turned to Forrest Ramos and said, "This can't be right. The boats must have got lost. This is just a big ass open field!" Dong Tam was even more spartan than Bear Cat had once been, just 40 acres of bare river silt with no structures at all – a desolate scene dominated by two giant dredges still spewing river-bottom mud. After the obligatory pep-talk from Company First Sergeant Crockett informing the men that if they wanted it, they were going to have to build it, Bradfield, Ramos, and the rest walked to the edge of the silt pile, about 8 feet above the surrounding rice paddies, and dropped their duffel bags, which served as a makeshift base perimeter. As he sat there on his duffel bag, Bob Eisenbaugh, a replacement from Shamokin, Pennsylvania, despaired that Charlie Company was going to have to sleep in this mud hole after having lived on those nice, clean ships. Suddenly a rat the size of a small cat crawled over his duffel and jumped off his shoulder and skittered away. Eisenbaugh gave chase, swinging his bayonet and yelling as men all up and down the line met with a similar fate amid something of a rat swarm. After a night spent sleeping under the stars, and fending off rodent attacks, the men of Charlie Company fell into a familiar rhythm of construction, assembling tents, digging trenches, and filling sandbags. Within a few days, Dong Tam began to take on an air of permanence, dotted with tents and criss-crossed with wooden walkways to keep the men from having to slog through the ever-present mud while the divisional engineers set to work on the construction of sturdier accommodations. The centerpiece of the base was a large basin, flanked by a narrow strip of land that could accommodate large cargo vessels and ATCs.

Within days of Charlie Company's arrival at Dong Tam, the local Vietnamese began to appear, walking to and fro among the bunkers along the berm, selling cokes, pineapples, and the ubiquitous Ba Muoi Ba beer. The civilian presence was especially strong near a complex of bunkers that guarded the entrance into the Dong Tam basin. Distant from the other bunkers, and technically not part of the base perimeter, men reached the basin positions by boat and remained there for three days, in close proximity to a small Vietnamese hamlet. One of the local women turned entrepreneur, converting her hooch into a bar, while children of all ages trekked to the bunkers to meet their new neighbors. Relaxed in what they considered to be "easy duty," the GIs took a shine to the children, offering them candy and the desserts from their C Rations. Although communication was difficult, several of the GIs came to know the children by name, and while Charlie Company was away on operations the children would pester the new occupants of the bunkers, asking them when their favorite Americans would be coming back. Cecil Bridges, a down-home country boy from east Texas, developed a close friendship with one of the little girls from the hamlet. Everywhere he went, she followed – eyes seemingly glued to his every move. Bridges joked with the youngster good-naturedly and loved to tousle her hair before giving in to her nearly constant demand for candy. While stationed in the bunkers, Bridges and his adoring follower were nearly inseparable. It was his way of finding peace and normalcy – something good – in the middle of a war zone.

As at Bear Cat, hookers soon followed the more legitimate Vietnamese vendors to the perimeter of Dong Tam. Having been through battle, and having realized how their lives could be cut short at any time, more and more of the young men of Charlie Company decided to seize what few opportunities they had to enjoy booze or sex, with their officers and NCOs in the main turning a blind eye. Initially the sex trade was a buyer's market with girls providing services in return for a pack of cigarettes, which cost only 11 cents, or for the main course taken from a GI's C Rations. The boys of Charlie Company could afford pretty much anything they wanted, until the navy turned up. When ships started docking in the Dong Tam basin, disgorging their complement of sailors, the local economy boomed. With fat wallets and boundless appetites, the sailors monopolized the trade, which nearly led to a riot when the soldiers of Charlie Company found that they now had to pay $5 for the services of a hooker.

The Mobile Riverine Force rotated its battalions every 30 days, with two based on ships running search and destroy operations throughout the Mekong Delta, while a third worked perimeter security at Dong Tam. The routine of day-to-day life at Dong Tam was much like it had been at Bear Cat; when not involved in construction labors, the men of Charlie Company spent time manning the perimeter bunkers, guarding the valuable dredges, and on local patrols designed to keep any Viet Cong in the area out of mortar range of the base. The patrols, which took place on both sides of the My Tho River, usually lasted for three days and involved scouring local villages for contraband by day and setting ambushes by night. Although from time to time the patrols discovered booby traps, and there were even mortar and rocket attacks on Dong Tam itself, operations in and around the base were considered "milk runs" that might net a few detainees of military age but only rarely resulted in significant contact.

While the GIs could speak hardly any Vietnamese and the locals were mainly "people we walked past, they might as well have been coconut trees," operating in the populous area around Dong Tam did result in observation of and interaction with local Vietnamese. For American boys at war, facing death so far away from home, seeing the locals going about their day-to-day lives – locals who might be Viet Cong by night – only days after a brutal battle, forced many to wrestle with the validity of what they were doing in Vietnam. Charlie Company, a unit made up of true believers, was undergoing a transformation, an internal argument. Vietnam was no longer an abstract idea. Men, their friends, had been killed and maimed. Was the war worth the cost? Were the Vietnamese worth the price? Jim Dennison wrote home:

> A couple of my buddies were transferred to the 4th today, and that leaves only 14 guys left who came over with me out of 40. Things just aren't the same without the old guys. As each mission goes on, I become more and more disenchanted with this war and its aims. The people don't care who wins, and a great majority are never affected by the war. They are the same as most of us back in the states, they just don't care. It just doesn't make sense to kill and destroy to "liberate" someone who doesn't care. They are like school kids who polish the teacher's apple and then go out and slash his tires. It stinks.

Most, though, still saw the cause as fundamentally just and worthy of the nation's continued sacrifice. Once, while caught in a thunderstorm, a Vietnamese peasant surprised John Young by inviting his squad to spend the night in his hooch:

> The man was very nice, we were very wet and cold, and he spread out a mat for us to sleep on, and even gave us some hot tea. His wife and children were sleeping in their bunker; all the Vietnamese have them inside their homes in case a fight takes place in their neighborhood... So there we were, with our machine gun looking out his front door, claymore mines out in his garden, and our gear and other weapons laid all over his house... I speak only enough Vietnamese to ask for I.D. cards ... and yet here were these families putting us up for the night and giving us whatever food they had to offer. They were so polite, so openly friendly, and so poor. If we can keep the VC from terrorizing these people, I'll feel that we've done something really worthwhile. At the house where ... [another] family gave us fruit, the father held his infant son out to me. The poor baby had awful leathery-looking scars almost the full length of both legs... Things like this point out why we must stay in Vietnam. In time, that baby will be treated by an American doctor, in time the parents will be taught how to increase their harvests and fatten their pigs, in time, they will be taught some elementary hygiene and medicine. Because we are doing all these things, and dozens more, right now. We can do so much, give so much to these people.

On June 1, Charlie Company also ran its first operation on Thoi Son Island, located in the middle of the My Tho River within sight of Dong Tam. At first the men thought it was going to be another "milk run," but within a few minutes they noticed that there were no male villagers to be seen and that the houses of the area were scrawled with Viet Cong slogans. Everywhere the men went there were signs of Viet Cong activity, so much so that the island simply became known as "VC Island." On edge and having snapped back into combat mode, Hoskins' 3rd Platoon walked point on the lookout for booby traps. Nearing what the point man thought might be a tiny base camp, Alan Richards, from rural Wisconsin, knelt down to radio the find to company headquarters just as Steve Hopper felt a tripwire tighten around his leg. The explosion peppered the back of Hopper's legs with hot fragments and blew Richards off the rice paddy dike. Joe Marr, a career soldier from rural Missouri who had served as Hoskins' platoon sergeant since Fort Riley, had been walking behind Hopper and took fragments from the booby trap in the groin. Elijah Taylor quickly bandaged Hopper before moving on to Richards, who was bleeding freely from wounds to the side of his head. If he had not been holding the radio handset he surely would have died; as it was a piece of shrapnel had missed his jugular by only a quarter of an inch. After reassuring Richards that his ear had not been blown off, Taylor moved on to Marr. The sergeant stood and stared in horror at a bloodstain on his crotch. He looked up at Taylor and then back down again, leaving the medic in no doubt as to the question that preyed on the sergeant's mind. Taylor gingerly pulled down Marr's trousers, and then gave him the good news. "Sergeant, them fragments done missed your dick by an inch." Marr almost collapsed in relief. He was wounded, but he was still a man.

Four days later Charlie Company returned to the area, with each platoon operating separately, only to find Viet Cong flags seemingly everywhere. Jack Benedick's 2nd Platoon slowly wended its way through the closely-packed countryside – a dense terrain of small rice paddies, hooches, and tiny streams. Bill Reynolds was walking point, taking great care with every step amid the hostile territory, with Bob Ehlert following closely behind. Nearing midday, the duo came across a well-used path flanked by a scattering of hooches. After checking the dwellings and finding them deserted, Reynolds and Ehlert continued down the path, both with the eerie feeling that they were being watched. Suddenly sniper fire erupted from the nearby jungle – Reynolds, who had heard the first round crack past his head, hit the ground and rolled into a nearby ditch. Elhert, though, was not lucky enough to find cover and got off only one shot from his grenade launcher before he felt something hit his foot hard, followed by a sledgehammer blow to his right shoulder and another searing stab of pain in his left. As Ehlert yelled for a medic, fire erupted from all around as 2nd Platoon hit back hard at the sniper.

The engagement lasted for only a few minutes before Benedick bellowed "Cease fire!" A quick search of the tree line netted no results. It was war as usual on VC Island – the sniper had squeezed off a few rounds, badly wounded a member of Charlie Company, and fled. A short, sharp battle with losses suffered but no payoff. Troopers from 2nd Platoon got down to the now-familiar business of cutting an LZ for the dustoff chopper, while Bill Geier stopped Ehlert's bleeding, and others commented that he had a "million-dollar wound." A few minutes later the chopper thundered in, amid a whirlwind of leaves and dust. A host of friends lifted Ehlert aboard, shouted goodbyes, and then another 2nd Platoon original was gone. Ehlert's first stop was the divisional hospital at Dong Tam, where doctors administered initial treatment. Company First Sergeant Crockett stopped by and complimented Bob on his service and wished him good luck. It looked like he was headed home. Doctors first in Long Binh and then Japan conducted further operations on Ehlert's foot and both shoulders but were unable to locate the bullet that had struck his left shoulder. Finally, 25 years later, it worked its way out.

As Charlie Company moved out once again, the platoons moved across the countryside with great care, but within minutes Robert Sachs of 3rd Platoon set off a "toe popper" mine. As Taylor dressed Sachs' minor wound, Hoskins warned 3rd Platoon to be on the lookout, just before automatic fire erupted from a nearby tree line. While the rest of the platoon hit the dirt, Terry McBride ducked into a hooch and was returning fire with his machine gun when he caught sight of the muzzle flash from the Viet Cong weapon.

Silently McBride motioned to his buddies outside and pointed at the bunker, and they took his meaning instantly. McBride depressed the trigger of his M60, sending a stream of fire at the enemy position while Bill Riley, the Indiana boy who had once sold booze to the thirsty Marines at Okinawa, ran forward under the covering fire and tossed two grenades into the bunker. After the two loud explosions faded, the short encounter was over. Riley, McBride, and Richard Rubio went to investigate and found three Viet Cong dead in the bunker, including a woman. Perhaps things would have been different earlier in the war, before the men had become so well acquainted with death. These dead VC were not people, just bodies. That one of them was a young woman made no difference. The trio gathered what weapons they could find and then were getting ready to move on when McBride had an idea. He took out his knife, bent over and cut the ponytail from the woman's head. He then affixed the ponytail to the back of his helmet; a gruesome reminder of death that he wore for the next month.

As the war took a growing toll on Charlie Company, and as the men became more hardened to the realities of combat, they turned to each other for support and formed closer bonds of friendship than ever before. Forrest Ramos and his friends Jose Sauceda and Fred Kenney couldn't help but notice that Willie McTear still seemed morose after the loss of Ron Schworer. Both Sauceda and Kenney were understandably distracted by distant family developments, but they would do anything to help a buddy in need. In an attempt to break McTear out of his malaise, Ramos, Sauceda, and Kenney took McTear aside and let him in on a secret. After looking around conspiratorially, Ramos whispered to McTear that he had asked Richard Rubio's cousin Patricia to marry him, and she had accepted. McTear couldn't believe his ears. He, like everyone else around, knew that Forrest and Patricia had been writing. But Patricia was beautiful; he had seen the pictures. Blonde, green-eyed beauty. What the hell was a woman like that doing with a guy like Ramos? Did Rubio know about this, that Ramos was going to marry his cousin? Forrest assured McTear that it was true and that Rubio was fully aware of what was going on. McTear countered, saying,

"Aww, man, but ya'll ain't never even met each other in person, right?" It was true, Forrest admitted, the couple had never met, but they were in love and were going to get married. To prove it, McTear was just going to have to come to the wedding once they all made it home. Fred Kenney, who was standing nearby, then warned Ramos that being married would make him all boring and grown up, just like him.

To celebrate the news, McTear and Rubio scored some beer, now readily available at Dong Tam, and got out the record player. Although reading, letter writing, and resting remained popular diversions during Charlie Company's precious and rare time off, listening to records and drinking were always high on the soldiers' list. The California guys, Kenney, Bill Reynolds, and the rest, had their own record player and liked to listen to Jimi Hendrix and surfer music, while the southern boys listened to Country and Western. For McTear and Ramos, though, along with most of the black and Hispanic crowd, there was no beating Motown. McTear put on a record by the Supremes while the others opened their warm beer, just as Butch Eakins, a farm boy from Cape Girardeau, Missouri, walked by. Eakins looked at McTear and asked him why the blacks never listened to Country. McTear, knowing a joke when he heard one, laughed and answered, "Blacks don't listen to Country because blacks don't play Country." Eakins shook his head and walked away, only to return with a record. McTear looked at the cover – Charley Pride, "Just Between You and Me." McTear looked down once again and then back at Eakins: "I'll be damned. Black folks do play Country music." Following Eakins over to the Country and Western group, McTear gave the song a listen. He liked it, but not enough to give up Motown.

The pressure cooker of war, along with the growing bonds of camaraderie within Charlie Company, blurred differences of race and class that had once seemed so important. Distinctions remained, ranging from language to music, but those distinctions paled in comparison to war-forged bonds of brotherhood. Men who had never before met people of other races, who had never before trusted people of other races, now depended on each other for their very survival. The differences of prewar life just didn't matter that much anymore. In response to hearing on the news about race riots back home, Steve Hopper, whose own wounds had recently been tended by a black medic, Elijah Taylor, wrote to his parents:

> Mom and Dad you know so many times I think about all the fighting going on at home. If all the people realized what they were doing I'm sure it would make a big difference. Over here my feelings towards a black man are the same as they are towards my buddies back home. Maybe people don't like me feeling that way, but you never know when you'll save his life and he'll thank you for it or in turn when he may save my life and I know I'll thank him for it and thank God for putting him on this earth. Maybe someday people will wake up, but I'm afraid it will be too late then.

Even as Charlie Company became more tight-knit, it also continued to change. Captain Rollo Larson's marriage was falling apart. His wife had been unable to come to grips with his busy schedule at Fort Riley, a condition that had only worsened during his absence in Vietnam. Larson had done what he could in letters to save the relationship, but by late May it had become clear that his wife wanted a divorce. With a family to save, Larson chose not to renew his commission and to return home to try to patch things up. It was one of the hardest decisions of his life. He had trained Charlie Company. He had led his men into battle. It was a good unit, a unit that still needed him. But he had to go. In early June, Larson processed out and command of Charlie Company shifted to Captain Herb Lind, who had been serving with Colonel Guy Tutwiler in battalion headquarters. Lind, who had always wanted a combat command, made his way to Dong Tam where he met with the officers and NCOs of Charlie Company, one of whom had only recently arrived in country.

Lieutenant Sheldon Schulman, who led the 4th Platoon of Charlie Company, was from the South Shore of Chicago – the grandson of eastern-European Jewish immigrants. Shelly, as he was known to family and friends, lived with an extended family including his parents, Harold and Sarah, and his sister Eunice, along with an aunt and uncle and their two children. The untimely death of his mother, though, in 1957, left the family, and Shelly's life, in personal and financial disarray. As a result, the young Schulman spent more and more time at the home of his best friend, Fred Rosenberg, and took on a job at Al's Delicatessen on 75th Street to help pay his family's bills. While he did not excel in schoolwork, Schulman threw himself into the Army Junior ROTC program at South Shore High School and joined the Al Shepard Chapter of the B'Nai Brith's AZA (Aleph Zadek Aleph) fraternal organization. With the help of his friends, both old and new, Schulman made it through the hard times and graduated high school in 1961.

After a short stint as a student at Southeast Junior College, Schulman took a job at a placement agency in downtown Chicago. On Friday nights, Shelly and his friends, including Fred Rosenberg, Bob Hirsch, and Billy Schatz, would pile into Shelly's old car and head out in search of girls to date. While his buddies always seemed to meet someone, Schulman never seemed to have any luck. In January 1964, though, Billy Schatz was hosting a poker game when Schulman walked in with a beautiful girl on his arm. Schulman sensed wonderment on the part of his pals, and said, "I would like you to meet Fern Davidson. We met at Mammy's Pancake House on Rush Street." After a quick greeting the group all became fast friends, and, by April 1964, Shelly and Fern were married. Knowing that he was a prime candidate for the draft, after his wedding Schulman went and enlisted in the Army, trained at Fort Dix, New Jersey, and was chosen for Officer Candidate School. After completing OCS during the spring of 1966, Schulman received his assignment to join the 9th Infantry Division for training at Fort Riley.

Living with Fern in a small, off-base apartment Schulman shepherded the men of 4th Platoon of Charlie Company through the training process and made ready to ship out to Vietnam. Fern, though, was pregnant with the couple's first child and developed complications with the delivery. As his men of the 4th Platoon shipped out to Vietnam, Schulman stayed behind to be with his wife and his new son Michael. Mother and child spend their recuperation time at the home of Fern's parents in the Chicago suburb of Skokie, giving Shelly time to reconnect with his old friend Fred Rosenberg. But their conversations were somehow different. Instead of talking about cars, girls, or sports, they now talked about Shelly's love of his new family and of his desire to make the army his career. Sheldon Schulman had discovered who he wanted to be and was ready to go and live life. Even with everything going on in his life and everything that he had to look forward to, Rosenberg could tell that Shelly wanted to be in Vietnam with his men – with the men who he had trained for war. With both Fern and Michael finally healthy and prospering, in March 1967 Sheldon Schulman kissed both wife and infant son one last time and departed for Vietnam to take up his command.

Among the enlisted ranks, replacements continued to arrive, new faces to take the place of lost friends. Peterson, Trcka, Nelson, Huntsman – they all had to be replaced. The war needed fresh bodies. Raised in rural Fowler, Michigan, just north of Lansing, James Rademacher had just graduated from high school and was thinking about popping the question to his sweetheart, Mary Ann, when his draft notice arrived in November 1966. After passing his physical in Detroit, Rademacher went to Fort Leonard Wood, Missouri, for basic and then to Fort Polk, Louisiana, for AIT. Finally Rademacher went to Fort Knox, Kentucky, for additional training in his specialty – driving Armored Personnel Carriers. Rademacher spent a few days in Fowler on leave before shipping out, devoting most of his time to Mary Ann. The night before his departure the couple was sitting listening to the radio and heard Scott McKenzie sing "If you are going to San Francisco," which brought tears to their eyes. James was going to San Francisco the very next morning, his first stop on the way to Vietnam. On May 22, 1967, Rademacher hugged his mother and Mary Ann at the Lansing airport, and promised to write to them often. As Carl Cortright had found out before him, Rademacher's MOS made little difference to a military in need of men. Upon his arrival in Vietnam he was reassigned as a rifleman and sent to Charlie Company.

Rademacher was true to his word and kept up a steady stream of letters to Mary Ann that chronicled his Vietnam journey.

May 22. San Francisco
Well I made it out here OK and seen some pretty country... And I remember that you said keep looking to the future and it really helped and I hope you do the same. Because when I get back I am going to

make you my wife. And the happiest wife on this earth. I know it's hard to keep from crying, because I feel like crying now. But that won't do any good. I still have to stay a year so keep smiling as much as possible. And believe me I will be back to marry you.

May 30. Arrived in Vietnam
Well I finally got here in Vietnam all right. It took 20 hours, which is a pretty long plane ride... It's also real hot. I sweat my ass off in no time at all ... it also smells all over around here. It's just unbelievable honey. I don't know how to describe it, except to say it's really a f__ked up place.

June 4, with 9th Infantry Division
Well I finally got a little time to write a few words of wisdom. I am ... here at the 9th Division... I can't wait until I start going out in the field and start fighting. It gets sickening around here working all the time. And them big guns shoot all night and keep me awake.

June 11
My company lives on a ship down here in the Delta on one of the big rivers. I am not on the ship yet but will be any day now. The ship is air conditioned and has hot and cold water, movies every night and nice beds to sleep on. So I guess it's just like home but it is not all that nice because there are a lot of VCs around here... This company, I guess, is a real good company because they only had two people killed in six months. But a hell of a lot of wounded. So my chances of getting wounded are pretty good. That sure is a lot better than getting killed as you already probably know.

June 15
I finally got on the ship, and it is a little bit crowded. There are a lot of guys on here. I heard that tomorrow we are going out into the field... Right now I don't know what to think of the whole idea. I just wish I was back home with you where I belong. I hate this damn country so much that I wish they would destroy the whole place. This country isn't worth fighting for. To me it is just one big swamp and jungle. It doesn't have much to offer anybody. So why it had to be this way I will never know. It doesn't make sense to me.

June 18

You keep asking me how it is out here... I wrote already that we went on a two day mission, and I told you we didn't see any VCs. Well A and B company lost about four men killed and I saw one man dead and about ten injured. I guess one guy had both legs blown off. So as you can see it's no picnic over here, and a man can only take so much and how much I can take I don't know. So far I have been lucky and haven't seen any real action yet. But I got the feeling we are going to get it one of these days just like the other companies on this ship... And now going out for six days we are eventually going to run into something, and most injuries come from the traps the VC have and they have a lot of them. So if I am at the right place at the right time I will get it also. I will never know and that's what gets on my nerves all the time is who is next in line, me or one of my buddies.

At the beginning of June, MACV in Saigon had received intelligence that the 5th Nha Be Main Force Viet Cong Battalion had retreated to an area near the village of Can Giouc south of Saigon to recuperate from a recent battle with the US 199th Infantry Brigade. Since the area was cut by several navigable waterways, the final destruction of the 5th Nha Be seemed to be a perfect job for the Mobile Riverine Force. After completing operations in the northern Rung Sat, on June 18 the Mobile Riverine Base moved to the confluence of the Vam Co and Soi Rap rivers, as near as possible to Can Giouc without giving plans away, to commence Operation *Concordia I*. The ambitious plan called for landing two companies of the 3rd of the 47th 1 mile to the south of Can Giouc, while three companies of the 4th of the 47th hit the beaches 1½ miles southwest of Can Giouc, and the 2nd Battalion of the 46th ARVN Regiment held blocking positions 3 miles away. The American troops, supported by a company of the 3rd of the 47th held in reserve, were to sweep toward the ARVN blocking positions, catching the Viet Cong in a trap.

When the entire MRB and all of the MRF's attendant war craft got underway, the men of Charlie Company realized something big was afoot. This was no platoon-sized sweep of semi-friendly territory; this was the real deal. Many, including Bill Geier, sat down to dash off quick letters home, knowing that they would not get another opportunity for several days. As usual, Bill gave his family some of the local unit gossip before asking about how his sister Jackie was getting along. Bill then went on to talk a little baseball with his father before signing off, promising to write again as soon as he had a chance.

As they gathered their gear that evening, Larry Lilley, Kenny Frakes, and Tim Johnson made time to get together and talk. Although the three high school classmates were all in Charlie Company and remained close friends, they served in different platoons: Lilley in 1st Platoon, Johnson in 3rd Platoon, and Frakes in 4th Platoon. With platoons often operating separately and serving as almost surrogate families, the trio had not been able to spend much time together since the battle of May 15. Standing on the slow-moving craft while they all enjoyed a smoke, Lilley asked Frakes and Johnson if they remembered the day that they had all gone to induction together. That day, and their civilian lives, seemed so remote. "Remember how you both said that you would not make it out of Vietnam alive?" Now that they were soldiers, real soldiers, both Frakes and Johnson laughed at that old notion. After living through May 15, they all realized that there was no such thing as fate. Soldiers make their own fate. Lilley had told them then that they would make it home, and now they believed him. Leaving the past behind, the group began to talk about what was going to happen on this operation. It sure seemed like a big one. It would probably just wind up being another long walk in the hot sun; even if they were there, the Viet Cong would just fire a few pot shots and run away like they always did. It was just going to be business as usual. Only one thing seemed different enough to be worthy of note. On recent operations, the MRF had begun using Plastic Assault Boats (PABs), 16-foot Boston Whaler fiberglass-hulled boats with outboard motors, to transport one of the company's platoons. The boats were seen as something of a mixed blessing. They provided a great deal of mobility, sure beat slogging through the mud, and were a convenient way to carry heavy mortar tubes. With no armor, though, the boats were extremely vulnerable to enemy fire, and the men on the boats couldn't shake the feeling that they were sitting ducks. The next day was 4th Platoon's turn in the PABs, and Frakes informed his buddies that he looked forward to not having to hump that damned mortar all over those freaking rice paddies.

Paris Fadden was the son of a car mechanic from Robbinsdale, Minnesota. He hadn't quite known what he wanted to do after graduation from high school in 1964, so he had drifted a bit, enjoying some time working on cars and drag racing. His draft notice in November 1965 had put an end to all that, and it was off to training with mortars for the 4th Division. As he departed on the train he noticed that is father, a tough veteran of World War II, had tears rolling down his cheeks. It was the first time in his life that Paris had seen his father cry. After a short stint with the 4th Division in Vietnam, in May 1967 Fadden received his transfer orders to report to Charlie Company. At first Fadden wasn't sure what to make of the transfer. Leaving his unit of buddies to become a new guy again in a new unit was a daunting prospect. Lieutenant Schulman and Platoon Sergeant Pedro Blas, though, had welcomed Fadden to Charlie Company, easing any possible tensions. And the guys – Ronnie Gann, Richard Northcott, Robert Cara, Hubert Fink – all quickly adopted Fadden as part of their unit family. They especially liked Fadden's helmet. On one side it read, in big, black letters, "Fuck the VC." When Richard Northcott wondered aloud what the chaplain might think of the inscription, Fadden replied, "I won't show that side of my helmet to the padre. I'll show him this side." Fadden then turned his helmet around so his new platoonmates could read the inscription on the other side – again in big, black letters – "Take a VC to church."

As mission followed mission in the Mekong, Fadden became more and more at home. There was Bobby Jindra, who always seemed to have a new story about his daughter Jacque back home. There was Kenny Frakes, who often shared the contents of his care packages sent by his family with Fadden in conversations about engine modifications for Chevys. But most of all, there was Hubert Fink. The Glendale, New York native had been shaken by the attrition going on all around him in Charlie Company. It seemed that more good men were going home killed or wounded each day, and one day his own number was going to come up. Fink was thinking of reenlisting – so he asked Fadden if the risk was worth it, if he should add more time to his enlistment in exchange for a ticket out of the field. Fadden couldn't believe his ears. More time in the army? Not worth it. They were all going to get home just fine. Reenlistment was not the answer.

The units of the MRF hit their assigned beaches outside of Can Giouc just after sunrise on June 19 and met no enemy resistance. As it had so often in the past, Charlie Company made its way off the ATCs and began the process of sweeping its assigned area of operations. There was nothing; no sign of the enemy, no civilians to detain. Nothing. As the men of his 1st Platoon trudged through the deepening heat, Lieutenant Lynn Hunt turned to John Young, one of his squad leaders, and remarked, "You know, Young. This could turn out to be a very boring day." Young replied, "Yessir, it could."

Unbeknownst to Hunt and Young, their battalion commander, Colonel Tutwiler, had just received orders to report to brigade headquarters. At the meeting the brigade commander, Colonel Fulton, informed Tutwiler that a local district chief had told them that a battalion of VC was dug in due east of the ARVN blocking force. Fulton ordered the US battalions to reorient their advances toward the reported enemy positions. In the 4th of the 47th, Alpha Company, which was closest to the new location, was to advance southwest overland, accompanied on its right flank by Bravo Company. Charlie Company, on the left flank and furthest from the reported enemy positions, reboarded its ATCs and moved southward to the junction of Nui and Ben Via creeks northeast of the reported enemy position. If all was well, and the intelligence was correct, the movement of Alpha and Charlie companies would drive the Viet Cong toward the waiting ARVN.

Just before noon, Charlie Company disembarked from its ATCs. Captain Lind, not expecting that his first major operation in command of the company was going to be anything out of the ordinary, surveyed the scene. It all seemed pretty typical – open rice paddies, crisscrossed by a series of dikes and dotted here and there with the ubiquitous thatched hooches of the local Vietnamese peasants. He assigned 1st Platoon to the right flank, near a stream that most of the men could not see, 2nd Platoon to the center and leading the way, while 3rd Platoon drew up the rear and took the left flank. 4th Platoon remained aboard the PABs and was supposed to shadow the movement of the ground forces by following up the

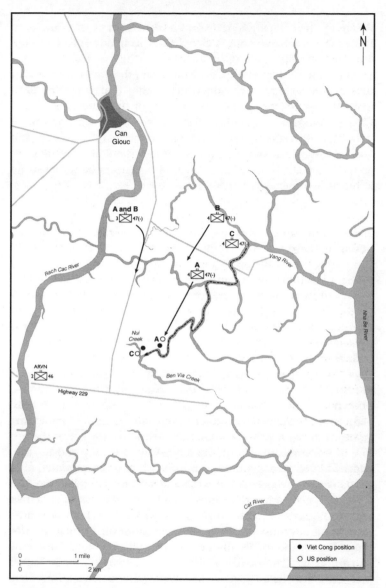

Tactical situation on June 19

stream on the company's right flank. As the men moved out, Larry Lilley felt just a bit envious. He could see his buddy Frakes and the 4th Platoon floating along in their boats while he had to trudge. Then he noticed something odd. The stream the 4th Platoon was in took a wide sweep to the left, which meant that when the PABs made the corner they would be in front of the other platoons of Charlie Company, not behind. The PABs were too vulnerable to be in front. Lilley yelled as loudly as he could for the boats to stop, and Frakes looked back and caught his eye, but the PABs kept right on going. Lilley got on the radio to call 4th Platoon back, but as he keyed his handset all hell broke loose.

To the north, Alpha Company, 4th of the 47th, under the command of Captain Robert Reeves, conducted its own sweep to drive the VC toward the ARVN blocking positions. Although the VC positions were supposed to be well south of his location, Reeves instructed his men to advance with care. The company moved with its 2nd Platoon on the right, the 3rd Platoon on the left, and the 1st Platoon and company headquarters taking up the rear. While negotiating the broken terrain, though, the 2nd and 3rd platoons strayed away from their assigned azimuth. Reeves called them back, which resulted in the entire company bunching up, with its reconnaissance elements perilously close to the main body of troops as the men entered a vast, open rice paddy surrounded on three sides by dense foliage. Mike Lethcoe of 2nd Platoon was walking point, and he noticed something strange as he approached a small mound and haystack near the tree line to the company's front. He looked more closely and his eyes widened in terror as he made out a 55-gallon drum mounted on a tripod flanked by grenades. It was a massive, homemade mine. Not wanting to make any sudden moves, Lethcoe looked toward the trees and saw hundreds of Viet Cong looking back at him. Lethcoe started to run and dove just before the monster went off. A total of three mines roared, and the VC lines erupted with fire, including the slow and distinctive THUD THUD THUD of at least two Chinese 50-caliber machine guns. The intelligence had been wrong. The Viet Cong were much further north than anyone had thought, and there were far more of them than anyone had believed possible.

Lethcoe was nearly deafened but otherwise unhurt, and dug in to what was left of the tiny mound. The Viet Cong were not shooting at him, thinking that he had died in the mine explosion, but instead were concentrating fire on the remainder of Alpha Company who were caught helplessly in the open. Lethcoe turned around to look just in time to see his team leader get stitched across the abdomen by 50-caliber fire. One by one men began to fall, their bodies ripped to pieces in the intense crossfire. There was no cover at all, except for bodies, and enemy bunkers surrounded Alpha Company on three sides. Unseen in his tiny hole, for a few moments Lethcoe could only watch in horror as his friends died all around him. Exposed as he was so near the enemy positions, Lethcoe realized that he had to do something, anything, and started to pick off Viet Cong gunners who were operating a nearby machine gun, getting a sense of grim satisfaction out of the fact that his victims could not figure out where the unexpected fire was coming from. After losing three gunners, though, the Viet Cong got a bead on Lethcoe's position and returned fire. As he curled up into a ball in his little hole, Lethcoe wondered why he was not being hit. It soon became clear that he was so close to the enemy positions that they could not depress their gun barrels enough to reach him. But there was nothing else he could do.

Toward the rear of the Alpha Company battlefield, Captain Reeves was able to find cover with a few of his men in a small ditch, and couldn't believe his eyes as his command was shot up all around him. Reeves grabbed the radio handset and frantically tried to raise his platoons, but there was no answer. There was nothing but static, because an RTO somewhere in the unit had died while his handset was keyed. Even had the radios worked, though, there was nobody left with whom to communicate. All of Alpha Company's platoon leaders, RTOs, machine gunners, and medics had been killed or badly wounded in the opening burst of fire. There was no Alpha Company left to command. Those still on board the nearby ATCs did what they could to help, including Navy Chaplain Raymond "Padre" Johnson, who left the safety of the boats to tend the wounded. All Reeves could do was radio the horrible news to Tutwiler who was circling above the battlefield in his helicopter. Reeves reported that Alpha Company had taken 75 percent casualties and that he had lost contact with his platoons, which were stranded in the open rice paddy. With the battle only minutes old, Tutwiler tried to order Charlie Company to the aid of Alpha, only to receive the news that Charlie Company, too, was under attack.

As Alpha Company was being cut to pieces, hundreds of weapons, including three 50-caliber machine guns from a separate Viet Cong bunker complex, opened fire on Charlie Company. While most of the men went to ground quickly, those on point with 2nd Platoon could not take their eyes off a terrible sight. Two of the PABs carrying the 4th Platoon had already made the turn in the river, and were caught in the open only 35 feet from the Viet Cong positions. Pieces of the tiny boats flew everywhere in the hail of automatic fire, and the men on board didn't stand a chance. John Winters, David Robin, Cameron Rice, Hubert Fink, Robert Cara, and Robert Jindra, who had tearfully left his wife and young daughter behind on that cold day at Fort Riley, were killed almost instantly, their bodies blasted into the water by the impact of the machine gun bullets, while the shattered boats turned wild circles in the river. The leader of 4th Platoon, Lieutenant Schulman, who had accompanied 2nd Platoon that day as a forward observer since there was not enough room on the boats for everyone, stood on the bank oblivious to the gunfire as he watched the bodies of his boys lurch as the bullets struck home. The leader of 2nd Platoon, Jack Benedick, only had time to yell "Get down!" before he saw Schulman's body pitch back as several bullets struck him in the chest. Schulman collapsed to the ground in a heap, his shirt already turning red.

On the bank of the stream Larry Lukes, the newly married draftee from Nebraska who had once had such a lucky break in the Rung Sat when he tripped a booby trap near his head that had failed to explode, saw Kenny Frakes floating by in the water badly wounded. Not even really aware of the heavy fire, Lukes crawled to the steep bank of the stream, reached in and barely caught hold of Frakes' arm. Frakes was so heavy, and the bank of the stream made the angle so awkward, that Lukes could hardly hang on, much less pull Frakes to safety. Lukes could see the fear in Kenny's face, which was covered in blood. While he shuddered from the pain, Kenny Frakes looked Larry Lukes squarely in the eyes and said, "You gotta let go Lukes, or they'll get you. I'll be OK. It'll be OK." It was the most difficult moment in Lukes' young life. The vision of Kenny Frakes floating there and saying those words would stick with him until the end of his days, but Larry Lukes let go.

Charlie Company's 4th Platoon had embarked on four PABs that terrible day, and, for the men in the trailing two boats, the scene was one that was almost unimaginable in its horror. Their friends – their brothers – with whom they had been joking only minutes before, disappeared around a tiny bend in the stream. Then followed a roar of a giant claymore mine and the deep bass pounding of automatic weapons. Then came the screaming. Ronnie Gann, one of the many Charlie Company originals from the Los Angeles area, hated the water and hadn't wanted to get on the boats that morning. But Platoon Sergeant Blas – who had been visibly upset at the prospect of placing his men in such an exposed position on the PABs – had taken Gann with him aboard the third boat in the file. When the firing began Gann watched as Blas' eyes widened at the sad spectacle of the destruction of much of his platoon. But Blas, ever the professional, did not give into the moment. Instead he calmly piloted his PAB to the bank of the stream amid the fire and got his men down behind cover, where they began to duel with a Viet Cong bunker hidden in a haystack. Richard Northcott, of Encino, California, was aboard the fourth boat, which beached near the position of 1st Platoon. Northcott and the others scrambled out of the boat, tumbled across the nearest rice paddy dike to relative safety, and did their best to help 1st Platoon with its own fast-developing fight. The remainder of the day was so busy – a constant, adrenalized balance between life and death – that Blas, Gann, and Northcott almost mercifully didn't have time to focus on the grim fact that much of their 4th Platoon – many of their best friends of a lifetime – had been killed in a single instant of murderous fire.

Jack Benedick knew immediately that 2nd Platoon was in serious trouble. The Viet Cong fire wasn't the familiar POP POP POP of individual weapons; instead it was a continuous and nearly overwhelming roar, a roar that included at least two 50-caliber machine guns. Benedick knew that the Viet Cong did not issue 50-caliber machine guns below the battalion level, which meant that Charlie Company was facing a dug-in enemy force of at least a battalion and perhaps more. Worse yet, the 2nd Platoon was stuck in place, unable to move toward the enemy bunkers because of the stream while a retreat through the open rice paddy against such heavy enemy fire meant certain death. The Viet Cong had them right where they wanted them. Of most immediate concern were the platoon's many wounded. While the point element of 2nd Platoon had made it to the cover of a paddy dike, Benedick realized that the trailing elements of the platoon, the majority of his men, had been caught in the open by the devastating fire. He yelled at the men closest to the dike to lay down covering fire to give the rest a chance to crawl to safety.

Mario Lopez couldn't believe what he was hearing. Bullets were cracking past his head, coming from every direction. Lopez hit the dirt, alongside Jimmie Salazar, and did his best to work out where the fire was coming from and how to fight back. Off to his left someone was hit in the neck, and Lopez yelled for a medic. Nearby Bill Reynolds fired with his grenade launcher as Ronnie Bryan opened up with his M60 machine gun. Nearby, Mike Cramer, one of the California draftees and an RTO with 2nd Squad, got off a round with a LAW, striking a hooch across the stream only to discover that the flimsy structure masked a reinforced enemy bunker. Noticing that one of his platoon's machine guns had stopped firing, Benedick glanced to his right to see that Bryan had fallen back into the rice paddy with a jagged wound in his upper thigh. Grabbing up the machine gun, Benedick got to his knees and continued to pour fire toward the Viet Cong even as he yelled for the medic. Unable even to see most of the enemy positions – set back as they were in thick undergrowth – there was little that Benedick and his men could do to stem the flow of Viet Cong fire. Seconds later, RTO Bob French started rolling around in pain, struck by a VC bullet in the waist just below his radio. At nearly the same time bullets hit Lieutenant Benedick in the wrist, throwing the machine gun from his hands. Without a weapon and unable to do much more,

Benedick hit the dirt next to Bob French and, as he bandaged his own wounds, said, "Well, I guess that's my first Purple Heart."

Bill Geier no longer had to worry about how he would react in a battle. The other medics, Taylor and Maibach, had already passed their own baptisms of fire, and now it was Geier's turn. Grabbing his medical bag, in which he had also squirreled away hot sauce for his C Rations, Geier crawled from the safety of his position behind the rice paddy dike and made his way to his fallen buddies. Saying that he was OK, Benedick waved Geier to Bob French, whom Geier quickly bandaged. Before moving on, Geier yelled to Benedick that French's wounds were serious and would require a medevac. Next the young medic from Chicago knelt over Ronnie Bryan. The wound was bad and required several of the field bandages from Geier's bag. While working on Bryan, Geier, ignoring the heavy incoming fire, put himself between Bryan and the enemy bunkers, shielding his patient from further harm. While calling in artillery strikes and a medevac, Benedick glanced over and thought to himself that he was going to have to put Geier in for a medal. There he was, so cool under fire, comforting Ronnie Bryan as he bandaged his wounds. The next second, Geier lurched as heavy machine gun rounds ripped through his chest, leaving holes the size of a man's fist.

Nearest to the scene, Bill Reynolds got up and ran through the fire to Geier and Bryan to see what he could do to help. In what seemed to be slow-motion, Reynolds could not help thinking, "Jesus, not Bill. Not Bill." Rolling him over to get a look at the wound, Reynolds muttered, "Shit, this is bad." Not knowing what to do, Reynolds yelled to Benedick, "Lieutenant, Geier has a sucking chest wound. What do I do?" With no medic nearby to help, Benedick yelled back that Reynolds needed to put plastic over the wound and then a bandage over that. Reynolds did what he could and then told Benedick that the medevac had better get there in a damn hurry.

Further down the line, near to where Mike Cramer was dueling with an enemy machine gun in a heavy bunker, Walter Radowenchuk, a Fort Riley original from a Ukrainian immigrant family, who had only become a US citizen in 1964, was shooting at a Viet Cong he had seen near a hooch across the stream. After only squeezing off a few rounds, two bullets struck Radowenchuk nearly simultaneously, one going through his right wrist and another through the upper portion of his left arm, severing the bone. Radowenchuk collapsed to the ground yelling, "I'm hit! I'm hit!" A few yards to the rear, Sergeant Ted Searcy, the heavy drinker who had prided himself on being so tough on the draftees in training, heard Radowenchuk's screams and ran to his aid. The fire was so heavy that, after only a few steps, Searcy had to drop to a crawl but made it to Radowenchuk's side. Having already been hit twice more, Radowenchuk told Searcy that he could not walk, leaving the sergeant to consider his next move. Before he could do anything, though, Searcy felt his own arm go numb – an enemy bullet had passed through Radowenchuk's lower leg and into Searcy's arm, entering at the wrist and exiting at the elbow.

Not far away, James Rademacher, the replacement who was on his first real operation with the men of Charlie Company, had also been caught in the open. He had watched in terror as Radowenchuk had been hit, and then felt an enemy bullet slam into his own chest and another strike his hand. Rademacher later wrote to his girlfriend Mary Ann:

> The bullet didn't really hurt at first. In my hand at the time I couldn't even feel a thing. It felt like it had no feeling at all. My chest gave me a funny feeling all over like you are going to die. It kind of knocked the wind out of me and my body felt numb all over, like it had no feeling at all. Then finally it started to hurt and breathing was a little hard, but I was so scared. The blood was running all over the ground into a little water that was there and finally the water was all red and my head was laying in that and I couldn't move because it hurt and I was afraid the VC would shoot at me again and really put an end to everything. I just had to lie there because no one could help me because the VC were shooting right over my head and I was too much in the open. So I just kept yelling for help, and they were behind cover watching me. There was nothing they could do at the time.

Hearing that 2nd Platoon had suffered severe casualties and had lost its medic, Gary Maibach, the conscientious objector medic of 1st Platoon, pleaded for and received permission from his own platoon leader, Lieutenant Hunt, to see what he could do to help. Hunt watched in admiration as this soft-spoken man, so committed to non-violence, calmly gathered his gear and then stood up and ran across the battlefield under withering enemy fire. A few seconds later, breathing heavily and wondering what to do, Maibach skidded to a halt under cover near someone he had not expected to see. Bernard Windmiller, the chaplain, had chosen that day to go out into the field with Charlie Company. With so much death and destruction around him, Windmiller, like Maibach, knew he had to do something to help. Seeing the desperate situation, Mike Cramer got on his radio and called in an artillery strike on the bunker across the stream, one of the first artillery strikes of the day. After a marking round let him know that the strike was incoming and was going to be accurate, Cramer, Windmiller, and Maibach rushed out under the cover of the explosions, which tossed shards of shattered palm trees skyward only a few yards distant. Windmiller wrote to his wife regarding the incident:

> The VC initial burst of fire wounded 3 men in our Charlie Blitzer element. So I dropped my pack and started up along the rice paddy dike to reach those wounded men. I was scared but kept my head. I knew I had to help those men. I would run like crazy and then dive behind a dike, run and dive. I made it to a shack and took cover behind it. [Two of the wounded] were right out in the middle of the rice paddies. After a couple of minutes the medic came and we both took off running out to the 2 wounded. We threw ourselves beside them and hugged the ground as the bullets went zinging over our heads. We got them bandaged. One boy had a chest wound and the other one was hit in the right wrist, left upper arm and left ankle. He had some broken bones and was in a lot of pain… I was able to talk with these boys to assure them of God's presence and that all would be well.

To the left and slightly to the rear, the leading elements of Lieutenant Hoskins' 3rd Platoon had also taken heavy fire and had seen many of their buddies in 2nd Platoon go down. Hearing that Geier was wounded and down somewhere near the hooch in the middle of the battlefield, 3rd Platoon medic Elijah Taylor, along with Bill Riley, ran forward to see what they could do. The pair first came upon the badly wounded Lieutenant Schulman and had just begun

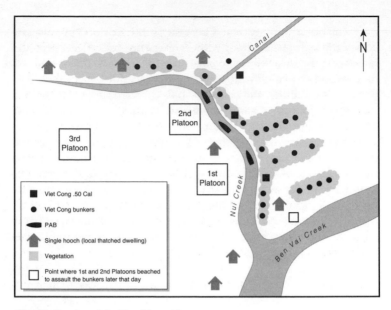

Charlie Company's battle of June 19

to drag him toward the hooch when a 50-caliber round struck Riley in the leg. Riley collapsed to the ground screaming in agony. With the bullets still zipping by, Taylor stooped and asked, "How is your leg, man?" Riley looked down amid the blazing pain and responded in horror, "What leg?" The huge round had blown most of the meat off of Riley's thigh and had shattered the bone completely. His leg, attached by only a few muscle fibers, had folded under Riley's body, with his foot lying nearly under his head.

In ones and twos Maibach, Taylor, Windmiller, Cramer, and Larry Lilley, who had also arrived from 1st Platoon, dragged what wounded they could find to the relative safety of a bit of low ground next to a nearby hooch. While Cramer, who had himself been wounded in the shoulder, went back to firing and working to call in support, Maibach and Windmiller, with Lilley's help, did what they could to tend to the wounded. When Maibach began to work on Lieutenant Schulman, he quickly realized that the wounds were so extensive that there was little he could do. Not even sure if he could hear his words, Maibach held Lieutenant Schulman in his arms and offered a prayer as he died.

Nearby, Elijah Taylor had crawled out to join Bill Reynolds with Bill Geier and was shocked by the severity of Geier's wounds. Taylor quickly realized that Bill didn't have much time left. His friend, the little guy who just had to be too young to be in the army, who had always regaled him about the Cubs during their medical training together at Fort Sam Houston, who always talked about his deep love for his family back home, was going to die on this God-forsaken field in Vietnam. Geier stared right into Taylor's eyes, his childlike face not seeming to comprehend what was happening to him, why he couldn't breathe. Although he knew that as a medic he should only offer hope and comfort and shouldn't cry, Taylor felt tears start running down his cheeks as he held Geier's head in the crook of his arm. He knew that he should say more, something profound, but all Taylor could do was stroke the hair on the back of Geier's head and say, "Stay loose, buddy. We are getting a chopper and you will be off to the hospital and be fine. Stay loose. Stay loose." A few seconds later, Taylor noticed that the body in his arms had stopped fighting for breath. Bill Geier was dead.

As 2nd Platoon had fallen under heavy enemy fire, 1st Platoon had been drawing near to the bend of the stream on Charlie Company's right flank. Lucky that his platoon was nearer to the stream bank's dike, Hunt ordered his men to take cover. While Hunt and his command element sheltered at the entrance to a small hooch, most of the men of 1st Platoon crawled forward and began to return fire across the stream, where they squared off against superior enemy forces and a Viet Cong 50-caliber machine gun located in a hardened and well-concealed bunker. On the extreme right of the Charlie Company line, John Young of 1st Squad couldn't believe his ears. The rhythmic THUD THUD THUD of a heavy machine gun couldn't be the enemy. The Viet Cong didn't have such things. Yet he saw the huge geysers of water as heavy rounds slapped into the flooded paddy behind his unit. In Young's mind that fire had to be coming from the navy boats' supporting fire that had overshot the enemy and endangered his men. Young got on the radio and asked Lieutenant Hunt to tell the navy to stop firing their 50s. Hunt simply responded, "That's not the navy." At that point Young realized that Charlie Company was in for a very rough ride.

Having taken no wounded, and since the Viet Cong heavy machine gun could not depress its barrel far enough to shoot through the dike, Hunt let Maibach go to the aid of 2nd Platoon while his men concentrated on bringing suppressive fire to bear on the enemy positions. Toward the right of 1st Platoon's positions, Frank Boetcher, a replacement who had already served his hitch in the army but who had re-enlisted to go to Vietnam, fought a duel with the Viet Cong 50-caliber bunker, waiting until its burst of fire had ended before popping up from behind the dike to fire a burst from his own M60 light machine gun. Up and down the line men watched the nearly suicidal display of bravery as Boetcher jumped up again and again in his deadly game of tit for tat. After a few minutes, Boetcher's helmet flew off, and he fell backward into the paddy bleeding badly from the head. Before anyone could rush to his side to see what was wrong, Boetcher sat up, tied on his own battle dressing, and got back to work. A bullet had holed his helmet on both sides and had laid open the top of his scalp. As the duel continued, Boetcher's assistant gunner, Jimmy Miller, a Charlie Company original from the hill country of Tennessee, fell into the water and clasped his hands to his face. Fearing that Miller had a bad face wound, John Young crawled to his side and pried his hands back only to find a tiny cut on the bridge of his nose. Young happily informed Miller that he was OK. His face was still there. He had only been "punched in the nose by a bullet." When Miller sat up, though, bright red blood began to spurt from his left arm where the bullet that had grazed his face had severed his brachial artery. Closer to the safety of the main river than the other, more exposed platoons, after applying a tourniquet, Young directed two of his men to drag Miller down to the nearby navy boats for medical care.

On the left side of 1st Platoon's line, at the bend of the stream, Hunt's men did their best to pour fire into the bunkers that faced 2nd Platoon. Ben Acevedo and John Sclimenti, who together had rescued Nelson and Ski in the battle of May 15, and James Nall blazed away at the unseen bunkers across the stream as Jim Stephenson worked with two replacements. Stephenson fired an LAW blindly at the bunker housing the 50-caliber, missing badly. Seemingly oblivious to the enemy fire, Fred McMillan, known to all as "Moon Mullins," crawled from cover onto the top of the dike to get a look around. Stephenson reached up and grabbed Moon screaming, "Moon, get down!" and pulled him back to safety. Stephenson barely had time to ask Moon what the hell he had been thinking, before he heard screaming off to his left. Successive rounds had hit Larry Morgan in the leg, and a replacement named Hammett, whom everyone referred to as Dammit, in the fingers. Dammit's wounds were the most serious – the young carpenter from Georgia had lost part of one finger and all of another. Nearby, Sergeant Bobby Balch got hit by a round in the shoulder. With no medic, Sclimenti and Stephenson told the wounded to make their way back to the boats, with Dammit hopping to his feet and leading the way. Moon Mullins, whose M16 had jammed, yelled, "Hey Dammit, toss me your M16, mine's shot!" Looking over his shoulder as he ran, Dammit shouted back, "If you catch me you can have it!"

When the firing began on June 19, 3rd Platoon was off to Charlie Company's left flank and toward the rear, and the men hit the dirt behind whatever cover they could find. With both 1st and 2nd platoons pinned down and unable to move, Captain Lind, who was watching events unfold from a position further to the rear, instructed 3rd Platoon to maneuver to relieve the mounting pressure on the stricken 2nd Platoon. With Larry Lukes, Bill Riley, and Elijah Taylor having already moved forward, Sergeant Marr turned to his left and to his right yelling to the remainder of 3rd Platoon to "lock and load." Getting up from cover and running forward was one of the hardest things that John Bradfield, Richard Rubio, Fred Kenney, John Howell, Jose Sauceda, and Forrest Ramos ever did. As soon as they had stepped off the boats that day, Forrest Ramos had turned to Jose Sauceda and remarked that, "this is going to be the shit." The scene around what had become their battlefield had been just *too* quiet. There had been no civilians in sight, a sure sign of impending trouble in the populous Mekong Delta. Marr's men didn't want to get up, but 2nd Platoon needed them, so they did. Jumping to their feet the men zigzagged across the paddy. Running for all he was worth, Bradfield just caught a quick glimpse of a machine gun round ripping a hunk of flesh from the hip of a soldier to his right before he heard Ramos yell, "I'm hit! I'm hit!" Skidding to a halt Rubio, Sauceda, Howell, and Bradfield got down beside Ramos and examined his wound. He had been hit in the arm, shattering his elbow. Although he was grimacing in pain, when he took stock of what had happened, Forrest Ramos cracked one of his famous grins. He had one. He had a real, honest to God million dollar wound. Bad enough to get him out of the hell hole that was Vietnam, but not so bad as to leave him permanently crippled. Ramos was going home.

Still sporting his Viet Cong ponytail, Terry McBride thrived on the heat of battle. He was in his element. Running forward with his M60, McBride and his gun crew found cover in one of the many hooches that dotted the battlefield. Ducking inside, McBride found several rice bags, some of which he stacked into a rough wall for cover while he stood on others to gain elevation. McBride then tore away some of the thatch in the wall facing the stream and peered out toward the enemy lines. From his perch McBride could see the tops of the heads of some of the Viet Cong in their bunkers, and opened fire. After McBride saw one of the Viet Cong heads explode, the rest dropped out of sight. A few minutes later, though, up they popped again until another head exploded. The Viet Cong obviously had no idea where the fire was coming from; how could someone be firing down on them? McBride kept firing in his private and deadly shooting gallery for nearly an hour before the first enemy rounds tore through the hooch around him. He thought to himself, "Oh shit, they figured out where I am," and got down to the floor just as a rocket-propelled grenade impacted at the base of the hooch. Shaken up, but uninjured, McBride, like most of Charlie Company, went back to trading fire across the stream with the Viet Cong.

Within minutes of being struck by the hail of enemy fire, the platoon leaders of Charlie Company made their first requests for artillery support and air strikes. Their own weaponry was ineffective against the hardened Viet Cong positions, and they needed something, anything, to suppress the enemy fire before they could call in medevacs and begin to maneuver their forces out of the kill zone. But there was trouble. Neither Captain Lind nor Colonel

Tutwiler knew the location of Alpha Company to the north, and could not risk ordnance striking among the downed troops. Also, the air force recommended that ground forces be approximately 1,000 yards distant from an incoming air strike, and Charlie Company was stranded just over 40 yards from enemy lines. But the fire was so heavy, and the situation so desperate, that Tutwiler gave Lind the go ahead, and Lind had artillery fire placed well behind the Viet Cong lines and then adjusted the fire, "walking" it toward the enemy positions. But Lind knew that the enemy bunkers were so well constructed that they could survive anything but a direct hit. The surest bet was airpower. Working closely with his platoon leaders, Lind took the risk of calling in the first air strikes, carefully alternating them with the ongoing artillery fire.

Warned of an incoming strike, the platoons of Charlie Company popped yellow smoke to mark friendly positions and got as low to the ground as possible. F100s shrieked in and dropped their payloads of 750-pound bombs, throwing shattered palm trees and waves of paddy mud into the sky. Across the stream, the men of Charlie Company were covered in a cascade of falling mud and felt the ground beneath them shake like Jell-O. One of the bombs scored a direct hit on the 50-caliber bunker facing 1st Platoon, vaporizing the machine gun nest and its occupants and leaving behind only a smoldering crater. The detonation had been so close that Ralph Wilson and two other men of 1st Platoon received shrapnel wounds from the bomb, a trade off that they were happy to take to get rid of that VC machine gun. But fire against the 2nd and 3rd platoons hardly slackened at all. Chaplain Windmiller wrote to his wife about the experience:

> Of course all this time they were having air strikes with 500-pound bombs and strafing the area; helicopter gunships came in with rockets and machine gun fire; and artillery was firing. It was all so close to us; the bombs just lifted us off our stomachs, and the shrapnel from the artillery fell in on us. I got hit several times, but it had lost all its "steam" each time. It scared me the first time it happened. They were pieces about the size of quarters and half dollars, some bigger. But the VC were dug in so well and their bunkers so thick even all this did not knock them out. They kept firing at us.

Seeing that the bombs had missed their primary targets, Lind called for a second strike and told his platoon leaders to pop smoke. As the yellow smoke rose into the sky, Lind watched in horror as the first of the incoming aircraft dove toward his men, not the enemy positions on the far side of the stream. Before Lind could react, the pilot fired an entire pod of 19 2.75-inch rockets directly at the exposed positions of the 2nd and 3rd platoons. Watching the rockets impact all around the friendly positions and expecting the worst, Lind radioed Lieutenant Benedick and Sergeant Marr, who was filling in for Hoskins in command of 3rd Platoon, for a report. After a few agonizing seconds both of the platoon leaders responded. They had been tossed around a bit, but there were no casualties. Almost all of the rockets had hit just short of their positions, and the deep mud had absorbed most of the impact. Some of the rockets had struck at the junction point of 1st and 2nd Platoons, where Clarence Shires lay behind a rice paddy dike next to Phil Ferro, a 2nd Platoon trooper from Northridge, California. The impact of the rockets left both Shires and Ferro dazed. When they came to, Shires wiped away some debris and felt a pain like someone had driven a nail into his arm. He looked at his arm and saw the culprit – a scorpion. Wondering if anything else could go wrong this day, Shires yelled over to Ferro, "If I'm dead in thirty minutes and there ain't no bullet hole, it was this damn scorpion!" Furious at the near disaster, Lind got on the radio with the Forward Air Controller, who was circling above the battlefield coordinating the air strikes, and learned that Charlie Company 3rd of the 47th Infantry, which was located just south of the battlefield, had also popped yellow smoke at the same time. The pilot had zeroed in on that smoke and had fired before he had realized his mistake. The confused position of so many American forces in such close proximity to each other was just too dangerous. Artillery could continue, but there would be no more air strikes in support of Charlie Company.

Burning through ammunition of all types in their continued efforts to suppress enemy fire, the platoons of Charlie Company quickly began to run low. Lind instructed each of the platoon leaders to take over their own radio and to send their RTOs and whoever else they needed back to the ATCs to gather what ammo they could. Up and down the line men left the safety of the rice paddy dikes and ran back to the ATCs amid the hail of fire, passing by the remnants of the 4th Platoon. The boats that had not made it around the bend in the stream had beached at the opening burst of fire, with many of the soldiers scrambling to cover behind the paddy dike while others sheltered behind the meager cover offered by the PABs. With many of their comrades killed, the survivors of the 4th Platoon pitched in where they could, often joining with 1st Platoon in its battle or working to carry ammunition to the other platoons.

The spare ammunition aboard the ATCs, though, could not hope to supply all of Charlie Company's needs. News of the ongoing battle had quickly reached the MRB, where soldiers loaded ammunition of all types onto helicopters to supply the stricken units in the field. Unable to land, or even to approach the field of battle too closely due to the intensity of enemy fire, the helicopters flew a few hundred yards behind Charlie Company's positions while the door gunners kicked out crates of ammunition. Danny Bailey, who had been so badly wounded in the same mine incident in the Rung Sat that had killed Lieutenant Black, had only recently returned to light duty on the barracks ships. Still on crutches, Bailey helped to load ammunition onto the resupply helicopters while he listened to the worsening reports of the battle over the ship's radio. Finally, Danny Bailey had just had enough. Those were his buddies out there getting shot to pieces, and, bad leg or no, he was going to be with them. Bailey went below decks, tossed his crutches aside, put on his gear and grabbed his M16. Bailey begged his way onto a resupply chopper and convinced the pilot to fly slowly enough above the rice paddies to allow him to jump out. Heavily engaged with the enemy, John Young was surprised to hear the faint sound of splashing behind him. Not knowing what he would see, maybe a sniper, Young wheeled to find Danny Bailey limping painfully through the paddy water as bullets kicked up tiny geysers around his feet. With a desperate look on his face, Bailey simply said, "Sergeant Young, tell me what to do."

For the chopper pilots of Delta Troop, 3rd Squadron, 5th Armored Cavalry, June 19 had begun just like any other day of flying missions in support of the ground units of the 9th Infantry

Division. The Crusader Fire Team of Captain Sam Slaughter had departed Bear Cat expecting a routine fire mission, until the call came in reporting heavy contact near Can Giouc. The background noise of heavy fire and men screaming and yelling during the radio contact told Slaughter and his pilot, First Lieutenant Evans "Sonny" Kayser, everything they needed to know about the gravity of the situation. As the choppers descended for their first attack runs, heavy ground fire rose to greet them, the heaviest fire they had yet witnessed in Vietnam. As bullets tore through their chopper, Kayser turned to Slaughter and yelled above the din, "My God. Those men down there are in awful trouble!"

First Lieutenant Wayne Lovell, a chopper pilot for the "Long Knives" lift platoon of Delta Troop, was already flying his second helicopter of the day, his own bird being badly damaged in a resupply run into the battlefield. Knowing that men of the 9th Infantry Division were down there, men who were going to die unless he could get them out, Lovell decided to buck the odds and do what needed to be done. Shortly after 2pm Lovell flared his chopper into an area by a small hooch where the wounded seemed to be located. As a hurricane of fire erupted from the nearby enemy lines, there was no time for niceties. With the door gunners firing continuous bursts just over their heads, Chaplain Windmiller, Doc Maibach, and several others rushed to throw what wounded they could on board, including Bob French, James Rademacher, Bill Riley, and Walter Radowenchuk. Within seconds Lovell gunned the engine and lifted off from the paddy, just as enemy rounds shot away the drive to the tail rotor. Beginning to spin out of control, Lovell slammed the aircraft back down, narrowly missing decapitating both Windmiller and Maibach, who still knelt nearby. Just as quickly as they had been loaded on board, the wounded were now dragged back into the mud. As Lovell and his crewmen joined in the fight, with his multiple wounds Radowenchuk crawled to a low point in the paddy and curled up in a fetal position, watching absently as the incoming bullets slapped into the paddy mud near his feet, and wondered what else could go wrong.

It was a desperate time for Charlie Company, locked in battle with a superior enemy force, unable to call in air strikes, unable to maneuver and with no way to evacuate several wounded men who were in danger of bleeding to death. Then reports began to filter in that made the already grave situation even worse as the RTOs of Charlie Company picked up bits and pieces of information on the destruction of their sister unit Alpha Company. Although it was strictly against military protocol to transmit such information over an unsecure network, word began to pass from man to man that Alpha Company had suffered over 80 percent casualties. Everyone knew that a unit that had suffered 10 or 20 percent casualties had been in a real fight. Suffering 30 percent casualties was a crippling blow that required a unit to stand down to be rebuilt; 80 percent casualties, though, was unheard of – beyond imagination. These were men with whom Charlie Company had trained at Fort Riley, and they were gone. Their unit had been destroyed. The men of Charlie Company had been locked in battle with an enemy force much bigger than they had ever realized – an enemy force that was now going to mass against them. When he heard the news at his end of the line, passed on by his RTO John Sclimenti, John Young, like many others in the unit, was gripped by a fleeting moment of sheer terror and thought to himself, "My God. They are going to kill us all."

Disease was an ever-present threat of soldiering in the Mekong Delta. Many, including Jace Johnston, had been disabled by foot problems caused by operating for long periods of time in septic water. In early July Stan Cockerell had fallen victim to a bad bout of Malaria, necessitating hospitalization. The more typical symptoms of the disease, including a raging fever, were bad enough, but Cockerell's lymph nodes also began to swell from his neck to his feet. The swelling ran out of control and failed to respond to any medication, and the doctors informed Cockerell that they were going to have to cut his lymph nodes open to allow them to drain. Happily, though, the swelling had finally begun to subside, and by June 19 Stan Cockerell was on the mend when he heard the first battle reports come in over the radio. Even as Danny Bailey made the same decision, Cockerell got out of bed, gathered his equipment, and made his way to the helicopter pad to try to make it to his buddies out in the field. A few minutes later Stan Cockerell was aboard a resupply chopper headed to the fight.

Army chopper pilots in Vietnam were a breed apart, often taking their vulnerable aircraft into the most precarious situations with little thought for their own safety. At 3.30pm, the resupply pilot of the Huey slick that was carrying Stan Cockerell decided he couldn't take hearing the radio reports any more. He knew that there were men on the ground who would die unless they were gotten out of there. He radioed to Colonel Tutwiler, circling in his own helicopter, that he was inbound to pick up the wounded. Tutwiler responded that it was too hot; he should not land. The pilot replied, "To hell with that, sir, I'm coming in anyway." Huddled on the ground below, Walter Radowenchuk could hardly believe his eyes. There was another chopper landing. The pilot landed the aircraft, with the main rotor still running full blast, in the lee of the downed chopper, using it for cover. Seeing the flurry of activity that followed, Radowenchuk realized that he was too far away for the chopper to do him any good, but he let out a tiny cheer knowing that others would make it to safety.

Forrest Ramos could hardly believe his luck; a chopper was landing. While Stan Cockerell exited one side of the helicopter, Ramos scrambled on board as quickly as he could before the helicopter gunned its engine and quickly took back to the sky. As the pilot wrenched the aircraft out of the mud, only a few hurried seconds since it had touched down, Ramos raised his good arm to wave at his buddies and yelled, "I'm going home!" The chopper rose more than 60 feet in the air, steeply nose down with door guns blazing as it sped away from the battlefield. As the men below shouted "GO! GO!" the aircraft lurched, struck by 50-caliber fire. Bucking wildly, the chopper stood nearly vertically on its tail, pitching the wounded around inside, before the pilot regained control. A second burst of heavy machine gun bullets ripped through the fuselage, and the aircraft rolled onto its side. The whole battlefield seemed to go silent, and time slowed to a crawl as the men of Charlie Company watched the awful scene. Forrest Ramos tumbled out of the chopper, which rolled over and came crashing down on top of him in the rice paddy.

Fred Kenney, Jose Sauceda, and Richard Rubio could only stare in frozen horror as they watched their close friend, and Rubio's cousin's fiancé, plummet to the ground. On the ATCs just that morning the group had talked about how great it was going to be when Forrest and Patricia finally met. Maybe they ought to meet

Willie McTear posing on an anti-aircraft gun, aboard ship in the Mekong Delta.

Ron Schworer on a break during a patrol.

Dave Jarczewski.

Top
Don Peterson (left)
and Doug Wilson
aboard ship.

Middle
John Bradfield and
friends crowding
around his record
player aboard the
USS Benewah.

Bottom
Charlie Nelson at
Bear Cat.

Opposite page top
At newly-established
Dong Tam, Ronnie
Bryan (left) and Bill
Reynolds; standing
behind them Butch
Eakins.

Opposite page
bottom
Carl Cortright
soon after arrival
in Vietnam.

Bill Geier.

Bottom Ben Acevedo (left) and Larry Lilley; top Kenny Frakes.

Elijah Taylor.

Larry Lilley (left) and Tim Johnson.

THE DAY WE MOVED OFF THE
COLLETON!
L→R ①FRONT: JIM DENNISON, NICK HAMMETT
DANNY BAILEY
②SECOND ROW: JIM STEVENS, ME, LARRY,
JIM McCAIN (BEHIND ME) RALPH WILSON
③BACK ROW: ERNIE HARTMAN, DUANE
DEWITT, BOB EISENBACH, JOHN
SCLIMENTI, JOHN BACHER,
JAMES OTIS NULL

Forrest Ramos flashing his famous smile.

up in a real special place like Las Vegas? Or maybe she should meet him as he got off the airplane from Vietnam when the boys came home in January? The helicopter crashed in a tangle of whirling metal, with bits of debris wounding Ronnie Reynolds, Jimmie Salazar, and Mario Lopez. Rubio and Sauceda both stood up, dropped their M16s, and Rubio took off his radio, and ran to the crash site, oblivious to the bullets whistling past from all directions. Forrest, their friend Forrest, was in the mud under the chopper. They could see his legs. A few other men gathered, including Fred Kenney, Elijah Taylor, and Ben Acevedo. First they tried to lift the tangled wreck of the chopper off of Ramos; then they tried frantically to dig him out. But it was no use. Forrest, and the pilots and crew of the helicopter, were all dead. It was the most jarring thing that most of the members of Charlie Company would ever see. There had finally been hope on this dismal day – some of the wounded were going to get away. And there had stood Forrest Ramos, flashing his usual smile and waving as he left. Richard Rubio sat by his friend in a daze for a few moments, before Elijah Taylor shook him back to reality. All across Charlie Company there was a moment of silence and doubt. Still lying curled up in a ball, Walter Radowenchuk said a little prayer for those who had been on the helicopter and thanked God that he had not been on it. Next he muttered aloud what everyone else in Charlie Company was thinking: "Oh God. Can things get any worse?"

During much of the day, men up and down the entire line of Charlie Company had noticed that they were taking occasional sniper fire from the rear, a bullet impacting here, a wound caused there. The fire was not continuous, but left the men with a singularly naked feeling. Not only were they facing death from unseen enemy positions to the front, but also someone was trying to shoot them in the back. In a lull after the downing of the second chopper, a few men caught sight of a muzzle flash from a hooch about a hundred yards to their rear. The sniper was in there, and in the fear and rage of the day the men of Charlie Company wanted that damn sniper dead. Calls went out from at least two places in the Charlie Company lines for a navy boat to fire a white phosphorus round at that hooch to set it on fire. That would solve the sniper problem in a big hurry. The round came whistling in and hit at the base of the thatched structure, setting it ablaze. At the same time several members of Charlie Company also pumped rounds from their M16s into the hooch. Although they were quite distant from the structure and the battlefield was a cacophony of noise, some men on the line heard screaming come from the hooch and watched as several civilians, presumably with the sniper in their midst, tumbled out of the inferno, scrambling and stumbling away.

Captain Lind was at a loss. His men had been locked in battle with the Viet Cong for four hours. Artillery and air strikes had not silenced the enemy positions. He could not maneuver his troops to flank the bunkers, two choppers had been lost, and there was no way to evacuate his wounded. At 4pm, though, a call came in from US Navy Commander Dusty Rhodes, aboard one of the monitor gunboats in the river. Rhodes was an experienced hand at navigating the rivers and streams of Vietnam, having served in the Brown Water Navy in Vietnam for nearly a year. He told Lind that, since the tide was high, he thought he could navigate his monitor up the stream between Charlie Company and the enemy positions. The move was very risky – the monitor, which at 60 feet long and nearly 18 feet wide was almost as wide as the stream itself, could run aground at any point. Even if it remained afloat, the ship would not be able to turn around and could only back down the stream if it got into real trouble. Rhodes and his men would be sitting ducks no matter what. Lind called back that it might be a suicide mission, but Rhodes told him that he thought the monitor's armor would withstand most of the enemy fire. And even if it didn't, he was coming anyway – so Lind had better tell him what he wanted him to do while he had his boat in that damned little stream.

True to his word Rhodes fired his engines and nosed into the stream, the commotion catching the attention of almost all the embattled survivors of Charlie Company. To their amazement the men watched as Captain Lind jumped to his feet and, ignoring the enemy fire, walked along the paddy dike with the radio to his ear directing the movements of the monitor. Although Lind was careful to keep the monitor between himself and the worst of the enemy fire, that's not how his men saw it. There he was, every inch John Wayne, walking along calmly amid the crackling fire pointing out targets to the monitor. After that performance, Lind would never again have to worry about winning the respect of his men.

With rounds continually pinging off its armored sides, the monitor made its way around the bend in the stream where the PABs had been shot up earlier in the day. The 40-millimeter cannon in the bow turret and the 81-millimeter mortar amidships opened devastating fire on the bunker complex housing the 50-caliber machine guns that had been ripping away at 2nd Platoon. Jimmie Salazar, whose wife Aurora was approaching the due date to deliver the couple's first child, watched in awe as the monitor blazed away at the Viet Cong and explosions threw bodies, trees, and mud several yards into the air all around. Despite being so tired and frightened, Salazar couldn't help thinking, "That's the prettiest sight I have ever seen." Only 25 feet away from its closest targets, fire from the monitor reduced the Viet Cong bunkers to smoldering holes in the ground. The men of Charlie Company let out a loud cheer, full of pent-up emotion and frustration, and opened fire on the enemy soldiers who popped up out of the ground and fled for their lives amid the inferno. Wanting his revenge, Jack Benedick asked if his platoon could charge across the monitor and into the enemy positions, but Lind and Tutwiler refused. They had other ideas.

While there were still hundreds of enemy soldiers on the far bank of the stream, Rhodes' actions had lessened fire enough for the men of 2nd and 3rd platoons to drag their wounded on air mattresses to the waiting ATCs along the river where doctors from both the battalion and the brigade were on hand to stabilize the worst patients before evacuating them to hospitals at Dong Tam and Saigon. With movement now possible, word came to the bone-weary men of Charlie Company that 1st and 2nd platoons were to withdraw to the river. There had never been more welcome news. Having survived the maelstrom, the men gathered up their gear and slogged back to the beach and to their Tango Boats. After they withdrew they knew what to expect: no longer limited by their presence, the air force would flatten the enemy positions.

Firepower would win the day, and the Viet Cong would be destroyed. But the men of Charlie Company did not know the big picture. Alpha Company was still out there, nearly destroyed, to their north. The bombers couldn't come in to pound the enemy positions into dust, and Alpha Company was in desperate need of assistance. 1st and 2nd platoons were not returning to the Tango Boats to rest and enjoy the show put on by the air force. They were going to launch an assault on the enemy bunker line and rescue Alpha Company.

To Captain Lind it seemed to be a David vs. Goliath mission. Two exhausted platoons were going to launch an infantry assault on a defended bunker line – a bunker line that might contain a battalion or even two battalions of enemy soldiers. Lind knew that infantry assaults, lining men up and yelling "Charge!" rarely succeeded. The situation had to be either totally perfect or unalterably desperate even to try such a thing. Either his men would be mown down trying to cross the open area in front of the Viet Cong bunkers, or they would get on top of the bunkers and kill all of their inhabitants. Once his troops were on top of the bunker complex, Lind knew that the enemy would have two choices – stay inside the bunkers and die or come running out and die. Either his platoons were going to get wiped out or they would wipe out the Viet Cong. There was to be no middle ground.

As the men of 1st and 2nd platoons climbed aboard their Tango Boats, and were beginning to come to grips with the events of the day, they were stunned by the barked orders: "Get all the ammo and grenades you can carry. We are going to beach you on the enemy side of the canal in two minutes!" As the engines of the ATCs roared to life, there was little time for the men of Charlie Company to think as they exploded into action frantically grabbing bandoliers and grenades. Before the men even really knew what was happening, the bow ramps of the ATCs dropped and Captain Lind, Lieutenant Hunt, and Lieutenant Benedick began to shout at them to get out. As the men disembarked, they gathered behind the safety of a paddy dike as the officers got them into battle formation. 1st Platoon would make the charge, while 2nd Platoon, on the right flank, would provide covering fire. There was about 30 yards of open terrain that the 1st Platoon would have to cover before it reached the enemy positions – 30 yards that meant the difference between life and death.

Hunt gave the order to move out, and the 25 dead-tired and terribly frightened men of the 1st Platoon got to their feet and moved forward. Ralph Wilson, the replacement who had arrived in May from New Jersey, had wondered how long it would take him to fit into the unit. After a full day of battle and as he struggled to make his feet move forward in what seemed to be a suicide mission, he wondered no longer. Wilson was one of the guys – a warrior. Firing on full automatic the men walked in line into the killing zone. Somewhere on the right flank someone started screaming – guttural, animal screaming. It swept the unit like a wave; all the men started screaming. A primal rage against death. As the line neared the enemy bunkers, so wrapped up in the moment that the men were unaware if the Viet Cong were even firing back or not, John Sclimenti watched stupefied as a Viet Cong emerged from the ground beneath his feet. Jumping up from a spider hole with his weapon above his head, the Viet Cong seemed to appear by magic out of nowhere. With his heart beating nearly out of his chest, Sclimenti leveled his weapon and fired, and the Vietnamese crumpled back down into his hole. Standing above the hole, with the young Viet Cong staring up at him, Sclimenti pulled the pin on a grenade and dropped it in. A few paces later, he turned back to see the grenade explode, followed by a pink mist and a shower of body parts. Then, seemingly almost before it had started, the 1st Platoon was on top of the Viet Cong bunkers. It was time for revenge.

To the rear, 2nd Platoon blazed away as the Vietnamese began to emerge from the bunker line and run away. Frank Schwan, the Cleveland native who had made one of Charlie Company's first kills in the Rung Sat, fired a round from a LAW that sent three Viet Cong spinning through the air, while Bill Reynolds fired at fleeing VC with his M16 until wounded by a mortar round. Spitting and cursing at his luck, Reynolds felt a hand on his shoulder. It was Chaplain Windmiller. Embarrassed, and moderating his language, Reynolds made his way to the ATC for medical treatment.

Atop the bunkers there was a chaos of killing. On all sides men were tossing grenades into the apertures of the bunkers, yelling, and firing at the Viet Cong who emerged all around them. On one corner of the bunker complex, Clarence Shires and Ralph Wilson worked as a team tossing grenades into firing slits. Nearby, Jim Stephens, the draftee from Morro Bay, California, who had helped lift Lieutenant Black aboard the medevac chopper on that long ago day in the Rung Sat, couldn't believe that he had made it. He, like most of his buddies, was so tired from a day of fighting; he was wounded; he had tied off an arterial wound for a replacement soldier whose name he didn't even know. But here he was, and there were the enemy. Everywhere. At first he gunned VC down with his M16, which had been hit by an incoming bullet during the charge to the bunkers. Even as he fired, he couldn't help but wonder how old these VC were – they just seemed so young. Stephens then got hold of a M60 machine gun and, with Fred McMillan as his assistant gunner, continued firing at the host of fleeing Viet Cong. He could see the bullets rip into one fleeing VC, making bright red holes in what had been a white shirt. He was reasonably sure that he also hit three others, given how their bodies lurched, before the M60 jammed.

Nearby, James Nall, the draftee from Fairfield, Alabama, who had never tasted "white water" before he joined the military, couldn't believe his eyes. He had hardly ever really seen the enemy before, and now here they were, everywhere. He couldn't help thinking, "We've got 'em now! We have them on the run!" The feeling was the same throughout 1st Platoon. These were the people who had terrorized them all day. These were the people who had shot down the helicopters. These were the people who had killed Geier, Schulman, and the mortar platoon. There would be no mercy. Viet Cong were shot down as they fled, as they crawled away. Some were women, but that didn't matter. These were the enemy. Bodies were everywhere. And then suddenly everything stopped. The Viet Cong were all dead, and there was nobody left to shoot at. 1st Platoon had only suffered one minor casualty. The audacious plan had worked. Breathing hard and running on adrenaline, 1st Platoon stopped to get its bearings amid the almost crushing quiet. Then John Young heard Benny Bridges call for him to come over.

There was a VC trying to get away, but his weapon had jammed. Young walked over, and, out in the rice paddy, sure enough there was a VC, covered in mud and perhaps wounded, crawling away. Young fired his M16 and missed, and then fired a burst on automatic. The impact made the body of the VC lurch and flip over. Badly wounded, the Vietnamese looked back at John Young and waved his hand as if to say, "I'm wounded. Don't fire." The simple act enraged Young. Here this man was asking for mercy, after what he had done to Geier, to Schulman, to Ramos? Young reloaded a new magazine and emptied it into the Viet Cong, whose body jumped and flopped like a rag doll. There was going to be no mercy this day.

When Charlie Company had become locked into its own battle, Colonel Tutwiler ordered Bravo Company of the 4th of the 47th to move to the aid of Alpha Company, which was still pinned down and taking heavy losses. Bravo made only fitful headway against fierce opposition, and was unable to reach the Alpha Company battlefield until nightfall. As the terrible day wore on, from the meager cover of a tiny ditch near the rear of the Alpha Company battlefield, Captain Reeves watched helplessly as his command was torn to pieces. Two Alpha Company medics died in forlorn efforts to reach the wounded stranded in the killing zone, and, without any further medical aid or hope, Reeves could only look on as several of his men bled to death. Reeves yelled at his men to scrape out hollows in the mud and hunker down as best they could against the enemy fire, while he worked to call in artillery and air strikes. Taking fire from nearly every direction in his exposed forward position, Mike Lethcoe was ecstatic when he heard the first CRUMPS of artillery explosions, and he hoped that the jets would not be far behind. Minutes later Lethcoe looked up at the first sound of the engine roar of the incoming flight of F4s and saw the fins pop out a 750-pound bomb that was hurtling right toward his head. The bomb screamed past the terrified Lethcoe and slammed into the VC positions 30 yards to his front, covering him in a thick cascade of suffocating mud. Lethcoe cleared just enough of the mud away to be able to breathe and could only wait as artillery and air strikes continued to impact all around. Although still in grave danger, Lethcoe figured that his luck had finally changed. Covered in mud, he was perfectly hidden. The enemy fire had lessened, and what remained was not aimed at him. For the second time that day the Viet Cong were sure that Mike Lethcoe was dead.

As darkness neared and the leading elements of Bravo Company arrived on the scene, Captain Reeves had a new fear. Once night fell Reeves was certain that the Viet Cong would leave their bunkers to flee, but not before they had killed the many Alpha Company wounded stranded out in the rice paddy. Unable to send help, Reeves yelled to those nearest him to pass the word – he was going to call in heavier air and artillery strikes to cover the retreat of anyone who could still move. At the front of the Alpha Company line Mike Lethcoe was surprised to see a helicopter pilot waving at him – waving him back to the rear. The pilot then made shooting motions with his hands. He was going to cover Lethcoe's escape. Figuring that the risk beat the hell out of being caught out in the open by the VC at night, Lethcoe jumped to his feet and took off as fast as he could. After lying for so long in the mud, Lethcoe's legs were tired and heavy, and a Viet Cong 50-caliber machine gun quickly opened up on him, the impact from its bullets throwing up mud in all directions. True to his word, the pilot of the gunship opened fire on the VC machine gun position and Lethcoe hurdled over the bodies of his dead comrades before skidding to a halt behind the cover of a small paddy dike. All around, the wounded continued to trickle in that night, the broken remnants of Alpha Company. Medics from Bravo Company and from the navy boats did what they could to help, some even crawling out into the open to reach the more badly wounded who could not move. For all intents and purposes Alpha Company had ceased to exist, having lost 28 dead and 76 wounded, a casualty rate of 90 percent.

At twilight on June 19, Lieutenant Hunt informed Captain Lind that his men on the enemy bunker complex were very low on ammunition. With only one tired platoon facing an unknown number of defenders, Lind called Hunt and his men back to the riverbank, where they dug in to spend a fitful night in the mud near the ATCs. Although the men were exhausted from their day of battle, few slept that night. Everyone expected an attack. Surely the Viet Cong would come at them in waves, cut off as they were against that riverbank. All through the night illumination rounds bathed the battlefield in an eerie glow, and the men caught glimpses of huddled forms darting between the trees – but nothing happened. There was no attack. Back across the river, on Charlie Company's original battlefield, 3rd Platoon had thrown up a perimeter around the two downed helicopters and traded sporadic fire with stragglers in the Viet Cong bunker complex. As the night wore on and it became more and more apparent that the VC were intent on fleeing rather than attacking, a sense of calm set in among the men of 3rd Platoon.

In the hooch that he had used as his personal machine gun firing position for most of the day, Terry McBride sat talking with Tim Johnson, who was having difficulty with the loss of his friend Kenny Frakes. Normally talkative, McBride thought it best to just sit and listen, to let Johnson unburden himself. "I can't believe it, McBride, just can't believe it. On our way to the draft office Frakes said that this was gonna happen, that he wouldn't come back from Vietnam. Frakes is gone." After a short pause, Johnson added, "You know something, McBride? On that same day, I said that I wasn't coming home either. I wonder if it's going to be my turn next?" Johnson then stood up and shrugged his shoulders. Seconds later, McBride heard a loud CRACK and watched as Tim Johnson's forehead exploded, struck between the eyes by a sniper's bullet. The men in the hooch rushed to Johnson's side, but there was nothing they could do. Johnson had died instantly, the last man killed in the battle of June 19.

The next day Charlie Company made its way through the maze of Viet Cong bunkers, not knowing what to expect. Everyone was on edge. Was the enemy going to fight? Had they left behind booby traps? The tension was made worse by the awful smell. There were not many enemy dead to find – the Viet Cong were experts at dragging away their losses – but there were congealed puddles of blood everywhere, puddles teeming with flies – and the heavy smell of death hung all around. The company walked on in an odd silence. Some were unhappy that there weren't more Viet Cong to kill after that horrible day. Others were glad that the fighting seemed to be over. But most simply went through the motions in a daze of exhaustion, lost in their own thoughts. Danny Bailey, who had thrown down his crutches to join his friends in battle, was walking point and called the column to a halt as he parted the Nipa palms of a shattered tree line. Without a word Bailey motioned Lieutenant Hunt to come forward. When he looked through the tree line for himself, Hunt could only gasp. He and his men were atop the Viet Cong positions overlooking Alpha Company's battlefield. The vast expanse opened up before them, covered in the bodies of dead GIs, soldiers cut down in almost perfect marching order, with the closest only a few yards away. His eyes sweeping the grim scene, Hunt noticed a lone man walking among the dead. Captain Reeves, the commander of Alpha Company, wandered the battlefield in shock, muttering incoherent words under his breath as he went from body to body. Hunt wondered what was running through the broken man's mind. He had lost his entire command in a single afternoon. What kind of pain could he be feeling?

Back on the river the crews of the ATCs were busy searching for the dead of Charlie Company's 4th Platoon, whose bodies had been carried away by the current. Paris Fadden, the recent replacement from Minnesota, had spent the battle aboard one of the ATCs working to adjust fire. It was up to him to identify the bodies of his friends as they were discovered. First the ATC neared a body floating freely, facedown. The sailors used a gaff to draw the body near and then hoisted it aboard by hand. Fadden looked down. It was Kenny Frakes. Fadden and Frakes were bunkmates back on the barracks ship where their clothes and gear were all mixed up in a pile, where their letters home were lying side-by-side only half written. By then the sailors were already wrestling with another body. Fadden again looked down. It was Bobby Jindra. Fadden closed his eyes and slowly shook his head. Bobby was never going to go home to see his daughter Jacque again. After a short time the ATC nosed into the small stream where so much of 4th Platoon had been destroyed. There, nestled in a bed of reeds, was one of the PABs – overturned and shot full of holes. Next to it was a body. The sailors brought it aboard, and Fadden looked down. It was 4th Platoon medic Robert Cara. There was so much death, so much loss. Paris Fadden had to go sit down. As he sat and stared into the infinite green depths of the Mekong horizon Fadden could only wonder at what had been lost that day.

Meanwhile, Charlie Company threw up a perimeter around Alpha Company's battlefield and then went about the task of gathering the dead. It was like a scene from a nightmare. Each body had its story to tell. Some lay where they had been shot, killed instantly. Others were at the end of pitiful trails through the mud, where the wounded had tried to crawl to safety before being hit again or bleeding to death. Working in pairs, the men rolled over each body from its own puddle of drying blood, hoping that it was not someone that they knew from Fort Riley, and collected dog tags. After identification, the men stripped the bodies of all useful materials, webgear, grenades, weapons and the like, before placing the body onto its own poncho and dragging it to the ATCs on the nearby riverbank. It was the worst day of the war for many of the men of Charlie Company. Even though they had all become rather well acquainted with death, June 20 was something different altogether. Something more horrible. Something more visceral.

Ray Thomas, a Charlie Company replacement from the Choctaw reservation in Newton County, Mississippi, never forgot what he saw that day. The first body he came to was curled in a fetal position. Somehow the man had gotten a picture of his sweetheart out of his pocket and had died while looking at it, and his open eyes still stared at his distant love even in death. As he wrestled another body onto its poncho, the thoughts that ran through Ralph Wilson's mind represented the thinking of many. He would make those lousy Viet Cong bastards pay for what they had done. He would make them pay. Nearby, Lieutenant Hunt made his way to the point section of Alpha Company and struggled to pull over a body by its arm that had become stuck in the mud. Finally the mud ripped free and Hunt found himself face to face with Lieutenant Fred Bertolino, who had commanded 1st Platoon of Alpha Company and had been Hunt's West Point classmate. Still holding his cold hand, Hunt went to one knee and said to his dead friend, "God, Fred. What happened?" Hunt looked around and saw a trail behind Bertolino's body. He had nearly made it to safety before he had died. Hunt was aware that officers were not supposed to do such things, but he sat there holding his friend's hands for a few moments. Fred looked fine, just pale. He looked like he was asleep there near that palm tree, but he wasn't. Bertolino was gone, leaving Hunt feeling helpless. But Hunt had to shake it off. His men were depending on him, and he could not let them see him like this. Hunt stood up and pulled out Bertolino's poncho. It was time to get back to work.

Nearby Larry Lilley struggled with a loss of his own. Ever since the PABs had rounded the bend in the river the day before only to be met with a hail of gunfire, Lilley had realized that his friend, high school buddy, and roommate Kenny Frakes had been killed. He had not seen the body, but Lilley knew that there were no survivors from Kenny's boat. But the battle had raged on, leaving Lilley little chance to dwell on Frakes' loss. Even during the night, when Charlie Company had been expecting a Viet Cong attack at any moment, Lilley had only had enough time to think that he and Tim Johnson would have to get together and have a drink and talk about their lost buddy when things calmed down. It was only upon reaching the Alpha Company battlefield, when 3rd Platoon had reunited with the remainder of Charlie Company, that Lilley learned the truth. Tim Johnson was gone too – shot between the eyes. The news hit Lilley like a sledgehammer to the chest, a real, physical blow. His two closest friends, lifelong friends, the guys who had hitched a ride with him and his mother to the draft board, had been killed. He remembered that day in May 1966 so vividly. He had sat in the front seat of the car with his mom Barbara, while Frakes and Johnson had ridden in the back. So young and innocent, talking about what army life might be like. Lilley remembered scoffing at his friends' fears that they would not return from Vietnam; remembered accusing them both of having dangerous negative feelings. But they had been right. They had both been killed on that forlorn paddy in Vietnam. Nothing would ever be the same.

As Charlie Company cleared Alpha Company's battlefield, Captain Lind, joined by Colonel Tutwiler, attempted to console Reeves and walked with him back to an ATC. Within hours it seemed that Reeves had shaken off the loss and returned to the effective command of what was left of Alpha Company. Shortly after the battle Reeves, in a normal rotation of command, moved to a staff position at 9th Division Headquarters while Alpha Company was rebuilt. Although Reeves performed well in his new staff duties, he could not shake the ghosts of the battle of June 19. Through no fault of his own, Reeves had lost virtually his entire company. He knew that he could do better. He had to do better. For months Reeves begged the commanders of the 9th Infantry Division, first General George O'Connor and then General Julian Ewell, for a combat command, always making the same request: "Sir, we trained that company for a year and brought them over here and I lost them. You can't let me go home with that on my mind. Please let me have another command." Finally General Ewell gave in, and Captain Reeves took over the command of Alpha Company, 2nd Battalion of the 60th Infantry, another unit within the 9th Division. Reeves joined his new command at the patrol base of Tran Tru in the Mekong Delta, where his methodical and serious nature quickly impressed his new troops. A few days later Reeves and his new Alpha Company moved to take over perimeter duty at a camp named Binh Phuoc. On February 21, 1968, less than two weeks after he had taken command of his new unit, during a mortar attack a shell fragment struck Captain Robert Reeves in the head, killing him. He was 26 years old.

In strictly military terms the battle of June 19, often called the Battle of Can Giouc or Ap Bac II, was a great success, despite the near total loss of Alpha Company. On that day the American units had cornered the 5th Nha Be Battalion, which was in the area rebuilding, following a sharp clash with the 199th Light Brigade. The restructured, rested, and resupplied Viet Cong unit, numbering 450 men, had expected an American operation in the area and had planned to intercept US forces as they moved across the rice paddies. The Viet Cong battle plan had worked well, with the 4th Company springing its ambush on Reeves' Alpha Company. The landing of Charlie Company, though, had caught the Viet Cong by surprise, threatening to flank the positions of both the 2nd and 3rd Viet Cong companies, which were dug in along canals. The American maneuver had effectively locked the 2nd and 3rd VC companies into place, leaving them subject to devastating US air strikes and artillery fire. The movement of Hunt's 1st Platoon across the river to attack the Viet Cong bunker complex had been the last straw. With their positions compromised, the Viet Cong attempted to flee and were cut down in droves by US small arms and artillery fire. During the fighting the Viet Cong lost 256 KIA and an unknown number of wounded from a total force of 450, a 57 percent fatality rate. The VC 4th Company, facing Reeves' Alpha Company, lost 50 KIA, while the VC 2nd and 3rd companies, facing Charlie Company, lost 100 and 46 KIA respectively, and local guerrilla forces lost 60 KIA. With its manpower shattered and its leadership killed, the remnants of the 5th Nha Be Battalion dispersed into small groups and remained on the run for months.* The 5th Nha Be Battalion had been destroyed.

Although the battle had been a victory, the losses within the 4th of the 47th had been heavy, 38 KIA and 101 wounded, with Charlie Company suffering ten dead and more than 40 wounded. June 19 changed Charlie Company and the 4th of the 47th. The difficult truth of the matter became crystal clear on June 21 when Charlie Company arrived back at the boats of the MRB. As the bone-weary men disembarked from the ATCs onto the ammi barge, the first thing that they saw was a pile of webgear, 4 feet high and 10 feet wide – helmets, pistol belts, ammo pouches – covered in mud and blood and crawling with flies. The webgear that had been salvaged from the dead of Alpha and Charlie companies. The men filed past the awful reminder of the recent carnage and made their way to their shipboard quarters, where nearly a third of the company's bunks were vacant. Worst, though, was mealtime. After filing past the eerie silence of Alpha Company's quarters the men of Charlie Company entered the galley to find the tables normally occupied by Alpha Company almost totally vacant. Nobody was there. Looking around at the scene, the thoughts that ran through Lieutenant Hunt's mind were echoed by many: "What happened to Alpha

---

*   2nd Brigade, 9th Infantry Division, Analysis of Captured VC After Action Report from the Battle of 19 June, 9th Infantry Division, 2nd Brigade, Assistant Chief of Staff S3, After Action Reports, 1967 through 1968, Record Group 472, Box 1, HM 988, National Archives, College Park.

Company can happen to us at any time. We are going to have to learn fast, or we are going to die."

For the next day of drying out on board ship there was little of the banter and horseplay that so typified Charlie Company during its precious downtime. As he walked aboard ship trying to process the events of the past few days Stan Cockerell was surprised to receive word to report to sickbay immediately. Cockerell had not had permission to leave his sickbed and join his unit when he had rushed off to the helipad on June 19 – he had just gone of his own accord. Instead of reprimanding him for his actions, though, the doctor just looked up and offered a half smile and said "I guess with what you have been through you must be well enough to return to duty." The doctor signed the needed paperwork, and Cockerell rejoined his buddies. As Cockerell returned, Steve Hopper, a farm boy from Illinois who had missed the battle due to injuries, noticed that a hush had fallen over the entire group and that the guys were all different somehow, more serious and more intense.

For many it was the sudden destruction of much of the 4th Platoon on board the PABs that weighed heavily, the entire scene etched vividly into their memories. Tim Fischer, the hard and tough hod carrier from Cleveland, could only sit in silence and mourn the loss of Bobby Jindra. How were his wife and young child going to get along without him? Ken Idle, who had been drafted from the same high school but was serving in Bravo Company, wrote to his parents and spoke for many:

> Dear Family,
> I hope that this letter I'm writing isn't a dream. If not, then I really am alive. How, I don't know. I imagine you have heard about the battle. I didn't receive a scratch, except my mind is shattered. Oh mom and dad, Bob Jindra is dead. Can't write anymore now.
> Love, Ken

Larry Lukes, who was still plagued by the guilt of having let go of Kenny Frakes in the stream on the morning of June 19, reacted to the loss by becoming emotionally cold, numb. Death was no longer some distant idea important mainly to the old or infirm, it was personal and immediate. It was there every minute, causing nightmares and cold sweats. For good or ill, Lukes and his brothers in Charlie Company had become well acquainted with death. John Young, the gung-ho enlistee, found himself questioning whether or not the whole war was worth it. Even though he was not religious, Young visited Chaplain Windmiller, stating, "I'm just tired of seeing ugly things happen to such good men." While Windmiller was able to help Young through his crisis of confidence, Young made an unspoken decision. He was not going to get close to anybody else. It just hurt too much to lose them.

In the farthest corner of Charlie Company's quarters, Larry Lilley spent hours just sitting on his bunk trying to remember everything he could about his friends Kenny Frakes and Tim Johnson – their faces, their laughs, their mannerisms, their jokes – holding those fundamental memories close while he could, knowing that they would soon fade. Larry couldn't help wondering why he had survived, why he would be going home one day while they had died, while their parents would be left to grieve their loss. What made him different? After reveling in the memory of his friends, Lilley slowly felt a new feeling creep in, one he had never felt before. He was going "quiet inside." His friends were gone, but if he was going to live to get home he had to go on, to get ready for the next operation. If he slipped up, or was overly consumed by grief, he too was likely to die. For all their love and friendship, he had to put Kenny and Tim behind him – he had to shut off feelings that come so naturally to civilians in time of loss and become emotionally tough. Tougher than he ever wanted to be.

Not too far away from where Lilley sat thinking, Willie McTear was doing his own soul searching. He had been hurt so badly by the loss of his friend Ron Schworer in April, but there had been Forrest Ramos doing everything he could to cheer McTear up, clowning, playing records – just being Forrest. McTear had allowed himself to open up and feel again, to feel close to Forrest, and now he could not get that horrible sight out of his mind. Forrest falling from the helicopter; Forrest being crushed to death. A small part of Willie McTear had died along with his friends. He would never feel the same way about anybody again, never feel as close to anybody again as he had felt toward Schworer and Ramos. Mario Lopez, the 2nd Platoon trooper from Calexico, California, couldn't shake the vision of the Alpha Company battlefield. Death had come to Alpha Company in an instant – in Vietnam you could die at any given second of any day. He swore to hold his friends and family more dearly; who knew how much time they had left? John Bradfield, who had been one of the first to reach Ramos after he had been wounded, channeled his sense of loss into anger. Expressing a feeling shared by many within the unit, Bradfield was "killthirsty" and wanted his revenge. The tough city kid from Cleveland felt a pervasive and almost directionless anger. The battle of June 19, all the fighting and loss of Charlie Company's experience in Vietnam, had hardened him. He was not a civilian anymore.

While the men of Charlie Company dealt with the reality of June 19 in their own ways, one common thread developed. In response to adversity and death, the members of the core group that had trained together at Fort Riley redoubled their commitment to each other. This family, shrinking and battered, had to keep its members alive, and Charlie Company's officers took careful note of the renewed commitment and deepened camaraderie of their men. Charlie Company as a whole emerged from the battle of June 19 stronger, and was now officially a battle-tested veteran unit. The men knew how to act and react in battle. They not only knew the pain of loss but also how best to avoid loss through competent and decisive action. Charlie Company, more of a family than ever in some ways, a mature family, knew how to fight.

With the door gunner slapping him from time to time to keep him awake and out of shock, a helicopter carried Bill Riley to two different hospitals, both of which were too busy with other casualties, before reaching the 24th Evacuation Hospital outside Saigon. With nearly his entire leg shot away by a bullet from a Chinese 50-caliber machine gun, the surgeons at the 24th could only get Riley stabilized before sending him on to Japan for specialist treatment. Not really knowing the extent of his wounds, Riley was still passing in and out of consciousness when he arrived in Japan, where a worried surgeon looked at the cast on his leg, which had already begun to smell bad. Cutting the cast away the surgeon looked at Riley's wound and mumbled, "Oh shit. Gangrene."

Producing a knife the surgeon began to probe the wound and asked Riley to let him know the first time he felt anything. Within seconds Riley was screaming in agony, and the surgeon only replied, "Good. That's what I wanted to hear." The surgeon then promised Riley that he would do all he could to save the leg, and then began to administer the anesthesia. Two months and three difficult surgeries later, the doctors gave Riley the good news. They had saved the leg, but he would have to undergo months of painful physical therapy and even then would never walk properly again. Still in a cast and awaiting his chance to begin his rehabilitation, Riley was transferred to a stateside hospital in September 1967. Wheeled from the aircraft onto the tarmac, Riley was surprised to see a group of people standing outside the fence to welcome the soldiers home, but when he got closer it all became clear. These people weren't there to welcome them, but to scream at them, to taunt them. One pretty girl made eye contact with Riley and shouted, "Serves you right. You should have died in Vietnam, you baby-killing son-of-a-bitch!" The country that he had left only a few months before had changed. What had it become? Riley could only wonder, "Why does she hate me so much?"

After his wounding James Rademacher, the new replacement who had been injured so badly on June 19, kept up a steady stream of letters to his sweetheart, Mary Ann:

Third Field Hospital in Saigon
June 27, 1967
Hi Honey,
I hope you're not mad because I got shot. Well today is the best I felt since I have been hit so I figured I could write you.

Well I am doing real good and will be all right in a month or so. I got hit in the left hand and then the bullet just went to the right of my heart and came out of my right side so God was with me out there.

The doctors also put a few extra holes in me. One hole in my right side is so the infection can all drain out which is still open. I will have four marks on my belly. One is about a foot long where they cut me open to fix up my insides like my liver and a few other small items inside. I also got a cut on my left arm just above the elbow where they had a tube in me so I could eat. Well I can eat all right all by myself.

I don't know what my left hand is like because it is all bandaged up and I can't see what all is wrong with it. But it sure looks funny. But the doctor said it will be all right also. So I will be as good as new before I know it. I got my Purple Heart. It really looks nice but I would rather not have gotten one the hard way.

I never hurt so much in my whole life. It hurt so bad at the time that I wanted to die. But now it don't feel too bad anymore. It still hurts only when I laugh. So I never laugh. The doctor might send me to Japan unless he changes his mind. I was hoping maybe they will send me back to the states. I will just have to keep hoping and praying that they do send me back home.

I hope you get this letter before your birthday because I'm going to wish you a very Happy Birthday. I am sorry I can't give you anything but I am sending you all my love which you need.

Maybe you can write to me. My address is on the envelope so maybe I will still be here yet.

Well, honey, I'm getting tired right now so goodbye for now.

Love, Jim

P.S. I love you and Happy Birthday and don't worry about me because they are taking real good care of me.

Camp Zama Japan
July 4, 1967
Hi Honey,

Well it's been sixteen days ago since I got shot and I am doing real well. They have been moving me around the last couple of days. They flew me to the Philippines where I stayed one night. Then I took a jet to the air base in Japan and stayed there over night. Then I went on a helicopter and flew to Camp Zama Japan where I am at right now in an Army Hospital.

I got a couple of broken bones in my left hand but I guess it will be all right. It's just a matter of time. My chest wounds are just about all healed up. I am sure a lucky man to be still alive today.

I will probably stay here for now until I get all healed up. Then they probably will send me back to Vietnam which I don't want to go back there as long as I live. I had enough fighting even if only there a couple of days and my first big battle. I never did get to shoot my rifle. I never got a chance to. The VC got me the first couple of minutes before I could get to some cover to hide behind. Well honey you can write me. I guess my address is on the envelope so write as soon as possible. I haven't got any letters since I got shot. Well that's about all I know for right now so good bye.

Love, Jim

P.S. I love you very much and wish you were here by my side and don't worry because I am going to be all right.

Camp Zama in Japan

July 6, 1967

Hi Honey,

Well honey I am still just taking it easy. I can get up and walk but there isn't any place to go to. The doctors said today that it would take three months before my liver would be all healed up so it looks like I will have three months of doing nothing except taking it easy.

I just wish they would send me home then I would be much happier. I forgot to tell you in my other letter that I saw Floyd Patterson, the boxer who fights against Clay. Then after I wrote you the last letter, I saw Hugh O'Brian. I will send you one of his buttons.

I guess I was pretty lucky to shake hands with those important people. I still don't like it here in the hospital. I sure would like to be alone with you. Wouldn't that be just great just you and me. But I am afraid it's going to be a while before I see you again. Anyway 11 more months.

Because I am healing up too good to be sent home, it looks like I will be back in that damn country again.

I guess it isn't good enough that I almost died once, so the army has to give the VC another chance at me. But I am not giving up hope yet I just might get back home yet. Well anyway this time of lying around counts as time in Vietnam so I would at least have four to five months in already which isn't just too bad. But it seems that I just have to see you again. I want to go on living. It's too hard to be without you this long but I will make it and then nothing is going to bother me ever again.

You ought to see all the scars I am going to have. I am going to have three scars just on my left hand and four scars on my belly and chest. One is about 12 inches long so remember I told you I would get a few scars and a purple heart. But I could do without them a lot better. Well honey I must be going. I ran out of things to write so good bye for now.

Love, Jim

P.S. I love you very much.

Eventually the military decided that Rademacher should not return to battle in Vietnam. Instead he served out the remainder of his tour in Okinawa, returning to the United States in October 1968 where he married Mary Ann.

On June 21, when most of the men of Charlie Company were resting and recuperating, Steve Hopper received orders to board a chopper for Vung Tau. There was a body in the morgue that didn't have dog tags. The authorities thought that it was from Charlie Company and needed positive identification. Reluctantly, Hopper climbed aboard for the short ride. He was so nervous that he was shaking. An attendant met Hopper and walked with him to a wall full of metal doors. The attendant first checked some numbers and then opened a small door, pulled out a drawer, and unzipped a body bag. Hopper looked in. It was Forrest Ramos. He only saw his face, and it looked like he was sleeping. After telling the authorities who it was, Hopper went outside and sat down on the pavement. He had known Ramos, who was always so alive, always making people laugh, since the earliest days at Fort Riley. The two had bunks near to each other and shared everything, from letters to cookies. And now Forrest was just a body in a bag. But yet he wasn't. He was still his friend, still his buddy. Alone, Hopper just sat there and thought about Ramos, about how he loved to spin yarns about his boxing days, about his newfound love of Motown music, about his incessant jokes and infectious good humor. Now all of that was gone, just gone. At that moment the price of war became real to Steve Hopper. After the identification of the body it fell to Jose Sauceda to gather up and send home Forrest's belongings. During the whole process Sauceda couldn't get the pictures out of his mind; the image of the helicopter being hit; Forrest falling out;

being unable to save him. Sauceda sighed, wiped away the tears, and closed his eyes. At that moment he swore a silent oath that he would make it home to see his wife Noemi and his new daughter Belinda. He swore that he would better himself and live a good life for his family in honor of Forrest Ramos.

On June 20, 1967, Narciso Ramos answered a knock at the door of the family home in Yakima and found a lieutenant standing there in full dress uniform. In hushed tones the officer informed Mr. Ramos that his son had been involved in a battle in Vietnam and had been declared MIA. Clearly shaken, Narciso had to go sit down while the lieutenant finished his story. After receiving the news, the seven Ramos children gathered together at the family home to await further events. MIA? Certainly that meant that there had to be some hope. Maybe Forrest was still alive? Two days later, though, the lieutenant returned with an NCO by his side. Forrest was dead, and his body had been identified. Narciso was disconsolate. His son, his dear son, was gone.

On June 20, 1967 two army officers arrived at the Skokie, Illinois home of Leonard and Bernice Davidson, searching for Fern Schulman. Fearing the worst, Fern came to the door and received the word that Shelly was missing in action. Distraught at the possibility of losing her beloved husband and father of her young son, Fern shouted, "Don't come back here until you find out whether Shelly is alive or dead!" She then slammed the door in their faces. Within hours family members were arriving from all over the Chicago area, along with a Rabbi, all there to console Fern in her time of need. At noon the following day, two more officers arrived, and this time, having had time to compose herself, Fern invited them in. The news was grim; it was confirmed that Lieutenant Sheldon Schulman had been killed in action in Vietnam.

On June 27, 1967, services were held for Schulman at Piser Funeral Home on the north side of Chicago. Sadly, during the service, a dispute broke out between the Schulmans and the Davidsons regarding the place of Shelly's interment. Shelly's father, Harold, wanted his son to be buried at Waldheim Jewish Cemetery, while Shelly's will stipulated that he be buried at Arlington National

Cemetery. The situation degenerated into a series of shouting matches as emotions boiled over for family members having to come to grips with losing someone who was so young and full of life. Following the rancor and the ceremony Fern, her parents, and Fred Rosenberg boarded a flight for Washington, D.C. The next morning they were met by an chaplain, who informed them that the Army had been unable to provide a Jewish military chaplain for the ceremony, but that arrangements had been made with a local Rabbi from one of the Reform Jewish Congregations in the area to officiate at the gravesite.

Arriving at Arlington National Cemetery, the small group was met by the Honor Guard Platoon from the 3rd Infantry Division and a horse-drawn caisson upon which rested the casket of 1st Lieutenant Sheldon Schulman, with a pair of black boots turned backwards in the stirrups of one of the black leather saddles. Following the procession, the Rabbi performed the traditional Jewish interment service, followed by the pall bearers' folding of the flag that had draped the casket. The chaplain then brought the flag to Fern and said, "On behalf of the President of the United States, the Secretary of the Army and the Chief of Staff of the Army, please accept this flag as a token of your loved one's service to a grateful nation." Next followed the traditional 21-gun salute and the conclusion of the ceremony. The Rabbi, plainly quite moved by the occasion, walked over to Fern who was distraught at the loss of her beloved husband. Searching for the right words of comfort the Rabbi said, "I'm sorry, Mrs. Schulman. This is the first time I've done this." Through her tears Fern replied, "This is the fist time for me, too."

It was a clear and beautiful day in Maywood, Illinois. A sharp rain shower had ended just before dawn, leaving a clean smell of spring in the air. As Bernice Geier looked out of the window to take in the young day, she noticed two well-dressed servicemen coming to the door. Jim, the youngest in the family, answered their knock, immediately worked out what was going on, and ran upstairs to his room to cry. With her husband Jack away at work, Bernice listened alone – her son Bill had been killed in battle in Vietnam. Nearly collapsing at the news, the officers helped Mrs Geier to a chair and waited until Jack arrived home. As the family made ready for the funeral, letters came in from the president and the governor, but none were more valued than those sent by Bill's many friends in Charlie Company. One letter was from Idoluis Casares, Bill's oldest friend in the unit. It was addressed to Bill's beloved sister Jackie.

26 June 1967
Dong Tam
Dear Jackie,

As I write this letter I feel as though I am writing to someone I've known for a long time. So close was I to Bill that I feel as such from the many times he talked to me about you and the pictures he showed me of his family.

I was hit very hard [by Bill's loss]... Every night since I have said a prayer that the Good Lord have him rest in peace and asked Him to give his parents, sister, and brother the strength to face these hard times. All of us in the 2nd Platoon took it hard, but I don't believe that there was anyone else in the platoon who will miss him as I will for a long time to come. I can very well imagine how hard it was for you, because somehow I still can't accept Bill's absence. I can speak for myself personally and for the platoon, Bill was the kind of friend anyone would respect and admire. My close association with your brother goes all the way back to May of '66 in Fort Riley where he and I had bunks together. It's been my experience that you tend to have closer and lasting friends with those whom you work together thru good and bad times. Together we faced many hard and difficult times, and it will not be easy to go on without Bill.

There are no words in which to express our sympathy for Bill's loss, but all of us here in the 2nd Platoon know we lost a friend that we will **never** forget. If there is ever anything (and I do mean anything) that I can do for you or your family, I will do so if humanly possible. So please do not hesitate to ask of me any good deed I can render.

Again my prayers are with you and your family at this moment of sadness.

Respectfully, Luis Casares

Most poignant, though, was a letter from Bill himself. Knowing that they were going to be out in the field for an extended period, many of the men of Charlie Company had taken time to dash off letters home on June 18, and Bill's letter did not arrive until after his family had received word of his death.

Dear Dad and Mom,
Well I came to find a happy surprise; a letter from mommy and a letter from daddy.

So I thought I'd answer you both. Because the next mission is six days, so they say. They said it last time too. Oh well! It's a division operation between Long Binh and Saigon so maybe something big is up.

The golf kick is back on huh! I can tell dad's heart is still with softball, though. Always will be. And I hope Arnold Palmer, I mean Bob, got his letter in the mail. I wouldn't want to deter his pro status in golf, but its time he wrote.

I got a letter from Jackie yesterday too. Haven't gotten grandmother's package, but I'll let you know as soon as I do, I know she'll worry.

The next package send some more tamales and chili. Peaches too. Makes for a great lunch. I used that Insta Shave a couple times, it works pretty well. I don't use it that often, though.

Now that the boys are out of school, I guess things are pretty hectic around home. Let me know when you receive Jim's watch.

So Jackie's growing up. No censor here. She keeps that up, it won't be long before the boys will be asking her out. Then she won't be needing her car. Ha! Ha!

Something's definitely wrong with dad, wanting to send Ken Holtzman and Glen Beckert [Cubs players] over here. Where would the Cubs be? Would he settle for Cassius Clay?

I'm still waiting for those snapshots. I've got a couple of girls who want pictures. Did I tell you I was writing this girl in California, Cindy? It's been a couple months. Writing the RTO's sister in Florida, Ginger. One in Singapore I met. I've got girls in every port if I ever get there.

Well all my buddies are still hanging on. They all say Hi! Some of them have been lucky enough to get those million dollar wounds. Still waiting for mine. I think I'll probably have to endure the whole excruciating tour. Say Hi to everyone. Missing you all, especially my family.

Love, Bill

6 THE STEADY DRUMBEAT OF WAR

Company C
4th Battalion 47th Infantry
APO San Francisco 96372

14 July 1967

Subject: Small Unit Action Report

To: Commanding Officer, 2nd BDE, 9th INF DIV

The Enemy will attempt to choose the battleground whenever possible. He has an abundance of positions, usually, to choose from. He utilizes his defensive positions as an ambush.

The enemy can be and is, in most cases, a well-trained and dedicated soldier. He has good fire discipline and chooses his positions with an understanding of fields of fire.

The enemy will police the battlefield and does a very thorough job of it. He will keep track of your movements and positions. Positioning for a night stand should not be accomplished until after dark.

Charlie will in most cases break contact and slip away during the hours of darkness.

Never cross an open area with the main body until recon elements have thoroughly searched areas of cover ahead. Keep point elements at three men or less. In some areas they will have to precede the main body by 1,000 meters. Never pull them in more than 500 meters in rice paddy areas.

Herbert E. Lind

CPT Commanding*

Ernie Hartman was born in the tiny community of Sugar Grove in northwestern Pennsylvania to Margaret and Albert Hartman. Soon after Ernie's birth, Albert and Margaret divorced, and Ernie and his older brother and sister lived with their mother at the home of her parents while Albert relocated to Florida. The family had little money to spare, and at the age of ten Ernie began working odd jobs for local farmers to help pay the bills. Picked on by many of the boys in town because of his family's status, Ernie grew up having to know how to fend for himself. By the time Ernie reached high school he was tough enough that he was winning his fights, and the bullying soon stopped. Not particularly interested in scholarly pursuits, Ernie turned much of his attention to sports, excelling in both football and track. Now popular, and even a bit brash, Hartman met and started to date a beautiful girl in his class named Jeannie, and was even offered a scholarship to run track at Allan Hancock College in California. Everything seemed to be looking up for young Ernie.

In his senior year Ernie, who served as president of the varsity club, was busy trying to get the attention of one of his friends during study hall when a teacher approached and told him to be quiet. The teacher then informed Ernie that someone was "going to kick his ass one day," and Ernie responded, "that might be so, but it's sure as hell not going to be you." A fight ensued that resulted in Ernie's expulsion from school. It was the moment that changed his life. There would be no scholarship to Allan Hancock College, and Ernie had to work hard with an individual tutor at nights just to keep up and graduate with his class in May 1966. With his college dreams dashed, Ernie took what jobs he could find, eventually settling in as a precision grinder in a nearby factory. Ernie began to make good money, and, in the late summer, proposed to Jeannie. The couple wed on September 17, 1966, and then went on a short honeymoon to

---

* After Action Report 1967 4th Battalion, 47th Infantry, 2nd Brigade, 9th Infantry Division, National Archives, College Park.

Florida to visit Ernie's father, Albert. Very much in love, the young couple enjoyed wandering the beaches and planning their future far from the blustery weather of the gathering autumn in New England. While on the honeymoon Ernie was surprised to receive a call from his mother Margaret. In a bit of a shaky voice, she said, "Guess what? Your draft notice came in today." Ernie had to sit down for a second to process the news, and Jeannie was devastated. They had only been married for a few days and now Ernie was going to have to go to Vietnam? Maybe he shouldn't go. Maybe there was some other solution or way out. But Ernie was adamant. Serving when their country called was what men were supposed to do, and he was a man. He didn't have to like it, and she didn't have to like it, but he was going to serve his country.

Hartman first went to basic at Fort Dix, New Jersey, and then to advanced infantry training at Fort Jackson, South Carolina. Athletic and smart, Hartman did well in his training, scoring the top marks in his entire company with the M16. Before shipping out to Vietnam, Hartman went home for a short leave and reassured his mother and bride that everything would be fine. He was a good soldier and was bound to wind up in a good unit. After a long and boring plane ride, Hartman arrived in Vietnam on June 10, 1967, and made his way to the replacement depot at Long Binh to receive his assignment. He could have gone anywhere, but when he reached the front of the line Hartman learned that he was going to the 9th Infantry Division as a machine gunner. Apart from wondering why he, an expert with the M16, was going to carry a machine gun, Hartman was happy. He had heard good things about the 9th, and quickly found himself surrounded by other replacements headed to the same unit. The group of newbies remained at Long Binh for several days as more and more replacements arrived. They talked about how the units of the 9th lived on boats and used landing craft instead of helicopters to move around. They talked about what battle might be like. They talked about hometowns and sweethearts. They began the bonding process.

On the evening of June 17 the news came in to be ready to ship out in the morning, but as the helicopters roared in readiness to take Hartman and his new buddies to Charlie Company of the 4th of the 47th, Hartman was pulled out of line. There had been a paperwork problem, and he was going to have to wait a little while longer. The other replacements got there just in time for the battle of June 19, but Ernie Hartman did not arrive with Charlie Company until the following day. Having heard that his new unit had been involved in a major battle, Hartman got off of the helicopter and noticed a huge pile of bloody webgear covered in flies on the ammi barge. The whole place smelled of death. Staring at the webgear, the charred and battered remnants of soldiers' lives, Hartman thought to himself, "My God. What have these guys been through, and what have I gotten myself into?" The next day the survivors of the 4th of the 47th came on board from their ATCs, battle-weary, quiet, and some obviously in shock. Even though many were in mourning for lost friends, these guys looked tough. And mean. How the hell was he going to fit in? Hartman reported to his squad leader, John Young. Even though he was muddy and distracted, the little NCO from Minnesota was every inch a soldier. Young began to teach Hartman and the other replacements about life during war – how to be on the lookout for booby traps, how to work in the jungle, how to recon a tree line, how not to die and get others killed out of stupidity. It was so much to take in at once. The information, and the danger, seemed almost endless. During the learning process, Hartman and the other new guys hung out together while the old hands from the days at Fort Riley mingled in tight-knit groups of twos or threes going over the events of the past few days. Several things hit Hartman all at once. He wondered if he would ever fit in with these guys, or be accepted. They seemed so comfortable with each other, but seemed to have so little trust for anyone new. They also seemed to have an intimate relationship with death. They talked about their own possible deaths, the deaths of their friends and the deaths that they had meted out, and it all seemed so matter-of-fact. It all seemed so banal. Then Hartman wondered if he ever wanted to fit in.

After only a few days on board ship, Charlie Company was back out in the field, running operations in the Rung Sat Special Zone and in the Mekong Delta proper. For Hartman there remained so much to learn. It was one thing to talk about booby traps and how to hunt for Viet Cong; it was another thing to remember everything while slogging through the mud on operations. Mercifully, Hartman's first two missions were "walks in the sun" with no meaningful enemy contact. Even so, Hartman could not help feeling a day late and a step behind. Everyone else just naturally seemed to know what to do, while he had to struggle with every step. Pulling his trailing leg from the endless sea of mud, Hartman realized that his learning process was really going to take some time. On July 4, while sweeping an area in Go Cong Province south of Saigon, it fell to Hartman's squad to set an ambush. To him the whole idea of an ambush seemed brave and even frightening. Charlie Company had just moved through an unoccupied village and was making ready to dig in for the night. As seemed to be usual procedure, the company sent out four squads in different directions, each about 1,900 yards distant from the main force, to set ambushes. John Young led the 1st Squad back the way the company had come. He looked at Hartman and explained that the VC usually shadowed US movements in the Delta, sometimes just to keep track of the American units and other times to launch night attacks. The 1st Squad was headed the right direction if it wanted some action on its ambush.

With Hartman placed in the middle of the column of men, where a newbie could do the least harm, 1st Squad made its way down a wide trail through the abandoned village it had passed through earlier in the day. It was really more a scattering of a few raggedy hooches than it was a village. Everybody else seemed almost casual about things, walking among the hooches apparently without care, but Hartman felt the hair on his neck standing up. Ten guys wandering through a village in enemy territory seemed almost laughably dangerous, and the sun was sinking as twilight gathered. What if they didn't reach their ambush position before nightfall? But the others had been through all of this before, and if they didn't worry why should he? A sudden commotion at the front of the file snapped Hartman back into the moment. John Sclimenti, who was just behind the point man, was nearing a T-junction in the trail just as two armed VC walked out of a nearby hooch. After the tiny group stared at each other in amazement for a few seconds, the VC took off running, one to the left and the other to the right. The point man lit out after one, while Sclimenti first shouted then lowered his M16 and squeezed off a couple of rounds before chasing the VC who had run to the right. When he reached the hooch, Sclimenti hurdled over a tiny fence – and smacked his head on the top of a small archway over the gate. There was a sickening THUD, Sclimenti's helmet flew off, and his body rose parallel to the ground before he came crashing down on his back. John Young, who, along with the rest of the squad, came running up as Sclimenti fell, couldn't stop laughing. There was Sclimenti lying on the ground with his arms folded over his chest mumbling, "I've been shot. I've been shot." Still laughing at the absurdity of the sight, Young replied, "Sclimenti: you haven't been shot! Now get up and go get that guy!" As Sclimenti felt around his head, realized what had happened, and scrambled to his feet with a sheepish grin on his face, Hartman couldn't help wondering at the coolness of his new comrades. Here they were in battle, with bullets flying around, and they were laughing and joking. These guys were the real deal.

After getting his helmet back into place, Sclimenti led the group through a dense tree line into which the VC had disappeared. He told them that he wasn't sure, but he thought that he had hit the VC and that he couldn't have gotten far. Hartman's heart nearly beat out of his chest. They were chasing after a real, honest-to-God VC who could open fire on them at any moment! When Sclimenti got clear of the undergrowth he saw the VC hobbling through a wide open rice paddy toward a small stream. A quick burst of warning fire brought the wounded Viet Cong to a halt, but he made sure to throw his weapon away into the stream before stopping. Sclimenti and a few others went over and were searching the prisoner when the point man returned, gasping for breath, to report that the VC he had been chasing had gotten away. Young muttered, "Shit. Now they will all know we're here." At nearly the same moment Sclimenti looked up and told Young that the prisoner only had a through and through wound to his calf and asked what he should do with him. Hartman felt his blood run cold at Young's two word reply: "Kill him."

Hartman stood and watched as Sclimenti shook his head and refused to kill the prisoner. For just a moment everyone stood still, all was quiet, and not even a breeze rustled the Nipa palm. The spell was broken by the machine gunner, Gerald Tanner,* who shrugged, said "Goddamn it," slowly leveled his M60, and poured 30 to 40 rounds into the VC at point-blank range. Hartman watched as the bullets ripped the tiny Vietnamese to pieces; the impacting rounds made the VC appear to dance before hunks of his flesh began to fly away. Hartman's mind raced. Should he have done something? What could he have done? This kind of shit was not supposed to happen. This was wrong. It went against everything he believed. What the hell was he doing here? Who were these guys – soldiers seemingly filled with such hate? Soldiers who were so immune to death. Would he become like them after a few months of war?

While Hartman grappled with his thoughts, Young got on the radio, reported a VC KIA and told the men to get ready to move out. They still had to get to their ambush position before nightfall. As the men made their way toward their destination Young had to come to terms with his own decision. Had it been right? It had to be right. His ten men were in the middle of enemy territory, and had no way to get a VC prisoner back to the company perimeter before nightfall. The other VC had escaped and Young had to assume that he was at that very moment telling his buddies about 1st Squad's location. That information made Young's men incredibly vulnerable. An entire enemy platoon or even a whole company might attack them that night. Facing such odds, caring for a VC prisoner was an unacceptable risk. Even if they tied him up – two of the men would have to watch the prisoner all night. And what if he yelled out? What if he broke free? If the VC attacked, and Young had to assume that they would, 1st Squad was going to have a tough enough time surviving that night without a VC prisoner giving away their location and taking up the attention of two of the men. Young knew that killing a prisoner was against the rules, but he had decided that the safety of his own men took precedence. People had been dying in Charlie Company for months all around him, but none had been in his squad. Amid the death and suffering, Young was more determined than ever to bring all his boys home safely. It was his job, his responsibility – a responsibility that wore on him just a bit more every day. John

---

*   Fictitious name.

Young was himself just a 21-year-old from Minnesota. He had never expected to have to make such difficult moral decisions, to weigh the lives of his friends against that of a Vietnamese prisoner, but he had done what he felt was best. It was cold comfort but Young thought to himself, "Sometimes in war there are no right decisions. You can only choose between bad and worse."

The men of 1st Squad were on 100 percent alert that night, but no attack ever came. The next morning the squad returned to the company perimeter and operations continued as normal. The next night, in the safety of the company defensive position, Hartman began to wonder again. Eventually he fell asleep, only to watch the machine gun rip into the VC again in his dreams – a memory that would haunt him for years to come. A memory that would even intrude unbidden into his daytime routine. Little did Hartman know that a few foxholes away John Young wrestled with his own demons. He still wondered whether he had made the right decision. This was not the kind of stuff that he had signed up for. Young, too, dreamed of the killing that night – a nightmare that he, too, would live with forever. But Young could never share his doubts with his squad. He was their leader and could not show any hint of weakness. He had to be hard. He had to be right so his men would have confidence in him and follow him, so he could get them home safely. They could have doubts and fears, but his own had to be locked away.

For the next three days Charlie Company continued to operate in Go Cong Province as part of a multi-battalion operation aimed at disrupting local guerrilla forces in the area, who, intelligence reported, were busy raising recruits for the 514th Main Force Viet Cong Battalion. The operation had plainly caught the local guerrillas by surprise and resulted in several contacts with small VC units, often only one or two enemy soldiers, who were trying to flee the area. During the four-day operation, the MRF accounted for 105 enemy KIA, most from air attacks. For Charlie Company the operation was a four-day deadly game of cat and mouse with an enemy who did not want to be found. On the day after the completion of the operation, Clarence Shires, the son of a Virginia shipyard worker who had given Lieutenant Duffy Black mouth-to-mouth resuscitation on that long ago day in the Rung Sat, wrote home regarding the on-again, off-again nature of the fighting:

Dear Mom and Dad

Well everything's o.k. I am doing just fine. We just got in off of a three day operation. It was not a quiet operation. We killed a lot of V.C. and captured a lot. They did not fight us most of them we caught by surprise…

One of my team leaders shot a guy coming out of a house the other night. The next morning his little boy and wife came up and started crying. We felt sorry for the family so we changed his bandages and gave him a cigarette and lit it. His wife helped me make him a stretcher. So we carried him 800 meters through mud and water to our C.P. We sent him off in a chopper.

We slept in a house the other night. One guy woke up with a pig chewing at his shirt sleeve. There were a dozen or so rats (big ones) in the house. They were trying to catch the baby chickens. There were three hens with baby chickens in the house. There were pigeons in the house. And every few minutes they would get into a fight. If they wasn't fighting somebody was throwing or shooting grenades at noises or people running outside. Then about the time you would get to sleep again a Willy Peter round would burst over your head. We were standing guard every hour and half. One time a squad leader called me on the radio and told me to get my men down, that he was going to fire in my direction. He like to have shot the house down that I was in. Then I got off guard again and went to sleep. About that time one of the men in my position shot the man at the house. And believe it or not this is a typical night on operation in Vietnam. If you get four hours sleep a night you are lucky.

We blew up over 200 bunkers these past three days. We used up all of our hand grenades and demo. We found their C.P. and tore their flag pole down and took their flag. A lot of us started whistling a tune as we tore it down.

We took a whole boat load of bananas from a V.C. and we found a house full of bananas. We ate them for two days. I killed a chicken and roasted it. One guy fried some eggs he found. There is always some fun mixed with work and believe me we take full advantage of it.

> Well tomorrow we go on a one day operation. We come back tomorrow evening.
>
> Yours, Junior

Small, fleeting contacts, like those of 1st Squad on July 4, were the rule of the day. VC would pop up, fire off a few rounds, and run away, with the units of Charlie Company giving chase. An event typical of the operation took place in 3rd Platoon when Terry McBride and Larry Lukes were investigating a hooch. Finding nothing but a wet pair of sandals, the duo was about to depart when Lukes caught sight of a perfectly round circle on the floor. McBride flipped the trapdoor open and, seeing a VC clutching a grenade, opened fire. After reporting the VC KIA and searching the body, McBride went outside where two other members of the platoon opened fire on a small group of VC who were crossing the road. Getting there just in time, McBride squeezed off a few rounds, and thought that he had hit the last VC in the file in the hand.

Later that night Charlie Company set up its defensive positions and sent out its normal squad-sized ambushes. Jim Stephens took his squad out from 1st Platoon and spread his men out in an "L" shape along a stream for the night. Stephens and his RTO, Fred McMillan, sat in the middle of the group to wait. Jim Dennison later wrote home about the experience:

> I had a little excitement this last mission, which you might find interesting. My company set up for the night, and I went on an ambush about 500 meters from their perimeter with 8 other guys. We set up along a woodline in 3 – 3 man positions about 10 feet apart. One man at each position was to be awake at all times. I sacked out since it wasn't my watch, and about 9:30 this new kid wakes me up and says, "7 guys with weapons just walked by about 10 feet from us, but I didn't shoot because I thought they were South Viet soldiers." I felt like wringing the guy's neck since the only thing that moves around here at night is VC. We all stayed awake after that since God only knew where those 7 guys went. About midnight a guy walks out of the bushes 20 feet in front of me and starts coming my way. I held my fire because I wanted to see if he was alone or what. By the time I had made sure, he was only 3 feet away not having seen me lying

there, so I tackled him. It turned out that his hand had about 5 holes in it already and he'd already ditched his weapon. But I didn't know that. It sounds sort of funny now, but it wasn't then.

The VC fell on top of Dennison, who was expecting a real fight. Already wounded, though, the VC just asked for a doctor. The next morning the VC was choppered to the rear for questioning, and Dennison felt every inch the hero. As more and more of his old buddies questioned why he had captured the VC and not killed him, Dennison's feelings began to change. He felt scared. Scared for who he and his buddies were becoming. He wondered when they had all abandoned the trappings of civilization and had become warriors instead.

As the drumbeat of war went slowly on, the men of Charlie Company spent their off days on the *Colleton* drying out, cleaning weapons, and resting. These short stays were important, allowing the men to deal with the loss and the killing in their own ways. Even though liquor was banned aboard ship, there was always some available, and several of the men turned to alcohol to help them through the dark times. Others wrote home as often as they could, pouring out their thoughts and pains to their loved ones. After June 19, Barbara Kenney noticed a distinct change in the tenor of her husband Fred's letters. He continued to ask questions about little Freddie. Was he sitting up yet? When would that happen? Would Freddie be walking before his father got home in January? Fred also still mused about what their lives would be like as a family once he came home. Would changing diapers and other fatherly duties mean that he wouldn't have time anymore to ride motorcycles? But his letters had seemed to take on a tone of despair. The fighting of June 19 had shaken Kenney to the core, especially the horror of watching his friend Forrest Ramos fall to his death out of the dustoff helicopter. He just couldn't shake the vision from his mind. He had to get home. He just had to make it home safely for little Freddie, but he wasn't sure anymore if he would make it out of Vietnam alive. Barbara was worried for her husband, but covered it up in her own letters. He would be fine. The loss was fresh now, but he would get over it. As long as he kept his head down and wasn't a hero he would get home safely, their little family would have a happy life, and Vietnam would fade into a distant memory.

Charlie Company's hard fighting over the past two months, which showed no signs of letting up, underscored the dangers of war. As young draftees most of the Charlie Company originals had been quite sure of their immortality. People might die in Vietnam, but it would not be them. By July 1967, though, everyone in the unit knew that death could strike anyone at any time. The common realization of their own mortality drew the Charlie Company originals closer than ever before. They were determined not only to see each other through the war safely but also to get everything they could out of life and to enjoy each other's company along the way. In 2nd Platoon the camaraderie of war and shared mortality drew together an unlikely group of friends. Two within the small 2nd Platoon circle were drawn together in part due to a common background but also because of a love of cars. Mike Cramer was one of the California draftees, a middle-class kid from Pacoima, part of Los Angeles and only a few minutes down the road from Canoga Park and Lancaster – home to so many others in Charlie Company. Too skinny for sports, during high school Cramer mainly hung around with other members of his church youth group. In his spare time Cramer tinkered on cars, especially Fords, and decided that he wanted to be a car mechanic. After high school, Cramer had been taking classes part-time toward his mechanic's license when he received his draft notice.

It was natural that Cramer would buddy up with Phil Ferro, a tall, good-natured draftee from just down the road in Northridge, California. Born in Bristol, Connecticut, Phil was the eldest child of Tony and Helen Ferro, children of Italian and Russian immigrants respectively. Tony made a good living as a mechanic, but Helen had her heart set on moving to California, so when Phil and his sister Diane were still in grade school, the family pulled up stakes and moved west. In their new world of the San Fernando Valley, Phil and Diane became ever closer, turning to each other for support. The Ferro children, seemingly always together, did well in school. Strong and fast, Phil became a popular athlete, winning the Los Angeles city championship in high hurdles during his senior year while Diane was selected as "Miss Northridge" of 1963, both receiving college scholarships.

Phil and Diane enjoyed hanging out with their friends on the beach during the summers, but more than anything the brother and sister team shared a love of cars born of long afternoons helping their father in his garage. While Phil was a student at Grover Cleveland High School, Tony bought the family a project, paying $10 for the burned-out shell of a '57 Chevy. Father and son spent months rebuilding the car from the ground up, elbow-deep in grease and oil nearly every weekend, restoring it to mint condition. Now with a stylish ride to go with his athletic fame, Phil joined the southern California cruising culture and loved to spend evenings slowly driving up and down Van Nuys Boulevard. To celebrate the completion of work on the car, Phil asked his girlfriend, Linda, to the event of a lifetime to see the Beach Boys in concert at the Hollywood Bowl. Linda, though, fell ill and suggested that Phil take her friend Sandy as his date instead. The concert was magical, and the two fell in love. Within months Phil proposed, and the couple were married shortly after Phil's graduation from high school in 1965. Wanting to be a mechanic and to open his own garage, Phil went to Pierce Junior College, where he majored in business, and planned to go on to California State, Northridge, to complete his studies. Phil, though, had to work to afford an apartment for himself and his wife, and could only go to school part-time. Only a few weeks after shifting over to part-time status, Phil received his draft notice.

Wanting to spend as much time with her new husband as possible, Sandy went with Phil to Fort Riley, where they lived in a small apartment. The couple, sometimes inviting Phil's new friends over to a welcome home-cooked meal, quickly became popular among the boys of Charlie Company. Even though Ferro liked Chevys and Mike Cramer swore by Fords, the two had quickly bonded over their love of cars and talked about everything automotive from rebuilding engines to body work. Sometimes their conversations deteriorated into an indignant debate over the relative merits of Ford and Chevy, a topic of never-ending fun, which the two decided needed to be settled with a race right after they got back to southern California for good.

While it was cars that had brought Cramer and Ferro together as friends, it was a shared rural upbringing that formed a bond between two other members of the 2nd Platoon. Butch Eakins was a country boy from Cape Girardeau, Missouri. He had grown up in a rural environment far removed from the city life so familiar to Cramer and Ferro in Los Angeles. From a poor family, Eakins had to go to work doing odd jobs at an early age and never had thought much about school. Maybe he would go to a big city or maybe he would work on farms, but he knew that his future held hard work, not college. As a teen Eakins had been a bit rough around the edges, frequenting taverns and riding a motorcycle that he had rebuilt himself. After graduation Eakins took a job at the Caterpillar plant in Peoria, Illinois, where he worked until he was drafted. At Fort Riley, Eakins, hard working and sometimes too honest for his own good, met Henry Burleson, a country boy from Texas who had grown up hunting and singing gospel music. Even though their accents were different, and Eakins preferred Country and Western to gospel, the two quickly became close friends. The two seemed to share everything together, including their escape from the mock POW camp. During AIT Eakins and Burleson had to work closely with Cramer and Ferro, receiving training together to learn to use recoilless rifles. Although the city slickers and the country boys seemed to have little in common, they bonded almost instantly, with Eakins even winning Cramer over from rock-n-roll to country music. It was playing his favorite song, Buck Owens' "Above and Beyond," that did the trick.

The others in the small group of friends all knew that Henry Burleson was religious. Henry didn't flaunt it, or preach it. His deep faith was just evident in how he held himself and spoke. Cramer, Ferro, and Eakins respected Burleson's faith and appreciated the fact that he was not aggressive about it. One early morning on the trip to Vietnam aboard the *John Pope*, Burleson had found Eakins sitting off in a corner alone. It was obvious that Eakins was scared. Burleson sat down beside Eakins and asked if he could do anything to help. Eakins looked up at him and said, "Henry, I just don't know if I am gonna make it back from Vietnam, and I don't know if I'm ready to die or not." Burleson took the copy of the New Testament that his mother had given him on his leave after training and asked Eakins if he had heard about Jesus. Eakins responded that he knew the story but had never given it much thought. Burleson then put his hand on Eakins' shoulder and said, "Do you have the Lord in your heart? He died for you, and if you have him in your heart you will spend eternity in heaven." With tears in his eyes, Eakins asked the Lord for forgiveness and to enter his heart. Burleson sat with his friend for a few moments longer and assured him that everything would be all right.

In Vietnam, the friendships between the members of the small group became even closer. They seemed to share everything, from pictures of their loved ones to care packages from home. Everyone especially enjoyed the cookies sent by Phil Ferro's mother, which they always gobbled up within minutes of their arrival. Because of their popularity, Phil wrote and told his mother that his buddies all hoped that she could send more. Helen responded by gathering together women from all over her community, including Bill Reynolds' mum, to bake and buy goods for packages to send not only to Phil and his friends but also to soldiers throughout 2nd Platoon. Soon Helen Ferro's group had expanded so much that it was sending care packages to many of the servicemen from the San Fernando Valley, often writing to those same soldiers so that they would always get something at mail call. Helen Ferro kept up her care package and letter-writing work for years, becoming the adopted mother of many young men who served in Vietnam.

Due in part to a hearing loss, Burleson was put on construction duty at Bear Cat and Dong Tam while in Vietnam, and became somewhat separated from the group. They all remained close, though, with Eakins, Ferro, and Cramer informing Burleson of their doings after every mission. The experiences had been difficult, from trudging through the Rung Sat to several near misses from booby traps and mines. On June 19 the trio had worked hard to lay down fire on enemy lines and to aid the wounded, with Ferro even receiving a Bronze Star for his actions. But even with all of the death that surrounded them, the little group seemed blessed. They had all avoided injury, and their circle had even expanded. Harold Wayne King was from the small town of Copper Hill, outside Roanoke, Virginia. Graduating from Floyd County High in 1966, King was drafted in August of the same year. Arriving in Vietnam in February

1967, King was one of the early replacements in Charlie Company and found himself in 2nd Platoon, where he joined Eakins, Ferro, and Cramer. The group got along together well, with Butch Eakins especially taking King under his wing. Both country boys, Eakins and King just seemed to hit it off and became nearly inseparable.

At the beginning of July, Phil Ferro had received great news. He was going to get his R and R to Hawaii to see his wife and family, and none too soon. He was ready for a break. He wrote home proclaiming his good luck and told everyone to make plans to meet him there on July 21, where they would have the time of their lives. On July 10, just after word came down that Charlie Company was headed out on another operation, Butch Eakins told Henry Burleson that he didn't think that he was going to come back from this one. Burleson put his arm around Eakins' shoulder and told him that everything was going to be OK. The two men then prayed together for a few minutes before Eakins had to go and join Ferro, Cramer, King, and the rest aboard the ATC.

On the morning of July 11, the 4th of the 47th began a battalion-sized operation near the old battlefield of June 19. Intelligence indicated that VC company-sized elements were in the area trying to raise recruits to reconstitute the 5th Nha Be Battalion. Enemy activity appeared to be centered in the villages along the Rach Song Cau and the Song Duong La rivers. In the early afternoon Alpha and Charlie companies moved by ATC to the east bank of the Rach Song Cau, where Alpha landed to the north at a bend in the river while Charlie beached in the south. At the same time Bravo beached on the west bank of the river. As Bravo swept its bank of the stream, Charlie moved north to act as a blocking force, while Alpha swept to the south, hoping to catch any Viet Cong in the area in a vise.

It seemed like every time Charlie Company went out there was good intelligence that indicated a large enemy force in the area, but most of the time nothing happened. Either the intelligence was faulty or the enemy slipped away without a major battle, so July 11 was just another day. Captain Lind had heard the reports, knew the enemy was supposed to be in the area, and acted with appropriate caution. But he had little faith that the reports were accurate. When Charlie Company beached, just after 1pm, Lind got his troops into order. On such operations the task of serving as lead platoon rotated, and it was 2nd Platoon's turn. Shouldering their gear and readying their weapons, Lieutenant Benedick's men took the lead in the unit's sweep to the north to its blocking position, flanked by 3rd Platoon on the right, with 1st Platoon on the left and bringing up the rear. After only a few steps a single round buzzed in, striking Idoluis Casares above the left kneecap. There hadn't really been that much of a noise, and several men wondered if Casares had just tripped until they saw the wound on his leg. A spent round had struck Casares, and when he struggled to his feet the bullet simply popped out of the wound. But still the injury was bad enough to require a dustoff. A few moments later, after 2nd Platoon had renewed its march, Mario Lopez was nearing a small ravine when a Viet Cong soldier erupted from the water almost beneath his feet. Standing only inches away with his rifle at the ready the VC, water streaming in rivulets from his body, locked fearful gazes with Lopez. After a split second that seemed like an eternity, Lopez opened fire, dropping the VC back into the water with another tremendous splash. Locked in a singular moment of fear and surprise Lopez kept firing until it finally registered that someone, perhaps Platoon Sergeant Kerr, was yelling at him to cease fire. Shocked back into reality, Lopez' finger slacked on the trigger, and he stood in semi shock as other troopers from 2nd Platoon searched the dead VC. Lopez was shaking uncontrollably, and he almost abstractly noticed that he was covered in water. The VC had been so close that the splash he created when he leapt to his feet had soaked Lopez. How the hell could he have been that close? How could death have been that close? As Lopez gathered his thoughts the troopers of 2nd Platoon began to wonder if they were being watched, if the VC were out there all around. The afternoon was off to a bad start.

Once the dustoff departed, 2nd Platoon resumed its move northward across the rice paddies. After what had happened to Alpha Company on June 19, Charlie Company had altered its tactical regimen. It was too dangerous for the entire company, or even a platoon, to move across a rice paddy in the open; if the enemy were dug in at the tree line on the far side, the results would be disastrous. Instead the lead platoon would send out a single squad to recon the tree line while the remainder of the company lingered to the rear, enjoying a quick break, to await events. It was a standard routine that the company employed countless times each day. Every squad of every platoon took its turn. Normally there was nobody dug in at the far tree line, nothing happened, and men of Charlie Company put out their smokes, shouldered their weapons, and moved out. A few minutes later the company would come to another open rice paddy, and it was another squad's turn to recon while the others rested for a bit. But everyone knew that one day, as had been the case on May 15 and June 19, the Viet Cong would be in the next tree line, and it would be the recon squad that would pay the price.

At 1:30pm Lieutenant Benedick brought 2nd Platoon to a halt and called over Sergeant George Smith. It was his squad's turn to recon a tree line about 200 yards away across an open rice paddy to Charlie Company's north. Smith went and got his men, Butch Eakins, Bill Varskafsky, Harold Wayne King, Henry Hubbard, and Frank Schwan. Varskafsky, a Charlie Company original from Washington who had worked in a shipyard but had secretly hoped to become a doctor, had been humping the radio all day. Having struggled from one mud hole to the next, Varskafsky was exhausted. It was OK; Phil Ferro volunteered to take his place. It would give him more time to hang with his buddy Butch Eakins. Hubbard was a relatively new replacement, and Frank Schwan was one of 2nd Platoon's machine gunners, a Hungarian draftee from Cleveland who had made one of the company's first kills when he had shot up a sampan in the Rung Sat. With Eakins and Ferro chatting amiably, the six men started forward across the expanse toward a scattering of hooches and the far tree line. They walked in a staggered formation, with Schwan intentionally lagging a bit behind knowing that machine gunners were the VC's favorite target. It was just like so many recons before, a boring and hot walk in the sun. As the group neared the hooches, about 200 yards in advance of the remainder of Charlie Company, Smith swung toward the left avoiding the hooches themselves and making straight for the tree line. The shift in direction placed Schwan uncomfortably close to the front of the line as the soldiers closed to within 100 feet of their goal. Suddenly there was a sharp CRACK of an AK47 firing, and the bullet struck Schwan in the midsection.

The entire tree line then blazed with enemy small arms and automatic weapon fire. As he was falling, another bullet struck Schwan in the shoulder, which spun him around and wrenched the M60 machine gun from his grasp. Without cover, Sergeant Smith, Eakins, and Ferro, who were at the very front of the line, dropped to their bellies and returned fire toward the unseen foe. Feeling no pain, only a strange sense of numbness, Schwan began to crawl but noticed that his movement among the rice attracted new enemy fire. He thought to himself, "I had better be still, or they're going to shoot me again." As he lay there, Schwan wondered what he could do, wounded, without a weapon, and stranded in the open, as the VC fire came in so heavily that it sounded like a continuous and deafening roar. Wriggling just a little bit, Schwan was able to look behind him and noticed that King and Hubbard had taken refuge behind a small dike in the paddy. He yelled at them to give him some covering fire, and that he was going to come in. Hubbard and King opened up with their M16s, and Schwan, in agonizing pain, scrambled to his feet and ran the short distance to the dike and dove to the ground, briefly passing out after the impact.

Waking up a few seconds later Schwan looked up at the agonized face of Harold Wayne King. His friends were out there in the open, screaming for help. The Viet Cong had them dead to rights, and they were going to die unless he did something. His eyes widening at the sight, Schwan watched as King jumped over the dike and ran *toward* the enemy fire to retrieve Schwan's machine gun. Then, engulfed by a new wave of pain, Schwan passed out again. After he came to, Schwan noticed that King was back, lying wounded on the ground next to him, while Hubbard administered mouth-to-mouth resuscitation. Try as he might, though, Hubbard could not raise a pulse. Schwan then rolled over to see what he could do, and after opening King's shirt he saw a clean hole through King's neck just below the Adam's apple – a fatal wound. Schwan then took note of the scene around him – all of the machine gun's ammo had been spent. King had retrieved the fallen weapon and had given his friends Ferro, Eakins, and Smith what cover he could until his ammunition was gone and he himself was killed. Snapping back to reality,

Schwan's skin suddenly went cold. The battlefield had fallen eerily silent. There was no firing from the Viet Cong bunkers; no firing from Smith, Eakins, and Ferro. It could only mean one thing: they were dead. It was just him and Hubbard out there in the open, 200 yards of open ground from their own lines and safety. They were stranded only 100 feet from an enemy unit he guessed to be of company size. What the hell were they going to do? Making matters worse, Schwan finally got a good look at his own wounds. Both bullets had passed clean through his body, but there was not much blood. Instead the wounds only oozed pinkish bodily fluids. Hit by a wave of nausea, Schwan vomited – vomited blood. He was bleeding internally. Unless he could get help, he was going to die.

Lieutenant Benedick had been sitting on a rice paddy dike next to his RTO, Mike Cramer, watching the advance of Smith's squad while the rest of the men took a short break. When the firing began, Benedick and Cramer jumped to cover behind the dike and took stock of the situation. The enemy fire was intense, but there were so many small dikes between them and Smith's squad that Benedick could not see what was happening. Given the volume of enemy fire Benedick feared the worst. The point squad was so far out that Benedick was helpless. Every time he tried to maneuver part of his own platoon out into the paddy, it fell under heavy fire and could not get forward. His men could not even lay down much covering fire; there were too many small rice paddy dikes in the way, and they were afraid of hitting their own fallen friends. Benedick called in artillery, but, since his own men were stranded only a few feet from the enemy positions, he couldn't call the fire in close enough to do much good. Air strikes came in as well, one almost hitting 3rd Platoon, but again the distances were too close to allow for a direct strike on the VC bunkers. With the men around him increasingly desperate as the afternoon wore on, and with several, including Mike Cramer and Bill Reynolds, volunteering to try to reach Smith's men, Benedick called in a salvo of smoke rounds to give cover to a rescue attempt. There was brief hope when the smoke rounds went off on target, but that hope was dashed by a brisk breeze that quickly blew the smoke away. Intensely frustrated, but not willing to let it show to his men, Benedick gave them the bad news. There would be no rescue. He was not going to sacrifice the living in a suicidal

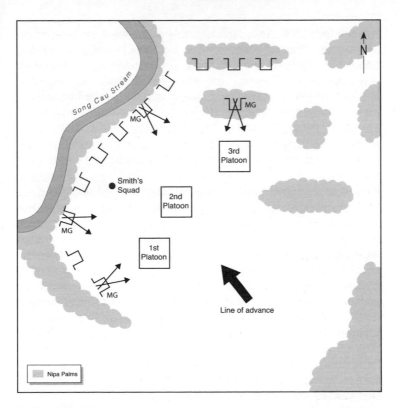

Battle of July 11

attempt to reach the dead. Instead he gave the most difficult order of his career: 2nd Platoon was to fall back into a nearby tree line and set up a night defensive position. Mike Cramer could hardly believe it. Eakins, Ferro, and the rest were out there, maybe wounded and needing help, just a few feet from the enemy. And now they were going to be marooned out there alone all night.

Within moments of the opening burst of fire, Captain Lind realized that Benedick, with 2nd Platoon pinned down and a squad perhaps lost, needed help. Lind radioed the situation to battalion. Both Alpha and Bravo companies, though, had also met dug-in enemy forces of company strength. Neither would be able to reach Charlie Company that day. With no help, and with artillery and air strikes largely ineffective, Lind ordered both 3rd and 1st platoons to move to try to flank the Viet Cong position and take pressure off 2nd Platoon. On the company left flank, 1st Platoon, under Lieutenant Hunt, moved to make up the distance and linked up with 2nd Platoon. But when Hunt's men moved past the final tree line and out into the open, they, too, fell under heavy fire and were pinned down. The enemy bunker line was so extensive, running for about 300 yards in a gentle U shape, that 1st Platoon was unable to maneuver and could only offer covering fire. While the others in 1st Platoon went about the business of war, newbie Ernie Hartman couldn't help just lying there a moment and wondering what the hell was going on. Those were real bullets cracking overhead and slamming into the rice paddy dike. Those were real Viet Cong, and they were trying to kill him. Getting his bearings, Hartman joined his platoon mates in returning fire, and realized that he was trying to kill someone. The noise, the confusion, the yelling, and the fear. It – war – was real in all its awful beauty. Hartman began to realize what the veterans in his platoon felt and why they felt it. Hartman began to fit in. Further down the line, two of the 1st Platoon originals, John Young and John Sclimenti, were also hard at work pouring fire onto the enemy positions. As "old" veterans, they reacted to the battle differently. Realizing that 2nd Platoon had taken casualties, Sclimenti looked over at Young and yelled above the din "Young! Man, I hope that they didn't get any of the old timers."

While on the ATCs that morning making their way to the battlefield, Fred Kenney sat with Tom Conroy in 3rd Platoon sharing the newest pictures of his son. While Conroy looked at the pictures, and Kenney regaled him with stories about what Freddie was going to be when he grew up, a replacement walked by to take a look as well. The newbie looked at Kenney and then at Conroy and then back again before asking if the two were brothers. Both Kenney and Conroy got a good laugh at that. Before the pair left the ATC, Conroy, who was newly married himself, couldn't help but wonder what it would be like to get home to his wife Vivian and start his own family. It seemed like this new operation was off to a good start. There had been no contact early in the morning, maybe there wouldn't be any in the afternoon either. As Smith's squad of 2nd Platoon worked its way forward into the open rice paddy, Hoskins' platoon was a bit more bunched together as it moved forward through a dense but small tree line on Charlie Company's right flank. Richard Rubio, who had been so close to Forrest Ramos and had grown up with Fred Kenney, had been walking point that day, followed closely by Fred Kenney and Larry Lukes. Just after 1:30pm, Kenney relieved Rubio of his duty on point and made his way ahead of the rest of the unit and into the narrow tree line. As soon as he stepped between the trees, a burst of fire caught Kenney full in the chest. Kenney crumpled to the ground with his arms folded tightly to his chest, yelling, "Someone help me! I'm hit! I'm hit!" Caught out in the open, Rubio and Lukes dropped where they were amid the heavy fire. Rubio screamed, "Kenney! NO! NO! NO!" He had lost two of his closest friends in only a matter of weeks.

Before the firing began, Hoskins' 3rd Platoon had closed to within 30 yards of the Viet Cong positions on the right side of the U-shaped Viet Cong bunker complex. The fire was intense and so heavy that it forced everyone to drop in place. Those lucky enough to have fallen behind some sort of cover did their best to return fire. Terry McBride did what he could with his M60 machine gun, but was not in the best of positions and could not even see the enemy bunkers. Rubio and Lukes, having been near the point, were exposed and vulnerable. McBride, though, was near a small sampan in the semi-flooded paddy and dragged it forward just far enough for Rubio and Lukes to use it as cover to fall back behind a small dike. Rubio then opened up with his M16, firing at VC who were visible for fleeting moments moving between their bunkers, but it jammed. Rubio then got another rifle from Tom Conroy, who was busy on the radio, and fired until it blew up in his hands, leaving him temporarily deafened.

Having dropped in the open off to the left of his point element alongside Tim Fischer, Hoskins looked around and noticed how close he was both to where Kenney had fallen and to the enemy positions. Always aggressive, the poet-soldier yelled to Fischer above the din, "We are close enough to assault that bunker line!" Watching as incoming fire kicked up dirt all around them, Fischer responded, "Are you sure about that?" Hoskins just yelled "Yeah!" Too far from Conroy and the radio, Fischer yelled as loud as he could to his right and left, "We are gonna go!" Seconds later Hoskins and Fischer jumped up and started running, but, having taken only three steps, Hoskins went down with a bullet in the thigh. Fischer flopped down beside him and asked, "What do you think now? Do we still need to do this?"

John Bradfield, the Cleveland draftee who loved to play soul music for the guys on his record player, had hit the dirt when the fire had started and switched his M16 to full automatic. He was crawling through the rice looking for the enemy bunkers when he caught a glimpse of movement: the enemy. He moved forward just a bit further and came face-to-face with Lieutenant Hoskins, who was carrying a revolver and a hand grenade. The two held their fire and Bradfield stifled a laugh. He had nearly killed the lieutenant! As Tim Fischer crawled into view, Hoskins told Bradfield to lay down covering fire. Seeing that Hoskins was wounded, Bradfield replied that he was going to get him some help. Hoskins shot back, "Son, I've got that under control. You start firing toward those enemy positions!"

Having taken cover wherever they could when the firing started, the other men of 3rd Platoon were scattered all over. Some were able to reach the meaningful cover of paddy dikes, while others, like Ron Vidovic, the divorced soldier with two children who had been drafted from Tacoma, and Jim "Porky" Johnson, were firing from vulnerable positions that were little more than small depressions in the ground. While Vidovic, McBride, Larry Lukes, and the other soldiers of 3rd Platoon swapped fire with the unseen enemy, the platoon medic Elijah Taylor yelled over to Hoskins, pleading to be allowed a chance to go and get Kenney. Taylor screamed that he might still be alive, but Hoskins refused. The lieutenant knew all too well that getting up and trying to move under that fire meant certain death. From behind what cover they could find, all over the battlefield members of the 3rd Platoon fired everything they had at the enemy positions, but nothing seemed to do any good. The Viet Cong were too well entrenched and too numerous. What few artillery rounds and air strikes came in had no effect. The VC fire simply would not slacken. In desperation Hoskins yelled to Conroy to get on the horn and call in smoke rounds; maybe a smokescreen would allow someone to reach Kenney and give any others still stranded in the open a chance to reach cover. The rounds detonated on target, but the smoke blew away too quickly to be of any use.

With night closing in and the paddy flooding as the tide rose, Hoskins knew that he had to get his men back to some kind of cover and form a coherent defensive position. Orders were screamed from man to man. "Hoskins is calling in smoke and we're all gonna pull back!" Terry McBride, Tom Conroy, and many others shouted back that they wanted one chance to crawl out to Kenney. How could they pull back and just leave him there? But each time they moved, the enemy fire was too intense. Kenney was too far away, too exposed. They would have to fall back without him. Since Hoskins was wounded and could no longer crawl, Tim Fischer came up with the idea of blowing up his air mattress. When the smoke came in, Vidovic and Johnson provided covering fire as Fischer dragged Hoskins away. Before all of the smoke cleared, Vidovic and Johnson scrambled to their feet and ran to cover in the rear, diving over a final paddy dike as bullets slapped into the mud all around.

The unit gathered in the safety of a small tree line and dug in for the hardest night that many of the men would ever know. Richard Rubio was disconsolate. He had been so close to Kenney when he was hit, had seen it so clearly. He knew that his friend was dead; nobody could have survived that wound, but he had to try to get to him. He couldn't just leave Kenney out there all alone. In the intermittent flashes of artillery fire and the ghostly glow of illumination rounds, the men of 3rd Platoon caught glimpses of the VC moving around on the battlefield. What would happen if they found Kenney? Rubio, Lukes, Fischer, John Howell, Terry McBride, and Elijah Taylor just couldn't take it anymore. The little group part crawled and part swam through the paddy water toward where they knew Kenney to be. As the group crawled along, John Howell, who had spent much of the day so close to enemy lines that a US air strike had coated him in mud, heard someone whisper Kenney's name. But the Viet Cong must have heard it too, because a blaze of fire erupted from the enemy positions. It was just too dark, the fire was too heavy, and the risk too great, so they pulled back to wait for morning.

Frank Schwan had kept fading in and out of consciousness during the afternoon, often vomiting up blood. But as darkness began to fall a growing fear snapped him fully awake. There was going to be no rescue attempt by 2nd Platoon or anyone else. He and Hubbard were alone. Schwan knew what would happen when it got fully dark – the Viet Cong would come looking for them. Rolling over on his side, Schwan looked at Hubbard and said, "We had better get ready for them. I ain't planning on dying without taking a few of them with me." Schwan then took out two grenades, looped his finger through the pin of one and gave the other to Hubbard. Having fought bravely alongside Schwan all day, Hubbard gritted his teeth and nodded. He knew what they had to do. The two men slid down low behind the rice paddy dike, with little but their heads sticking out of the water, and listened. Here and there were the sounds of tiny splashes and hushed voices. The Viet Cong were combing the flooded fields looking for them. As the voices came nearer and nearer, Schwan and Hubbard tried not even to breathe. The Viet Cong paused only a few feet away and stood silently for a few seconds. The tension was unbearable. Then the Vietnamese began chatting again and their voices and splashing receded into the distance. Letting out a long, quiet sigh, Schwan realized that they had gotten lucky. If they stayed put they were dead men; they had to risk sneaking away before the VC came back. Schwan whispered to Hubbard, "Come on. I'm not going to die in this shit hole."

The two crawled with agonizing slowness through the paddy water, moving as noiselessly as possible toward what they hoped were friendly positions. After crawling for 30 yards, and what seemed an eternity, Schwan and Hubbard reached a sizeable paddy dike, which allowed them to walk stooped over without being seen. Hubbard helped Schwan along, who had to stop on occasion to throw up blood. Several times the pair had to drop in place and hold their breath to avoid notice of the wandering Viet Cong patrols. Schwan and Hubbard had only just gotten to their feet again after a brush with the Viet Cong when an illumination flare lit up the entire battlefield. The two threw themselves down in near panic, hoping that they had not been seen. The sudden movement set Schwan's body afire with pain, and he writhed silently in the water as the flare slowly went out. To the pair's surprise, the VC didn't come, and their journey could continue. After what seemed like hours of crawling and stumbling in the darkness, Schwan and Hubbard came to a raised burial mound dotted with graves and small bushes. Estimating that they had covered hundreds of yards, Schwan reasoned that they were nearing friendly lines and told Hubbard that they should stop and take cover. Moving any farther meant running the risk of being shot by their own friends. Huddled behind one of the larger grave mounds, Schwan and Hubbard waited for first light. Far too frightened to sleep, Schwan kept vomiting blood and wondered if he would survive the night.

It was a long night for the members of Lieutenant Benedick's 2nd Platoon. Everyone had known the members of Sergeant Smith's squad well, knew their hopes and dreams, wives and girlfriends – and they had left them behind. Benedick put a stop to all thoughts of any rescue mission. It was too far and too dangerous. Those guys were dead, and there was no use in losing more men to retrieve their bodies. Mike Cramer didn't quite know how to handle it. Three of his best friends were out there, maybe wounded, and here he sat doing nothing? It was almost more than he could bear. Then he saw the lights. Red lights – the red map lights on the end of every GI flashlight. The lights were pointing in the direction of the 2nd Platoon and waving slightly. Somebody was alive out there and signaling for help! They just had to go now, had to launch a rescue mission. Benedick calmed Cramer down and told him that the lights were not being waved by anybody in Smith's squad. It was the VC, who were looting the bodies, trying to lure them out.

At the first hint of light Schwan and Hubbard crawled as far toward the lines of 2nd Platoon as they dared, and then Schwan took a chance and yelled "Hey Lopez, this is Schwan, Frank Schwan. Don't shoot!" Mario Lopez, a Charlie Company original from Calexico, California, couldn't believe his ears. Schwan and Hubbard both stood up after they saw Lopez lift his head just above the rice paddy dike. Lopez yelled, "It's them! They're alive!" Seconds later several members of 2nd Platoon jumped over the paddy dike and helped Schwan and Hubbard to safety, buzzing with questions about how they had survived. Cramer was happy to see anyone from Smith's squad; it was a true miracle. But he didn't see his buddies Eakins, Ferro, and King. His hopes had been raised, only to be dashed again.

A few minutes later 2nd Platoon moved out across the rice paddy toward enemy lines. The men walked slowly, not knowing what to expect. Were there booby traps? Were the Viet Cong still there in force? Was there going to be another firefight? As Benedick neared the site of the previous day's fighting, it became apparent that the Viet Cong had fled during the night. He first found the body of Harold Wayne King, surrounded by bullet casings where the young draftee had fought to the death. Benedick then came upon the bodies of Smith, Ferro, and Eakins. All of their weapons were gone, their shirts were open indicating that their bodies had been looted, and two had been shot in the head by the Viet Cong during the night. Mike Cramer walked up and knelt between the bodies of Eakins and Ferro, such good friends who had died only feet apart in Vietnam so far away from home. With tears in his eyes, Cramer couldn't help humming a bit of Eakins' favorite song, "Above and Beyond," as he covered his best friend with his poncho. Just the day before, Cramer had walked with Eakins and Ferro in the heat talking about seemingly everything under the sun, and now they were gone. It was all so quick, and all so painful. He wondered how Phil's wife and family would feel, learning of his death even as they were getting ready to visit him in Hawaii. He wondered if he would ever have friends as good as these again. He wondered if he could ever have friends at all again – it hurt so bad to lose them. Cramer remained with Eakins and Ferro until the dustoffs came to collect the bodies. Then, in a whirl of rotors and a downward blast of air, they were gone, and the war went on.

Benedick and his men then went on to sweep through the Viet Cong bunker complex. It was massive, and from it the men could see that Smith's squad had been caught in a deadly crossfire. They never had a chance, making the survival of Schwan and Hubbard all the more miraculous. That the VC were gone filled the men with rage – 2nd Platoon had lost an entire squad. Everyone had lost friends, but there were no dead VC, none. There were not even blood trails – just a few pitiful bullet holes around the bunkers. Their friends were dead and the VC had gotten away scot-free. The sons of bitches didn't even stand and fight like men. It was an impotent and frustrated rage with no outlet. The men of 2nd Platoon explored the bunkers by fire – shooting into them or tossing in grenades before they looked in. They hoped that there was someone inside, hoped that someone would die. Lieutenant Benedick was right there with his men, carrying his sawed-off shotgun. When he reached one small bunker, he thrust the barrel of his weapon inside and fired. After the deafening report, there was a bit of moaning and then silence. Benedick looked inside to find the body of a Viet Cong soldier he had just shot. Someone, at least, had paid the price.

With Sergeant Joe Marr now in command since Lieutenant Hoskins had been wounded, 3rd Platoon also made its way slowly back across its own battlefield that morning against little resistance. One sniper round managed to strike home, though, wounding John Howell badly in the thigh. After the fire and commotion ceased, everyone searched the still-flooded paddy for Fred Kenney. After nearly an hour, Tim Fischer yelled "Over here!" He had nearly stumbled over Kenney, who was half-submerged in the water. Fischer took Kenney's legs, and Tom Conroy took his arms to hoist Kenney out of the mud. The paddy water drained in a torrent from a gaping wound in Kenney's chest, a wound directly into his heart. He had died almost instantly. When Fischer and Conroy shifted the body to carry it to higher ground, a spurt of blood jetted out and hit Conroy. It is his last coherent memory of his time in Vietnam. He remained in country until January, and fought in more battles, but because of the shock of that single moment, the rest of his tour is just a haze. Fischer and Conroy carried Kenney to a nearby paddy dike and put him back down to wait for the dustoff. His weapon was gone, as were his watch and his wedding ring. Richard Rubio, Larry Lukes, and several others just stopped where they were and sat down in the mud to cry. Soldiers, tough soldiers like them who had been through so much, were not supposed to act that way. But Fred Kenney, "Cool Wig," was special. He had been everybody's friend. So happy, so ready to lend a hand to anyone who was down. So full of unbridled joy in his fatherhood. Fred Kenney more than anyone else was supposed to make it home, supposed to meet his child, supposed to teach Freddie how to ride a motorcycle, supposed to live. For just a few fleeting moments the Vietnam War stopped as Fred Kenney's friends in 3rd Platoon paused to mourn his passing.

Enraged by what they had found, the men of 3rd Platoon went on to search the Viet Cong bunker complex hoping that someone would be there, spoiling for a fight. But, as with 2nd Platoon, there was nobody there, no focus for 3rd Platoon's anger. In the battle area near where Kenney had fallen, there was a scattering of hooches, not really a village or even a hamlet – just a few, solitary dwellings. Nobody really knows who did it first, but soon one of the hooches went up in flames. Then they all went up in flames. It wasn't the revenge that 3rd Platoon wanted, but it was just going to have to do.

Frank Schwan drifted in and out of consciousness on the helicopter ride to the hospital outside Saigon while battlefield scenes of Eakins, Ferro, Smith, and King kept replaying in his mind. He was safe and reasonably sure that he was going to live. But had he done enough for them? Could he have done anything more? Hustled off of the helicopter, Schwan first met a nurse who asked him where and when he had been wounded. He replied that he had been hit in the stomach and shoulder but that it had happened the day before. Her expression changing, the nurse shoved him through the other patients, saying, "He is next for surgery!" The doctors took a quick look at Schwan's wounds, but there was little that they could do but stabilize him; injuries like his needed to be treated by military specialists in Japan. With drains in both his stomach and back, and an IV hooked up to his shoulder, Schwan was placed on a jet bound for the military hospital in Camp Zama, Japan, where a doctor looked him over and immediately broke into a string of cursing. Schwan's chest drainage tube had been placed incorrectly, and, if it had fallen off during transit, his lung would have collapsed, which might have resulted in his death. After a string of surgeries, which he was sure would leave him one heck of a scar, Schwan was finally able to contact his parents, who were so concerned that they threatened to get on the next plane to Japan. After talking his father out of the idea, Schwan went on to a lengthy recuperation, weak both from his wounds and from a significant loss of weight after his surgeries. Young and healthy, Schwan recovered relatively quickly, which raised the prospect of him returning to Vietnam in November to serve out the remainder of his tour. Still concerned with his weight loss, though, the doctors decided to keep him in Japan for a while longer, after which he returned to Cleveland before serving out his time at Fort Knox, Kentucky.

Phil Ferro's sister Diane had just given birth to her second son, so she knew that something was wrong when she had gotten word to rush over to her parents' house. When she pulled up she saw too many cars, many of which looked official, outside her family's Northridge home. The scene when she opened the door told her all she needed to know. Two immaculately dressed military officers were sitting on the couch, while her mother Helen sobbed uncontrollably nearby. Tony, normally stoic, was sitting in his favorite chair in front of the fireplace, slumped over with his head held in his hands and weeping openly. Phil, her brother, best friend, and protector, was dead. It was the worst day of their lives. The officers did their jobs well, consoling everyone and promising that a military escort would be with Phil during his entire journey home. Amid her own grief, Helen Ferro was determined to look out for the needs of others. Helen realized that Marie Reynolds, who had helped her with her community care packages, would read about Charlie Company's recent battle in the newspaper. Not wanting Marie to worry about her own son, Bill Reynolds, Helen got on the phone and told Marie that there had been a battle, and, that while her own son Phil had been killed, that Bill was fine. A few days later, Tony had to go identify Phil at Lorenzo's Funeral Home. He went in alone and came out shaken. It was Phil, but that was all he said. The funeral service was beautiful, with a big crowd of Phil's many friends and admirers coming out to pay their respects. Phil Ferro was laid to rest in Chatsworth, California, and the Ferro family would never be the same. Two weeks later Diane received Phil's last letter home from Vietnam congratulating her on the birth of her second child. Diane knew that life would go on, but much of the joy of life was gone.

Barbara Kenney had recently moved to Cottonwood, California, to be with her mother. She didn't really like the small town; all of her friends – the Kenney circle of friends – were still in the San Fernando Valley. She wanted to be with them and to be part of their lives, but she needed her mother's help with little Freddie. To have some fun, Barbara's mother suggested that they all drive to San Francisco to see her grandparents. The day started well enough, and it was a pretty drive. But they arrived to find Barbara's grandparents in tears. They had just received a telegram that Fred was missing in action. Holding on to little Freddie tighter than ever, Barbara felt her blood run cold. Missing in action? That meant that there was a good chance that he was still alive. Together the family drove back to Cottonwood to await news. It was the longest drive of Barbara's life; the hours passed in silence, uncertainty, and fear. The next morning there was a knock at the door, and Barbara opened it to find two officers in their dress uniforms. They regretted to inform her that her husband, Elmer Kenney, had been killed in action. The whole family began to weep as Barbara slumped into the nearest chair. Fred, her Fred, was gone. He had been everything to her. Now he was gone, and he had never even had the chance to meet his son. She then looked at little Freddie, mercifully asleep, and despaired that the poor little guy was going to have to grow up without his dad. It all settled on her like some great weight. She was 21, had a five-month-old son, and was now alone. In a fog of grief Barbara Kenney did what she had to do: return to Canoga Park, go to the funeral home, help plan the funeral, and go to the ceremony. People came from all around to pay their last respects to Fred Kenney. It was a beautiful service. The military honor guard presented Barbara the folded flag with great dignity and respect before the 21-gun salute signaled an end to the ceremony. Barbara could not stand to leave Canoga Park again. She had to be near Fred and those who shared his memory. It dulled the pain to have someone with whom to share it, someone to talk to about Fred and the good times. At first Barbara and little Freddie moved in with Fred's sister Mary Lou, but after only a few months she moved again, this time to live with her own sister just down the road in Woodland Hills. Barbara was among friends and family, people who had known and loved Fred, but still she felt so terribly alone. All of her friends were planning their lives, had relationships, were thinking of marriage, and were looking to the future. But for Barbara, at the age of 21, life seemed to be over. She wanted normalcy and happiness, not only for herself but especially for her son Freddie. But she was not sure how she would ever be able to find normalcy and happiness again.

While families in the United States mourned the loss of the young men who had been killed on July 11, life for Charlie Company, and the war, continued. There was little time for Cramer, Burleson, Conroy, Fischer, and all the other men to process events. The unit kept up its daily routine of running search-and-destroy missions both near Can Giouc and in Long An Province – missions that could prove deadly to anyone who lost focus. Mourning and grief would have to be left until later. Living took precedence.

After a series of cat-and-mouse operations in which the MRF and the 4th of the 47th tried to corner the Viet Cong again, only to run into booby traps and ubiquitous sniper fire, wonderful news filtered down to the tired soldiers. It was their turn to rotate out of the field; they would spend August on perimeter duty at Dong Tam. While it was still a war zone, the men all now saw Dong Tam duty as gravy. There would be patrols and bunker duty, but there would be no battles. Charlie Company would finally be able to rest and recover from its wounds. The news came in, though, while the unit was engaged in a search and destroy operation in the Cam Son Secret Zone, an area known as a hive of Viet Cong activity. Whenever it operated there, Charlie Company always seemed to take losses, especially to snipers and booby traps. Despite the good news, nobody could let his guard down.

As night fell on July 28, 1st Platoon set up its defensive positions around a clutch of hooches near one of the Mekong Delta's many small streams. The day had been tense but had passed without serious incident. As usual the company had found signs that the Viet Cong might be near, locating and destroying 52 bunkers and detaining for interrogation 26 civilians suspected of being Viet Cong. For the veteran soldiers such finds were nothing new. The Mekong was honeycombed with bunkers, and Viet Cong sympathizers were everywhere. Viet Cong main force units could be anywhere, in bunkers in the next tree line or nowhere at all. It was all part of the deadly game of war in the delta. With no special reason to fear, only the constant possibility of death, 1st Platoon spent the night on 50 percent alert. The next morning welcome news arrived. Helicopters were on the way to pick up Charlie Company; maybe to take it to its anticipated downtime at Dong Tam. The men of 1st Squad began to get ready for the move. Inside one hooch, which was really just four poles with a thatched roof, Ernie Hartman chatted with one of the other replacements while getting in a quick shave. In the far corner James Nall, who had been the first to learn of the birth of Don Peterson's son on the train ride back to Fort Riley, sat cleaning his weapon and getting ready to move out.

A few yards distant, John Young, the squad leader, was sitting on a log that stuck out over the river sipping coffee, his feet nearly dangling in the water. With his sleeves rolled up to cover his sergeant's stripes, a common practice in the delta where snipers always aimed first for those in positions of command, Young gazed absently at the dense tree line on the far bank of the stream, only 20 yards away. Young enjoyed the rare moment of calm. There was nothing to fear, and the choppers were on their way to take them to the safety of the division base. Hell, it was not even quite as hot as usual. Back near the hooch where Young had spent the night, John Sclimenti was finishing his watch. As Sclimenti walked back toward the hooch, Benny Bridges came out, carrying a stool, and sat down in an open area next to a small trail to take his turn as sentry and hollered back over his shoulder for Sclimenti to bring him some chow when he had the time.

Cecil Benny Bridges was a lanky 20-year-old from Carthage, Texas. Raised on a farm, Bridges was a country boy and an original

Charlie Company draftee who was reputed to have the best southern drawl in the entire unit. While on leave after training, Bridges had returned to east Texas to marry his high school girlfriend. In Vietnam, Bridges stood out as a competent and hard-working soldier, always performing well and without complaint as Charlie Company moved from one battle to another. Bridges became especially close to Danny Bailey, the country boy from Arkansas who had been wounded by a booby trap in the Rung Sat during April in the same incident that had killed Lieutenant Black. The two loved to talk about hunting, fishing, and farming, chatting in a slow cadence and with a twang that made the others in the platoon smile nearly every time they passed by. In June 1967, John Young decided to replace John Bauler as his 1st Squad RTO. The Viet Cong saw RTOs as prime targets, and Young believed the position to be too dangerous to leave in one man's hands for too long. Knowing that his new RTO had to be a thoroughly dependable veteran, Young immediately thought of Benny Bridges. When asked to serve as an RTO, Bridges jokingly put on his best southern drawl and replied, "But sarge, I ain't no RTO, 'ahm a rafleman!" After Young got through laughing, Bridges had taken the radio, and the two had become a nearly inseparable team, with Bridges sometimes even answering Young's questions before he asked them.

While Sclimenti was in the hooch trying to scare up some grub, Bridges got a call on the radio. The helicopters were inbound, and it was time to form up. Instead of walking the few feet to Young, who was finishing his coffee, Bridges just stood up and said, "Get ready to move out." Bridges had given an order. Young dumped the dregs of his coffee in the river, Hartman finished his shave, Sclimenti finally located some breakfast, and the rest of 1st Squad began to shoulder its gear. Young walked back to Bridges to pat him on the shoulder before getting his own equipment. One step before Young reached Bridges, a single shot rang out, followed by a BRRRRRRRRP of automatic fire. A Viet Cong sniper had been lurking in the tree line across the river, just a few feet away from where John Young had been sitting. He had 1st Squad dead to rights. Trained to take out the leaders first, the sniper had waited to see who would give an order. It was Benny Bridges.

The side of Bridges' head exploded with the impact of the first round, covering John Young's arm, which had been extended toward him, with blood and grey matter. The quick burst of automatic fire blasted through the hooch, sending thatch and dust flying everywhere. The rounds wounded Joel Segaster, a replacement sent from another battalion, in the stomach and struck Ernie Hartman in the leg and the back. For just a moment, John Young was in shock as he watched Benny Bridges collapse next to him. Inside the hooch James Nall didn't even flinch. Firing that close had to be outgoing friendly fire. Then he saw Segaster and Hartman. Hell, it was enemy fire! Nall ran to Segaster and Hartman, while Sclimenti grabbed his rifle and ducked outside with Danny Bailey, who had been talking to Bridges just before he had gone on guard duty. They emerged to find Ben Acevedo pointing at the tree line across the river and shouting, "He's right there! He's right there!" With the seconds slowing to a crawl in the adrenaline rush of battle, Sclimenti and Bailey looked on as Bridges slumped to the ground and Sclimenti thought, "Oh my God. I was there only a couple of seconds ago," before lowering his rifle to fire into the tree line. With his M16 on full automatic, shell casings flew everywhere, one striking a replacement named Nelson in the eye while he stood firing his own weapon.

Recovering from the initial brutality of the moment, John Young grabbed up Ernie Hartman's fallen machine gun and shot the entire belt into the far tree line in one continuous burst. There was no target for anyone to aim at, no bunker or enemy silhouette. In a blind rage they all just shot – at anything. Death had been so near, so immediate, and it had come in such a rare moment of calm that it had nearly unhinged everyone. Bits of trees and mud flew everywhere, and then the firing stopped. In the silence that followed there was no sign of the sniper, only the moans of Hartman and Segaster, and a weak gurgling from the fallen Bridges. Young ran the few steps back to Bridges, and, using the radio that was still on his back, informed Captain Lind that 1st Squad had four men down and needed a medevac. Young then looked down at his RTO and could only mumble, "Jesus, Benny." Young elevated Bridges' head to ease his shallow breathing and sat there with him until the medics arrived. A small group gathered to look at the scene in silence. Nall, Sclimenti, and Bailey could only stand and stare at their dying friend. They were helpless. Sitting there holding Bridges, the thoughts blazed through Young's mind like a white-hot light. "Goddamn it, Young! It's your fault. That sniper shot Benny because he thought he was you. You should have given that order. You should have had your men farther from the river. You should have… It's all your fault."

Medics and several volunteers carried Ernie Hartman, hit several times by the brief burst of fire, back to a landing zone where they would meet the medevacs. As the medics went about their business, Hartman took stock of his situation. He was bad, but not too bad. His dull pain, though, quickly turned to near panic when he finally noticed that his crotch was bloody and hurt like holy hell. Had his dick been shot off? Too afraid to look, Hartman called for the medic, who pulled down his trousers to find a small, but horribly painful, wound to Hartman's testicles. The medic assured Hartman that the wound was nothing to be worried about and that he would be OK. Relieved, Hartman looked up from his pain to take in the scene around him. Waiting for the helicopter were the other 1st Squad wounded all around him. Nelson couldn't believe his own bad luck. Hit in the eye by a shell casing? It wasn't bleeding badly, but he couldn't see. His eye was pretty much gone. Joel Segaster had a large bandage across his stomach and was plainly in agony. But Jo Jo, as he was known to the guys, seemed oddly calm and even happy. He looked at Hartman and told him that this was his third Purple Heart. He was gonna get the hell out of Vietnam. Hartman then thought back to everything he had been through since he had joined Charlie Company on June 20 – the incident with the VC prisoner, the battle of July 11, and now this? It had only been five weeks. How was he going to survive another 11 months in Vietnam?

Captain Lind had always liked Benny Bridges. The country boy from Texas had been a good soldier from the start, hard working and dedicated. To Lind, Bridges just seemed to represent the best of American youth. After hearing that he was badly wounded, Lind made his way to the landing zone and sat with Bridges while waiting for the helicopter to land. Lind knelt next to Bridges and took his hand, shocked by the severity of his wounds. Bridges opened his eyes for just a brief moment and asked, "Sir, I'm not going to make it, am I?" Amazed that Bridges was able to talk at all, Lind replied, "No, son, I don't think so." It was the hardest thing that Captain Herbert Lind ever had to say. Just a few seconds later, as a violent downblast of air blew leaves and bits of thatch in every direction heralding the arrival of the medevac, Lind felt Benny Bridges' hand go slack.

The next morning, safely back on the barracks ships, John Young went into the galley to get a cup of coffee. He had not been able to get any sleep that night and had a feeling that sleep might be hard to come by for a long time. Every time he closed his eyes, he saw Benny Bridges. His job had been to bring his boys home safely. He had worked so hard, worked his men so hard. And now in a flash, in a matter of a couple of seconds, he had lost half of his squad. He had failed. He was responsible. That responsibility, a tangible weight on his shoulders, was crushing. Strangling. Taking the first few sips of coffee, Young noticed that he was not alone in the galley. There, sitting at a table all alone, was Danny Bailey. Young walked over and sat next to Bailey, who was busy writing a letter. Young glanced down at the script, big, clumsy letters – almost childlike handwriting. Young then noticed what Bailey had written: "Dear Mom, Yesterday my best friend got killed." The phrase hit Young like a physical blow. "My best friend got killed." Big tears rolled from Danny Bailey's eyes as he struggled with the words. Young put his hand on Bailey's shoulder and said, "Danny, I'm so sorry I lost him, so sorry I lost him." Danny Bailey looked up from his letter, brushed away the tears and responded, "Sergeant Young, don't worry about it. It wasn't your fault." But the responsibility, all that weight, remained.

7 CHARLIE TRANSFORMED, BATTLEFIELD CODA, AND THE FREEDOM BIRD

Sept. 24, 1967

Dear Mom, Dad, and Kids,

We got back from a mission yesterday. Everyone was so damn tired cuz we walked around 14,000 meters in three days in this area that was so thick at times you couldn't see ten feet in front of you. We had to use machetes all the way, and we ran into booby traps, punji traps, and sniper fire all the way also...

How is everyone at home? I pray this letter finds all of you in the best of health. I wonder about all of you so much. Sometimes I just sit and wonder if everyone looks the same as they did when I left. Over here, though, a guy thinks about almost anything.

Well I wonder when I'll be home. I don't know if I'll be home for Christmas or not. I really hope I am. I heard we'd rotate the 22nd of December, but that was just a rumor... God I hope all of us make it home for Christmas. That's all anybody ever talks about.

Mom and Dad, you know we only have around 30 guys left in our company that came over here the same time I did. We came over with 160 or something like that, and we only have 30 left... I think if I hear about much more fighting I'll lose my mind. I'm so sick and tired of hunting and being hunted. All I want is to come home and lead a normal life...

Well, it's about closing time I guess so tell everyone I said, "Hi."

Your loving Son in Viet Nam,

Steve [Hopper]

The Charlie Company that returned to Dong Tam in August 1967 had seen over two months of almost constant combat since its initial battle of May 15 – sometimes in great waves of destruction, as on June 19 or July 11, but more often than not it had been a slow soul-wrenching grind of death, maiming, and killing. It seemed like a lifetime to the bone-weary men who unloaded their gear from the ATCs and trudged, in ones and twos, across the sea of mud to their barracks. Some of their conversations centered on how good it was to be back at Dong Tam. They knew that there would be mud and tedium, but working in the Dong Tam Area of Operations (AO) was gravy. Nobody would die. Instead of looking forward, though, many of the battle-hardened veterans of Charlie Company looked back – back at what they had lost. Back at who they had once been.

So many good men were dead – Lieutenant Black, Ron Schworer, Don Peterson, Kenny Frakes, Robert Cara, Hubert Fink, Robert Jindra, Cameron Rice, David Robin, George Smith, John Winters, Lieutenant Schulman, Bill Geier, Forrest Ramos, Tim Johnson, Phil Ferro, Butch Eakins, Harold King, Fred Kenney, and Benny Bridges. Then there were the men – too many for most to remember – who had been lost to brutal, ghastly wounds. It hurt too badly to try to remember them all. Medic Elijah Taylor had to go and sit alone for a few moments to gather himself amid the foreign silence – a calm without battle seemed so odd. He tried to remember the faces of his buddies, men he had held as they breathed their last. His memories of men who had once been so vibrant and happy, playing jokes and speaking of their loved ones, all seemed to end in blood and despair. It all seemed so wrong. Turning inward, Taylor realized that for everyone who had died, everyone who had been badly injured – a little bit of his soul had died as well. He was hollow.

The commonly held pain of losing friends, of the final brutalized moments of young lives, bound the men of Charlie Company together. Across the unit men like Ben Acevedo, John Sclimenti, Bill Reynolds, Clarence Shires, and Tim Fischer agreed that the mission, some nebulous idea of freedom for South Vietnam, no longer mattered. Their draft-day motivations no longer mattered. Who they had once been no longer mattered. Caring about and for each other – their few surviving friends – is what mattered. Being good soldiers, preparing for missions, and paying scrupulous attention to detail mattered, because by doing those things the men of Charlie Company would make it through the next patrol, the next day.

Many of the men refused to think about the fact that they still had four months left in country. Surviving for that long seemed impossible. Looking forward to the freedom bird home was a fool's game that could get you killed. It was better not to look beyond the next tripwire, the next tree line, the next sniper. Vietnam was alive with death, and the men of Charlie Company would have to pull together more closely than ever to cheat their fate. James Nall, who had come to the army from Fairfield, Alabama, was a changed man. Everything that had happened – charging the bunkers and killing so many VC on June 19, standing there while John Young held a dying Benny Bridges on July 29 – it all weighed him down. He played some James Brown on the record player, but it didn't help. So many of the guys he had known, the guys he had trained with, were gone – some with terrible wounds and others dead. The unit just wasn't the same any more. He wasn't the same anymore. All he wanted to do was to survive, to go home.

In a military sense, the unit's shared sense of professionalism and cohesion meant that Charlie Company had grown up, was an experienced and lethal military force. That maturity was due in part to resignation. Richard Rubio, who had watched helplessly as his buddy Forrest Ramos had fallen from the dustoff helicopter on

June 19, sat alone for a few minutes on the edge of his bunk lost in thought. He knew that he was going to die. Having seen the dangers, having seen so many of his friends broken and lost, he knew he was going to die. But with that realization came liberation. He was close to death – it was not frightening or shocking. It was just there. Death was no longer anything to be feared. For that reason, he no longer would be nervous in battle. He wouldn't make any mistakes. Resigning himself to death was his best chance for living.

Many also had to wrestle with the darker parts of their beings, especially among the members of 2nd and 3rd platoons. The loss of friends was one thing, but, in looting Fred Kenney's body and shooting two of the wounded left out on the battlefield on the night of July 11, the Viet Cong had crossed an invisible line. As the months and the battles had passed, many of the men of Charlie Company had developed a grudging respect for their resilient foes, but, for several, July 11 was the date on which that respect transformed into a primal hatred and desire for revenge. For Terry McBride, who had once sported a Viet Cong ponytail, the change was simple in its brutal elegance. Unable to find sleep as the events of the past month replayed on a continuous loop in his memory, McBride embraced the violence of the visions and decided: "After this I am going to make sure that any Viet Cong I meet are going to be dead." There would be no prisoners, no mercy, only death. Only a few bunks away lay Ron Vidovic, the divorced father of two from Tacoma, Washington, who had watched Fred Kenney fall on July 11. Kenney had been such a good guy, a good friend, and had so much to live for. Now some damn Viet Cong was out there with his wedding ring, having taken it from his lifeless hand. Vidovic felt his sorrow change to a quaking rage. Someone was going to pay. But then Vidovic came up short. What had happened to him? He had gone into the army hoping to find a better opportunity in life. He had gone to Vietnam to fight for a cause – to defend freedom in a faraway land. All of that was gone, and he felt himself becoming some sort of animal. What could he do? What kind of person had he become?

John Young, the enlistee from Minnesota, had always known why he was in Vietnam. He had chosen war, chosen the infantry, in an effort to honor the spirit of John F. Kennedy's generational call to service. Young had always pushed himself to be perfect, to do everything right – to lead. He had believed in the cause and had understood his responsibility as part of the military machine. Winning battles and defending the freedom of South Vietnam was the cause; the responsibility was to ensure the survival of the men under his care. As battles came and went, and the war shifted from an intellectual notion to a bloody reality, Young's understanding of his role in the conflict had subtly changed. With more old friends being killed or maimed every day, ephemeral notions of victory or freedom had faded into the background. The survival of his men had become everything for John Young. On July 4 Young had even decided that a Vietnamese prisoner had to die to avoid risking the lives of his own men. The decision had clashed with a lifetime of civilization, a lifetime of shared morals. The decision had hurt Young deeply. But it had been worth it. His men had survived. But with a single shot followed by a short burst of automatic fire from a sniper's rifle on July 29, John Young's world had come to ruin. Nearly half of his squad had been shot down in a matter of seconds. Those men had been his responsibility – he was supposed to bring them home safely to their loved ones and friends. He had failed. The cause that he had once believed in was gone, and the responsibility he had shouldered was now a crushing weight. Sitting outside the barracks in Dong Tam, while the cigarette dangling from his lips slowly turned to ash, John Young realized that he had nothing left to hang on to. Like so many within Charlie Company, John Young was adrift. He tried to put his feelings into words for his parents:

Dear Mom, Dad, and Girls,
My radioman died of the head wound he got on the 29th of July (he was shot by a sniper as I stood about 18 inches from him), another friend of mine lost one leg below the knee to a booby trap, and one of my men, who is from Minneapolis, lost an eye. Every time one of our men gets hurt or killed I wonder a little more whether or not this country is worth it. Being in the infantry is the best way to become a pacifist. I suppose that if I were not so close, so personally involved in the war, I would have no doubts about it all; but from where I stand the view is a little different. Men I have lived with for

a year and a quarter are not easy to lose. It is difficult to keep working when a friend dies.

I've been on the line since 18 January, and I've seen enough... I guess I've never told you, but being a combat leader is enough to drive anybody crazy. The responsibility, the pressure, and the necessity to lead 10 men, to make them get up and move when you yourself have trouble making your legs move because there are bullets flying all around you; well it's a damn hard job, and I've had the course. If I can get off the line, I'll sure do it...

Well, that's about it for now. Hope everybody is OK.

Love, John

Gary Maibach, Charlie Company's conscientious objector medic, had witnessed several soul-wrenching scenes in Vietnam. He had prayed with dying men and tried to comfort men who, at 20, would never walk again. But the scene he witnessed as the men of Charlie Company returned to Dong Tam hurt and frustrated him worse than any other he had yet encountered. So many of his friends, who such a short time ago had been carefree youths, had been spiritually wounded, morally battered and broken. Maibach, buoyed by his own deep faith, did what he could, which often meant just listening as his friends poured out their stories of sorrow, loss, and killing. Carefully, like a doctor gingerly probing the fresh wound of a trauma patient, Maibach offered what spiritual help he could. The violence and destruction had been more than some of the men could bear, leaving behind what Maibach thought to be a "God-shaped hole" in their lives. For the devout Maibach, it was the most crushing blow of all. The war had left these boys, and they were just boys after all, with a void where faith should have been. In the worst cases the souls of the men had become spiritually fallow fields. Beauty, hope, and godliness had been replaced by darkness and fear. It broke Maibach's heart to see these men – men who asked him to pray for them because they were too far gone to pray for themselves.

Charlie Company needed downtime – time to draw a deep collective breath after the exertions of war. The Dong Tam to which the company returned had changed a great deal since May and seemed to be the ideal place for Charlie Company to regroup. There were clubs for the officers, the NCOs, and the men, perfect for having a few drinks without being too worried about military discipline. The food was good. Heck, there were even cookouts with real steaks. There were volleyball courts, a place to play football, a rudimentary miniature golf course, and even a USO show starring Barbara Mandrell. But what everyone looked forward to most was the pool. On the day of its opening the soldiers of Charlie Company stripped down, sweaty and dirty, and gathered for an impromptu swimming party. Waiting at the gate, though, was a REMF (rear echelon motherfucker) of the highest quality. With feet splayed out to his sides he announced that the Charlie Company soldiers were not going to be allowed in the pool because they had ringworm. As his men grumbled and began to leave, Captain Lind got on the horn with the Dong Tam base commander who quickly made his way poolside and informed the REMF in question that the pool was for the benefit of combat soldiers. It was not his pool. It was their pool, and, ringworm or no, they were going for a swim. With the gates thrown open, the men of Charlie Company rushed the pool, in a flurry of cannonballs and belly flops. For a few happy minutes the teenagers within the warriors emerged. Splashing, diving – having fun. The water accepted them, didn't care about their sins. They were back on Pismo Beach, the banks of Lake Michigan, the local pond.

While the pool remained open to Charlie Company during the remainder of its stay at Dong Tam, the idyll of those first few golden moments soon passed. There was still a war out there. Lurking. A war to which Charlie Company would soon return. But for now there was Dong Tam. Sure there were patrols outside the berm. Sure a few mortar shells fell from time to time, forcing men to run for the bunkers. There were even a few brave snipers who risked taking pot shots at the berm or the upper stories of the larger buildings. There was both work and danger aplenty at Dong Tam. The military indeed seemed to specialize in inventing useless jobs to take up the men's time. Digging, building, guarding. But for the veterans of Charlie Company, the hard physical work at Dong Tam and the operations in the local AO seemed so easy as to be somehow relaxing. They weren't in mud up to their necks. They weren't waiting for an ambush from the next tree line. They weren't putting friends into body bags.

Each day a small human avalanche struck the soldiers manning the berm at Dong Tam: Vietnamese entrepreneurs selling everything from cold Cokes, to girls, to packs of cigarettes. More specialized vendors peddled cigarettes that looked perfectly normal, they even came in a real pack, but the tobacco had been removed and replaced with marijuana. Everything was for sale, and – determined to enjoy their relative freedom – many of the boys of Charlie Company were buying. Gary Maibach could certainly understand why his friends had to let go, had to forget. They were young, and they were lost. But he feared that some would become so badly lost that they might never find their way back. He realized that pushing them too hard would only push them further away, so he prodded gently by trying to set an example. He also used curmudgeonly good humor, often throwing his hands in the air and telling the malefactors in feigned indignation that "cats and dogs at home have better morals than you!"

While the men of Charlie Company still enjoyed the illicit pleasures of youth, there was no denying that they had been changed by their months in the field. Combat and fear had engendered a new and more somber outlook on life among the men. One task that most men in Charlie Company loathed was garbage detail. Every day men gathered the flotsam and jetsam of American life – spoiled food, old newspapers, discarded letters from home, tattered clothing – and hauled the resulting small mountain of refuse away downriver. As soon as each boat had dumped its load into the landfill and pulled away, hundreds of Vietnamese would emerge from the nearby tree line – old men, mothers, and children – to clamber over the steaming, rotting pile in search of something to eat. It was the children, filthy and clothed in little more than rags, that broke the men's hearts. After a few trips to the dump these hardened warriors, who were so closely acquainted with death, decided that they had to do something for those kids and chose to adopt a local orphanage. They brought the children rice, C Rations, and candy. They brought school supplies, and even managed to build the children a real swing set. The orphans and the warriors needed each other. Amid all the violence of their lives, several men in Charlie Company were brought to tears at that tiny orphanage. Especially for the parents who had left young ones behind in the States, while they were standing and pushing swings for laughing children, they felt – human.

As during their first stay at Dong Tam, the closest interactions between the GIs and the local population took place at the small bunker complex guarding the river entrance to the Dong Tam basin. The men reached the isolated positions by boat and remained there, near a small Vietnamese hamlet, for at least three days. One woman had turned her hooch into a bar, and children swarmed the bunkers to welcome the soldiers back. For Ron Vidovic, returning for a stint of guard duty at the bunker complex was like a tonic. The local children, one of whom Vidovic had dubbed "loudmouth," ran down to meet them as they emerged from the landing craft. Amazingly the children remembered each of the men from their last stay in the bunkers in May. They remembered what the men liked, and even what kind of candy they usually had to give away. Feeling some of the pain of the last two months ease, Vidovic stood there with his best friend Tim Fischer and talked with the children in pidgin English while the squad got settled. The proprietor of the local hooch bar soon turned up with warm beer and freshly peeled pineapples, and the group sat down and spent a wonderful day in peace. Tim Fischer added to the feast by shooting coconuts out of a nearby tree, and then trained his rifle on a passing rat. The children screamed at him not to shoot. They wanted to catch the rat for dinner. Even Terry McBride, who had always stood out as one of the toughest men in the platoon, couldn't help laughing.

In a bunker nearby, John Bradfield sat chatting with his buddy James "Smitty" Smith. The two had been close friends since Fort Riley. Both of the young black men were from the Cleveland area, they liked the same music, and were good soldiers. Their individual experiences over the past two months, Smith having been wounded in the fighting on May 15 and Bradfield having lost his close friend and running buddy Forrest Ramos in the fighting on June 19, had somehow brought them even closer. Whether absent-mindedly giving bits of their C Rations to the local children or just walking in file down a rice paddy dike, Bradfield and Smith hung together. Alone in their bunker, Bradfield told Smitty that he felt down; couldn't shake the idea that he was somehow responsible for his buddies dying or getting "mangled up." There was one particular vision he couldn't get out of his head – a horrible image that haunted the edge of his consciousness. He knew that it was there, waiting. Waiting for him to close his eyes, and then he would see it. The body of one of the mortar crew who had been lost on the PABs on that horrible day of June 19. A body floating in the water, without a shirt – staring vacantly at the sky in death. A body that mocked Bradfield. It was the body of someone he should have saved. Smitty cracked open one of the mamasan's warm beers, handed it to Bradfield, and said, "Don't worry man, it wasn't your fault. Ain't nothin' but a thing. One day you're gonna close your eyes and that body won't be there no more." Bradfield took a swig, grimaced a bit, and said, "Sure hope you're right."

During those few days in the bunkers near the tiny Vietnamese hamlet, the veterans of 3rd Platoon became an even more closely knit group. Vidovic and Fischer. Bradfield and Smitty. Terry McBride. They were closest to each other, but together they formed something of an exclusive group of friends. There were replacements around who were mostly good soldiers. But somehow they didn't count. Only the originals could remember the good times at Fort Riley, or the stop at Okinawa while on the *John Pope*, or Fred Kenney bragging on his beautiful wife. Only they could truly share the pain – losing Tim Johnson, Fred Kenney, Forrest Ramos. The originals were family. They kept to themselves, hung together – shared hopes of returning home and fears of never leaving Vietnam.

After nearly a week in the bunker complex, Vidovic, Fischer, Bradfield, Smitty, and the remainder of their squad got their gear together to leave. It was their turn to run a local patrol in the Dong Tam AO. As Vidovic and the others climbed aboard the ATC, John Young led his squad off the vessel. After all of the events of the past few months, Young looked forward to the normalcy, the peace, of spending time at the bunkers. There would be rest and time to reflect on things with a few of the remaining veterans of 1st Platoon. But most of all, there would be the children. Somehow he needed them, their innocence. They were an unmitigated good in a world that had been so bad. Maybe they could help him forget. Maybe they could help him dull the pain. Then the moment came. The children came running up and mobbed the men. While others were hugging soldiers or begging for candy, one little girl seemed a bit lost. She looked around at them all again and again. Finally she walked over to Young and said, "Where Benny?" The breath caught in Young's throat. It was the little girl who had become so close to Benny Bridges during their last stay in the bunker complex in May. Stooping over, Young placed his hand on the girl's shoulder and said, "I'm sorry honey. Benny's dead." The little girl broke into tears and ran back to her home in the small hamlet. As Young watched her run he realized that even here, where everything seemed so peaceful, there was no escaping the war.

While at Dong Tam, the component units of the 4th of the 47th were responsible for patrols meant to flush Viet Cong from the area and deter mortar attacks on the base. Such patrols hardly ever netted meaningful contact with enemy forces, which, especially in the run-up to the Tet Offensive of 1968, chose to steer clear of major engagements. However, local guerrillas often set mines and booby traps along the trails and paddy dikes that the US patrols travelled most heavily. Even if it was a "safe" area, nobody could let down their guard. On August 16, Jimmie Salazar was walking point as 2nd Platoon filed down a rice paddy toward a scattering of Vietnamese hooches. Somehow it didn't seem quite fair, walking point. He was doing a perfect job, watching closely for everything, but knew that his mind could wander at any moment. Only days before he had received a letter from home. Aurora, Salazar's young wife, had given birth to the couple's first child, a boy named Richard. The delivery had been complicated, but both mother and baby seemed to be doing well. He didn't have any pictures yet, but had celebrated his good fortune with the 2nd Platoon originals, complete with beer and a few cigars. It comforted Salazar greatly that day to see that the local farmers were hard at work. When civilians were around everything was likely to be OK. It was when they left, scurrying off into their bunkers and hiding places, that every GI in Charlie Company knew that something was wrong.

Searching hooches for contraband in the relatively peaceful Dong Tam AO was gravy, Salazar thought to himself, but he was still happy when his squad rotated off point duty and Ronnie Reynolds, nicknamed "the Penguin," took his turn at the lead of the file.

Ronnie Reynolds was from Malvern, Arkansas, where his father worked for a local shoe company. After high school Ronnie had spent a few adventurous months working in California, conveniently living next door to a tavern that he often frequented. Reynolds had just returned home to Arkansas in an effort to land a better job when he was drafted in the spring of 1966. One of the dwindling number of Charlie Company originals, Reynolds had been through it all; he had just made it across the stream in the Rung Sat when the helicopter had made its attack run and 2nd Platoon lost Ron Schworer. He had been returning fire across the canal on June 19 and had watched as Bill Geier was hit by enemy fire. He, along with the other men of 2nd Platoon, had not been able to get to the men lost on July 11. He had walked point countless times in Vietnam, on days that had been far more foreboding than August 16. He was on alert, but all was calm. It all seemed so routine, leading the platoon from one nondescript hooch to another. The next was, what, the 20th hooch they were going to search that day? As he drew near he saw a woman and her children sitting outside smiling at him. Nothing to hide. Then he felt the tripwire tighten and heard a short FIZZ of a fuse, and the world went black. Reynolds' body jerked above the first booby trap, a smallish device known as a "toe popper," and fell on top of a larger mine. The two detonations peppered Reynolds with hundreds of shell fragments, shattered one of his legs, and tore a chunk of meat out of the thigh of the other.

Bill Reynolds, the California draftee who had labored in vain to staunch Bill Geier's bleeding on June 19, took Ronnie Reynolds' hand and tried to remain upbeat. "Hey, buddy! You've got the million dollar wound. You're going home!" The medic was on the scene quickly and began to bandage the worst of Ronnie's wounds while waiting for the medevac. Following a path blazed by so many Charlie Company unfortunates before him, Ronnie Reynolds first went to a hospital in Saigon before making his way to Camp Zama, Japan, for extensive surgery. For days Ronnie couldn't bring himself to write to his parents to tell them that he had been wounded. He knew that they would be so worried. He was shipped home in November, in a wheelchair, and remained in a cast until the following March. For Ronnie Reynolds, August 16 had heralded the start of a painful recovery process. For the veterans of Charlie Company, August 16 was just another day – a day like so many in Vietnam – a day when another friend was lost.

Back at Dong Tam, 3rd Platoon made ready to move out on its own sweep of the Dong Tam AO. But Lieutenant Hoskins was still recovering from wounds he had received on July 11 and Sergeant Marr was away on leave. Since it was going to be just a walk in the sun, Tim Fischer, a squad leader, volunteered to take the platoon out on its mission. But Fischer was overruled, and 3rd Platoon got a fill-in commander – Lieutenant Sam Thompson. The same officer who had sent Dave Jarczewski's squad too far out into the rice paddies on May 15. The same officer who had put his pistol to Lance Morgan's head and ordered him forward on May 15. Thompson had been moving from job to job in the divisional base area back at Bear Cat since that difficult day in May, and now he was supposed to lead another platoon of Charlie Company into the field. Fischer knew Lieutenant Thompson's reputation for deadly inefficiency, and protested that he was better suited to lead 3rd Platoon on what was, after all, going to be a milk run. But there was nothing Fischer could do.

Thompson was in a hurry. In a hurry to fight the VC. Fischer knew that there were no VC out there, not in the Dong Tam AO anyway, but let the lieutenant have his way. After an uneventful day of walking through the heat, 3rd Platoon settled down in a night defensive position around a cluster of small hooches. The next morning much of the platoon stayed put, while a few fire teams scoured the surrounding area. The teams reported in on a regular rotation, and by late morning one got on the radio and told Fischer, who was acting as platoon sergeant, that the local farmers had begun disappearing. Fischer knew that meant land mines and radioed back for the team to be on the lookout for tripwires. Thompson excitedly jumped up from the ground saying, "The farmers are leaving? That means there are VC out there! Get the platoon together and ready to go!" Fischer couldn't believe how naïve and green one lieutenant could be. He tried to calm Thompson down and told him that there weren't any VC to get out there. They were too close to Dong Tam. The area was too open. There were no VC, just mines and booby traps waiting to kill unwary soldiers who went rushing into places they didn't need to go. The two men began to argue, but Thompson was adamant. As he gathered his gear Fischer thought helplessly to himself, "Christ. Someone is going to get hurt – and bad."

Ron Vidovic had been resting alone in the heat near where John Bradfield and Smitty were munching on bits and pieces they had taken from their C Rations – just another nearly inedible lunch on a hot day in the delta. There were a few water buffalo grazing nearby, and some local mamasans were having an animated discussion in their singsong language as they worked in the rice fields. As Vidovic absently wondered whether he should join Bradfield and Smitty, he couldn't help thinking that the scene was almost peaceful. Lieutenant Thompson, with Fischer walking closely behind, emerged from the hooch and yelled, "Get ready to move out!" With a few obligatory complaints, the members of 3rd Platoon got to their feet and began to slog through what seemed to be an unending series of paddies, dotted with dikes and a few raised grave mounds.

Thompson and Fischer, who was still fuming about the situation, watched from near the back of the file as 3rd Platoon inched across the paddies toward where Thompson hoped to find VC. After searching in vain for bunkers and other signs of enemy activity, the lead elements of the platoon were on their way back to report negative contact when, near the middle of the platoon's formation, a thunderous roar lifted Ron Vidovic skyward. Coming to after the explosion, Vidovic felt a pain in his chest. Was he about to die? No, the fall back to earth had only knocked the wind out of him. But then he looked at his legs, because, even though they didn't hurt, he knew something was wrong. They just didn't feel right. Then, for just a few seconds, Vidovic was unable to breathe. The lower part of one of his legs was gone, while the other was little more than a black, oozing mess. All he could do was sit and stare at where his leg used to be.

Tim Fischer couldn't believe his eyes as he watched his best friend Ron Vidovic go flying through the air. That goddamn lieutenant had ordered 3rd Platoon out on a wild goose chase, and now Vidovic might be dead. Cursing, Fischer took off through the rice paddy to reach his fallen friend. Thompson followed a little way behind, as many from the platoon moved in the direction of the action. Bradfield and Smitty, together as usual, had witnessed the explosion from a nearby rice paddy dike and had taken only a few steps toward Vidovic when there was a second explosion. Fragments from the grenade booby trap tossed Bradfield in one direction and Lieutenant Thompson in the other. After briefly blacking out, Bradfield looked around for his weapon, only to find out that it was still clutched in his hand. Somehow comforted that he had not lost his weapon, Bradfield sank into unconsciousness again. The last thing he heard was someone yelling, "Vidovic's leg is gone!"

Fischer had just reached Vidovic when he heard the second explosion. Looking around he saw Bradfield, Smitty, and Lieutenant Thompson all sprawled out and obviously wounded as the last of the smoke from the detonation drifted away on a slight breeze. The medic was busy with Vidovic, so there was little that Fischer could do but pat his buddy on the shoulder and assure him that everything was going to be all right. Certainly Fischer felt sorrow for his wounded comrade – they had shared so much and become so close – something they both knew to be dangerous in Vietnam where friends could disappear so quickly and painfully. What Fischer felt most, though, was rage. There was no way in hell that they should have been out there. There were no VC in this area. He had known it; all the veterans had known it. There were only mines. That idiot lieutenant had ordered them out. It was his fault. Fischer walked over to where Thompson lay. He had a few fragment wounds in his legs, and was kicking and wriggling an awful lot – but he would be fine. Fischer locked his gaze on Thompson and softly said, "I hope you're happy now, you son-of-a-bitch. You got what you deserved. I told you we didn't need to be out here." Thompson made no reply and instead struggled to break away from Fischer's accusing stare.

Ron Vidovic was joking around; he had to do anything he could to keep his mind off being a cripple – or worse. Terry McBride was there, tough-as-nails McBride. He wore a wry smile, no doubt in an effort to keep Vidovic's flagging hopes up. McBride leaned in saying, "Here Vidovic, take a smoke. In the John Wayne movies wounded guys always want smokes." Vidovic refused and glanced towards his crotch. McBride picked up on the meaning of that glance. He leaned in again and whispered in a stage voice, "Don't worry. Your little fella is still there." Some of the worry was gone. Vidovic knew that he was still a man. But he still couldn't bear to look at his legs again. Instead he chatted with the medic. Poor guy. It was his first operation with 3rd Platoon. Here he was, green as grass; no doubt expecting an easy mission with no casualties. Now he was dealing with a traumatic amputation, another leg that might be lost, and three other casualties as well. Vidovic said to the medic: "Doc, it's OK if you want to puke." The medic just chuckled and informed Vidovic that the medevac was on the way before asking him if there was anything else he wanted. Vidovic replied that he could use another shot. The medic obliged and Vidovic drifted off to sleep.

Bradfield and Smitty had received mostly minor wounds and were back to normal service in a matter of days. Lieutenant Thompson's wounds were more serious, but nobody ever went to the hospital to check on him. He got on the chopper and was gone and, like a bad dream, became a memory that most of the members of Charlie Company simply tried to forget. Ron Vidovic, though, was another matter. He woke up in a hospital in Saigon, where a nurse told him that the surgeons had been able to save his right leg, but it was going to hurt like hell. It did hurt like hell. But, with the help of a prosthesis, he was going to be able to walk again. Several of Vidovic's friends dropped by to wish him well. Lieutenant Hoskins, who was still recovering from his own wounds, brought an entire carton of cigarettes. Tim Fischer, who couldn't quite hide the fact that he partly blamed himself for Vidovic's condition, visited for a long talk. It was Terry McBride, though, who was there in Vidovic's hour of greatest need. McBride noticed that something was wrong. Vidovic was shaking. He asked if there was anything he could do. Get the nurse maybe? Vidovic didn't want the nurse – he was too embarrassed. He had to shit and didn't know how to do it. McBride did what he could to help, but the two succeeded in making a stinking mess of the whole procedure – just in time for the visiting USO showgirls to pop their heads in the door. The girls put on their bravest smiles, apologized for the interruption, and hurried away, leaving McBride and Vidovic laughing uncontrollably.

After being stabilized, and after writing a letter home to tell his mother the bad news, Vidovic was taken to Japan, where he found himself in a bunk only a few feet away from Bill Riley – who was still in a full body cast after nearly losing his own leg on June 19. The two swapped stories for a few hours, with Riley wanting to find out all he could about his old buddies of Charlie Company, before Vidovic left aboard a medical flight first to California and then to Madigan Army Medical Center at Fort Lewis, Washington – only 6 miles from his home. Placed in a ward with other amputees, Vidovic quickly realized how good he had it. Many others had lost more than one limb. He had just lost one leg below his knee. His mother had a very hard time seeing the bright side of his injury, but he knew that he was going to make it just fine. As the months crawled by, though, Vidovic began to feel a bit trapped and finally asked his doctors when he would be going home. They responded by telling him he could leave just as soon as he could get up and walk. He didn't have a prosthesis yet, and was weak due to weight loss, but Vidovic thought to himself, "What the hell. I can walk now." So when everyone had left the room, Vidovic threw his good leg, which itself was still pretty badly damaged, over the side of the bed, grabbed his crutches and tried to walk. It was too much, too fast, and Vidovic nearly blacked out from the exertion. He crashed to the floor and splintered the bone on the end of his leg stump.

The doctors rushed Vidovic back into surgery, where he lost another 3 inches of his leg. When he awoke, his surgeon was standing there staring at him and yelled, "If you ever try that again I will cut your other leg off!" After the surgery, Vidovic got with the program. He was just going to have to wait to walk again until the doctors said it was all right. It really wasn't all that bad in the hospital. The nurses were cute and his buddies from the

Tacoma area often came to visit, always sneaking him some beer. First his good leg had to heal. Then he had to go through physical therapy to build up his muscles and endurance. Only then would he receive his prosthesis. By the spring of 1968 he was ready. His mother was there for the big day when he took his first few, halting steps. She mentioned that it was like teaching him how to walk the first time, all those years ago. Ron Vidovic finally walked out of the hospital in May 1968 – exactly two years after he had received his draft notice.

As the summer of 1967 wore on, and Charlie Company went about its business of Dong Tam base security, a significant concern arose in the halls of MACV in Saigon and at the 9th Division's headquarters at Bear Cat. Since many of the units within the 9th Infantry Division had arrived in Vietnam on the same day in January 1967, the originals of those units would all rotate home on the same day in January 1968, effectively gutting whole battalions of their veteran cadre. Such a massive turnover of experienced troops threatened the effectiveness of the entire division. After numerous attempts to devise a plan to deal with the problem, MACV staffers developed the infusion program, which involved shifting men around within the 9th Division so that no one unit contained too many men who shared the same DEROS (Date Eligible to Return from Overseas Service) date. For Charlie Company infusion meant that, at random, many of the Fort Riley originals received orders to transfer to other battalions within the division. For each soldier lost in that manner, Charlie Company received a soldier in return who had a different DEROS. All across the unit, men packed up their things to leave – James Nall, Jim Dennison, Terry McBride, Elijah Taylor, Larry Lukes, Willie McTear, Richard Rubio, Idoluis Casares, James Smith, John Bradfield, Jim Stephens, and so many more were suddenly just gone. Friends who had trained, lived, bled, and suffered with their brothers in Charlie Company just were not there anymore. There were new guys from other battalions in their bunks and walking point.

To the command elements of Charlie Company, infusion was a necessary evil. For Company First Sergeant Crockett, who referred to the whole process as "confusion," the constant coming and going of soldiers necessitated an administrative nightmare of papers to be filed and soldiers to be assigned. Some of the new soldiers were veterans, while others were as green as the grass, but Crockett and Captain Lind had no choice – they had to fit the new men as best they could into the existing structure of the unit. Lynn Hunt and the other platoon leaders quickly became frustrated with the process. While Charlie Company had lost many of its best men, its long-service veterans, it seemed to them that other units saw infusion as a chance to empty their manpower cupboards of their least effective soldiers – their malcontents and malingerers. Even many of the best men infused into Charlie Company proved difficult to absorb into the unit's culture. They were already trained and part of a team, meaning that they all had preconceived notions of how things should be done. All too often they grumbled or questioned their new leaders. While working in Dong Tam to rebuild his platoon around these new men, Hunt could not help thinking that he actually preferred replacements fresh from training in the States; at least they were blank slates.

For the soldiers who left Charlie Company for new units, infusion was a jolting process. They had been members of a family and suddenly found themselves as the new guys in strange surroundings. Infusion usually began with hope – with the thought of maybe being assigned to a noncombat position. All too often, though, the reality was that the Charlie Company draftees found themselves isolated in their new units, serving among men and for officers who did not measure up to the exacting standards of Charlie Company. Jim Dennison, the Chicago native who had once tackled a Viet Cong during a night ambush, at first wrote home regarding infusion with enthusiasm:

Dear Mom, Dad, and Fran,
I've been with my new unit about 3 days now, and things aren't too much different... It would have been nice if I could have gotten a different job when I was transferred, but such is life. I miss the old gang too, but I'll make new friends here... Since I'm in a recon platoon we work independently of the regular infantry companies and pull more security jobs than they do... The terrain down here is

100% better than in the delta, very little mud, no rice paddies, mostly rubber plantations. Some of the guys complain because they think they've got it rough. But this is almost heaven compared to where I came from... I'll keep in touch with my old buddies... I just hope that they get a lucky break pretty soon.

Love, Jim

Within days, though, Dennison's opinion of infusion had changed. In its first firefight since his arrival, the new unit did "everything wrong," and his new sergeant seemed to be an "idiot" who could not control his troops in battle. Dennison decided that it was going to take all of the effort that he could muster simply to survive the remainder of his tour.

Dennison was not alone in his dissatisfaction. Richard Rubio found himself appointed squad leader in his new unit, which was bad enough. Worse, though, his platoon leader was an untested newbie, while his platoon sergeant was a long-service REMF who was going to see combat for the first time in his military life. Since neither man seemed to know his ass from a hole in the ground, it was up to Rubio to lead the platoon from behind the scenes if he wanted to live. As a combat veteran, Idoluis Casares, whom Bill Geier had known simply as "Bear," also became a squad leader in his own new unit. Casares figured that he could adapt and deal with the situation, until several men in his squad flatly refused to go out into the field on operations. After a mix of cajoling and threats, Casares got the men up and started, but the tension only worsened as his first day as squad leader went on. The worst of his new men refused to walk point when his turn came. He just stood there, looked Casares in the face, and said, "Hell no, man. I ain't movin'." The platoon leader flew into a rage and threatened to blow the man's head off with his shotgun. Casares watched the standoff and wondered what the hell he had gotten himself into.

Willie McTear was one of the lucky ones. Having developed a debilitating foot infection, McTear first went to the hospital before being infused. When his orders finally came it seemed he had hit the jackpot. No more combat for him. He was going to be a truck dispatcher. A real, honest-to-goodness REMF. At first the new assignment was a dream come true – nice food, air-conditioning, plenty to drink, and even Vietnamese to make the bunks and clean the barracks. Even though he was safe, McTear found himself missing Charlie Company, even missing combat. These new guys around him were worse than REMFs; they weren't even soldiers. They were worried about the polish on their shoes, the precise length of their hair. What the hell was he doing here with a battalion of pencil pushers while the real soldiers, his buddies, were out in the field fighting? How was it fair that these guys had the easy life, while Charlie Company slogged the rice paddies? Amid the drinking, polishing, and pencil pushing Willie McTear isolated himself. He didn't want to get to know any of these paper soldiers. He would just do what he had to do to get home.

Back in Charlie Company everything had changed. The few remaining original draftees, now old veterans, hung together now more than ever before. All around them were new guys. Whether replacements from the States or veterans from other units – they were new guys. Some of the veterans did their best to ignore them, others tried to show them the ropes, but hardly anyone tried to get close to them. Friendships in Vietnam were just too hard to make, and too easy and painful to lose. Sure the veterans worked with the new guys – their survival depended on it. But the old closeness – the old camaraderie – while it was there in an even stronger measure for those originals who remained, was gone from the unit. Charlie Company was strong and experienced. It was battle-tested, but it was different. It was no longer the band of brothers that had emerged from Fort Riley. It was now, in many ways, just another American unit in Vietnam. A hodgepodge of soldiers from everywhere and nowhere, of soldiers with little in common other than a violent job.

Dave Jarczewski had nearly been killed on May 15 in the same battle in which Don Peterson had died. A Viet Cong bullet had left him with a sucking chest wound, after narrowly missing his heart. In August, after two months of painful recuperation in the military hospital in Camp Zama, Japan, Jarczewski received some unwelcome news. His recovery was so far ahead of schedule that he was going to be sent back to Vietnam instead of to the States. Jarczewski wasn't happy with the situation, but he knew one thing: if he was going back to Vietnam he sure as hell didn't want to go to any other unit. He wanted to go back to Charlie Company. A quick call to Company First Sergeant Crockett was all that it took, and the orders were cut. In mid-August Jarczewski climbed out of the chopper in Dong Tam. The place looked so different than it had the first day he had arrived there in May. Then it was one vast, open field of mud. Now there were buildings everywhere and something that even looked like a swimming pool. Still walking somewhat gingerly, and only approved for light duty, Jarczewski found First Sergeant Crockett, who smiled and welcomed him back, and then made his way to his new barracks. It was going to be so good to see the guys again, to shoot the breeze and get caught up. He located the barracks and went inside to see if he could find an empty bunk. Only then did he realize his mistake. He had wandered into the wrong barracks. As politely as he knew how Jarczewski asked one of the guys in the room where he could find the 1st Platoon of Charlie Company. Almost absentmindedly one of the soldiers looked up from a book he was reading and informed Jarczewski that he was in the right place. They were the 1st Platoon of Charlie Company. Jarczewski looked around again at all the faces in amazement. There was nobody there whom he knew.

There wasn't much ceremony, certainly no pomp and circumstance, but on August 20, 1967, the normal command rotation in Vietnam hit the 4th of the 47th with a vengeance. After serving a standard stint in the field with a battalion, Lieutenant Colonel Guy Tutwiler moved on and was replaced by Lieutenant Colonel R.M. Rhotenberry. Everyone knew that Tutwiler was going to be a tough act to follow. He had been there since Fort Riley and during that time had developed a strong relationship with his company commanders and platoon leaders. The younger officers uniformly looked up to and admired Tutwiler, who was something of a father figure to the entire unit. Tutwiler had also been there for all of the battles, large and small, and had proven his competence. Even before Rhotenberry arrived there were rumors. Somehow all of the officers had heard that Rhotenberry had been a tough platoon leader in Korea, barely escaping with his life in the fighting near the Yalu River. In Vietnam, though, it was rumored that he had bounced around from military pillar to post, never quite earning the coveted position of battalion commander, in part due to inefficiency but also because of alcoholism.

Captain Lind, the commander of Charlie Company, didn't much like what he saw in his new battalion commander. Rhotenberry was indeed a heavy drinker, and a stickler for spit and polish. One of Rhotenberry's first innovations was to demand that the men of the 4th of the 47th shave every day in the field. Lind and the platoon leaders were very conscious of such matters while in base camp – but to require men to shave when on patrol? Who was going to be there to inspect them? He knew that the men would consider such an order to be nothing more than "chickenshit," so Lind chose to ignore it.

Worse, though, was that Rhotenberry seemed to believe that he knew everything about warfare in Vietnam. Lind and his platoon leaders were delta veterans. They had been there since the formation of the MRF and had helped to develop its tactics. But they felt ignored by Rhotenberry. He seemed arrogant, aloof, and determined to do things his way – no matter what the cost. Command relationships within the battalion were strained from the start. Lind did what he could to shield his platoon leaders from the fallout, taking the blame for anything that Rhotenberry felt went wrong. In the field, Lind and Rhotenberry had a frosty working relationship. The command tensions were not without a level of humor, though, resulting in Benedick, Hunt, and the other platoon leaders nicknaming Rhotenberry "Pop Smoke." Unlike Tutwiler, Rhotenberry hardly ever set foot on the ground with his men, choosing instead to circle overhead in a command helicopter. From his position on high, Rhotenberry liked to micromanage the unit, but he never could see things on the ground very well. Like clockwork, Rhotenberry would call in to his platoons, "This is Crooner 6. Have your lead elements pop smoke." The first few times the calls came in were simply annoyances, but they kept coming – regularly every day, every operation. Hunt, Benedick, and Hoskins knew that it was all well and good that Rhotenberry know the location of his troops, but popping so much smoke was also a very easy way for the VC to track Charlie Company's movements. Within a few days the platoon leaders began to pretend that they did not hear Rhotenberry's orders. When that didn't work they crackled paper near the radio handset to mimic static and reported communication difficulties. Rhotenberry's voice would jump a couple of octaves as his demands for smoke became more shrill, but the communications difficulties continued.

Hoskins, Hunt, and Benedick knew that they were bucking the odds. The standard combat assignment for a platoon leader in Vietnam, for those who lived that long, was six months. The Charlie Company trio had already overstayed their military welcome, having been with their platoons for over seven months. With the standard date for rotation having come and gone, though, they dared to hope that since Charlie Company had trained together and served together they would be allowed to remain with the unit for its entire tour. Their hopes were in vain, and in late August all three were summoned to Rhotenberry's office to receive their new orders. They were all headed to staff jobs scattered across the division. They were officers. They knew the score, but the news hit them hard. Charlie Company was their unit; these were their boys. They had been with them from the beginning. They had made them into soldiers; fought with them, bled with them. And now they had to leave them behind.

On the short walk back to their quarters, the group fell into a discussion about the timing of their rotation. Maybe it was simply a matter of military paperwork finally catching up to them, but they suspected that Rhotenberry had a hand in the matter. Maybe they had pissed him off just a bit too much. Well, they agreed that he deserved it. He was a menace and somebody had to stand up to him. Now that was Captain Lind's job, and they all agreed that it was going to be a hard one. Hoskins, Hunt, and Benedick still had a few days remaining with Charlie Company, days devoted to training their replacements. The new platoon leaders were all green, untested, and gung-ho. They didn't know Vietnam; didn't know combat. Hoskins, Hunt, and Benedick did their best to give the young lieutenants (one of whom immediately earned the nickname "John Wayne" because of his propensity to rush forward into trouble) a crash course on how to keep themselves and their men alive in the Mekong Delta – tripwires, recon of tree lines, cloverleafing, ambushes, fire missions – the tricks of survival learned over seven months of war. The trio met for one last drink in the officers' club before shipping out, and the conversation turned to their new pupils. They all tried hard to remember that they had been green once, but these new guys seemed greener than green. Maybe the training at home had gotten worse? Who knew? Absently staring at his glass of whiskey, Jack Benedick, not known for holding back his thoughts especially after a few drinks in the Officers' club, blurted out, "These new guys don't know shit from Shinola! John Wayne is going to get himself killed. Christ, he's gonna get some of the men killed." Hunt and Hoskins agreed. The whole thing stank. It was dangerous. But they had no choice. The next morning Hoskins, Hunt, and Benedick boarded a helicopter and departed. Charlie Company was under new management.

While dealing with the results of infusion by breaking in its fresh complement of new officers and men, during September, whether by design or by sheer happenstance, Charlie Company caught a break. The Viet Cong were lying low in the relative calm that preceded the Tet Offensive of 1968, leaving Charlie Company with little in the way of enemy contact as it left Dong Tam and began once again to operate from the ships of the MRF. With little to show for its search and destroy sweeps, except for a few booby traps and minor injuries, the 9th Division and the MRF shifted more of its tactical emphasis to "hearts and minds" operations. For much of the next two months, Charlie Company worked in and around "friendly" Vietnamese villages in support of local South Vietnamese elections and as security for Medical Civil Affairs Program (MEDCAP) operations. On such missions the soldiers of Charlie Company would set up a defensive perimeter around a village, often in the Dong Tam area, standing guard against any Viet Cong incursion. In the case of elections the company often remained dug in near the village for days of electioneering and voting, while MEDCAP operations usually only lasted a single day, or sometimes two.

The MEDCAP missions were often rather raucous affairs. Protected by the cordon of troops, the battalion medical team, accompanied by the individual platoon medics, would set up shop in the village square to provide medical and dental treatment of all kinds – vaccinations, wound debridement, prenatal care, pulling abscessed teeth – it was all part of the program. Civilians would flock in from miles around to receive care the likes of which they might never see again in their lifetimes. Having witnessed so much death, after having taken part in so much killing, helping so many people as part of the MEDCAP missions served as a powerful tonic to many of the men of Charlie Company. There were smiles of gratitude and handshakes from grateful civilians instead of booby traps and sniper fire. And then there were the children, who seemed to appear as if by magic as the Americans settled into their defensive positions. Some just stood and stared at the fearsome giants in green. Others begged for candy or sold trinkets. Some of the more jaded even tried to sell the services of their sisters. But they were there – tiny and often wearing infectious grins. On some occasions ARVN troops accompanied Charlie Company to serve as interpreters during MEDCAPs, which allowed the soldiers to actually speak with the children instead of just communicating through pantomime. It turned out that these children were just like kids back home – they went to school; they loved to play; they argued with their siblings; they wanted to live and deserved to live. The short relationships between the warriors and the children were reassuring. The soldiers could still feel, still care. At the same time, though, the relationships were like a great weight. The soldiers would leave the next day and the war would be there waiting. Who knew whether the soldier would live – whether the child would live? It didn't pay to get too close, to care too much.

As the end of September drew near, many of the Charlie Company originals began to feel something alien – a sense of hope. They were getting short and would go home no later than the end of December. Rumors flashed around the company that, since they had suffered so badly and for so long, Uncle Sam would surely get the originals out of the field and to some safe job as REMFs in a cushy base camp somewhere. But home – eating dinner with mom and dad, shooting pool and enjoying a beer, going to school – seemed so distant. Some wondered if, after what they had been through, they would ever really be able to go home again. John Young spoke for many when he wrote to his parents on September 27:

Dear Mom, Dad, and Girls,

Sorry I haven't written in several days. Things have been pretty hectic here lately. We're on a new ship, the LST USS *Whitfield County*. It isn't much of a ship... December 20 is the date by which all the "originals" in the battalion will have rotated... This is the best thing I've heard in a year. Even without the fighting, an infantryman's tour here is terribly hard, boring, dirty, sweaty work, and there is no way to make another, who has not been through it, understand.

For a long time after I'm home, I'll jump at sharp noises and watch for tripwires when I walk, and I know that the mention of certain names will take me back to this place. I don't think I'll be able to watch a war movie again. When I answer the phone, I know I'll say "Akron One" (my radio call sign) instead of "hello."

Imagine the ugliest sound, the ugliest sight, the ugliest smell you can. This war (all wars) is a continuum of events far more revoltingly ugly than it is possible to describe. It will be so unbelievably good to enjoy beauty again, whether it is just good hot coffee in the morning with the paper, or a Christmas tree or a painting in a museum, or simply the beauty of sleeping safely in my room at home. It will be very nice.

Well, it's late and I'd better stop. Hope everybody is ok.

Love, John

While involved in local security operations, Charlie Company continued to receive new members, both as replacements and through the ongoing infusion process. Steve Hopper, the Charlie Company original from Illinois who had to identify the body of Forrest Ramos in the morgue following the battle on June 19, was surprised at the nature of a couple of the replacements they received. Gale Alldridge and Danny Burkhead were fresh to the company, but both were short-timers, with only 30 days to go before they rotated home. Hell, Burkhead had been a truck driver for nearly eight months and had never before seen combat. Both were good men, and willing soldiers. Hopper, in his position as squad leader for 3rd Squad, taught them everything he could about the new war they had suddenly found themselves in, but he couldn't help but wonder about the military absurdity of it all. These guys should be in an REMF job somewhere, packing their gear, drinking their beer, and dreaming of home. Instead here they were learning a new war; one was learning about combat for the first time. What the hell kind of sense did that make? Hopper did what he could to help out, and the men became relatively close in a short span of time, with Burkhead especially happy to talk about his native Minnesota. Maybe that new football team of theirs, the Vikings, would be decent one day?

At the end of September, Lieutenant Charles Davis, an Alabama native fresh from officer training, arrived to take command of 3rd Platoon. Captain Lind met Davis briefly before leaving for some well-deserved R and R, and could only give the most basic of briefings on combat operations in the Mekong Delta. Things were quiet, so it shouldn't be too bad. Most of the important issues could wait until Lind's return. Until then, Lind gave Davis the most important advice that he could – stick close to Sergeant Marr. He was a pro, and had led the unit several times through difficult battles. If Davis listened to Marr – did exactly what Marr said – everything would be fine. With that, Lind made his way to Saigon and boarded a flight to meet his wife Becky in Hawaii.

As members of the mortar platoon, Alan Richards and Ronnie Gann occupied special positions in Charlie Company. Sometimes the platoon accompanied Charlie Company on operations in its mortar capacity, as it had on the terrible day of June 19 when so many had been lost in the PABs. On other occasions the platoon remained behind in a defensive position, with a few of its members out as forward observers, to help provide firepower support for the maneuver platoons. Sometimes, though, the mortar platoon carried rifles and acted as a fourth maneuver platoon for Charlie Company. On October 6, Richards, Gann, and the other members of the mortar platoon were carrying M16s and humping through the rice paddies on a search and destroy mission in the Mekong Delta just like everyone else. Charlie Company was back to the familiar routine of working off the boats in its search for the Viet Cong, but they seemed to be lying low. Richards, a country boy from Wisconsin who had been wounded by a mine on VC Island and missed the fighting on June 19, and Gann, from California and whose father had sold his car before he left for Vietnam figuring that he wouldn't return, had been close friends since their time at Fort Riley. They had been through a lot together and had come through reasonably unscathed, which they largely attributed to their platoon sergeant, a tough Guamanian named Pedro Blas. Even though Blas wasn't with them that day, the duo felt fairly at ease as they slogged through the rice paddy. Crossing the paddy first was 3rd Platoon, with Steve Hopper's squad on point. Any trouble would come their way. But nothing would come. For some reason, the VC had been hiding, not fighting. Still Richards, Gann, and the rest of the platoon didn't take anything lightly. They were professionals and knew that death could be anywhere. Their guard was up, on the lookout for tripwires or bunkers. Even so, it was late in the afternoon; the day had been a long walk in the hot sun. Nothing was going to happen before the call came in to prepare a night defensive position.

While crossing through the open paddy, with a dike off to his left, Alan Richards felt something slam into his shoulder and then turned a near somersault in the air before landing on his back in the muddy water. Only then, dimly as if through a thick haze, did he hear the reports of rifle fire from nearby Viet Cong positions. All of the training from Fort Riley and the hard lessons learned from battle just kicked in; almost without knowing what he was doing Richards reflexively pulled the quick release strap on his pack, wriggled free and crawled through the muck to the cover of a paddy dike. Within seconds the medic, a new guy – Richards didn't even know his name – was by his side asking Richards where he was hit. Gritting his teeth through the pain Richards replied, "my back," and the medic cut his shirt away to get a look at the wound. The young medic didn't say anything, his training was too good for that, but a passing look of surprise and concern let Richards know that his injuries were bad. The Viet Cong bullet had struck Richards just below his shoulder joint, shattering the bone before travelling through his chest cavity and lodging near his spine.

When the Viet Cong opened fire, 4th Platoon hit the dirt with some men returning fire while others made for any cover they could find. With so many men caught in the open, the call went out to fall back and regroup. Ronnie Gann looked around from where he had gone to ground surrounded by the high rice in the middle of the paddy. He caught quick glimpses of men hustling back to cover and knew that he should go as well. But he couldn't. Richards, his buddy, had just been standing there and then his shoulder had exploded, tossing him backward. He couldn't just leave him out there. So instead of moving back to cover, Gann crawled forward to find his friend. By the time Gann arrived, the medic was hard at work, and Richards looked bad. Maybe he wouldn't survive. Almost without thinking Gann looked around to take stock of the situation. Where was the enemy? What could he do to cover Richards and the medic? Then the world went black. A few minutes later Gann came to and watched detached as the medic frantically worked on him. On him? What the hell had happened? Then he felt the pain – a searing jet of heat – coursing through his body. He could barely breathe, and his legs – his legs wouldn't move. A Viet Cong bullet had entered Gann's shoulder, collapsed his lung, nicked a kidney and had damaged his spine. Gann had always wondered what it would feel like to be wounded, and he was surprised to be so calm. He just sat there lost in thought as the medic worked. The more Gann thought about it, the more it felt like his body was on fire. But what worried him the most was that he couldn't move his legs. Then, as if from a long way away, Gann heard the medic yell that they had better get a chopper in quick if they wanted these men to live. These men? Could the medic mean him and Richards?

Steve Hopper's 3rd Squad had been walking point for Charlie Company that day. It was nothing unusual. Moving with care, Gale Alldridge had led the men forward, about 100 yards in advance of the main body of troops. It was just another recon of just another open paddy while nearing just another tree line. Realizing that the day was almost at its end, the men had even chatted a bit about sharing C Rations that night as Alldridge was the first to make his way over the last paddy dike before the tree line, followed closely by Burkhead. Their turn as the recon element was nearly done. Suddenly fire blazed in from both the left and from the front. The Viet Cong were impossibly close, and Hopper

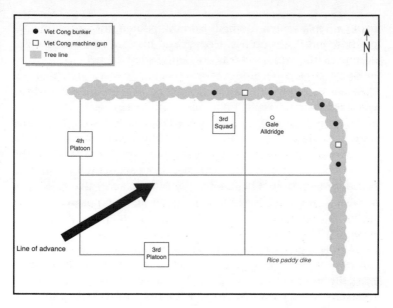

Battle of October 6

and his men had been caught near the corner of an L-shaped ambush. Hopper's RTO, a young replacement named Ybarra, was wounded in the opening burst. Hopper crawled over, took the radio, and began to drag Ybarra to safety. Yelling over the din of the incoming fire, Hopper ordered his men forward to the base of a paddy dike only 40 feet away – the same paddy dike Alldridge had just crossed. With bullets buzzing overhead and slapping the mud all around, Hopper and his men moved to the dike. It offered them cover from the Viet Cong fire from the tree line to their front – but did nothing to protect them from the fire coming from their left flank.

The enemy fire was intense, but most of it seemed to be passing above their heads. Hopper looked to his left and discovered why – he and his men were only about 10 yards from the nearest enemy bunker. They could see the VC – their eyes and their gun barrels. The firing slits were too narrow for them to get a good shot because Hopper and his men were so close. Hopper shouted quick orders to his men; they had to keep fire on that bunker; he and the nearest man, a replacement named Horney, poured fire into the VC position, but it was no use. Hopper and his men had been caught dead to rights. As Hopper was wondering what the hell he could do, he saw it. A grenade. Somehow the VC had tossed a grenade from their narrow firing slit, and it had landed next to himself and the wounded Ybarra. Getting up to run meant certain death, so the pair curled up in fetal positions and waited for the explosion. There was a short, loud FIZZ – but nothing more. The grenade was a dud. On the one hand almost unable to believe his good luck, and on the other hand nearly quivering with rage, Hopper got on the horn and called for help from a helicopter gunship. He knew that they were so close it would be like calling in fire on his own position, but he had to take the risk. Hopper and his men weren't going to live long dueling with that VC bunker.

Hopper told the pilot what he wanted, a rocket put right on the junction of two paddy dikes. He then tossed a smoke grenade to mark the enemy position and told the chopper pilot that he and his men were only a few yards away and for God's sake to shoot straight. Hopper, Ybarra, Horney, and the rest of the squad hugged tight to the ground as the helicopter made its first run. Machine gun fire? It spattered all around them. Hopper was livid. Amazingly nobody had been wounded, but that fire could get them all killed and was of no use whatsoever against an enemy bunker. What the hell was that pilot thinking? Hopper got back on the radio and yelled that he didn't want any damn machine gun fire – they needed rockets! A few seconds later the chopper made another run. The rocket scored a direct hit on the VC bunker, tossing mud in all directions.

After the smoke cleared, 3rd Squad quickly took stock of the situation. With the fire from its left having ceased, the tree line to the front seemed to be the only real danger. Safe behind the paddy's final dike, though, Hopper and his men could just pull back and let the artillery hammer the remaining Viet Cong positions. But Gale Alldridge and Danny Burkhead weren't there. They had crossed the dike and were between it and the enemy positions in the tree line. Burkhead had gone to ground just on the other side of the paddy dike, but nobody in the squad had any idea of Alldridge's location, let alone whether he was alive or dead. Something had to be done, and Danny Burkhead, Alldridge's closest friend in the unit, volunteered to go out and find him. As the rest of the squad did what it could to lay down covering fire, Burkhead crawled out into the open. He could only have been gone for a few minutes, but, with the tree line erupting into fire, it seemed like an eternity. Then Burkhead was back, shouting that Alldridge was dead. The news hit 3rd Squad hard, and there was a momentary silence. Burkhead then raised up to repeat his news. His head jerked violently, struck by a Viet Cong round. Burkhead sank back to the ground and then disappeared out of sight on the far side of the paddy dike. Hopper couldn't believe it. Alldridge and Burkhead were so short that they should have been in some cushy REMF job, not out here in the field. Now they were both gone – Alldridge in the opening burst of fire and Burkhead lost in an attempt to save his buddy. It all just seemed so wrong. Gritting his teeth, Hopper fired an entire clip of tracer rounds at the nearest VC bunker, and, though he never got the satisfaction of seeing any enemy bodies, he was reasonably certain that he had avenged Burkhead's death.

Hopper got on the horn and started calling in artillery fire, hoping to take care of any additional bunkers, but there was nothing further that anyone could do for Alldridge or Burkhead. With darkness falling and facing an enemy unit of unknown strength 3rd Squad had to pull back or risk being overrun. It was amazing that they had survived this long. Hopper, Ybarra, Horney, and the remainder of 3rd Squad crawled toward the rear, hugging the spider web of rice paddy dikes for cover. Any movement through an exposed area brought immediate Viet Cong fire, which struck so close that it spattered the men with mud. After a harrowing journey, 3rd Squad neared what it hoped were friendly lines. Yelling that they were coming in, Hopper and his men jumped to their feet and ran the last few yards with enemy bullets whizzing past all around. Finally behind some decent cover, Hopper quickly located Platoon Sergeant Joe Marr and gave him a report on events. He pointed out the enemy positions and where he had lost Alldridge and Burkhead. Marr, ever the professional, processed the information while preparing to call in the first artillery strike. Marr then looked up into Hopper's eyes and asked, "But where's Lieutenant Davis?"

Tim Fischer's squad had been some 75 yards behind Hopper and his men and had gone to ground in an open rice paddy when the firing had broken out. Marr had been further to the rear near the cover of a large paddy dike and had turned to Lieutenant Davis to coordinate the action, but neither Davis nor his RTO were anywhere to be found. After some yelling, Marr located the RTO, Tom Conroy – who had been so shaken by the loss of Elmer Kenney on July 11 – who was stranded behind Fischer's position in the open in the rice paddy. The two communicated the situation to the company headquarters, but couldn't undertake much in the way of meaningful action other than coordinating small arms fire. Nobody knew where Lieutenant Davis was, and nobody knew the exact location of Hopper's downed squad. Hopper himself was coordinating air strikes, and that would have to be enough. In the open paddy, a few yards to Conroy's front, Fischer and his men had a much better view of the unfolding battle. They could see Hopper and his men locked into place by enemy fire. They could even fire at the enemy positions, but to little effect. Then Fischer saw the most startling thing. A lone man running forward. Was that Lieutenant Davis? What the ever-living hell was he doing out there on his own – running toward the downed recon element? There was little time to wonder, because Davis' body soon jerked two, perhaps three, times – as Viet Cong bullets struck home – before collapsing to the ground.

Marr could hardly believe what he heard from both Fischer and the men of Hopper's squad. That new, gung-ho lieutenant had been under orders from Lind to stick by his side – to listen to him. But he had run off after the recon element and was down in the rice paddy? With twilight fast approaching, Marr felt helpless. Viet Cong fire was pouring into 3rd Platoon's position, with a bullet blowing off Marr's ring finger and another destroying Conroy's radio, so a rescue mission was out of the question. Even Steve Hopper was wounded. It was so ironic; he had survived unscathed a few feet from an enemy bunker, and was hit by shrapnel once he had reached safety. Amid the heavy fire, all Marr could do was call in artillery missions and hope for the best. All night the men huddled under their ponchos in a relentless rainstorm, under constant attack from ravenous mosquitoes, while artillery rounds hammered nearby and the landscape was lit with the ghostly glow of falling flares. During it all the men of 3rd Platoon knew full well that their friends were out there. Burkhead and Alldridge weren't Fort Riley originals, but they were good guys – guys who were about to go back to the world. Davis hadn't been with the unit long. It was one of his first combat missions. But he was out there somewhere, and nobody knew whether he was dead or alive. His was the nightmare fate that had long haunted the men's dreams. What if they were out there wounded, surrounded – begging for help? What if nobody came to get them? Although they were exhausted, the men of 3rd Platoon didn't get much sleep that night.

The next morning Charlie Company moved toward the Viet Cong tree line, and, as usual, there was no enemy resistance. The enemy had fled during the night, dragging their wounded and dead with them. 3rd Platoon first came across the body of Lieutenant Davis, nearly submerged in the rice paddy water. He had been wounded in the upper thigh and groin area, meaning that he had bled to death out there alone in the paddy. It was difficult for the men to take. Should they have helped him? Could they have helped him? It seemed to be such a bad way to go. How long did Davis lie there, fully aware of the fact that he was dying and praying for help? Next the men reached the bodies of Burkhead, still slumped against the rice paddy dike where he had been shot, and Alldridge – who had been killed instantly. At least they hadn't suffered. At least the Viet Cong had not had time to loot any of the bodies. All Steve Hopper could do was stand there and stare as the body bags were brought in. These had been his men. He was responsible. He had been unable to bring them home safely. Death and killing had been part of the tour in Vietnam, but this time it had struck so close to home. On one hand Hopper felt an incredible sense of loss and guilt, while, on the other, he felt an oddly conflicting feeling – a numbness. He couldn't feel like he had before. Somehow he was a part of death, and death was an all-too real part of his own existence. The contradictory feelings rushed together, leaving Hopper confused and altered. He was not the same boy who had enjoyed watching movies and drinking chocolate malts after a day of baling hay in rural Illinois. He was not even sure he knew who he was. After writing letters to

Burkhead's and Alldridge's families apologizing for failing to bring them home safely, Hopper wrote about the battle to his parents. In the letter, Hopper was careful to assure his parents that his own wound was minor before giving them a blow-by-blow account of the action. Hopper closed the narration:

> There's one good thing about it, though. Since I have received two Purple Hearts I shouldn't have to go into the field any more. I really hope so. Mom and Dad, sometimes the tension gets so great that I feel like I'm going to lose my mind. Oh well. Maybe it will be the last time something like this happens. That's what I said last time too, though.

Alan Richards waited on a gurney in the hospital in Saigon for hours while other, more urgent, cases received treatment. Finally a doctor came to his side and touched his back, which left Richards writhing in pain. Apparently just realizing that the bullet was still in Richard's back and was lodged near vital organs, the doctors rushed him into emergency surgery. Richards awoke without much of his shoulder blade and with an open incision in his back to allow for drainage. It hurt far worse than getting shot – the pain was almost unbearable. The doctors gave Richards the good news first. He had been lucky – the bullet had nearly killed him, leaving a wound bad enough to be sent home for treatment. But the extent of the wound combined with the surgery meant that he would never regain full use of his arm. The doctors then put Richards into a full body cast and sent him to the hospital in Camp Zama, Japan. After only a week in Japan, Richards received the best news of all. He was going to be sent to the hospital at the Great Lakes Naval Station just north of Chicago – the nearest hospital to his home in Wisconsin. Richards was elated to see the white mountains when his medical flight touched down for refueling in Alaska. Many of the ambulatory patients disembarked during the short stay to kiss the ground – they were so happy to leave Vietnam and return home. Richards contented himself with gazing out the window and wondering whether it was really possible. Was he really back in the United States, or was it all some kind of dream? But it was all true, wonderfully true. A few hours later Richards arrived at Great Lakes, and there were his mother, sister, and brother waiting to see him. His war was over.

Ronnie Gann woke up in the same hospital ward in Saigon with Alan Richards. After running through the events of the last day in his head for a few moments (had he really been shot?), Gann remembered everything and looked toward his feet. After a few tries, he was able to wiggle his toes. He wasn't paralyzed. The doctor came in and informed Gann that the bullet had lodged between his kidney and his spine, and it was the force of the blow and swelling in the area that had led to an initial paralysis. It was going to take a long time, and he was going to go home, but he was going to be fine. Just a few minutes later Gann had to shake his head, because he didn't believe what he was seeing. General William Westmoreland had entered the ward and was pinning Purple Hearts on all of the wounded soldiers. Not quite knowing what to say to someone of such exalted rank, Gann simply informed Westmoreland that it was his second Purple Heart before the great man moved on. The doctors were concerned that a flight could result in Gann's lung collapsing again, so they first sent him to a hospital ship off the Vietnamese coast. On October 15, Gann celebrated his 21st birthday, lying there in a hospital bed, barely able to move. But it was OK. He was going home. He had survived the Vietnam War. Gann spent Thanksgiving in Camp Zama. The treatment there was good, but all Gann could think of was the stink. Everybody on his ward was in a body cast, so they couldn't take baths. The whole ward smelled of unwashed soldiers. Finally Gann was airlifted to Letterman Army Medical Center outside San Francisco. Gann had not told his family that he had been wounded, and finally called them from Letterman. It was the first time they had heard from him in a month. His parents drove to see him, and Gann thought that he was going to have to work hard to get the pieces of his life back into some kind of order, a life that had been interrupted and altered by war.

After the battle of October 6, Charlie Company stood down at Dong Tam for a few days before going back out on the ships, continuing to hunt for the ever more elusive Viet Cong. As the originals neared the end of their tours, the operations took them back to places they had not been for months – places that were so foreign yet so devastatingly familiar. Operations in some areas drove home how much the unit had changed over its deployment. After spending two weeks in the mangrove swamps of the Rung Sat, where the unit had once cut its military teeth, Clarence Shires, who had brought Charlie the cat – who was still alive and well – to Vietnam, wrote home:

> When we first saw this worthless, muddy place we hated it. Now we think of it as a vacation... The thing that got me the worst were leeches. We got them all over us. I had one four to five inches long and an inch in diameter hanging from my you know what... I lit a cigarette and burned him off. The place bled for about three hours! Everybody laughed at me. Some of the guys had them that big to tiny ones all over them. I was lucky that I had only four.

In early November, the ATCs beached Charlie Company at the same location where it had fought the battle of June 19. To the many replacements the Can Giouc area was just another collection of rice paddies. Sure, they had heard that a major battle had taken place there, but to them it was ancient history. To the originals, the boys from Fort Riley, walking those paddies again was like walking through some kind of nightmare. Memories of friends who didn't make it back from that day were everywhere. Memories of who they had once been. For Mike O'Gara, a 2nd Platoon original from Minnesota, it was another stage of an emotional see saw ride. At the beginning of his tour in Vietnam he had wondered if he would ever make it home. After the fighting of June 19 he had accepted the fact that he wouldn't make it home. Now he was daring to hope that he might live to return home, but still feared that the end could come at any time. John Young wrote to his family and spoke for many when he attempted to explain his feelings:

> Dear Mom, Dad, and Girls,
> I really don't know how much I'll be able to write because there just isn't much to say.

Not long ago we ran an operation through the area in which we had our big fight on 19 June. On that day my company had 13 killed and about 25 wounded. A Company had 14 men out of 134 who were **not** wounded or killed. It lasted 23 hours, and it was the most violent, frightening, exhausting, ugly thing I shall ever see. When we got to our old battlefield this time, I was able to look and say "this is where Lt. Schulman died"; "this is where that VC machine gun was"; "here is where our medevac chopper was shot down"; "over there, 9 men in the mortar platoon died – Jindra, Frakes, Winters, Fink, Robin, Cara, Rice and two others I didn't even know"; "inside that shack Tim Johnson died"; "right there Geier, the 2nd Platoon medic, was killed while he tried to aid a wounded man." I could see the tree line that my platoon finally assaulted and where I killed four men and one woman as they ran out of their bunkers. I could also see the big open area in which A Company was destroyed, and could remember with perfect clarity how it looked on the morning of 20 June when we moved to it to help police up the dead. There were dead GI's scattered in the mud everywhere, and it was easy to see which ones were lucky enough to have died instantly because they didn't have the pathetic trails in the mud behind them.

Now it is all changed. Where there were bare mud flats, the rice is now four feet high, and sugar cane now grows around the peasant shacks. The shell craters in the paddies have been filled in, and, except for the still-standing shattered trunks of coconut palms, there is no way to tell that 1,200 men fought there on a clear, hot day last June.

There is a hamlet called Ap Bac close by, and we drew fire from it all day on the 19th. This time we walked down its main street. In most villages the people smile at us, and they smiled this time in Ap Bac, too. But the smiles were acid; these people smiled a paper smile that said "we have seen you before, American soldier, just a few hundred meters out that way, and we hurt you very badly that day." Ap Bac is a VC hamlet in a VC area and faces tell the story. They hate us there, behind their thin smiles.

We spent the night there, and it was hard to believe that any of it had ever happened. But I know that it happened, because this battalion hasn't been the same since.

After writing all this, I feel a little empty. There just isn't much to say...

Guess I'll sack out. Hope everybody is OK. Say hello to everybody.
Love, John

In early November, the MRF received intelligence indicating that some of the main VC units in the Mekong Delta were regrouping in the Cam Son Secret Zone, the base area in Dinh Tuong Province near the site of Charlie Company's first battle on May 15 in which Don Peterson had been killed. The entire 4th of the 47th went out on the hunt, with Lieutenant Colonel Rhotenberry circling above the scene and still asking his units periodically to pop smoke. The sweep began on November 15, and for two days the companies of the 4th of the 47th turned up little, except for leeches and red ants. The Viet Cong didn't seem to be anywhere around; the intelligence had proved faulty once again. On November 17, slated to be the last day of the frustrating operation, Charlie Company swept down the bank of one of the Mekong Delta's many canals. John Young's 1st Squad of the 1st Platoon walked point, looking for anything out of the ordinary. The banks of canals were favorite locations for Viet Cong mines and booby traps; there were even signs posted reading "danger" and "do not enter," so Young and his men took special care. The men had been moving for just over an hour that morning when an explosion tore through the middle of the Charlie Company column. Everyone stopped reflexively to await news, and word slowly filtered up to Young's point squad that a man in the 2nd Platoon had tripped a toe popper mine. The explosion had only broken the man's foot, but Young was still mad at himself. It was the duty of him and his squad to locate the mines and booby traps, and somehow they had missed one.

Young, who was third in line, gave the order for his point man to rest easy. During the next 20 minutes, while the medevac came and went, Young decided to share a smoke with the second man in line, Brookins, an African-American replacement from the Houston area. Brookins had been with the company for such a short time that Young knew next to nothing about him. So the two chatted, and Young learned that Brookins was married with three children – but had been divorced from his wife just long enough to be drafted before patching things up and remarrying. Of all the damn luck. And now here he was, humping through the heat of the Mekong Delta trying to learn how to survive. As the two men finished their cigarettes, word filtered back up the line that it was time to move out. Young got to his feet, patted Brookins on the shoulder, and told him and the point man to get moving when there was a flash and a roar, which sent Young flying through the air and slammed him against the base of a coconut tree. The entire thing couldn't have taken more than a second or two, but Young had time to think, "Christ, I can go home in a couple of weeks and I've just blown my leg off."

After Young's head cleared, he looked down – his legs were still there and seemed to work well enough. Then he glanced off to his right where he heard an odd thrashing. It was Brookins. He had been the one who had stepped on the mine, not Young, and it had blown him clean into the canal. Young scrambled to his feet and, with the help of some of the other replacements, dragged Brookins out of the water. As soon as Brookins' leg cleared the canal, Young knew it was bad. His boot and his foot were gone, severed just above the ankle. Battered, white bone jutted from the jagged wound, and blood ran freely from the stump. The new platoon medic arrived on the scene quickly, gave Brookins a morphine shot, and applied a tourniquet to his leg. Young knelt by Brookins' side, lit a cigarette, and gave it to the young man. Brookins was shaking and afraid to look at his battered leg. He could only look at Young and ask, "My leg's gone, isn't it?" Young swallowed hard and replied, "Well, part of it is." Brookins closed his eyes, sighed, and said, "Well, get me the hell out of here then." He had been in Vietnam for only a few days and was now going back home to his children without part of his leg. As a team of men hauled Brookins off to a landing zone to await a medevac, Young crawled over to the side of the trail and vomited uncontrollably. He didn't like showing emotion or weakness in front of his men. They depended on him for their lives. But Young couldn't help it. After so long in Vietnam, after so many deaths and mutilations, men were still being lost. The price was still being paid. Somehow it hurt so bad that it made John Young sick.

Young quickly regained his composure – complicated feelings like these had no place out on an operation. They could get you killed. Bob Eisenbaugh came to the front of the file, along with his close buddy Ralph Wilson – the New Jersey native who had joined the unit as a replacement in May. As the unit moved out again Wilson led the way, while Eisenbaugh followed a few feet to his rear. Wilson was shocked to hear another explosion, and he whirled around just in time to see Eisenbaugh falling out of the sky and into the nearby canal. With `a shudder Wilson realized that he had walked right over the mine that had blown Eisenbaugh sky high. Men from the 1st Squad rushed to drag him out and Eisenbaugh fell into a fit of hysterical laughter when he looked down to see that both of his feet were still in place. He has stepped on a toe popper. Once again the company held in place to await the arrival of a medevac chopper.

Charlie Company had strayed into a minefield. Movement any direction might result in injury or death. Back at the company command area, Captain Lind was becoming aware of the full gravity of the situation. The minefield was vast. Charlie Company had lost six wounded, while Alpha and Bravo companies, operating nearby along the same canal, had lost five and 11 men respectively. Taking such heavy casualties while accomplishing something would be one thing, but there were no VC around – no damage to inflict. The 4th of the 47th was just bleeding for no good reason. Lind, who already had a rocky relationship with Rhotenberry, agreed to take the heat. He got on the radio and told Rhotenberry that the companies of the 4th of the 47th were going no further that day. Rhotenberry was livid and responded by yelling into the radio, "Damn it! You get a move on! If all of those mines are there they must be guarding something. There must be something to find. I want you guys to find whatever it is right away! I either want a big body count or a large cache!" The built-up animosity between the two, the changes in Charlie Company and the 4th of the 47th made manifest, quickly came to a head. Lind shouted back, "No Sir! I will not move. If you give me a direct command I and my company will sit here until you relieve me. But I warn you, there will be a chain reaction. The lieutenants who would take command from me will do the same. You can't win it!" A moment later, another voice broke in on the conversation, that of the new 2nd Brigade commander Colonel Bert David, who had been monitoring the entire exchange. Calmly, but quite forcefully, Colonel David said, "Rhotenberry, you listen to that young captain. He is on the ground and knows more about the situation than you do." A few minutes later the ATCs were on their way to pick up the troops of the 4th of the 47th and take them back to their barracks ships. The brief foray into the Cam Son Secret Zone was over. Once behind closed doors on board, Rhotenberry let Lind have it. What the hell was he thinking, disobeying orders? He had better get his head straight. Lind just stood there and took all the abuse that Rhotenberry could dish out – he was confident that he had done what was right and had helped to save the lives of the men under his command in Charlie Company.

Nobody could have known it, but the mining of November 17 was the last significant contact for most of the Charlie Company originals. There was to be no climactic end to their tour in Vietnam, no seizure of an enemy capital or cathartic victory. Instead, Charlie Company's war fizzled inconclusively – really no end at all. The draftees of May 1966 would leave Vietnam with the job unfinished, with nothing to show but memories of war, departed friends, and enduring questions. Like most, John Young knew that the end of his tour was close at hand and wrote about the experience of November 17 to his parents, trying to put it all into context. After recapping the action from that day, Young closed his letter:

We evacuated him [Eisenbaugh], then were extracted by the navy ATC's. There is no way to describe how glad we were to get out of there. We were afraid to take a step anywhere.

The entire operation was called off a day early. It had cost my company 6 wounded men, two of whom lost a foot to mines.

Nothing about this mission will make the newspapers, but one of my good men is going home to his wife and family with no right foot, and three days ago he told me that his wife was getting crank letters from someone, telling her that her husband was in grave danger in Vietnam; so where, I ask myself, is the moral behind this small episode in this great tragedy of Vietnam?

I wish I knew. To doubt is to be without a foothold, and I look now at Brookins' empty bunk and doubt. I really don't know what to think of this whole war.

A few days later, Young wrote another letter with a solemn statistic given all too matter-of-factly:

There are 6 of us left from the platoon who came from Fort Riley. Of the other 39, two are dead and the rest badly wounded.

For the Charlie Company originals everything just felt different. Most of their old friends were gone – killed, wounded, or infused. Sure, there were new friends, and a job to be done, but nothing was the same. When they had first arrived in Vietnam they had been spoiling for a fight and ready to make a difference in the war. After the fighting had come, and the losses had begun to mount, feelings had shifted. Some were motivated by longing for revenge, some by grim determination to succeed, most by loyalty to their comrades. By December, though, the originals were so close to home they could almost physically sense it – the snow of Chicago, the waves beating on the California shoreline, the wonderful aromas from mom's kitchen, hugs from wives and children. With so few days remaining in country the purpose of the Charlie Company originals shifted to survival. Everything else – the mission, the war – fell into the background. They had to live to make it home.

The originals of Charlie Company had already seen their once extensive family shrink to tiny, cohesive groups of a few men at the heart of each platoon. But in December, even that changed – shattering the original company seemingly for good. As the originals neared their DEROS, most were transferred to REMF positions scattered throughout the 9th Division. Some of the unlucky remained in the field on operations, virtually alone in what had once been "their" platoons, fighting until very nearly the end. Charlie Company had arrived in Vietnam together – as a family. It would leave Vietnam in ones and twos – as lonely individuals.

There were as many experiences of those final days in Vietnam as there were men. The new company first sergeant pulled John Young off the line and put him in charge of "horticultural beautification" of the company base area, leaving Young to spend his final days in country bartering C Rations with Vietnamese locals in exchange for banana trees and flowering plants to spruce up the drab landscape of Dong Tam. Tim Fischer came off the line to lead some of the old hands in clearing brush around Dong Tam, an easy – if sweaty – job that led to several bull sessions and visits from the local working girls. While sitting there one day with not much of anything going on, still missing his buddy Ron Vidovic, a shot rang out. A sniper. Fischer was a professional. He knew that the sniper was far away and didn't pose a real threat. A few months back it wouldn't have bothered him at all – but it was December. It was almost funny. After all he had been through, that little piss-ant sniper got him more nervous than anything had during the whole year. He had to get home.

Larry Lilley, the California draftee who had lost his two classmates and close friends Kenny Frakes and Tim Johnson on June 19, remained out on operations with 1st Platoon until the middle of the month, when he had jumped over a small stream and heard his knee pop. After a visit to the doctor, Lilley found himself on duty in the PX back at Bear Cat waiting for the freedom bird home. Jimmie Salazar, who had finally let himself hope that he was going to make it home to see his son, had worse fortune. He was out on operations with 2nd Platoon until almost all of the other originals had gone. Finally he went to Captain Lind to see what was up; was somebody mad at him? No. Everything was fine, and his turn was next. Relieved, Salazar made his way to Bear Cat, but the job he found there for his last day in country again made him wonder whom he had pissed off. Young was planting trees; Lilley was working the PX; Salazar was burning the shit cans from the latrines. Mike Cramer, another of the California draftees, was out with 2nd Platoon, serving as its RTO, until December 23, when he finally received his orders to report to Bear Cat. Just in time! Bob Hope was coming to Bear Cat to put on his famous Christmas show for the troops. Now Bob Hope was just fine by Cramer and the rest of Charlie Company, but they all really wanted to see Hope's special guest – Raquel Welch. Cramer and some of the other lucky Charlie Company originals got there early – really early. It was a huge production that took a great deal of time to get organized, so Cramer and his buddies had to get there at 5am. But they were sure it was going to be worth it. But this was the army; this was Vietnam. The television crews came and constructed a massive camera platform right between Cramer's group and the stage. They couldn't see a damn thing.

As the remaining Charlie Company originals gathered in Bear Cat to await their flights home, there were several reunions – men who had stayed with Charlie Company and those who had been infused; reunions that took on lives of their own on New Year's Eve. Most of the original officers were there – Lind, Benedick, Hoskins, Hunt – led by Colonel Tutwiler himself. They all headed to the officers' club and talked about their latest assignments. Benedick had been a liaison officer with an ARVN unit, where he never felt safe. Hunt had been a junior aide to the commander of the 9th Division, and had even gotten a chance to meet Raquel Welch and Bob Hope. But they both had felt odd, even depressed, in their new assignments. Charlie Company was their family, their boys, and leaving had been harder than they ever admitted. The group gathered at a huge table on a concrete patio, and Tutwiler kept the champagne flowing. They toasted everyone they knew, shattering their 8-ounce glasses after each shot. They then started swapping stories, some bawdy, others of tearful loss, of the past year. Charlie Company had been something special. The men had been golden. But so many had been lost. Tutwiler didn't let the group linger overlong on the pain of war. His young officers had done well, as well as any officers in any war. They were there to toast survival. More champagne came, and, running out of glasses, the group started a drinking game. POP went the top of a new bottle. Whomever the cork landed nearest to had to chug as much as he could.

The night had been epic. Benedick and Hoskins were awoken the next day by a voice saying, "I wonder if they are dead?" Shaking the cobwebs away as best they could, the two young lieutenants noticed that they were lying in the bottom of a muddy ditch. Slowly it all came back to them; they had been walking home from the O club, singing loudly, when there had been a mortar attack. The duo had then tumbled into the nearest ditch for cover, where they had promptly passed out and snored the remainder of the night away. Hunt, for his part, had made it all the way back to his own bed, where he came to the next afternoon. He was badly hungover – he had expected that – but he didn't know why his arms and legs hurt so badly. He looked down to see that his trousers were torn and that he had cuts and bruises all over. Finally he remembered; thoroughly drunk, the lieutenants had challenged each other to a low-crawling competition across the gravel outside the O club. It seemed that he had won. Hunt sat and thought, through a blinding headache, back on the rest of the night. They had all let their hair down. It had been all of the pent-up emotion of an entire year coming out all at once. It had been a funeral dirge for men who would never return to see their families – men lost under their command. But it had also been a celebration – a celebration of survival. They had beaten the odds.

For the enlisted men of Charlie Company, New Year's Eve was very much a mixed bag. John Sclimenti, who had been so badly shaken when the Viet Cong soldier had jumped up from a spider hole when 1st Platoon had charged the enemy positions on June 19, knew that there would be a lot of drinking going on that night. But he wasn't going to take any risks. He was only a couple of days short of going home to California. The chances of being hit by a mortar round at Bear Cat were laughably low, but he was damned if he was going to take any risks now. Instead of drinking, Sclimenti, joined by a few others, slept in the protective bunkers that night. It wasn't comfortable, but it was safe. For Sergeant Daniel Kerr of 2nd Platoon, the time called for reflection. He remembered back to "Parents' Day" at the end of training at Fort Riley. It had been an occasion where parents could come visit their soldier boys – an occasion that Kerr relished. What a pleasure it had been to meet the parents of the men he had helped to train. But now he could only think about how much it hurt. He kept seeing those parents in his mind – parents of the boys who had been lost in Vietnam. Parents who would never see their children again.

Jim Dennison, who had been infused in late August, was so happy to be with some of his old Charlie Company buddies again that he wasn't going to let fear get in the way of a last good drink. The army owed him at least that. Dennison, Jimmie Salazar, Bill Reynolds, and a few others could hardly believe their luck – it was like somebody wanted them to get drunk. Who did they meet manning the PX but Larry Lilley? The group drank the night away, and, while their celebration did not reach the epic level of the officers only a few tents away, it got the job done. The next day Dennison wove his way unsteadily to the holding area that represented the first real step before the freedom bird. Through an alcohol-fueled haze, Dennison became dimly aware that an REMF was telling him that he couldn't bring his half-full bottle of scotch into the holding area. There seemed to be few options, so Dennison calmly drank what was left of the bottle and passed out on the spot. A few feet away, Gary Maibach, the conscientious objector medic who had also been infused, watched Dennison collapse and sighed. Even though they sometimes fell short of the ideal, Maibach knew how good these men were – his men. They had been through hell, and some had not made their way out unscathed. Maibach walked over to Dennison, got him up onto unsteady feet, and signed him in – they were going home.

John Young had started drinking heavily, but in secret, after the battle of June 19. On New Year's Eve he knew that he would need a fair amount of booze to be able to get any sleep at all – it was the end of one year and the beginning of the rest of his life. On the way to the NCO club he had run into Buford Hoover, who had been Young's platoon sergeant and mentor for most of the year. It was too early; the NCO club was not yet open, but the duo talked themselves in and sat down to a long, steady afternoon and night of drinking. They sat in a corner, very aware that their close relationship that had begun at Fort Riley was coming to an end, and shunned the company of the REMFs who crowded into the club at opening time. Hoover and Young realized that it might be the last time that they would ever sit down with another person who shared the same memories. They, like the rest of Charlie Company, were headed to different places – different lives, among people who would never truly know or understand what had happened to them, to Charlie Company. As the drinks kept coming, the two did their best to

Lynn Crockett (left) and Herb Lind.

Terry McBride and his M60 machine gun.

John Hoskins on board ship in the Mekong Delta.

Phil Ferro during a break in a patrol.

Alan Richards (left) and Ronnie Gann shown here on the right of the picture.

Fred Kenney (left) and James "Smitty" Smith.

Jerry Specht (left) and Gary Maibach.

Frank Schwan on board the John Pope.

Ron Vidovic posing for a hospital photograph.

Steve Hopper.

Larry Lukes (left), Tim Fischer, and Ron Vidovic aboard ship.

Carl Cortright.

Jimmie Salazar with his grandchildren.

Gary Maibach (photo courtesy of Bill Ganzel).

The indomitable Jack Benedick.

John Young in 2002.

Jacque Bomann (Peterson) upon her graduation from nursing school in 1985.

Charlie Nelson after his return to the reservation.

Charlie Company's first reunion, 1989 – left to right, Tim Fischer, Jim Cusanelli, Joe Marr, John Howell, Tony Caliari, John Bradfield, Steve Hopper, and Tom Conroy.

remember every battle, every encounter, every loss of the year – to burn them into their minds.

There were the losses outside of Charlie Company. "That one guy fell off of the boat." "How about the mortar squad that got blown up at Bear Cat?" There seemed to be so many; people who got sick and never came back, people who had fallen off the ammi barge into the river never to be seen again. But most attention was given to their own combat losses. "Remember Lieutenant Black, blown up by the VC mine?" "Ron Schworer, what a tragedy. That guy was a genius, really going places. I wonder if they ever found his body?" At nearly the same time Hoover and Young remembered Don Peterson. "He was a good man; the best." "I wonder how Jacque and little Jimmy are doing? Must be tough on them. Maybe we should look them up when we get home?" "I wonder how Nelson, Ski, and Cortright are doing?" June 19 was almost too difficult to bear. The mortar platoon lost on the PABs; Lieutenant Schulman getting shot after his command was destroyed; everybody's friend Bill Geier dying while helping a wounded man; Forrest Ramos falling out of the helicopter; Tim Johnson being killed after everything seemed to be over. All of the wounded. "No way to remember all of the wounded – too damn many of them." "Yeah, seems like everybody got hurt at least once." Eakins, Ferro, and King – all killed together on July 11. "And what about Fred Kenney?" "Damn, that was tough. Never even got a chance to see his kid. Do you remember how he liked to show those pictures around all the time? He loved it when we got a replacement in, so he could show those pictures off to somebody new." Young opened up and let Hoover know how much losing Benny Bridges on July 29 had hurt. How he had never quite been the same since. Then, when it had all seemed like it was over – Burkhead, Alldridge, and Lieutenant Davis – all killed on the same day. Maybe in the same burst of fire.

The conversation had taken hours. It was well past dark and the club was full of REMFs intent on celebrating New Year's. But Young and Hoover just sat there and drank in silence, trying to process the now shared pain and loss. Young passed out on the table, and Hoover kept on drinking. A few minutes later the club's Master-at-Arms came by and shook Young. It was obvious that he didn't want passed-out drunks in his bar. Hoover looked at the MA and calmly said, "Touch him again and I'll kill you." The MA glanced up and Hoover continued, "I mean it." The entire club went quiet, and the MA pled with Hoover: "Look, Sarge, I can't have people passed out on the tables. He can't stay here." Hoover glared at him and shouted, "Is this a 9th Division NCO club?" The MA replied that it was. "Well this is a 9th Division NCO. You stay the fuck away from him!" Deciding to leave well enough alone, the MA retreated to his office. Hoover looked around at the silent REMFs who were all staring at him. He yelled to the throng, "Spread out men. One grenade would get you all." A few minutes later Young woke up, and the pair ordered another round of beer.

Some of the Charlie Company originals had the good luck to fly home together; however, though arriving in Vietnam had been a shared experience, leaving Saigon and returning home was intensely personal and individualistic. Charlie Company was no more. Yet even as the young men prepared to return to lives and families in a different world, there remained a few shared experiences. Like many in the company, Steve Hopper watched anxiously as the freedom bird touched down at Tan Son Nhut airbase. His excitement turned to introspection, though, as hundreds of fresh-faced replacements, wearing starched fatigues, disembarked the aircraft. They looked so young. Had they looked that young just a year ago? He couldn't help wondering how many of them wouldn't survive to see their own freedom bird and flight back to the world. Then he saw how they were looking at him and his buddies. To these newbies they must have looked so old, so worn, so jaded. Hopper could just see that they were all wondering, "What the hell happened to these guys? I wonder if I will look like them after a year over here?" A few of the veterans wished the replacements good luck, and received congratulations in return before boarding the plane, but it was a sobering experience.

On the different flights home, the boys of Charlie Company slept, ordered glass after glass of cold milk, and flirted with the stewardesses. There were great cheers when the airplanes took off, and even greater cheers when they touched down. Some of the men hustled off the aircraft to kiss the ground, while others lingered to talk to old friends. Some were met by protestors and catcalls of "baby killer!" Elijah Taylor couldn't be bothered by such foolishness. He was in too much of a hurry to get home and just ran right on past. Tom Conroy, who still could not shake the memory of picking up Fred Kenney's body after the battle on July 11, had to be held back by MPs when he tried to get at the protestors in San Francisco. Larry Lukes, who had been right behind Fred Kenney when he had been shot, narrowly avoided getting hit with a rotten egg thrown by one of the protestors. He didn't get angry; he just stood and stared at the screaming mob. He couldn't even move. He could only wonder why they hated him and the boys of Charlie Company so much. Lukes hadn't expected a parade when he got home. He knew that there was unrest in the country, but he hadn't expected anything like this. This wasn't the America he had left. He had lost so many good friends in Vietnam; had lost so much of himself. This was their welcome home? Somehow that one rotten egg had hurt Larry Lukes more than the sum total experience of an entire year spent in Vietnam.

Stan Cockerell, who had ignored his Malaria and abandoned his sickbed to join the battle of June 19, flew alone into San Francisco where he too was met by protestors. Making matters worse, Cockerell had to report in to receive starched new fatigues and a proper regulation haircut. Looking strictly military, Cockerell stuck out like a sore thumb and was shunned on his next flight to Los Angeles. Trying his best to ignore the many slights offered by his fellow countrymen, Cockerell then took the bus to the North Hollywood station but was still 2 miles from home. Hoping to surprise his parents, Cockerell didn't call for a ride home; instead he hailed a cab. One by one, though, the drivers turned their backs on him; they refused to serve a Vietnam veteran. With a sigh of resignation, Cockerell shouldered his duffel bag and trudged home. As he finally neared his parent's house, Cockerell stopped to gaze at the house across the street where Linda Walters lived. Stan had used to love to watch Linda and her friends walk past on their way home, and, even before he had left for Vietnam, he had told his buddies that he would marry that beautiful girl one day. But he had never worked up the gumption to ask her out. Cockerell was a changed man, though, and he knew what he was going to do. After reuniting with his parents, Cockerell was going across that street to ask for that date.

For Jack Benedick and Lynn Hunt, the flight home was the best of times and the worst of times. They were going home to see their families, but they had left behind a job undone. They were officers, trained to lead – to win. But the war was still going on – their platoons were still going into combat without them. For them there was no closure. After the two parted ways in San Francisco, Benedick caught a connecting flight to Fayetteville, Arkansas, where his wife, Nancy, and his young son Jack Junior, who had been born in March 1966, were living with her parents. When he stepped off the aircraft, he couldn't help but notice how cold it was before he made his way inside the terminal. Expecting his arrival, Nancy ran to him, and the couple embraced. Watching their reunion, the assembled travelers broke into a round of applause. Nancy then drove Jack home and threw the door open, where Jack Junior was waiting. Excited to see his son after so long, Benedick opened his arms wide for a hug, but Jack Junior ran and hid behind the door, asking his mommy, "Who is that strange man?" Benedick realized that he had missed so much – so much that he didn't even know his own son. But at the same time, he wondered what he was missing in Vietnam.

John Young had not let anyone at home know that he was coming. Instead, after landing in San Francisco and catching a connecting flight to Minneapolis, he caught a cab home from the airport and hoped to surprise his parents and sisters. The blinds were open, and his mother, Myrl, and his sisters saw the cab pull up and saw John get out in his uniform – they rushed outside and mobbed him with hugs and kisses long before he could make his way into the house. John had arrived too late, though, to catch his father, Wilbur, at home. He was already at work down at the International Harvester plant. After more hugs and a quick meal, Young donned his dress uniform and went to surprise his father. He walked into the plant and up to the foreman and simply said, "I'm looking for Wilbur Young." It was a plant full of World War II veterans – they knew what the stripes on Young's arms meant. They knew what the ribbons on his chest meant. They knew what was going on. The foreman ran out onto the floor and yelled, "Bill, get over here! Your son is home!" Wilbur Young walked over and gave his son a bear hug. He then stood back, and the men standing all around began to clap and walked forward to pat father and son on the back. John Young could see the pride in his father's eyes as he showed his son off to his work friends. It was a brief, happy moment after a year of pain.

Jimmie Salazar couldn't wait for his flight to land; he wanted to get home and see his baby. Couldn't airplanes go any faster? In San Francisco, his group was held up by a protest and stood shivering on the tarmac before being hustled inside to meet their connecting flights. Salazar located his flight to Dallas on the board and realized that he was going to have to run fast or miss it. He took off and passed someone he recognized running for the same gate. It was Colonel Tutwiler. He slowed down just a bit to keep pace with the man who had been his commander, and the two reached the gate barely in time. Tutwiler checked in, but there was a problem with Salazar. Evidently he had reached the gate so late that an REMF captain was in the process of being booked into his seat. Salazar pleaded his case, but the captain made it plain that it would be him flying to Dallas – Salazar would have to wait for the next available flight. Having seen the entire incident, Tutwiler walked back to the gate area and made the captain snap to attention. He gave the unfortunate officer a classic military dressing down. What did he think he was doing, taking the seat of this combat veteran who was trying to get home and see his wife and child? After making the captain apologize for his transgression, Tutwiler walked with Salazar aboard the aircraft. The two, one who had been the battalion commander, the other an enlisted man, sat together on the flight, sharing booze and stories of Vietnam. Only after the flight touched down in Dallas did Jimmie Salazar remember that in the rush in San Francisco he had not had time to call his family to let them know he was coming home. Well, there was nothing for it now. It was only 6am, but he managed to catch a cab to his mother's house. Not quite knowing what to expect – how does a father prepare to meet his child for the first time – Salazar rang the doorbell. The door opened. It was Aurora, up early to take care of little Richard. She let out a scream and jumped up and down before giving Jimmie a hug. Then she opened the door just a bit further, and Jimmie saw Richard – walking around in one of the little baby saucers with wheels. Aurora had done her best over the months to show Richard pictures of Jimmie, pointing to the pictures and saying, "Papa, Papa." It had become such a ritual that papa had been one of Richard's very first words. It had worked. When Richard saw the man at the door he began yelling over and over, "Papa, Papa, Papa," while his chubby little legs churned the wheeled saucer forward toward the father he had never met. It turned out that Jimmie didn't need any lessons on how to meet his child – he just picked Richard up from the saucer, gave him a hug, and held him. That hug and those little arms – little arms that didn't care what he had seen or what he had done over the last year, little arms that loved him unconditionally and only knew him as papa – set Jimmie Salazar free.

8 HOME FROM WAR

Sad Times

Oh, Vietnam. The memories, it's been so long ago
The sounds of bullets, bombs, and the cry of the wounded
At night, when I sleep, the dreams and nightmares

It has been so long ago, twenty years or more, but the memories make it seem like yesterday

How can you forget the hot, smelly, and sticky jungle, and the many flying insects?

The mud after a monsoon?

The many friends you made, and so few coming back

When you sleep, the dreams, nightmares, and waking up in a cold sweat

Saying to yourself, it's over now, but how can you forget the memories of Sad Times?

Charlie Nelson

Remembering Fred Kenney

I saw your name upon The Wall and I cried so many tears
It seems just like yesterday, but it's been so many years
I saw so many faces of veterans with welting eyes

We never told you how we felt, or got to say our goodbyes
Your memory etched in our minds, you were so brave and bold
Stories of your young lives still need to be told
You were eager and full of life, and waiting to go home
I'm sorry for not getting to you while you were lying all alone
I've cried so many tears my friend, I cannot forget that awful day
I heard your cries and screams for help, but then you heard God say
You're coming home to be with me, I'll guide you through the light
Your life was gone, you had gone home and I cried through the night
My life has been filled with sorrow to remember how you died
But I know that you are in heaven and looking down with pride
When we meet again someday, I hope you will take my hand
For we will be Brothers again and together in the Promised Land.

Tom Conroy

After Fred Kenney's funeral in Canoga Park, Barbara Kenney and her young son Freddie moved into a condo in nearby Woodland Hills. Only 21, having lost the love of her life, caring for a young son, and feeling terribly alone – Barbara was adrift. All of her friends were preparing for the beginning of their lives and marriages, and she was a war widow. Everything seemed so dark. Through it all, Barbara remained close with the Kenneys, who did what they could to help, but nothing seemed to make a difference. But then amid her grief and only a few months after Fred's funeral, Barbara began to hear from Don Hill, a family friend of the Kenneys whom she had once dated in high school. Don made it clear that he never stopped caring for her, and let it be known that he wanted to marry her and to help care for her young son. Initially Barbara was unsure of what to think. It was all so sudden. But when Don returned from his own stint in the military, Barbara saw him at a welcome-home party where the two talked and later began to date. To Barbara it was almost like someone had thrown her a lifeline. She craved nothing more than normalcy and a loving family for Freddie, and Don was there – a good man, a man she had known for much of her life. She talked her decision over with the Kenneys. They knew and liked Don Hill, and fully supported Barbara's desire to get married and to start her life over again.

A few months later the couple wed. Don Hill was a good father and worked hard on his relationship with young Freddie. Don did his best to understand Barbara's grief; after all, Fred had been his friend too. The little family even kept a picture of Fred Kenney on the wall to keep his memory alive. When Freddie turned four years old, as soon as they thought he could process the information, Barbara and Don sat him down and told him about Fred – his real father. Freddie sat through the explanation as best he could as tears began to roll down his cheeks. It all left the boy with so many questions. Don wasn't his real dad? His real dad had been in the army and was dead? It broke Barbara's heart to see little Freddie so distraught and so confused. It was like having to deal with the pain of losing Fred all over again. Barbara and Don helped Freddie deal with his sorrow as best they could, and, over time, he seemed to come to peace with the pain. As the years passed and Barbara and Don had four other children of their own, Freddie learned to balance a fatherly love for Don Hill with a growing curiosity about his real father. In the process, Freddie came to know and become close to his Kenney relatives, and developed a fierce pride in both his father and his sacrifice.

Through it all, though, Don and Barbara began to grow apart. Perhaps it was simply due to the many strains that so often doom marriages. Perhaps, though, the end of the marriage was rooted in its beginnings. There was still love there, and both parents cared deeply for their children, but the couple divorced in 1986. Although Don did his part to provide support, Barbara was once again alone – and without a job – but this time with five children. The important thing in her life was caring for her "babies," but to do that she had to go and find work. Within a few months, Barbara was lucky enough to find a position with a friend who worked for a title company, a job that she would hold for 22 years. Barbara worked hard to raise her children and kept up a thriving relationship with the Kenneys along the way. All the while, the picture of Fred Kenney, lovingly cared for, hung on Barbara's wall. Both she and Freddie did what they could to honor his memory, including visits to decorate his gravesite, but something was always missing. Barbara had kept Fred's letters home from Vietnam, but she knew that they didn't tell the whole story. Both she and Freddie wanted to know more.

As Vivian Conroy stood there waiting for the airplane to touch down in January 1968, she could hardly contain her excitement. Her husband Tom was coming home from Vietnam. The couple had married just after Tom's basic training at Fort Riley, and had spent some time living together in a cramped apartment there before he had shipped out for war. But now he was coming home for good and their life together could finally begin. There were the tearful hugs and the sentimental moments that define any homecoming, but Vivian quickly realized that the Tom who had come home was not the same man she had sent to Vietnam only 12 short months ago. He seemed more distant, smiled less, jumped almost uncontrollably at loud noises. It hurt all the more because there was nothing Vivian could do. She knew that she would never understand what he had been through, and Tom certainly didn't want to talk about it. She had to hope that this somber, dark time in Tom's life would pass – that his wounds would heal on their own.

Tom Conroy never could escape from the visions of Vietnam – especially the memory of picking up Fred Kenney's body on the morning of July 11 and getting covered in his blood. Then there had been the protestors in the San Francisco airport and the ongoing controversy over the war that had somehow conspired to cheapen the loss of so many good friends. Tom had done his very best to put the war behind him, and, like so many veterans, thought he was doing a reasonable job of hiding his pain. But Vivian knew him too well and could sense his suffering. The couple had three children, and Tom worked hard to support his burgeoning family, first in a chicken rendering plant and then as a truck driver before settling down to work in construction in the Los Angeles area until his retirement in 1999. Along the way, Tom began to hear more and more about something called post-traumatic stress disorder (PTSD), but he knew one thing for sure: he didn't have it. Finally, though, one of his co-workers, who was a fellow veteran, handed Tom a pamphlet on PTSD. Mainly in an effort to please his well-meaning friend, Tom leafed through the brochure and, to his great surprise, discovered that the symptoms he was reading described him perfectly. Nightmares, quickness to anger, hyper alertness, dislike of crowds, feelings of guilt; they were all there.

With Vivian's full support, Tom Conroy went to the Veterans Administration (VA) to receive counseling, where he shared his experiences in Vietnam with another person for the first time. It had all been bottled up in him for decades, festering. The doctor encouraged Tom to confront his fears. To remember Vietnam was a good thing, not a bad thing. Slowly, tentatively, Tom Conroy began to explore the memories of his past, memories that conjured horrible images and brought such pain – it hurt, but he kept trying, kept moving forward. In his own process of coming to terms with his past, Tom Conroy got back in touch with some of the many Charlie Company veterans who lived in the Los Angeles area. He even began to write about his experiences. But something was still missing. He had to confront the image that was seared so vividly into his consciousness. He had to confront the memory of Fred Kenney.

The younger Fred Kenney was at his home in the Simi Valley one evening when the phone rang. A voice on the other end asked, "Is this Fred Kenney, the son of a Fred Kenney who served in the 9th Infantry Division and who died in Vietnam?" After a short pause, Fred answered that he was. The man identified himself as Tom Conroy and said that he had served with Fred's father. They had been friends, and he had been with him the day he died. Conroy expressed an interest in meeting Fred, and his mother Barbara if she was still in the area, to talk about what had happened that day. Fred took Conroy's contact information and said that his mother did indeed still live in the area and that he would talk to her about it. After Conroy hung up, Fred called his mother and told her of the conversation. Neither Fred nor Barbara was at all sure about what to do next. They both wanted so badly to know about Fred's time in Vietnam and about his friends. But could they bear hearing the story of his loss? After several conversations, though, Barbara and Fred decided that they shouldn't pass up this opportunity.

A few days later, Barbara and Fred Kenney met with Tom Conroy, Bill Reynolds, and Stan Cockerell. To the Charlie Company veterans it was like a moment frozen in time. Barbara still looked just as beautiful as she did in the pictures that Fred delighted in showing off, and in Freddie they saw the image of their long-lost friend. For Barbara and Fred, the meeting was a cathartic experience. These men had clearly loved Fred Kenney. They remembered him so fondly and spoke of him in a way that almost seemed to make him come to life again. There was a shared joy in the room, until the men began to talk about the events of July 11. The details brought everyone to tears – with some reliving old pain while the others absorbed it anew. During it all, Barbara noticed something. It seemed to be making Conroy, Reynolds, and Cockerell feel better to speak to her; like they were finally transferring a burden they had carried alone for so long – finally delivering a message from the past that had weighed on them so heavily. Although hearing of the manner of Fred's death was difficult, the knowledge was tempered with a feeling of calm. Fred had died surrounded by friends; friends who cared so much about him that they still held his memory dear after so many years. While Barbara sat detached from the conversation going on around her as the three men spoke further with Fred, her memories strayed back to the day she had first met Fred Kenney. There he stood, young and so good-looking. It was love at first sight. They were supposed to have had such a good life together, but he had fallen in that rice paddy so far away in Vietnam. The love of her life was truly gone, and she would never find someone so thoroughly nice ever again.

Two days after his wounding in the fighting on May 15, 1967, Carl Cortright struggled to come to terms with the idea that, at age 21, he would never walk again. For the remainder of his two-week stay in Vietnam, the hospital staff were very encouraging, stopping by twice a day and asking him to wiggle his toes. Although his brain fired, nothing happened. Ever. At the first hospital Chaplain Windmiller had been there holding his hand and offering comfort. At the next hospital, another chaplain informed Cortright that his family had already received a telegram informing them that he had been wounded and suggested that Cortright pen a letter home. Cortright obliged, but hid the worst from his parents. He told them that he had been wounded, but was going to live and would soon be home. From Vietnam, Cortright was flown directly to California and taken to Letterman Army Medical Center in San Francisco. The next morning, the door to Cortright's hospital room opened and there stood his parents Aubrey and Dorothy. For a few moments they just stood there, unable to react, as the reality set in. They had known that Carl was badly wounded, but they had not expected to see him strapped into a Stryker frame – a narrow, rigid cot for use in paralysis cases.

Their son, their beloved son, was paralyzed. There was no chance that he would ever walk again. But he had been fine only such a short time ago. It was so difficult for them to take, but the family worked through the bad times and was constantly at Cortright's side during his eight weeks at Letterman. Next Cortright made his way to the Veterans Affairs Medical Center in Long Beach, California, where he was housed in a ward with 50 other spinal injury patients. The very next morning a nurse came into his room with a wheelchair and told Carl to get out of bed. He was not sure whom the nurse was talking to. He had been in bed for ten weeks and was somehow sure he would be bedridden forever. But, no, that nurse was talking to him. At only 100 pounds, Cortright struggled even to sit up, and the nurse had to wrestle him into the wheelchair. But it felt so good. He was up. He was mobile. Regardless of his newfound mobility, though, Cortright was in critical danger of lapsing into a depression. There were so many hard questions. Would he ever drive his white Impala again? Could he ever have a job or would he just be a "cripple?" Would he ever have a date or get married? But as he looked around the Long Beach VA, Cortright discovered something. There were so many people there who were worse off than he was, quadriplegics who would never have use of their bodies from the neck down. At least he could sit up. At least he could use his arms. His epiphany came when he noticed who was cheering him on the most – a veteran completely paralyzed except for partial use of one arm. Damn it! If this guy who was so much worse off was so optimistic why was he sitting there so damn depressed? From that moment Carl Cortright swore never to feel sorry for himself again.

By 1968 Carl Cortright was out of the hospital, living with his parents, and trying to figure out a new direction for his life. The first thing he had to do was get mobile – he had to get a car to fit back into the able-bodied culture of California in the late 1960s.

Nobody thought he could do it, but Cortright went down to a local dealership and bought a car with hand controls, and, after a few lessons with the unwieldy setup, was back going to drive-in movies, flirting with girls, and generally living life. In the simple act of driving, Carl Cortright felt liberated, whole. His newly mobile life was not without its difficulties, though. At the time there were no such things as handicapped parking places, and Cortright could not get his wheelchair into the narrow spaces between standard parking spots. Sometimes the parking situation meant that Cortright could not go where he wanted or needed; worse was that sometimes when he was lucky enough to find a parking spot he would return only to find that the parking spaces around his car had been taken, leaving him stranded until the owners of the vehicles returned to depart. And there was always the matter of his wheelchair itself. Initially Cortright's father, Aubrey, accompanied him almost everywhere to fold and load the cumbersome wheelchair into the back seat and then unload it when Carl was ready. But having dad along was no way to be successful on the social scene. Cortright practiced nearly every day, wriggling from the chair into the driver's seat and then folding the chair and loading it into the back with one arm. The process involved trial and error, and a few spills, but in short order Carl Cortright was back looking for girls without his father in tow.

For a few months after his return from Vietnam, Carl Cortright suffered from vivid nightmares; the Viet Cong were shooting at him in slow motion. The bullets were kicking up mud and searching him out, but no matter how fast he ran he didn't make any headway. He usually woke up before any bullets struck home. But Cortright was determined not to let one month in Vietnam get the best of him. He was determined not to live a life of bitterness and what ifs. He was paralyzed and that was that. No use being bitter, he just had to keep on living as best he could. While getting used to his new life, Cortright was determined to take some time off – to get his bearings. He didn't need a job; he was on government disability. He could take some time to make up his mind about his future. In 1970 Cortright bought a house in Oxnard, California, on a government grant. Then he and his parents set out to discover America. As the decade of the 1970s unfolded, the Cortrights became inveterate travelers, driving in an RV across the country to Maine, traveling the trans-Canada Highway, and generally seeing what the continent had to offer. By 1979, Cortright had met a woman and had fallen in love, and the couple wed in 1981.

Cortright spent much of the 1980s helping to raise his stepchild and as an on-again off-again college student, working on a degree in photography. After his graduation in the early 1990s, Cortright put his skills to work in the field of computer photo imaging and also developed an interest in working in stained glass. His life, interrupted by a divorce in 1989, was full, but Cortright always found time to go and visit with other veterans at the local VA. While the social workers at the VA were happy that Cortright had so much to keep him busy and seemed to be in no danger of slipping into depression, one social worker in particular kept bugging him. Every year veterans like him from the Los Angeles area competed in the National Veterans Wheelchair Games, and she thought that it would be a good idea if he trained and went with them. It became something of a running joke. Every year she would ask Cortright to come with them; every year he said he would think about it. In 1996, when the games were scheduled to be in Atlanta, Cortright finally gave in – after all he wasn't doing much of anything else that week. What the hell?

The games in Atlanta were beyond anything Cortright could have imagined. With the event being used as something of a dry run for the upcoming Atlanta Olympics, the disabled veterans got the best of everything – fancy hotels, great food, and wonderful hospitality. Cortright competed in a few events, including bowling, air gun, and table tennis – but it was the company that had the greatest impact. The life of a wheelchair-bound veteran can become very lonely. Other than visits to the VA, Cortright had never before met someone else like himself. He was always the odd man out – the different one, alone in a crowd. But at the National Veterans Wheelchair Games, everyone else was like him. There were 500 veterans in wheelchairs! For a week, instead of being singular, Carl Cortright was part of the norm, the majority. There weren't stares or questions left politely unasked by the able bodied. Everyone else understood what it was like to live in a wheelchair, what it was like to be so badly wounded in battle. Carl Cortright had found a home.

The games became an increasingly important part of Cortright's life, returning every year to rekindle bonds of camaraderie with those with whom he shared so much. But it was more than just friendship and bonding; Carl Cortright wanted to excel in the games. In 2008 his dreams became a reality when Cortright won the gold medal in trapshooting. Winning the gold, a symbol of his victory over the debilitating, life-long effects of a single Viet Cong bullet fired during a single battle during a single month in Vietnam, meant the world to Carl Cortright, especially surrounded as he was by a caring family of veterans who were striving to achieve their own victories over grievous wounds suffered in their own wars.

While others were celebrating and drinking, Willie McTear spent the flight home from Vietnam lost in thought. He tried again and again to remember the faces of his friends Ron Schworer and Forrest Ramos. Already it was getting harder to recall them vividly, which saddened the big man greatly. He didn't want to forget his friends. He never wanted to forget. When he filed off the aircraft in San Francisco he finally smiled. There was a crowd there cheering, welcoming him – and the memory of his friends – home. It all came crashing down when McTear realized that those weren't cheers. The crowd was booing and yelling things like "baby killer!" What the hell had he been doing in Vietnam? Who had he been doing it for? McTear boarded the flight home more confused and saddened than ever. After landing in New Orleans, McTear made his way back to his tiny hometown of Newellton, Louisiana, where his family treated him to a party and a good, down-home dinner. For the next few days, McTear's parents did everything they could to make him feel at home. His mother, Mary, cooked all his favorite dishes, while his father once again tried to talk Willie into joining him in the family logging business. "Real men work with their hands and sweat, son." His father, grandfather, and uncle even took him hunting, which had been one of his favorite pastimes. It was there that it struck Willie McTear. Nothing was the same. Hunting wasn't fun anymore. He had hunted people. Somehow hunting animals didn't measure up, didn't seem right. Nothing seemed right. He couldn't reclaim the past, and it was of no use to try. He had changed too much.

Realizing that he had to get away, to make some kind of change, Willie McTear returned to Las Vegas and the college studies that had been interrupted by Vietnam. After some struggles, McTear graduated from community college in 1972 and went to work as a corrections officer in a juvenile detention center. He had also fallen in love, gotten married, and had two children, a girl and a boy. There he was, Willie McTear, living the American dream. Middle class, nice house, growing family. He had it all. But all the while his life was spiraling out of control. Willie McTear had never shaken the pain of Vietnam; he had simply covered it up. Alcohol and drugs were his defensive mechanisms, but they also threatened to destroy his life and the lives of his wife and children. The signs of his deterioration were all around. He often drank until he blacked out, only to have his children wake him. His best friends were gangsters, dope dealers, who were far too comfortable in his home. He was spending all his money on booze and drugs. He was a disgrace to his family. His so-called friends were a danger to his family. He saw no way out.

In January 1985, Willie McTear simply left. He took off his tie, walked away from his job, bought a pistol, and went to live on the streets. He stalked the mean streets of Las Vegas, looking for handouts to score his next shot of booze or next way to get high. He generally lived in flop houses with other homeless veterans. It was a dirty, difficult, demeaning existence, but somehow McTear felt at home among the other homeless men. Routinely McTear would pass out on the streets for days at a time. When he awoke he would often just stagger to the nearest bar, where sometimes he was received well and sometimes violently. On two occasions he was nearly kicked to death outside of bars, and another time a drug dealer stabbed him in the face, narrowly missing his eye. While he was on the street, his wife applied for and was granted a divorce, all without his knowledge. He was too high, too lost, to care. Willie McTear was slowly committing suicide. After five years of violent, besotted street life, Willie McTear hit bottom. He passed out in the back of a "shooting gallery" high on dope and wracked with pneumonia. While McTear tossed and turned on a cot, the purveyor of the gallery noticed that he was about to die. Not wanting a corpse on his hands, he hauled McTear to the hospital and dumped him, where he was eventually picked up by the Las Vegas Police.

While serving time on an outstanding warrant, Willie McTear sobered up. After so long on booze and drugs, going cold turkey was excruciating, leaving McTear with the cold sweats and panic attacks of withdrawal. But as his sentence was nearing its end, Willie McTear looked at the world clearly for the first time in years. He had lost everything in his life. He wanted to stay sober, but what was he going to do? Perhaps it was fate. Soon after his release from jail, when he was at his most vulnerable, Willie McTear received a visit from Richard Vincent, with whom he had worked in the juvenile detention system. The two had always gotten along well, and Vincent had since moved to Orange County, California, where he oversaw several of the Care Unit hospitals on the west coast. Seeing his old friend in distress, Vincent offered McTear a job and a place to live in California. It didn't take Willie McTear long to decide. He took Vincent up on his offer. It was the best decision that he had made in years. McTear stuck to Vincent like glue, learning everything he could about hospital administration while coming to terms with his own future. What he saw, and who he had been, pushed McTear toward a natural career path. In 1994 he enrolled in Saddleback College to study the treatment of chemical dependency and alcohol abuse. In every page of his studies he saw himself; he saw the desperate faces of the other veterans living on the streets of Las Vegas. Willie McTear had found his calling. In 1998 he graduated at the top of his class, and then went on to work in several hospitals throughout California caring for those with chemical or alcohol dependency.

McTear had his own dependencies in check, working through them in part through Alcoholics Anonymous. While the meetings and camaraderie of AA were central to his recovery, they had only been a conduit to something greater and more meaningful. In one of his first nights at AA, McTear heard another member's testimony that it was God, not AA, who had reclaimed his life. In his memories McTear was transported back to a tiny church in Newellton, Louisiana. His parents were there, his grandparents – his whole extended family. All singing. All praising. He remembered that he had once been close to God. War, death, and drugs had pulled

McTear away from faith. He had been "in the belly of the beast." After the meeting, Willie McTear visited and joined a small church in Santa Ana, California. It wasn't going to be like church back home. He wasn't the same, but somehow he knew that God welcomed him no matter what.

Even alcohol free, with a meaningful job, and with a renewed life of faith Willie McTear wasn't right. He kept waking up at night in a panic. The nightmares were so vivid – the jungle smells, the lifeless faces, the gripping horror. He could hardly stand it. He had friends, but he didn't want to be around them. He had a life, but sometimes he couldn't face it. Willie McTear knew that he wasn't crazy, but he sure didn't know what was wrong. He just felt so alone, so desperate. What if he went back to his old ways and lost everything he had fought so hard to gain? Nobody else was having these problems. Maybe it was him. Maybe he was losing it. Finally Willie McTear swallowed his pride and spoke of his problem with one of the doctors he worked with at the hospital. It didn't take long for the doctor to reach his diagnosis. Willie McTear exhibited the classic signs of PTSD. As soon as he had returned from the war, Willie McTear had turned to alcohol and drugs to numb his pain; he had never dealt with Vietnam – the friends he had lost, the things he had done, and the national rejection he and his generation had received for their sacrifice. Now that the alcohol and drugs were gone, Willie McTear finally had to deal with Vietnam. The doctor patted Willie on the shoulder and told him that there were medications to help and therapy he could receive, but, most importantly, he was not alone.

On his doctor's instructions, Willie McTear began to get VA counseling for PTSD, which involved intense group therapy sessions with other veterans. His PTSD didn't go away; the doctors had warned him that that's not the way it works. Treatment and counseling didn't eradicate Vietnam from his memory – he didn't want to do that. He didn't want to forget Vietnam, because that would have meant forgetting the good along with the bad – and there had been so much good. Friendships, camaraderie, laughter; Vietnam had been one of the most meaningful times of Willie McTear's life. He didn't want to forget Ron Schworer and Forrest Ramos. Losing them had hurt so badly, but he wanted to cherish the memories of who they had once been. No, Willie McTear didn't want to forget Vietnam, but treatment helped him to learn to live with Vietnam without it threatening to consume him. With newfound hope, Willie McTear worked out the remainder of his career and in 2004 retired back to Las Vegas. He did what he could to patch up his relationships with his children, relationships too long ignored while Willie McTear wandered alone in the wilderness. In retirement, Willie McTear found the first true peace and contentment that he had known since his childhood. With his savings, military pensions, and social security, McTear had enough to buy a small house and a nice car. He devoted much of his time to AA and PTSD groups in the area, and set out to find the homeless veterans who had once been his only companions. He knew their lives, and they trusted him. McTear took those who would go to the VA and to AA meetings. Others he knew to be more hard-core and less trusting. For those veterans, the ones more thoroughly lost, McTear bought another small house to provide them with what shelter he could. With the sun having finally risen on his life, Willie McTear was determined to walk as boldly in the light as he had once stridden through the darkness.

With all of the hustle and bustle that surrounded the holding of a military funeral, Narciso Ramos could almost get lost in the moment, surrounded as he was by friends and relatives, and shield himself from the reality of his loss. But after the cars drove away and the crowds dwindled, Narciso and his youngest son Jesse were left in the silence of their small house outside the Yakima Indian Reservation – alone with the sad truth that Forrest was never coming home. Jesse had idolized his older brother Forrest; he had even carefully tucked away Forrest's favorite slacks and shirt. When Forrest came home he had planned to have them ready, so the two could go to one of the community dances in Yakima that Forrest liked so well. Forrest could dance and flirt with the girls just like the old days; the only difference would be that this time, for once, Jesse would be old enough to go with him. But now the slacks and shirt would go unworn, destined to remain lovingly folded and tucked away in Jesse's closet for years. For the sake of his youngest son, who was so obviously shaken by Forrest's loss, Narciso tried to put on a brave face. Narciso threw himself into his work, kept up his normal routine of being both a father and mother around the house, and generally tried to hide his sorrow.

Although young Jesse never let on, he knew full well that Narciso was stricken with grief. Smiles came far less often to Narciso Ramos; he seemed locked in a world of melancholy, and there were the moments of quiet sobbing when he didn't think Jesse was watching. Narciso's pain returned afresh not even a month later when the news hit Wapato that two of Forrest's high school classmates had died in Vietnam. There was another round of military funerals, more folded flags, and more grief – a refrain that would become all too frequent as the war in Vietnam lingered. The greatest family shock, though, came in early 1969 when Narciso was absent-mindedly sorting through the mail only to find an all-too-familiar government envelope. Jesse Ramos' draft notice. Nearly beside himself with fear and worry, Narciso was frantic. He couldn't lose another son in Vietnam. He just couldn't. Jesse, though, took the news calmly. Young men his age all over the country were burning draft cards or running away to Canada, but he was going to Vietnam. He looked his father in the eye, and with no small measure of pride, told him that he was going to war like his brother before him. He was going to avenge Forrest's death.

Jesse Ramos served in Vietnam as part of the 101st Airborne Division, fighting in the jungles of the Central Highlands during the latter part of 1969 and early 1970. He returned home to a proud and relieved father – a father who had been denied the opportunity to welcome another of his sons home. Looking up at the wall, Jesse noticed that the picture of him in his uniform now hung beside that of Forrest amid the many family photos. For Jesse there had been no single moment of revenge, no soul-purging catharsis. His part in Vietnam was over. The war just kept going. But Forrest was still gone, and the void in his life was still there. In a world left more bleak, the members of the Ramos family went on about their lives, getting jobs, falling in love, raising families of their own. All the while, though, the family did its best to remember Forrest, to not allow his memory to dim. Every holiday, when the family gathered, they swapped stories about Forrest. Forrest boxing.

Forrest laughing. Forrest alive. But every year the past receded just a bit further, and the memories dimmed just a bit more – until 2003, when Vincent Ramos, son of Forrest's older brother Paul, was sitting at his computer one evening and stumbled across a website for the 9th Infantry Division. Wasn't that Uncle Forrest's unit? After entering the site, Vincent could hardly believe his eyes. There was a picture of Uncle Forrest and a note asking anyone who had known Forrest Ramos to contact webmaster Bill Reynolds. Vincent dialed the number and talked to Bill, who later talked with Paul, Jesse, and the other Ramos siblings. Charlie Company was going to have a reunion, and he invited them all to come – the boys of Charlie Company would love to meet them and tell them about Forrest, about their lives with him, and about how much he had meant to everyone.

After receiving news of Bill Geier's death, his mother, Bernice, fell back on her religion to keep her strong through making the funeral arrangements and the rigors of the service itself. Yet, just to keep going – to get up, to put one foot in front of the other, to live out the day – was so difficult. Somehow Bernice Geier not only had to go on living but also had to console the other members of her family, to plan the funeral, to welcome well-meaning friends and relatives. Through it all, though, she knew that God stood by her, a comforting and comfortable presence, like that of a dear and trusted friend. As Bernice Geier sat at her son's funeral, she looked at the solemn beauty that surrounded her. The stillness of the cemetery, the stock-still military honor guard, the throng of friends and relatives that had come from all around. It was so sweet; Bill's old high school newspaper even ran a special edition in his honor.

While Bernice dealt with the loss with quiet grace, Bill's father Jack wore his sadness for all to see. The pair had always been so close, inseparable, cheering from the bleachers at Wrigley Field, setting up the tents on the family camping trips, coaching little league together. For Jack, there would be no more Cubs games with Bill, no college graduation. His life with his son was over. Jack still loved his family fiercely, and in some ways held them closer than he ever had before, but there was a void in his life – a wound that would not heal. His pain was so great that the family realized it had to do something for him. It was Bernice who hit on the idea. They had promised Bill that they would buy a travel trailer for his return from Vietnam and go camping in Colorado – which Bill had agreed was a far sight better than their normal routine of camping in tents in Wisconsin. To honor Bill, the family would still do it. The Geiers went and picked out a 14-foot Shasta travel trailer and went on vacation in Colorado in 1968 on schedule – in homage to Bill. For a week the Geiers took in the beauty of the West, talked about Bill, and dealt with their collective loss. At the time of the writing of this book, that travel trailer is still in use by the Geier family, owned now by Bill Geier's eldest nephew and his family who travel the byways of the West with a picture of Bill on board.

As Jimmie Salazar stood there, holding his son Richard for the first time on the porch of his parents' house in January 1968, he felt a strange sense of peace wash over him. The war was over, and his life as a father and husband could finally begin. It didn't take Aurora long, though, to realize that Jimmie had changed. He was not that happy-go-lucky boy that she had fallen in love with at age 14. There was something different, more dark, about the new Jimmie Salazar. The simplest part of the change was that Jimmie had become a heavy drinker, almost like he was using booze to cover something up. The family spoke of Vietnam, something Aurora realized that she would never understand, and everyone hoped that Jimmie would just need a little time to readjust to his new life after what he had seen in that faraway land. On the surface Jimmie seemed to be doing everything right. He rented a small house a few blocks away so that he and his new family could move out of his parents' home. He served out the remainder of his enlistment at Fort Hood and then returned home to serve as a member of an engineering battalion in the army reserve and got a job working on hydraulic systems for the Lower Colorado River Authority. Jimmie Salazar worked hard to achieve the American dream for his family, but the nightmare of Vietnam just wouldn't go away.

Try as he might, the drinking couldn't keep the pain at bay. Most visibly to others, Jimmie sometimes hit the dirt at loud noises. More personal, though, were the cold sweats, the whispered voices of friends who had been killed, and the terrible nightmares. Sometimes Jimmie would wake up in the middle of the night screaming and punching – punching Aurora. When he came to, Jimmie was horrified. How could he be hitting his wife? He loved her. What the hell was he doing? Aurora didn't know what to do. She was only 18, was raising a child, and the kind and happy boy she had fallen in love with was gone. The new Jimmie still cared for his family deeply with a love that almost ached with tenderness, but his life was tinged with a constant sadness, a new and volcanic temper, and ever-present alcohol. Sharing a bond of true affection, the Salazars were determined to work through their problems; Aurora spoke with the family priest, while Jimmie went to see a physician. Surely someone would understand their troubles, understand the darkness that threatened to engulf Jimmie's life. But in the 1970s there were no answers. Both the priest and the doctor remarked that many Vietnam veterans seemed troubled, but neither could offer much advice other than telling the young couple to remain strong.

The Salazars were strong. They, like so many others of Jimmie's generation, fought on alone – misunderstood in a country that seemed so desperate to forget both Vietnam and its veterans. The good moments that they had were great – welcoming two more children into the world and sharing times of happiness that blazed all the brighter due in part to their comparative rarity. Jimmie worked hard to make certain that his family wanted for nothing, even though his anger often got him into trouble at work. But the bad times were still there, and were too frequent. The constant alcohol-fueled friction finally became too much for Aurora to bear, and the couple divorced. Then something miraculous happened. During 11 months apart, Jimmie gave up the booze and gained more control over his life. The bad times of nightmares and pain were less frequent; the old Jimmie Salazar who had won Aurora's heart was back. The couple remarried and lived in peace.

Vietnam never totally went away, but the Salazars were now its master, until the terrible day in 1992 when Jimmie suffered his first heart attack. The war and the strains of its aftermath had taken a devastating physical toll on Jimmie, who suffered further heart attacks in both 1994 and 1996. With his heart failing, Jimmie had to give up his job – and, without either work or alcohol to serve as buffers, Vietnam came back into his life full-force and unbidden. The nightmares, the anger – it was all there. But this time there was an added and all-pervasive feeling of hopelessness. Aurora felt helpless as she watched her husband slip away a second time; often he would just sit in his chair and stare at the walls for hours. At least this time there was a name for their problem and pain – Jimmie was diagnosed with PTSD. Although Jimmie had never seen any of his Charlie Company buddies since 1968, he had always been active in local veterans' groups like the American Legion and the Veterans of Foreign Wars, but after 1992 he became involved in a different kind of group, a PTSD support group.

Although he entered treatment with high hopes, Jimmie Salazar was sorely disappointed. Sure he and the other veterans discussed their problems and issues, sure the doctors cared – but nothing got better. He felt like the docs were using him as a guinea pig, all while not really knowing what they were doing. For her part Aurora Salazar felt completely and bitterly alone. The American people had finally admitted that veterans were having problems with Vietnam; that was wonderful, but nobody seemed to realize that it was the wives and children of those veterans who bore the brunt of an all-too-often silent sorrow. The families of troubled veterans were in a no-win situation; they tried to understand, only to learn that they would never understand. They desperately tried to help, only to learn that they couldn't help. All too often they could only stand by and watch their husband and father slowly disintegrate before their very eyes. Both Jimmie and Aurora, though, were determined not to fall into the same pervasive sorrow that had once destroyed their marriage. This time they were going to win, but they would have to find their own way forward.

With more time on his hands than in the past, Jimmie Salazar did what he could to attack PTSD head on, including taking a trip with a veterans' group in 1999 to visit the Vietnam Veterans Memorial in Washington, D.C. Perhaps seeing those names after more than 30 years – Geier, Ferro, Kenney, Peterson – would in some way help him. But as soon as the group arrived in D.C., Salazar began to feel that ominous and all-too-familiar tightening in his chest. When his friends asked what was wrong, Jimmie told them that he was fine. He didn't want to ruin everyone's trip to the wall. A few days later, Jimmie was at a veterans' group meeting back home, ready to tell everyone about his experience at the wall, when the heart attack hit full out. He managed to drive the 5 miles home, weaving in and out of traffic. Shocked by how pale Jimmie looked, Aurora rushed him to the hospital where doctors made ready for an emergency quadruple bypass. As Jimmie lay there on the gurney being prepped for surgery, it all hit him. The only guys who could understand him, the only guys who could help him were those men who knew the true meaning of those names etched in the black granite of the wall. With tears rolling down his cheeks, and teetering on the brink of death, Jimmie Salazar apologized to his wife Aurora for what he had put her through over the years, and whispered, "I'm so sorry that I am going to die without seeing my brothers of Charlie Company ever again."

Jimmie Salazar survived the surgery, only to be diagnosed with diabetes so severe that it resulted in neuropathy from the waist down, leaving him with badly deteriorating function in both of his legs. With mounting physical problems, in addition to his ongoing PTSD, Salazar went on 100 percent disability. Now almost a prisoner in his own house, Salazar knew what he wanted to do – what he needed to do: to find Charlie Company. He wasn't quite sure where to start looking for his old friends, so the process was slow. However, in 2002 Salazar hit pay dirt. He located a website for the 9th Infantry Division – a site that, when opened, was chock full of pictures of his old friends. There they were, all so young, all so vibrant. There was Fort Riley; there was Dong Tam; there was Kenny Frakes and Tim Johnson; there was – everything. Somehow sure that it was too good to be true, Salazar fumbled for the telephone to call the number listed on the website. The "hello" came from a voice instantly recognizable even after 35 years – Bill Reynolds, Salazar's old friend from 2nd Platoon. Reynolds couldn't believe his ears. The boys from Charlie Company had been looking for Jimmie for years – how the hell was he doing? The impromptu chat went on for nearly an hour as memories of the endless mud of the Rung Sat, the steaming heat of the rice paddies, the sudden fear of stumbling across a Viet Cong sniper, and of lost friends all flooded past. Then Reynolds gave Salazar the best news of all. Charlie Company was having a reunion, and he ought to come. It didn't take Salazar even a minute to decide. Heart attacks, diabetes, and neuropathy be damned. He was going to Las Vegas to see his brothers once again.

Upon his arrival back in the world Elijah Taylor had sprinted through the protesters in San Francisco without a second glance. The war, with all of its blood and mud, was over, and he was headed back to Dallas and his own life. Those long-haired people who seemed so angry could worry about Vietnam all they wanted; he had been there, done that, and it was time to move on. When he arrived home, there waiting for him were both a proud father and his old job in the post office. After a short leave, during which he ate as much as he could of the southern delicacies that he had so missed while eating C Rations in Vietnam, Taylor served out the remainder of his enlistment at Fort Hood. But none of that really mattered; he was ready to get back to the life and job that he had enjoyed before Vietnam, like slipping on an old, comfortable shoe. When his hitch was over, Taylor went back to work as a window clerk in the main Dallas branch of the post office. While everything was familiar, including his old car, Taylor slowly realized that he had changed. Where there had once been a happy-go-lucky youngster who enjoyed chasing girls and drinking, there was now a more sober and dedicated young man. He had grown up while he was gone. For Elijah Taylor, Vietnam was there, and important – but the war did not define him. There was bitterness, especially when Saigon fell in 1975. With South Vietnam gone, had the whole war been for nothing? And there were painful reminders. Every January, Taylor reminded himself that another year had passed and that Fred Kenney's son had had another birthday without his father. Working in the post office, Taylor was surrounded by other veterans who understood and valued his wartime experience. They talked about it, joked about it, and overcame it. In Vietnam Elijah Taylor had been gung-ho. He was proud of his service; proud of what he and Charlie Company had accomplished, and, working in the Dallas post office, it was OK to be proud of Vietnam.

By the 1970s, Taylor had moved to a better position in a sub-station of the main Dallas post office, had bought a house, gotten married, and started a family. His wife, a beautiful young woman named Precious, was everything he could have hoped. She took great care of their three daughters, all of whom had Elijah wrapped around their little fingers. And, while she never pressed the subject, Precious tried to understand what Vietnam was and what it meant to her husband. The couple talked about the war, with Precious patiently listening to all of her husband's many stories, and relegated Vietnam to a tiny, well-tended corner of their married lives. There were bigger things to worry about; the children were growing up, and it was time to get their eldest daughter, Kim, ready for college. But in August 1990, Kim gave them the news. She didn't want to go to college just yet. She wanted to follow in daddy's footsteps and go into the military. Initially Precious didn't like the idea very much, but Elijah knew firsthand how the military could help a young person gain maturity, so he supported Kim's plan. Elijah and Precious saw Kim off to basic training in Fort Jackson, South Carolina, only to learn a few days later that Iraqi forces under Saddam Hussein had invaded Kuwait.

Elijah Taylor knew that his eldest daughter was likely off to war, especially when the family learned that she was not going to be granted leave after basic training but instead was slated to go straight to advanced individual training (AIT) for her specialist duties as a quartermaster. Proud, but somewhat apprehensive, Taylor wasn't going to miss Kim's graduation from basic for the world. Fort Jackson seemed so familiar to Taylor – the drill sergeants, the harried trainees. And Kim seemed so familiar, reminded him so much of himself. She was gung-ho, one of the top trainees in her battalion. Taylor's heart beat just a bit faster, and he had to choke back a tear as she marched past with her unit. Was that how his own father had felt all those years ago in 1966? During AIT, Kim kept up a steady stream of letters home, and received some fatherly advice. Elijah warned Kim that he could take it – all the news that she had to send, the good and the bad. But Precious was already losing weight with the worry of sending a daughter to war. In letters home to her mother, Kim should only write about the good things, her surroundings, her friends, her hopes. There was a lot of praying going on in the Taylor home after Kim's departure for Saudi Arabia. The family rushed to read Kim's latest letters, all of which seemed so happy. The build-up for the war was really going well. This was going to be a cinch. With each new letter, Elijah Taylor suppressed a quiet chuckle; he had a smart daughter.

In January 1991, the bombing of Iraq began – build-up had become war. The prayers in the Taylor home became ever more fervent as the family gathered around the television to watch the war unfold before their eyes. When the ground war began in February, everything in the house came to a halt, but the war was going so well, surely everything would be fine. On February 25 the reports came in that an Iraqi missile had slammed into a quartermaster corps barracks in Dhahran. There were bodies everywhere. But Kim was in the quartermaster corps! It just couldn't be. The Taylors hurried to gather what little information they could, but it was still hours before they learned that Kim was not at Dhahran, but in a station farther out in the desert. Elijah and Precious could hardly take it, and for a moment Elijah stopped short and hoped that his parents had not been as worried about him for his entire year in Vietnam.

Shortly after learning that Kim was safe, the war in Iraq came to an end. In May 1991, there she was, getting off her own freedom bird and coming back to the world. The Taylors met her flight at Dallas-Fort Worth International Airport, the same airport to which Elijah had returned in such a hurry 24 years before. Taylor looked around and liked what he saw. There were no protestors. There were crowds, waving flags, clapping, hugging. Joyous crowds reveling in victory. Crowds welcoming the soldiers home from war. Elijah Taylor's chest swelled with pride. But underneath it all was a faint tinge of jealousy. His soldiers, the brave men of Charlie Company, had never received a welcome home. There was no victory. They had been greeted with curses instead of applause. But seeing his daughter getting off that aircraft and hearing the cheers, it all seemed worth it. It seemed that America had learned from its mistakes. If America had learned never to treat its returning soldiers that way again, well, it was a price that Elijah Taylor was happy to have paid to see the look on Kim's face as she ran toward them amid all the cathartic applause. Maybe it was his welcome home too.

As the children began to grow up and move out, and as he began to consider retirement, Elijah Taylor would sometimes wake at night with Precious shaking him by the shoulders. He had been thrashing around and yelling out in some kind of nightmare. He never could quite remember the dreams; the faces and events remained just beyond his waking grasp, but Taylor knew that they were about Vietnam. The memories didn't distract him from his work, or derail his life – Vietnam was just more, well, there. More at the front of his consciousness rather than safely tucked away. Precious had heard about PTSD and asked Elijah to go and talk to a doctor before things got any worse. A doctor? A VA doctor? Elijah agreed to go, but he couldn't shake the notion that VA doctors were for veterans dealing with serious injuries, like the loss of a limb. When he had his first meeting, Taylor was surprised to learn that many veterans first exhibited symptoms of PTSD when they got older and were dealing with a major life change like their children leaving home or retirement. Without those elements of life that normally keep adults so busy, work and children, memories of war are more able to percolate to the surface and take a place of greater importance. The doc assured him that it was OK; it was normal. Elijah Taylor went to his treatment meetings, and he and Precious made a determined effort that, while Vietnam was going to be a bigger part of his life, it would not be the biggest. The family moved forward, welcoming three granddaughters into the world. Elijah Taylor retired from his beloved job in the post office in 2004; shortly after he had received the heart-breaking news that Precious had cancer. With the help of Elijah and the entire family, Precious Taylor fought that disease tooth and nail, living long enough to know that her eldest daughter had given the Taylors their fourth grandchild – this time a grandson. It was a difficult time for Elijah Taylor, a time of mixed and powerful emotions. He had to say goodbye to his best friend, but he also had to welcome his grandson into the world. Elijah Taylor knew just what to do. After the funeral he went to the sporting goods store and bought a baseball glove.

He knew it was going to be a while, but he just couldn't wait for T-Ball to start.

Finally touching down in New Jersey, Gary Maibach went, along with the other soldiers returning from Vietnam, for out-processing at Fort Dix. After he and his compatriots had turned in their summer uniforms, and while they were standing there in their underwear, a group of some 200 new recruits – so new that they had not even received their inaugural military-regulation haircut – came traipsing from the opposite direction in their collective underwear. A few looks and mumbled greetings were exchanged between the two files of men, separated as they were by the vast gulf of experience. Maibach sympathized with the soldiers-to-be, and offered a silent prayer for them as he stepped back into his own civilian life. Gary's father and wife, Mary, met him, and the group decided to stay the night in a hotel in Pennsylvania rather than hazard the long journey back to Sterling, Ohio, in the dark. When they opened the door to the hotel room, Maibach remarked that they might have to move to another room. This one smelled a bit funny. Mary sniffed the air, with something of a quizzical look on her face, and said that it smelled just fine to her. Then Maibach realized what it was. It was he that smelled. He smelled like Vietnam, like war. He had never noticed the smell while he had been there, but now that he was back home it was unmistakable. It seemed like it was going to take some time to get used to being home.

The smells of "civilization," though, were the least of Gary Maibach's concerns. He and Mary had only been husband and wife for a few months before he was drafted. She had accompanied him to Fort Riley, where, in November 1966, she had presented him with a daughter named Karen. Gary Maibach had always taken his duties as a husband and father very seriously, but, with all of the training and his looming departure for war, everything had been so rushed. When he returned to Sterling in 1968, Gary Maibach had to reacquaint himself with his young family. His daughter had not even been two months old when he had departed for Vietnam; now she was a happy toddler – not just a pretty face in a tattered snapshot, but a real little girl. To Karen, who had lived with her mother's large family during Maibach's absence, this new adult on the scene was just another face in a big crowd. Gary took her into his arms, and their life together began anew.

Gary Maibach went back to work in the family store, taking on roles of ever greater importance, and launched himself back into the religious life of his church. Through it all he had a wonderful support group. So many of his relatives had served in past wars, and with his church having such a strong tradition of providing its members to serve as corpsmen in the military, Maibach was surrounded by people who could understand what he had been through and people who held his service in very high regard. Still, it hurt to see mounting protest in the country. Gary Maibach, more than most, understood and valued individual conscience and the right to protest; but it saddened him greatly to see so much of the vitriol aimed at the soldiers themselves – young men like his brothers from Charlie Company who were only doing what their nation had asked them to do in the most difficult of circumstances. But Vietnam could not have a hold on his life – he was far too busy dealing with the present to become mired in the past. By the time Saigon fell, Gary Maibach was president of a rapidly expanding family business, while he and Mary were also busy raising four children – Karen, Mark, David, and James. His faith had also led him toward a new and challenging spiritual future – in 1971 Gary Maibach was chosen to be a minister of the Apostolic Christian Church of America.

There were five democratically chosen ministers in Maibach's congregation, a rapidly growing flock that totaled nearly 700 worshippers each Sunday. The ministers divided the church's work as evenly as they could – but with three weekly services, spiritual education, ministering to the ill and shut-ins, and counseling, there was more than enough work to go around – especially for a father of three who was also running his own business. More than anything else, it was Gary Maibach's enduring faith, combined with his work in the spiritual vineyard of his church, that allowed him to transform the legacy of Charlie Company's service in Vietnam into a tool for good. One piece of scripture kept returning to Maibach's mind over and over again when he thought of Vietnam. Romans 8:28 – "And we know that all things work together for good to them that love God, to them who are called according to his purpose."

Maibach realized that wars sometimes destroyed the souls of men; he had seen it happen all too frequently in Vietnam. It had left him feeling so helpless to see young men lost in a spiritual wilderness. These same young men, in their tens of thousands, had returned from war. Men with God-shaped holes in their lives. Men just like many of his brothers in Charlie Company. Maibach earnestly believed that it was only the peace of God, freely given, that would be able to mend these men, to make them spiritually and physically whole again. To Gary Maibach, Romans 8:28 called upon him to use his Vietnam experiences, as difficult as they were, to work for God's good. Whether it was by preaching, counseling, or just living his life, Maibach hoped to reach out to other veterans – those who were still lost – and bring them home. The bad of Vietnam could become a good, a tool in the reclamation of others. Over the years, Maibach has slowly regained contact with many of his brothers from Charlie Company, and does what he can to help. Often, as it was in Vietnam, he only listens. Faith is not something you can push onto somebody, after all. When help is asked, he gives it freely. And every night, Gary Maibach prays for the boys of Charlie Company, especially for those who still cannot pray for themselves.

While recovering from the wounds to the neck and leg that he had suffered in the fighting on May 15, Charlie Nelson received a visit from his sister. She gave him news that the young Navajo already expected – his parents would not be coming to visit him in the hospital in San Francisco; it was just too far away. But they sent word that, as soon as he was well enough, Charlie needed to return to the reservation to undertake the age-old cleansing ritual of his people – a type of powerful medicine reserved for warriors. But Charlie had a stubborn streak; while his parents had given up on life in Los Angeles and had returned to herding sheep on the reservation, he wasn't about to trade Hollywood for a hogan. After his release, Nelson hobbled to a friend's house in LA – he was ready to be young again. For the next year and a half Nelson worked odd jobs, crashed on his buddy's couch, and hit the local drinking scene with a vengeance. Through it all, the drinking became an ever more dominant part of his life. Spending what little money he made on booze, Nelson drank to go to sleep, drank to have fun, drank to wake up – drank almost constantly. But still Nelson needed more booze, because the drinking wasn't doing its job. The constant nightmares and day-mares, the inability to sleep, the fear of crowds, the jumping at the slightest sound, the jitteriness, the numbness; no matter how much he drank it just didn't work. The memories were still there.

Charlie's parents had already seen Vietnam take a terrible toll on the reservation's youth, and feared for their son's life. Several of the reservation's veterans who had returned from Vietnam had taken to drink, sliding into a tortured oblivion. One had gone out with his sheep one morning and had never returned. The next day a rescue party found him dead at the watering hole – he had shot himself in the head. Two others, cousins back from the war, committed suicide by walking together in front of a speeding semi-trailer. Realizing that his life was hopeless and in response to the pleading of his parents, Charlie Nelson returned to the reservation in 1969. Strong in support of their warriors, Navajo gathered from all around for Nelson's cleansing ceremony – especially from the Salt Clan of his mother and the Big Water Clan of his father. The ritual – part celebration, part mourning – lasted for four days of dancing, feasting, and praying. At the center of events stood the ritual hogan, where Charlie Nelson sat with a single medicine man. With infinite care and elaborate ceremony, the medicine man had crafted two small, but powerful, balls of medicine. At the height of the ceremony, as the fire burned low and the smoke gathered, the medicine man instructed Nelson to eat the first ball of medicine. Nelson placed the ball in his mouth and began to chew, and promptly gagged on the bitter substance. As the crowd gasped, the medicine man leaned in and whispered to Charlie – in English. Charlie didn't even know that the medicine man spoke English! He instructed Nelson to flatten the second ball against the roof of his mouth with his tongue before he swallowed it – it would taste better that way. Nelson looked at the medicine man, who seemed to be wearing just the slightest grin, and then followed his whispered advice. The second ball of medicine went down without a hitch, as the assembled crowd looked on approvingly.

For all of the powerful magic and the acceptance of his grateful people, Charlie Nelson still wandered, still couldn't put Vietnam into the past. At first he departed the reservation for Phoenix, where he went to college on the GI Bill to become an elementary school teacher. But during his studies his father passed away unexpectedly, leaving the family without a patriarch. As the eldest son, it fell to Charlie to return to the reservation to care for his mother and the family flock and farm. At first it was a letdown – to go back to herding sheep, splitting firewood, and hauling 50-gallon drums of water for the crops. Charlie Nelson had wanted more, had seen more, and was now right back where he had started. Sure he was disappointed, but there was nothing for it. This was his future, so Charlie Nelson worked hard. His garden was the best for miles around, with friends constantly dropping by and asking for some of his squash or corn. The family flock prospered, and Nelson learned to do much of the work for himself – the shearing and the castrating – so he didn't have to pay someone else. He became so skilled that his services were in constant demand from his neighbors. Charlie Nelson settled down into a simple life that followed the rhythm of the seasons.

Through it all, though, Vietnam remained. The nightmares continued, and, after his mother passed away, Nelson became a loner. He had given up the booze, because it simply wasn't working. An accustomed sight, silently tending his herd and garden, Nelson didn't need anybody. Didn't need friends. Didn't need a phone. Someone in the closely knit community, though, was keeping tabs on Charlie Nelson and contacted the Northern Arizona Veterans Affairs Hospital in Prescott, Arizona, on his behalf. The doctors brought Charlie in for a meeting where they talked about PTSD. Charlie was happy enough to talk – these docs seemed really to care about his experiences. He was happy enough to go to group meetings with other veterans. But Charlie Nelson was not happy to hear the docs' advice that he ought to forget Vietnam. He didn't want to forget – either the good times or the bad. Forgetting Vietnam would be forgetting himself. No. Charlie Nelson had another way to deal with PTSD, if that's what you call it. The vast openness of the desert plains, surrounded by his flock, was Nelson's cure. Under a canopy of stars, with only the soft bleating of his sheep to interrupt the deep stillness, Charlie Nelson was gloriously, singularly alone. In that pure solitude, he sat beside a single companion – Vietnam. In some ways his worst enemy, but in others his only friend.

After a short leave in Fayetteville, Arkansas, spent getting to know his wife Nancy again and trying to convince his young son Jack Junior that he really was his daddy, Jack Benedick returned with his family to Fort Riley, where he worked as part of the post operations section. Jack, Nancy, and Jack Junior settled down into a comfortable routine, and even wondered together what civilian life would be like after Benedick's military career ended in May 1968. As his separation date neared and Jack and Nancy first began to think about where they might move and what they might do when he left the service, Benedick received a telegram from the parents of his best friend John Hoskins. From the time that they had first met in Fort Riley in the spring of 1966, the two young Charlie Company platoon leaders had formed an inseparable bond, Hoskins the warrior-poet graduate of West Point, Benedick the hardscrabble OCS graduate. John Hoskins, then a company commander serving his second tour in Vietnam, had died, killed by the detonation of a land mine he had been trying to disarm. It was while he was serving as one of Hoskins' pallbearers on a dreary, gray afternoon at West Point that Benedick made his decision. He wasn't going to leave the army. He was going to go back to Vietnam to get revenge for his fallen friend. There was no chance at all that he would catch Hoskins' killers, but even an impersonal revenge was better than doing nothing at all. Nancy was not happy with her husband's decision, but she had been expecting it. Even she couldn't really see Jack Benedick as a civilian. He was a military man. It had been nice to dream about playing house together and having a normal life, but she had always known deep inside that he would return to Vietnam.

Following a period of refresher training, Jack Benedick got the news in the early spring of 1969; he was headed back to Vietnam to command Charlie Company, 3rd of the 60th Infantry – a familiar position since the unit was part of the 9th Infantry Division and operated in the Mekong Delta. But as soon as he arrived in country, Benedick realized that much had changed. The war in the delta was no longer much of a "shooting war." Having suffered heavy losses during the Tet Offensive, the Viet Cong was lying low. There were no more bitter clashes of sizeable units. It was now more than ever a land-mine and booby-trap war. That was fine by Jack Benedick. He had helped develop the 9th Infantry Division's tactics for dealing with land mines. On April 30, 1969, after just a month in his new command, Benedick called his new Charlie Company to a halt. The unit had reached a sharp bend in the tree line it was patrolling – a perfect spot for an ambush or a minefield. Benedick motioned for his RTOs to follow and stepped out into the rice paddy to get a look at what was awaiting Charlie Company around that ominous bend. To get to a point where he could see the way forward clearly, Benedick had to break one of his own rules of delta warfare; he had to step up on a rice paddy dike. He had just barely gotten his trailing foot onto the dike when the world erupted into a massive explosion. A few seconds later, Benedick came crashing down out of the air into the murky rice paddy water. After checking his crotch to make sure that his "jewels" were intact, Benedick looked at his legs. One was gone below the knee, a jagged piece of bone protruding from a stump that was bleeding freely, and the other leg was mangled beyond recognition. Cursing wildly, Benedick got on the radio to order his own medevac helicopter. Both of his RTOs had been injured, and, though he allowed the medic to give him a morphine shot to ease the pain, Benedick demanded that the RTOs be choppered out first. He could wait.

Benedick left on the last helicopter, bound for surgery in the divisional hospital in the familiar confines of Dong Tam. The scene was something of a blur, with doctors and nurses hooking him up to IVs and discussing his shattered legs. Before they put him under, Benedick grabbed the lead surgeon by the throat, pulled him close, and said, "If you cut off my fucking knees I will kill you. I'm damned if I am going to sit around the rest of my life as a cripple!" With a look in his eyes that indicated he believed that Benedick would follow through on his threat, the surgeon promised Benedick that he would do his best. After surgery Benedick awoke to find a somewhat relieved surgeon waiting to give him the good news that, while he had lost both of his legs, the amputations had taken place below the knees. Benedick hurt like hell, and noticed that bone still protruded from the base of both of his stumps. The doctor told him that it was something about warding off infections – the stumps would have to remain open, perhaps for months. But none of that conversation really registered, because there was more bad news to follow. Wearing a very concerned look, the doctor informed Benedick that his kidneys had shut down, a condition that was not too rare given the circumstances, but one that could prove life-threatening. Ever the cantankerous patient, Benedick replied, "You say my kidneys have quit working? Well, damn it, you are the doc. Make 'em work!"

The next day Benedick was on a chopper bound for the 3rd Field Hospital in Saigon, where they had a dialysis machine. Whether due to a mistake in paperwork or pilot error, though, Benedick arrived at the wrong hospital. As the staff tried to work out who he was and what kind of care he required a helpful nurse asked Benedick if he was hungry. Benedick replied that he was famished and would love a cheeseburger. A few minutes later Benedick sat enjoying his first meal in three days, only to be interrupted by a doctor who rushed in and yelled, "You have to stop! Why are you eating?" Not even bothering to take time to swallow his mouthful of food, Benedick replied, "Because I'm fucking hungry!" The doctor then patiently explained that Benedick would not be allowed to eat, since his failing kidneys were in no shape to flush any toxins from his body. Heck, he couldn't even have pain medicine, much less cheeseburgers!

An ambulance finally delivered the disgruntled Benedick to the correct hospital, where he started on his dialysis regimen. Having no solid food and being hooked up to a kidney machine was one thing, but no pain medication was another. Benedick was tough, and he knew it, but the pain radiating from his wounds was agony. Almost like an awful addiction, the pain kept Benedick wired and awake. He knew that he was in the hospital's "to die" ward, and that nobody expected him to make it, but he wasn't going to give up easily. A few days after his arrival, there came a welcome relief to the monotony of pain and boredom – bullets came flying through the window. The hospital was under attack. It was almost comforting. Benedick thought to himself, "Now here is something I can deal with." But as he began the mental preparation for action he quickly came up short, thinking, "Crap. I can't do anything. I don't have any feet." A few seconds later, while the bullets were still flying and Benedick was wondering what to do, a medic entered the room carrying a carbine. Plainly, though, the medic was mystified by both the weapon and the situation, and Benedick asked him, "Son, do you know how to use that thing?" The medic responded, "Not really, sir." Benedick rolled his eyes and then barked, "Well then give it to me and get the hell out of here." Now armed, Benedick slid to the floor and turned his hospital bed over for use as a makeshift fort. A few minutes later, after the enemy firing had died down, a bemused doctor poked his head into Benedick's room where he saw the double amputee ready to fight in his own private Alamo. The doctor shook his head and told Benedick that the medic really needed the weapon back; Benedick was not going to need a weapon where he was going. He was headed home.

As it turned out what the military meant by "headed home" was that Benedick was first off to a hospital in Japan, where he endured more surgeries but got good news when his kidneys resumed their normal function, and then to Fitzsimmons Army Medical Center Hospital in Denver, Colorado, for another round of operations. It was only in Colorado, after he had been joined by Nancy and Jack Junior, that doctors finally cut off the last bit of bone protruding from his stumps, closed his wounds, and began the process of skin grafts that would get Jack Benedick ready for prostheses. After the skin grafts came the physical therapy, but then came the big day. Four and a half months after being wounded, Jack Benedick sat in the artificial limb shop in Fitzsimmons getting his new legs fitted. Once they were strapped on, the technician asked Benedick what he thought. In response, Benedick sat up, slid off of the bed and walked out of the room with a gruff goodbye. The technician watched Benedick's departure in horror before turning to the orderly who had wheeled Benedick into the room and saying, "Hey! He can't do that!" The orderly, all too familiar with Benedick's now legendary stubborn streak, replied, "You go tell him. I'm not." Leaving the bemused orderly behind, Benedick walked to his first session of physical therapy with his new limbs and opened the door. In the room sat an army doctor, who fully expected to see a man in a wheelchair – a man who was unable to walk. The doctor stared at Jack Benedick, looked him up and down, turned a bit red in the face, and said, "You can't do that! We have to teach you how to walk again!" Benedick calmly replied, "Well sir, I didn't forget how to walk." The doctor spluttered for a moment and then replied, "But what if you fall down?" Benedick answered, "Well, I didn't forget how to get up either."

Although he was up and mobile, Jack Benedick still had to undergo weeks of therapy to build up his strength – weeks of monotony that left the young lieutenant with a mounting case of cabin fever. He had to do something – anything instead of just lying in bed, practicing walking, and doing leg exercises. Relief came in the form of a pretty young nurse who asked Benedick if he would like to go skiing. It seemed that there was a program that twinned amputees with patients from the local children's hospital for ski lessons as part of their rehabilitation. Benedick made a show of looking at a calendar before answering, "What the hell. It doesn't look like I have anything else to do today." The trip to the slopes was fun, even though he had a hard time keeping his balance and fell down more than he skied at first, and the gruff warrior enjoyed the company of the children in the crystal-clear mountain air. It all seemed so natural, so peaceful, so right. Benedick filed it away – when he got out of the army, he was going to ski. The thought of having no legs never even entered his mind.

After returning to the hospital, Benedick received a visit from one of his doctors, who informed him that, since he was making such progress in his recovery, he was slated to be released, retired from the army, and turned over to the Veterans Administration. Benedick was indignant. They were going to retire him? No way in hell. He had lost his legs by playing army and he was going to stay in the damn army. The doctor let Benedick vent, but then told him that the decision was out of both of their hands. The army just didn't need double amputees. Seconds after the doctor had left, Jack Benedick was on the phone with his old battalion commander,

Colonel Tutwiler, who, in turn, called his old brigade commander General Fulton. The two men knew Benedick well; they knew that he was about the most hard-charging soldier they had ever met. If he said he could still serve without legs, they believed him. Tutwiler and Fulton placed a few phone calls and pulled a few strings, and Jack Benedick received his orders. He was off to Fort Benning for the advanced officer training course in preparation for his new command.

His Fort Benning classmates looked at Jack Benedick with a sense of awe – especially impressed when he decided to go on runs while wearing short pants. Hardly anyone complained about the difficulty of the course when Benedick was around. If he could do it, so could they. After training, Benedick, now a captain, reported to Fort Carson, Colorado, to serve as a company commander in the 1st Brigade of the 4th Infantry Division. He walked in the door at brigade headquarters, where the major who served as brigade executive officer was seated at a desk reading his personnel file. The major looked at Benedick, glanced down at his legs, and gave him the bad news. There was no place for a double-amputee officer in the 1st Brigade. Benedick looked the major square in the eye and said, "Give me a chance. If I can't cut it, I'll retire in six months. You have my word." Shaking his head and grimacing, the major replied, "All right. I'm going to hold you to it." A few months later, it was the major, not Jack Benedick, who retired. Before he left, the major sent Benedick a formal letter of apology. Not only had he been able to hack it, Benedick had proven to be the best company commander in the entire outfit.

After his time as company commander, Benedick served two stints in battalion staff positions before attending Command and General Staff College and receiving promotion to the rank of major. Budget cuts interrupted a slated tour in Germany, and in 1977 Jack Benedick transferred to San Francisco to work in the Office of the Inspector General. While adjusting to the new position, Benedick received jarring news. A cordial officer informed him that a change in regulations meant that remaining on active duty put his eventual military disability benefit in jeopardy. As the young officer closed his briefcase Benedick responded, "What? Does this mean that my legs will grow back? What a nice surprise."

Two weeks later Jack Benedick was out of the US military. Not knowing quite what to do with himself, Benedick decided to move with his family to Colorado, so that he could pursue a future as a skier, an avocation he had kept up since the day that kind nurse had entered his room during his initial rehab.

Jack Benedick soon became a fixture on the ski slopes of Colorado, at the same time that local resorts, business sponsors, and the international sports world were coming to realize the importance of competitive sports for disabled athletes. Benedick became a tireless advocate of disabled sports, skiing competitively from 1979 to 1986, helping to create the US Disabled Ski Team, and winning a silver medal in the Winter Paralympics in 1980 and two bronze medals in the World Championships in 1984. In 1986, Benedick took on a formal position of Director of the US Disabled Ski Team, which he held until his retirement in 1995. He was also a member of the United States Olympic Committee from 1984 to 1988 and was instrumental in having disabled skiing added to the 1988 Winter Olympics in Calgary as a demonstration sport, where the US team won four of the available six medals. Benedick also served as director of the able-bodied cross-country ski team and was team leader for the 1994 Winter Olympics in Lillehammer.

After retirement, Jack Benedick not only remained involved in skiing but also took up weightlifting and worked as a white-water rafting guide. What caught his attention most, though, was scuba diving. Entranced by the tranquility and near weightlessness of diving, Benedick decided that he had found his new avocation and quickly received certification as a dive master. Hoping to teach scuba diving to other people with disabilities, Benedick applied for his instructor's license. A few days later a call came in to Benedick's local scuba shop from a representative with the Professional Association of Diving Instructors. There was no way that they were going to let an applicant with no legs take the test. Sensing a challenge, Benedick got on the phone and spoke to a crusty old navy diver who informed him that, while he had squeaked through qualification to this point, this was the end of the line. Benedick shot back that he had not squeaked through anything, to which the diving instructor replied, "Be that as it may, you ain't ready for this test!" "Well, how about I get on a plane to California and challenge you to a street fight," Benedick retorted. "If you beat my ass, I quit. If I beat yours, I get to take the test. Since I don't have any legs, it shouldn't be too hard for you to beat me." Not quite knowing how to react to the challenge, the instructor relented, and within a few weeks Jack Benedick joined the Professional Association of Diving Instructors as a fully-fledged member.

It first came on as an odd feeling of imbalance while he was skiing during the Winter Olympics at Lillehammer. He wasn't sure, but something just didn't feel quite right, kind of like having had too much to drink. While the odd feeling did dim over time, it never went away, and sometimes came back even worse than before, so Jack Benedick did something he loathed – he went to the doctor. After a battery of tests the results were in – Jack Benedick was diagnosed with Parkinson's disease. While he immediately went on medication, over time the symptoms worsened and came to include the uncontrollable trembling so commonly associated with the affliction. The fighter, the man who had taken up skiing when he had lost his legs, had to give up the things that he loved. No more skiing. No more scuba. Maybe no more driving or walking. But Jack Benedick wasn't going down without a fight. He volunteered for an experimental procedure and had two electrodes implanted deep inside his brain designed to stop the tremors. The treatment worked, and part of the battle was won – but the vertigo was still there; no more skiing or scuba yet. Out of all the battles he had ever fought, it seemed that the struggle against Parkinson's was going to be the hardest yet. How could he fight something he couldn't even see?

After John Young's reunion with his father in the International Harvester plant in Minneapolis, he gave his family the news; he was headed back to Vietnam. There was still a war going on, and that was why Young had joined in the first place, to fight for his country. It just didn't make any sense to come home with a job still to be done. Following a short leave, Young made his way back to Vietnam, where he served another 18 months as a staff NCO in the headquarters of II Field Force. It was the summer of 1969 when John Young finally returned home for good. As he walked through the airport in Minneapolis wearing his uniform, Young couldn't help noticing that everyone looked away from him. They weren't yelling or screaming – they didn't care enough to pay him any attention at all, whether good or bad. Arriving home for a second time to the hugs and kisses of his family, with $800 saved up and nowhere in particular he needed to be, John Young settled down in his parents' basement to take something of an extended breather, which for him meant drinking. Young had started drinking heavily in Vietnam, to help him sleep – a habit that followed him home and became one of the central facets of his life. While drinking away his meager savings, Young explored a civilian world that had become both foreign and forbidding. He found that he had little in common with his old friends, who had moved on with their lives, started jobs, and gotten married. Life had gone on in an America that didn't seem to care at all about the young men it had sent off to war and destruction. To Young, the civilian lives that his one-time friends cherished so deeply seemed somehow mundane, even petty. All their fretting over mortgages, schools, and time clocks – all the needless civilian hustle and bustle. John Young and his friends in Charlie Company had lived the most difficult and rewarding life there could be – a life of overwhelming power and emotion. They had lived life-and-death decisions that really mattered, but their moment was gone. Homecoming had brought on a complex tapestry of emotions: guilt for not still being in Vietnam, anger at society's complacency, sorrow for friends long lost, guilt for having survived when so many had not. In the confusion, alcohol was his only constant.

In January 1970, John Young picked himself up, dusted himself off, and decided that it was time to get started on his own civilian life. He took a job as a still photographer with a Minneapolis television station, and eloped with a girl named Kathy after a whirlwind courtship. They rented a small house, and she had a good job; the Youngs were the perfect, well-adjusted middle-class couple. But all the while Vietnam remained close to the surface, ever-present in John Young's psyche. Every night he had to drink himself to sleep to ward off the nightmares but still woke up drenched in sweat. Every day was a struggle to find meaning and to avoid anger. Nothing seemed to matter anymore. The world seemed so inconsequential, and life seemed so numb. For the next few years, Young bounced from job to job – always achieving success, but never achieving happiness. Every Friday he would collect his paycheck, make his way to one of the local watering holes and start his drinking. He drank to sleep. He slept so he could work. He worked so he could make money to drink so he could sleep – a vicious cycle that quickly and completely destroyed his marriage. One night Young awoke in a haze and heard Viet Cong in the living room. He crept to his closet, grabbed his rifle, and low-crawled into the furniture-strewn rice paddy. A few minutes later a voice came from nowhere asking him what he was doing. It was Kathy. Young got to his feet and responded, "Bridges is dead. They shot Bridges." Kathy began to weep and helped her husband back to bed. Something – Vietnam – was eating him up on the inside. Something beyond her control.

A few months later the couple divorced – another failure. Everything John Young touched seemed to fall apart. Amid the ruins of his life, it struck Young that the only place where he had ever really found meaning and fulfillment was the military. With his discharge papers in hand, Young returned to the same recruiting office that he had visited on that long ago day in the spring of 1966. In 1974 the recruiting sergeant was different, but the results were the same. He could help Young join the military, and he could certainly help him join the infantry. In fact, Young was in luck. Due to the new Minuteman Program, he could skip training and go straight into service as a private E-3. For anyone else who had been a staff sergeant E-6 and who had worked in a corps-level tactical headquarters, the loss of three ranks might have been a deal-breaker; but not for John Young. He was ready to get to a place where others understood and valued his service. He was ready to get to a place where others understood Vietnam.

Within a month Young stood in a barracks in Bavaria, ready to report to his new unit. The army of the 1970s was different, full of discipline problems and drug use. But the officers and the NCOs were the same – honorable men who understood who John Young was – and why. Flourishing in the comfortable surroundings, he once again pinned on new ranks in near record time. Vietnam was still there. The pain was still there, but these guys understood why it was there, and that helped. There was also the institutionalized drinking culture of the army NCOs. Booze flowed freely, from bottles stashed in desks to the NCO club. Young was able to mask his growing dependence on alcohol behind a façade of boozy comradeship. The military was the perfect place for someone who was still troubled by war to hide in plain sight. Having met a pretty German girl named Helga, Young moved to an apartment off base. The couple was happy, and even spoke of marriage, but they both knew better. Young would eventually return to the United States, and Helga would never leave Germany. But still the years slipped slowly by, years that were almost happy.

In the late fall of 1977, orders came in that changed everything. Young was being transferred to Fort Ord, California. It was about the last place in the world he wanted to go, and about the last time he wanted to go – Christmas time. But, orders were orders, and Young said goodbye to Helga and shipped out to New Jersey, from where he would drive his car to Fort Ord. The parting was tough on Young, tougher than he was willing to admit. On the long, cross-country odyssey Young began to think – began to think of how alone he was. He had no family – no wife and children. He didn't even have any friends. As he thought about Helga, his mind went back to 1975, when they had watched the fall of Saigon together on the television. The war, the most meaningful thing in his life, had ended in defeat. All of the savagery and loss had been for nothing. The solitude of the journey west was devastating. John Young had nothing, had nobody – and the central event of his life meant nothing. Somewhere in Texas, Young stopped to pick up a few bottles of whiskey and drank his way to California. On December 23, Young reported in to his new company. He needed them – he needed somebody. But the company was on a Christmas stand down. The first sergeant welcomed Young aboard, but then told him that he might as well go and get a hotel room and report in after Christmas.

For any other soldier that would have come as great news – go ahead and have a merry Christmas and a few extra days off. But for Young it was nearly lethal. He bought more whiskey, checked into a cheap hotel room and drank himself into the depths of depression. He was tired – tired of life. Young just sat there, perched on the end of a rumpled bed, trying to drink enough to pull the trigger on his handgun. Nearby there was a phone book, and, through his blurry sight, Young noticed a number on the back cover, a number for a suicide prevention hotline. He called. A woman picked up, one who was well trained enough to listen to his drunken ramblings; one who was well trained enough to get his location and call the authorities. The feminine voice on the other end of the line told John Young, "You don't want to kill yourself. You are not a killer." Young could only reply, "But I'm already a killer. I'm already a killer." Seconds later there was a knock at the hotel door; it was the police. The officers, calm professionals, asked John Young for his gun. He gave it up voluntarily, and then rode with the officers back to Fort Ord, where he was admitted to the psychiatric wing of the base military hospital.

After a two-week stint in the hospital, and with a prescription for an anti-depressant in hand, Young returned to his unit, where he served as a training NCO. Needing the hard work, the comradeship, and the distraction, Young threw himself into his new job. He was the model soldier, always there when you needed him, and quickly rose in the estimation of his superior officers. After only a short time, Young was singled out for success and chosen to serve as part of a field team within the Inspector General's office. He even got married again and rented a home in Seaside, where he and his wife, Valerie, awaited the birth of their first child. In 1980 Young received even more good news. He had been chosen to attend Drill Instructors' School. He knew that a stint as a drill instructor would not be easy, but it was one of those things that you have to do in the military to get your ticket punched. DI school meant that John Young was on his way up. Young, his wife Valerie, and their young son Joseph, packed up and headed off to Fort Sill, Oklahoma, to start a new stage in their lives. The couple bought a small house on 5 acres of land outside the town of Fletcher; they even planned to farm a little bit. Having reached the bottom, John Young had clawed his way back. He had his career, his family – even a farm. But through it all, the drinking had continued and worsened. He didn't know that he had a problem. Hell, he liked drinking. It kept the demons at bay.

While he had known that life as a drill instructor was going to be demanding, John Young had no idea of the strain it would place on his marriage. He had to be up and out of bed at 3:30am to drive to Fort Sill and roust the trainees for reveille. He worked doing exhausting physical labor, including two 5-mile runs every day, seven days a week, and rarely made it home before midnight. Barely able to keep his eyes open, Young spent what little home time he had drinking and then sleeping before the alarm went off again. On the few short breaks that he received during gaps in the training cycle, all Young wanted to do was drink and sleep enough to get caught up a bit. It was no way to live. Caring for a toddler, and with her husband either drunk, asleep, or gone, Valerie felt abandoned. The couple grew apart, and what conversations they had were often arguments. Just when he needed it most, Young received some very welcome news. He had been chosen for the senior NCO course at Fort Benning, the last ticket that he needed punched before promotion to sergeant first class (E-7). He had fought through the tough patch, and things were looking up again.

The course of study at Fort Benning was slated to last six weeks, but almost immediately John Young sensed trouble. No matter when he called home, or how often, he couldn't get Valerie on the phone. He called multiple times a day, often in the dead of night, and still nothing. What the hell was going on? Not sure what to do, and in something of a panic, John Young just got in his car and left Fort Benning, without any orders. He drove back to his home in Fletcher and eventually located Valerie and Joseph. She said that she was sorry, but she couldn't take it anymore. She had filed for divorce and was going to take their son and leave. The next day Young was called before his battalion commander at Fort Sill for a classic military dressing down. Who the hell did he think he was just to up and leave the senior NCO school? It didn't matter what kind of damn personal problems he was having: NCOs in this man's military don't go AWOL! There was no way in hell that he was ever going to get another shot at senior NCO school. In fact, he was going to be relieved of drill instructor duty. Maybe that would teach him a goddamn lesson!

John Young's marriage was over. His short life as a father was over. His career was over. He had five days of leave before taking his new assignment, so he went home to drink. Sitting there among the empty whiskey bottles of his life, Young was back in his parents' basement in 1969. Everything since then had been for nothing. He hadn't moved one damn inch in 13 years. He was alone with no life, nothing except booze and pain. Young got up from his chair, and grabbed his whiskey and $300 in cash. He rummaged through the house for his weapons and as much ammunition as he could find, and then he went out the front door and got into his pickup truck. He didn't even bother to close the door, because he wasn't coming back. Randomly heading west, Young began to formulate a plan. He would find a lonely spot, perhaps among some rocks on a hill, take up a defensive position, and start shooting people. Someone was going to pay for his pain. After a while the police would respond, and Young would die in a hail of gunfire. He would die like a warrior – the way he should have died in Vietnam. For days Young drove west, spending the nights drinking in shabby roadside motels – through Colorado, Utah, and Nevada. But somehow or another he just never found the right spot, and then he was at the end of the road on a cliff overlooking the Pacific Ocean. He had run out of country. He stood there and watched the breakers for a few minutes and then just gave up. He couldn't even kill himself right. Crawling back into the cab of his pickup, Young drove down the highway until he saw a California State Highway Patrol office. He went in and surrendered to the surprised officer behind the desk.

A psychiatric team transferred Young to Letterman Army Medical Center, where a lieutenant colonel interviewed him for several hours. After grilling him with questions, some of which were about Vietnam while others seemingly made no sense at all, the officer leaned forward and said, "Well sergeant, you have PTSD and can't be a soldier anymore." PTSD? Young had never heard of that. What was it? The sympathetic colonel described the symptoms: nightmares, emotional numbness, hyper alertness, anger, guilt – it all seemed to fit John Young to a T. As he sat there trying to take it all in, the officer informed Young that he would be sent to Fort Sill for his discharge. As he left the room, the colonel poked his head back in for just a moment and added, almost as an afterthought, "Don't worry, sergeant, once you are discharged just go over to the VA. They will have some help for you."

The military couldn't wait to get rid of John Young – he was discharged within a week of his arrival back at Fort Sill. Everything in his life was gone, except for the booze, so Young went home to drink. It was about a month before he thought again about the colonel's final words and decided to go visit the VA. Even after all he had been through, John Young could barely admit it, but he needed help. Young walked up to the reception desk at the VA in Oklahoma City, where the receptionist looked up and said, "Can I help you?" Young replied that he was a career soldier who had been discharged due to PTSD and that the army had told him to come and talk to the VA. Although the receptionist looked sympathetic, her response was crushing. "I'm sorry sir, but the VA does not recognize PTSD as a disability. We really don't have anything to offer you." There was nothing left. Nothing. John Young went home to drink. Maybe he hadn't had the guts to kill himself with a gun or to die in a hail of gunfire, but he could damn sure drink himself to death. Young held down a job to pay for the booze – they even thought he was a model employee – but that is all he wanted to do: drink. And it was working. He began to have alcohol-induced seizures and blackouts. The pain was going to be gone.

One day, out of the blue, John Young's parents showed up and bundled him into their car. A friend had located them in their new home in Picayune, Mississippi, and had told them of John's condition. They went to pick him up before he died. In July 1985, John Young checked into an alcohol treatment program at a local VA and got clean. He didn't believe that he could go even a few hours without drinking, but after the 28-day program, John Young knew that he would never drink again. He got a job selling cars at a local dealership near his parents' home and began to make good money. But now, sober and alone, Young had no defenses against PTSD and the memories of Vietnam. Slowly they ate at him more and more. As usual he worked hard and well, but he felt isolated. He moved out of his parents' home and got his own place, but he became more and more of a loner. He couldn't trust himself to deal with people. They didn't understand. They didn't want to understand. It was 1993 before Young ran across a random advertisement in the local paper. "Vietnam Vets. Lonely? Depressed? Need help? Please call." The voice on the other end of the phone informed Young that the VA now had help for veterans with PTSD and told him how to gain access to treatment. Taking a gamble, and a major leap of faith, Young contacted the VA in New Orleans and applied for the inpatient program. A few weeks later, he was there, filling out forms and getting ready for who-knew-what. Then it happened. Dr Karen Thompson asked Young to her office. He sat in a comfortable chair, and she sat behind her desk. She leaned in, looked him in the eyes and said, "Tell me about Vietnam." A simple request, elegant and vitally important. It had been 25 years since John Young had served with Charlie Company – 25 long years. And finally someone asked – someone cared about it all. He had been holding it all in – the wonderfully good and the horrifically bad – for so long, alone. Someone finally wanted to know, and he could begin to let it all out. That single meeting saved John Young's life.

Having left the funeral in Arroyo Grande, Jacque Peterson sat alone in her apartment with her young son Jimmy and just cried. At age 18, she could still almost feel the excitement of her wedding day, of her marriage to Don – there was no way that it could be over; Don was still out there somewhere. As the weeks went by, Jacque moved to a farm that her family owned outside of Dinuba, California, near Fresno, where she and Jimmy were able to find some solitude. While there, Jacque watched from a distance as several of her relatives and friends came home from tours in Vietnam. Loved ones were coming back to everyone but her. She kept waiting for the knock on her own door, to see Don again, but the knock never came. She heard stories, stories of heroism in which Don had given his life to save others. But she so desperately wished that he would come back to her.

Alone, and in frantic hope of finding a future for both herself and her young son, Jacque met and married David Bomann, who promised to love and take care of little Jimmy like he was his own. In some ways, David loved Jacque and Jimmy too much, and that is where the trouble started. He didn't want to be Jimmy's stepfather; he wanted to be his dad. To avoid confusion, the couple cut all ties with the Peterson family and never spoke of Don

Peterson. He was the past; the Bomann family was the future. It pained Jacque greatly, but she went along with the charade. Down deep she knew that Don Peterson was the irreplaceable love of her life, her soulmate. But she had to put him and his memory into the past. It was for the best. It would give her and Jimmy a new life.

The rural life of the Bomann family, which quickly grew to include two more children, seemed idyllic. Jimmy enjoyed the acres of vineyards and going to the small local school. But as he grew up, Jimmy began to notice something odd. It didn't hit him all at once, but built slowly over time. A vague hint here, an unexplained oddity there. His father, David, didn't seem to treat him the same as he did his other children. The more he thought about it, the more curious it all became. He didn't look like David. He didn't think like David. He didn't walk or talk like David. Unsure of so much, Jimmy began to rebel – he drank and he got into trouble at school. Jacque didn't know the exact nature of the problem, but she had a pretty good guess. As her eldest son questioned his place in the world, Jacque came to her own realization that she had made a mistake. She tried so hard to make her marriage work, especially for the children, but she now understood that losing Don had left her incomplete. She had tried to fill the gaping hole that his loss had left in her soul – she had reached out for love and a future. But it had been a mistake. Nobody could replace Don Peterson. As her marriage to David crumbled, Jacque knew what she had to do. She had to tell Jimmy about his real father.

It was all so much for Jimmy to take in; David wasn't his father? He had a different dad who had died in Vietnam? There were so many questions. Who was he? What was he? Suddenly being Jimmy Bomann didn't make sense anymore. And the guy who could help him make sense of his life wasn't there – he was gone, lost when he was only an infant. Jimmy felt nothing but sorrow for his mother, who had plainly loved this man named Don Peterson so deeply, but who had been forced to push even his memory away so far. But he also felt betrayed and conflicted: betrayed by David posing as his father and forcing his real father into the past; conflicted because he loved and respected David. David was the only father he had ever known. Two fathers warred for his soul, but one was only a faint whisper on a barely remembered breeze. Jimmy had to learn, had to go back into the past and rescue Don Peterson.

As her divorce from David Bomann became final, Jacque decided to do what she could to help Jimmy on his journey by moving her family to Pismo Beach, where he could be reunited with the Petersons. For Don's parents, his siblings, and the entire extended family, watching Jimmy walk into the room was wonderful but heart wrenching. At age 16, Jimmy was a carbon copy of his father. It was as though Don had come back to them whole and young – unchanged – after so many sad years of absence. There were tears for what had been missed, but there was also great joy at a family reunited. Jacque went back to school, taking courses toward a nursing degree, as she and her children started life over again. Jimmy went to a much larger school now, a school that offered him more chances to indulge his rebellious side, and he was a constant presence at the doors of the various Petersons. He wanted to learn everything he could about his father. What had he been like? Was he athletic? Was he an artist? Was he a surfer? Everything. He heard all of the stories about his dad, comfortable and well-worn stories that other families swap over Thanksgiving or Christmas dinners to nods of group remembrance. But to Jimmy they were all so new. The thing that was most obvious was that the Petersons loved Don deeply and missed him dearly. After nearly 16 years their pain was still fresh, so near the surface and so constant. Vietnam to them was not the past but a living, organic part of their beings. The shared agony of the Petersons' unhealed scars opened new wounds in Jimmy. Instead of finding closure, finding a father, he was more confused than ever.

Jacque graduated as a Licensed Vocational Nurse in 1985, sometimes working three jobs to keep food on the table. She focused her remaining energy on her children, helping them in any way she could. Along the way, she slowly drifted apart from the Petersons again, but she has never forgotten Don. His love and the short time of contentedness that they once knew remain at the core of her being. Although she still works, is outwardly vibrant, and remains devoted to her family, in her soul is a stillness. It is only when she thinks or speaks of Don that she feels truly at peace.

Jimmy needed direction. The confusion that was his life, and the drinking that played an ever more important role in his daily routine, were threatening to get the best of him. Before he had even graduated from high school, Jimmy enlisted in the navy. Service would give him the discipline and the focus that he lacked. But his two years of service were a rough ride. He was still rebellious, not a trait valued by the military, and still liked to drink. He did, however, gain focus and maturity. Jimmy took back the last name of Peterson and decided to embark on a career in the music business. But there was still a hole in his life. He had collected shards of his father – like brightly colored bits of a shattered mosaic. The individual pieces were beautiful, but he didn't know how to fit them back together again. He still didn't know his father. But then came a call from his uncle Rich, his father's youngest brother. Some guys named Jim Dennison and John Bauler had found his name in a phone book. They had known his father, served with him, and had been there the day that he had died. They were going to have a reunion, and they wanted to know if Jimmy and the rest of the Petersons wanted to go. Jimmy didn't have to think long. Maybe this would be the way to put the memory of Don Peterson back together again.

After his drunken farewell to Vietnam, Jim Dennison had returned home to Chicago. For a while he just drank a lot and took in the world around him, before giving college a try and flunking out. Dennison was engaged for a while, but "treated his fiancée like shit," which resulted in him getting unceremoniously dumped. Dennison jumped around from job to job, drinking all the while, before settling down, getting married, and finding work selling construction equipment. Climbing the corporate ladder, Dennison was first transferred to Colorado in 1978 and then to San Diego in 1981. Ever since the end of the war in Vietnam, Dennison had remained in contact with John Bauler, one of the Charlie Company originals who had hailed from Chicago but was brought up in California. Since Bauler lived in the San Diego area, the two often got together over drinks and swapped reminiscences of their lives as part of Charlie Company. As one of the large California contingent in Charlie Company, Bauler had fleeting contact with others from across the unit. It was over drinks in the mid 1980s that Bauler and Dennison, both half in the bag, thought that they should try to get into contact with as many Charlie Company veterans as possible and have a reunion. They didn't even know where to start – so they began with John Sclimenti. That wasn't a very common last name. Surely there couldn't be too damn many Sclimentis crawling around? Wasn't he from the Simi Valley? They both thought so. One phonebook later, Dennison was on the horn. A male voice answered. Not quite sure how to proceed, Dennison apologized if he was wrong and then went on to say that he was a Charlie Company veteran looking for the John Sclimenti who had fought in Vietnam in 1967. The voice answered, "Damn! This is him. I'm John Sclimenti. How the hell are you doing, Dennison?"

From there the ball started rolling quickly. Every veteran they contacted seemed to be in touch with at least one other veteran. Lilley, Nall, Benedick, Wilson, Cortright; the contact list grew and grew. Every time there was a call, the voice on the other end was shocked and overjoyed. Where had everyone been all these years? Some people were just impossible to find – folks like John Young, Charlie Nelson, or Danny Bailey. Their names were too common, and nobody knew where they had wound up or even where to begin looking. It was Bauler's idea to place advertisements in the most popular veterans' publications. Hopefully somebody would read them and call. After months of work, the list of names had grown to more than 40. Someone had even found the Petersons. Holy God. They were going to get to meet Don's son. Then the letters started coming in. John Young wrote:

Well Hello fer Chrissakes,

The odds of all this coming about are too boggling to contemplate. I got home from work the other night and found my first copy of the DAV magazine since I joined a month or so ago, and I almost tossed it, knowing that there is rarely anything in it to actually read, but I sat down and ate supper while I paged through it. I got to the reunion page and began to glance down the list. I just damn near choked when I saw the ad. I read it five or six times before I believed my eyes. Just a Riverine Force reunion would have been a mild surprise. A battalion reunion would have been cause for some satisfaction. A company reunion would have been joyous. But to see the very platoon I belonged to was just too much. I'm still shaking.

For the first time in a long time I have something to live for.

My God, my God, the memories.

Enough of this for now – let me finish and get this mailed.

I simply cannot say how much this means to me. It has come at a crisis in my life.

The first reunion of Charlie Company was a rather small affair in Las Vegas in July of 1989 and mainly included members of the 1st Platoon – the men Dennison and his friends knew how best to contact. But as the years went by, Dennison and Bauler reached out to more and more people – the Geiers, the Kenneys, Tom Conroy, Colonel Tutwiler, Captain Larson, Willie McTear, John Bradfield. Only a few, once contacted, chose not to attend. Danny Bailey, who had been so badly wounded on the day that Lieutenant Black had been killed, sent a letter in the childlike handwriting that John Young remembered so well after the loss of Benny Bridges.

Jim Dennison,

This is Danny F. Bailey... I don't know what happened to all. I was wounded twice. Was in too many hospitals going home, I don't like talking about it. I know we all had it rough, we who made it. It was hard to forget. I'm married with two kids, both girls. I won't come [to the reunion]. I stay in one place. But hope all are well, I don't work anymore, had to give it up. I fish, keeps my mind off things the VA said. I've ben married for a long time. I treat my family super and they are always there for me.

Bill Reynolds, from 2nd Platoon and who had been the first to reach Bill Geier's side on June 19, came home from Vietnam to a wonderful marriage and landed a good job at Lockheed. All the while, though, he remained interested in Vietnam, in what had happened to him and his brothers from Charlie Company. Over the years, he remained in touch with only a few of his buddies from Fort Riley, but in the mid-1990s he got the idea to found a website that would serve as a clearing house for everything Charlie Company – a place for people to get together, a place for the unit's history, a place to remember. In his efforts to gather the unit's people and story, Reynolds made contacts across the company, and eventually came across the burgeoning reunions. He couldn't believe his good luck – the unit that he loved so much was back together, at least part of it. He went to the next reunion and got together with Dennison. With the help of Reynolds, and through the vehicle of his website, the reunions continued and grew to include almost everyone. Charlie Company, the family that had gone to Vietnam, was back together again.

The boys of Charlie Company, now graying, had shared the most energizing, tragic, heroic, happy, and soul-wrenching times of their lives in 1967, times that had come to an all-too abrupt halt, whether ended by a sniper's bullet or by a brief goodbye while running to catch a flight home. Now, after decades had passed – after an entire lifetime had passed – they were getting back together. Many were worried. Would they recognize anybody? So much water had gone under the bridge; they all had new lives, children – even grandchildren. Could they still share anything in common with these people they had known so long ago in a world that was so foreign and so violent? In their ones and twos the Charlie Company veterans began to drift into their Las Vegas hotel. Terry McBride, always so tough and always so irreverent, who knew that seeing his old comrades was going to be one of the saving graces of his life, broke the ice. He looked around and said, "Who the hell are all you people? I served with a bunch of young, skinny guys. But all I see here is a bunch of fat old turds!" From somewhere farther back in the crowd, Jimmie Salazar shot back, "These turds might be older than hell, but they all look damn pretty to me!" With the niceties out of the way, the boys of Charlie Company began to shake hands, shed tears, and hug one another. They were home.

Old friends sought each other out to speak of events that only they could remember. Tim Fischer and Ron Vidovic talked in a corner about the mining outside Dong Tam to which Vidovic lost his leg. What had life been like since then? Steve Hopper and Tom

Conroy quietly discussed the battle of October 6, when they lost Alldridge and Burkhead. What bravery Burkhead had shown by going after his fallen friend even when he was so short that he could have gone home in less than a month. Charlie Nelson ran into Dave Jarczewski, who was nursing a drink at the bar. Although he had given up drinking as part of his life of solitude back on the reservation, Nelson sat down and ordered himself a shot. The two got royally and exuberantly drunk while discussing the fighting on May 15 when they had both been so badly wounded. It had been such a terrible day, but as the drinks continued coming both men slowly came to better terms with their past. It just helped so much to talk to someone else who understood, who really understood. The two men, getting up from their barstools arm in arm, agreed that what they wanted most was to meet Don Peterson's son one day and to come face to face with Lieutenant Thompson. Wouldn't that be great? To give Thompson a piece of their minds?

Like a family getting together and swapping comfortable and comforting stories over a holiday feast, the boys of Charlie Company talked, wept, and shared just about everything – their pasts and their presents. Everyone had heard that one of their number had lost both of his legs, only to overcome adversity and become a skier. They couldn't wait to find out who it was, to ask him questions. From the middle of a small crowd of men, Doug Wilson, who had blown three VC out of a haystack with an LAW on the long-ago battle of May 15, turned to Jim Dennison and said, "Is the guy without the legs going to be here?" Standing only a few yards away, Jack Benedick piped up, "I'm him, and I'm here." Wilson looked him up and down, evidently not quite believing that a man with no legs was just standing there, so Benedick rolled up his pants legs to show his prostheses. Immediately a group of Charlie Company veterans crowded in for what was sure to be a good, and hard-drinking, story. Wilson fumbled for what to say next: "Geez, sir. I'm sorry, but I didn't recognize you after so damn long." "Well, I wouldn't have recognized me either," Benedick replied. "I used to be taller." Having ordered enough drinks to make it through the story, the group went to a nearby table – they just had to hear what had happened to Jack Benedick. How had he lost his legs? Benedick took a deep swig of his whiskey, looked around and began by pointing to his prostheses: "Well, fellas. I fucked up. I wished that my dick was closer to the ground, and this is what I got!" Benedick went on to share the real story, followed by others chiming in about their own lives, families, and brushes with the VA.

Nobody had noticed it – a sign at one of Charlie Company's first reunions. The hotel in Las Vegas had several events going on that weekend, with each function warranting its own black felt announcement sign with white plastic letters directing participants to the correct room. One sign steered Charlie Company veterans to a second-floor ballroom, while another read, "Thompson wedding." Perhaps if they had noticed it, the boys of Charlie Company would not have made the connection – it was just too outlandish even to consider. But, while Jack Benedick sat there telling the story of his lost legs, the door to the meeting room opened, and there stood a tuxedo-clad Sam Thompson – the man who had ordered Ski's squad out into the rice paddy on May 15. The man who had rushed 3rd Platoon into a minefield in August. His daughter was getting married in the same hotel. For a moment or two, Thompson just stood there and looked around. All conversation came to a halt and the room went totally silent as the men realized who it was. At a few tables animated conversations broke out – Tim Fischer, Ron Vidovic, Charlie Nelson, and Dave Jarczewski all wondering what the hell Thompson was doing here. One or two of the men got up and headed Thompson's way. Seated at one of the tables nearest the door, Jack Benedick got to his feet and was the first by Thompson's side. He looked Thompson in the eye and said, "You are going to have to leave. You aren't welcome here." The look on Benedick's face told Thompson everything, that if he hung around there was going to be real trouble. Thompson looked up and made an exaggerated effort to scan the room again and turned to Benedick and said, "Nobody I wanted to see here anyway," and turned to leave. As the apparition of the worst part of Charlie Company's collective past left the room, Benedick closed the door and announced that nobody was going to follow him. This was their reunion and it was damn well time to get back to it.

For many of the families of the men who never made it home, the Charlie Company reunions were a chance to get to know the last friends their sons, husbands, and fathers ever had. It was a chance to come to terms with the most important losses of their lives. Barbara Kenney was there to renew ties with Tom Conroy, Bill Reynolds, and Tim Fischer, who had already helped her better understand the loss of her husband. Jesse Ramos was there, a Vietnam veteran in his own right. He felt comfortable and comforted among his brother's friends in Charlie Company. He understood their pain, and they assuaged his. Bernice Geier was in attendance along with her son Bill's siblings and their spouses. They carried a collection of photos of Bill as a young man to share with his friends. They especially wanted to meet one of Bill's closest buddies, Idoluis Casares, whom Bill had known as "Bear," and to learn more about Bill's loss while acquainting his comrades with who Bill had been before he had been drafted. The reunions meant different things to each of the family members; Phil Ferro's sister, Diane Hawley, was deeply moved to see how everyone remembered her brother like it was yesterday. Barbara Kenney continued to piece together the story of her beloved husband, who had been everyone's friend. Jesse Ramos had met kindred spirits who loved his brother as much as he did. The Geiers were so pleased that everyone wanted to know about Bill, that they cared so much. It was also somehow comforting to learn how Bill had died – he had been lost doing what he loved, helping someone else. But what meant the most to each and every one of the family members was their welcome. Charlie Company was a living, vibrant family – a family that fully embraced both them and their cherished memories. Together with the Charlie Company family, the wives, mothers, and siblings of the fallen were finally able to mourn. Their pain would never fully diminish, but they could now share both the pain and the love with others who could truly understand their loss.

A hush fell over the room as the men of Charlie Company looked up from their drinks and conversations – the door to the banquet room had opened, and standing there was Don Peterson. It was like he had walked right out of that rice paddy in 1967 and into the Flamingo Hotel. For just a few seconds nobody could believe their eyes. It couldn't be true. Then, as people began to take in the faces of those surrounding the newcomer, faces that also resembled Don Peterson, it all became clear. At different tables in the room it all hit at the same time and murmurs went up: "Oh my God, it's Peterson's kid." "Peterson's son's here." Jimmy Peterson, along with Don's parents and siblings, were greeted by an enormous outpouring of affection, an affection so great that it initially threatened to overwhelm them. Moving from table to table and from group to group, Jimmy met with pats on the back and warm embraces – all of these people, these people who welcomed him so freely, were the key to putting the pieces of his father together again. Everyone, but especially those veterans of 1st Platoon, just couldn't wait to talk with him. For the next two days Jimmy soaked it all in, sitting with men who had for decades been rehearsing what they would say to him about that tragic day in 1967. Although his father's friends often wept when recounting the story of his days in Vietnam, it was evident that these men were overjoyed to see him, and that in telling their stories to Pete's son they gained some kind of closure, a sense of completeness. For Jimmy it was all so painful, to hear how his father had died, to hear of the love that these men had felt for him and still felt so long after his death. But in that pain was true understanding, a sense of who Don Peterson actually was. Don Peterson had been good, and had fought through the adversity in his own life to become the kind of man everyone in the assembled family of Charlie Company admired. Don Peterson, his father, had been loved. Was still loved. As the stories piled up – Don Peterson in Fort Riley, Don Peterson showing off Jimmy's picture to everyone, Don Peterson talking about how he and Jimmy would play football together one day – for the first time Don Peterson came alive to his son. Jimmy could almost see his father standing there, mirrored in the eyes of the men who remembered him where Jimmy could not. Jimmy Peterson finally had a father to look up to, a father complete and whole, to guide the remainder of his life.

For everyone the reunions were cathartic, and for some they were and are life-saving. While their families and friends at home certainly meant well, many of the boys of Charlie Company had felt alone with their pain for so long. There were well-meaning doctors, ministers, wives, and children – but these men had done so much, had seen so much, that they could not bring themselves to share. But finally, reunited with their brothers, they could let it all out – a tidal wave of emotion that had been building for more than two decades. It felt so good – to Jace Johnston, to James Nall, to Doug Wilson, to Steve Hopper – just to talk. Just to talk to someone else who had been there, who knew the smells, the fear, who had been bitten by red ants, who had seen the helicopter crash on June 19. For men like Willie McTear and Charlie Nelson, being with their old comrades was the only place where they felt truly free. No amount of counseling or PTSD rap groups could ever compare. For Jimmie Salazar the reunions were more than therapeutic. He had done it – survived heart attacks and diabetes to see his brothers again. While at the reunions his mental anguish, the nightmares, and the pain simply disappeared – sometimes for months at a time. Hearing the stories of his own past, adding stories of his own, was so powerful. He was not alone; he was part of a family – a family that would never be broken up again. Aurora Salazar, who had struggled to stand by her husband through it all, had suffered so long in silence. There was treatment for the men, the veterans, but somehow everyone had forgotten that for every veteran there were wives, children, parents, and siblings – who tried to understand, tried to help, but always fell so woefully short. There was such a hopeless feeling in not being able to soothe the pain of the one you love the most in this world. At the reunions, Aurora discovered that she, too, was not alone. There was Vivian Conroy, Karen Huntsman, Jeannie Hartman, and all the rest; wives who were also struggling to help their husbands and families cope with the fallout of war. Aurora now had sisters with whom to speak and to share. She had a new family that she never knew existed.

For John Young, the reunions were almost too good to be true. At home he hardly ever slept, especially since he had given up alcohol. He hated to travel, to be so far away from the familiar, from relative safety. But at the reunions he felt safe. He slept like a baby and wore a constant smile – a smile that his sisters once told him that they had not seen since 1967. Sharing it all with others who had been there – the terror of June 19, the shooting of the Viet Cong prisoner, the death of Benny Bridges – it meant so much. It also helped that these guys remembered the good times: the beer bust on the beach at Vung Tau when they had destroyed an entire bar, the Phantom Shitter at Fort Riley, the children in the little village near the bunkers at Dong Tam. It was important to balance the bad with the good, the tragic with the outlandish. Seeing them all again was like that New Year's Eve that Young had spent with Sergeant Hoover before they left Vietnam – the night when they had tried to remember everything. There was John Sclimenti who had bashed his head on a gateway arch while chasing a Viet Cong; there was Sergeant Crockett, still an imposing sight after so many years; there was Larry Lilley who now owned a motorcycle dealership in California; there was Steve Huntsman who he had last seen on May 15, 1967. Everything seemed right.

There was one person, though, whom John Young almost didn't want to see – Carl Cortright. It had been so hard – the memory of crashing down beside him in that rice paddy on May 15 – to discover that Cortright, so young, so new to the unit, was paralyzed. Young had never been able to forget the last few images of Cortright being dragged over the rice paddy dike and manhandled onto a medevac chopper. It must have been agony. Young was sure that Carl Cortright blamed him for his condition. What was it like not being able to walk? What was it like having your life end at 21? What would Carl Cortright say to him? As the pressure mounted, Young saw the wheelchair. Cortright was there and was making his way through the crowd. Finally facing the moment that he had dreaded for so long, Young walked over and stuck out his hand. "Carl, I'm not sure if you recognize me, but my name is John Young." Cortright replied that, even though he had been with Charlie Company for such a short time, he did recognize Young, and asked him how he was doing. The two exchanged pleasantries for a few moments before Young asked the question that had haunted him for years: "Carl, I just didn't know how you were going to react to me, to what happened on that day. I understand if…" But before the final, unspoken but understood words reached Young's lips, Cortright intervened: "John, if it wasn't for you, I wouldn't be here." Cortright didn't blame him. He was alive, joyously and happily alive. Heck, he was even an athlete. As Young sat down and heard the story that Cortright spun about his life since Vietnam, it was as though a great weight was lifted from his chest. That memory, the bloody memory of May 15, would always be there, seared into Young's consciousness. But after speaking to Carl Cortright, Young decided that he could now live with that memory. In coming together as a family again, a family that now included wives, siblings, and children, Charlie Company had taken the most important step in learning to live with Vietnam.

With much to process, Young went back to his home and solitary life in Picayune, Mississippi. He had returned from the depths of depression, depths from which few men have surfaced to tell the tale. Vietnam would always be one of the dominant forces in his life – perhaps the most dominant force. But, with the joy of looking forward to a Charlie Company reunion every year, John Young knew that he was going to live. But to what end? While he sat and contemplated the future, the telephone rang. Young absently wondered who it could be. Maybe a solicitor? He didn't have many friends and received few calls. Picking up the receiver, Young was surprised to hear the voice of Dr Leslie Root, his PTSD therapist at the VA. What was she doing calling him at home? It turned out that there was a college professor asking if his class could meet with a group of Vietnam veterans. She wanted him to participate in the discussion. Universities taught classes on Vietnam? That was news to him. Did these students really want to know the truth? After giving it some thought Young agreed, telling Dr Root that he would be there and that he had a story to tell. He didn't want to talk about himself but instead about Charlie Company: Bill Geier, Don Peterson, Kenny Frakes, Ron Schworer, Phil Ferro, Forrest Ramos, Fred Kenney, and all the rest. These students didn't know their story. America didn't know their story. The story of the boys of 1967, golden men, young draftees who had done everything that their nation had asked of them and had received so little in return – lost faces of a distant war.

GLOSSARY

AIT Abbreviation for advanced individual training.

AK47 The assault rifle of the communist bloc, first developed by Mikhail Kalashnikov. By 1967 the AK47 was standard equipment for Viet Cong units in the Mekong Delta.

Ammi barge A pontoon-type barge moored alongside the barracks ships of the Mobile Riverine Force (MRF). Used for docking and loading of the Armored Troop Carriers and for storing ammunition.

Area of Operations (AO) The area assigned in which a military unit operated. Often an area around a major emplacement like Dong Tam or an area assigned for a specific military operation or sweep.

Armored Troop Carrier (ATC) Known by the troops as "Tango Boats," the ATCs carried the men of the MRF from the base ships into battle. Each platoon had its own Tango Boat, a converted World War II landing craft, which was 56 feet in length and had a top speed of 6 knots. Each ATC was armed with one 20mm cannon, two 50-caliber machine guns, and two grenade launchers.

Army of the Republic of Vietnam (ARVN) The proper name for the South Vietnamese Army, the armed forces of South Vietnam that fought as allies of the United States.

Bear Cat A brigade base camp for the 1st Infantry Division 10 miles south of Long Binh that became the temporary home for the

9th Infantry Division while Dong Tam and the Mobile Riverine Base were under construction in early 1967.

Berm The raised area of earth, usually studded with bunkers and defensive emplacements, that surrounded military instillations such as Dong Tam.

Booby trap In the Mekong Delta booby traps were normally explosive devices set by the Viet Cong along trails frequented by US troops or as defensive measures near Viet Cong base camps. The most common types included grenades fixed to a monofilament line that hung slack in the water or on the ground. When a passing soldier's leg caught the line, the pin would be pulled from the grenade.

Brown Water Navy A term used to refer to naval forces that operated in riverine environments, as opposed to blue water navy forces that operated at sea.

C 4 A plastic explosive commonly carried in Vietnam that was impervious to shock and had to be set off using a detonator. When set alight it burned hot and slowly and was often used to heat C Rations.

C Rations Individual meals, usually containing canned, pre-cooked food, for use by US soldiers in the field. Came in several varieties, many of which were detested by the soldiers, and were often heated by burning C 4.

Ca Mau The southernmost province in Vietnam, which was heavily infested with Viet Cong during much of the Vietnam War.

Cam Son Secret Zone One of the main bases of operation for the Viet Cong in Dinh Tuong Province in the Mekong Delta south of Saigon.

Camp Zama A major US Army post located 25 miles southwest of Tokyo, Japan. Location of a major military hospital that housed many of the casualties of the Vietnam War who required treatment beyond that normally available in country.

Claymore mine A command-detonated mine, fired by remote control, that fires a pattern of steel balls like a shotgun.

Cloverleafing The practice of sending patrols out from the main line of advance in a cloverleaf pattern to avoid ambushes.

Date Eligible to Return from Overseas Service (DEROS) In Vietnam most soldiers served one-year tours of duty and counted down the days until their DEROS, after which they would return to the United States.

GLOSSARY

Dong Tam The main operations base of the MRF (and for much of the 9th Infantry Division) in Vietnam. Located 50 miles southwest of Saigon, Dong Tam (which means "United Hearts and Minds") was created by dredging silt from the My Tho River and creating a new, vast expanse of mud.

Dustoff A term that usually means a helicopter extraction mission to remove wounded men from the battlefield.

F4 McDonnell Douglas fighter/fighter bomber (often referred to as the Phantom) widely used by the US Navy and the Marines in Vietnam.

F100 North American Aviation fighter/fighter bomber widely used by the US Air Force in Vietnam. Often referred to as the Super Sabre.

Forward Air Controller (FAC) Circling above battlefields in a light aircraft, the Forward Air Controller was tasked with directing close air support strikes in aid of ground forces involved in combat.

Gravy Army slang for "easy", used in the context of an easy assignment such as Dong Tam duty.

Hooch The term used by many Americans in Vietnam to refer to almost any rural Vietnamese structure, which most often were the ubiquitous wood and thatch homes of the Vietnamese peasants that dotted the countryside.

Huey (Chopper) The common name used for the Bell UH1 helicopters that were widely used in Vietnam for troop transport, medical evacuations, and fire support.

Infusion The practice of shifting men around in the 9th Infantry Division to avoid too many men from any one unit having the same DEROS, which would have gutted units like Charlie Company of their veteran cadre.

KIA Abbreviation for killed in action.

Landing Ship, Tank (LST) A class of vessel originally created in World War II to allow for landing armor or other vehicles in support of amphibious operations. In Vietnam the LSTs were remodeled to serve as the barrack ships of the Mobile Riverine Base.

Light Anti-Armor Weapon (LAW) Shoulder-fired, single-shot anti-tank weapon. Fires a rocket carrying an armor-piercing warhead. Also used for dealing with hardened bunkers.

Long Binh A major US logistics center located just north of Saigon.

M16 The 5.56mm standard issue service rifle of the Vietnam War. When first introduced the weapon was notorious for jamming.

M60 The 7.62mm standard issue general-purpose machine gun used by American forces in the Vietnam War. Served by a crew of two or three: gunner, assistant gunner, and ammunition bearer.

M79 Single-shot, shoulder-fired, break-action grenade launcher. Fires 40mm rounds. Was known in Vietnam as the "blooper" for the distinctive sound it made.

Medevac In Vietnam the term generally meant evacuating wounded via helicopter.

Medical Civil Affairs Program (MEDCAP) A civic action program in Vietnam that involved doctors and specialists setting up a field clinic to offer medical care to local civilians.

Mekong Delta The area south of Saigon in Vietnam, dominated by the nine channels of the Mekong River. Comprised of 15,500 square miles of wetlands and traversed by over 3,500 miles of waterways. A very fertile rice-growing region and in 1965 home to over half of the population of South Vietnam.

MIA Abbreviation for missing in action.

Military Assistance Command, Vietnam (MACV) The unified command structure of all US military forces in Vietnam. Located in Saigon. During Charlie Company's year in Vietnam, 1967, MACV was headed by General William Westmoreland.

Military units The below figures are general in nature, and, since terminology and practice change over time, are most relevant to the Vietnam era.

> **Squad** Usually composed of two fireteams totaling ten men, led by a squad leader who is a staff sergeant.
>
> **Platoon** Usually composed of three or four squads roughly totaling 40 men, led by a platoon leader who is a lieutenant.
>
> **Company** Usually composed of four platoons roughly totaling 160 men, commanded by a captain.
>
> **Battalion** Usually composed of three or four companies often totaling 500-600 men, commanded by a lieutenant colonel.
>
> **Brigade** Usually composed of three or four battalions plus supporting elements often totaling 4,000 troops, commanded by a brigadier general.
>
> **Division** Usually composed of three or four brigades plus supporting elements often totaling 15,000 troops, commanded by a major general. The smallest combined

arms unit in the Vietnam-era US military capable of independent operation.

Corps Usually composed of three or four divisions plus supporting elements often totaling 45,000 troops, commanded by a lieutenant general.

Mobile Afloat Force The original name given to the concept of basing a brigade or more of men on ships for mobile operations in the Mekong Delta.

Mobile Riverine Base The barracks ships that housed the afloat forces of the MRF, eventually including the *Colleton*, the *Benewah*, and the *APL-26*.

Mobile Riverine Force (MRF) The combined navy/army force made up of the ships of the River Assault Force and the ground force of one (later two) of the brigades of the 9th Infantry Division designed to contest control of the Mekong Delta with the Viet Cong.

Monitor The main gunship of the Brown Water Navy in Vietnam. Heavily armored and carried a 40mm cannon, a 20mm cannon, an 81mm mortar, and two 50-caliber machine guns.

Mortar Muzzle-loading, high-trajectory small artillery piece. In Charlie Company the 4th Platoon was the mortar platoon, often tasked with providing close fire support for the other three platoons in battle.

MOS Abbreviation for military occupation specialty.

North Vietnamese Army (NVA or PAVN) The term used by most Americans when referring to the troops of North Vietnam. More properly termed the People's Army of Vietnam, which during the Vietnam War specifically meant the regular military of the state of North Vietnam.

OCS Abbreviation for Officer Candidates School.

Plastic Assault Boat (PAB) 16-foot Boston Whaler fiberglass-hulled boats with outboard motors sometimes used to transport one of Charlie Company's platoons in the watery terrain of the Mekong Delta.

Post Exchange (PX) A retail store that operates on US military bases.

PRC 25 The major field radio of the Vietnam War, weighing just over 23 pounds and worn on the back of the RTO.

PTSD Abbreviation for Post Traumatic Stress Disorder.

Punji trap A decidedly low-tech Viet Cong weapon. Often a hole dug in the ground on or near a heavily used trail with pointed sticks in the bottom designed to injure the unwary.

Purple Heart The medal awarded to members of the US military who are wounded in action.

Radiotelephone operator (RTO) The soldier tasked with carrying the unit's radio (usually a PRC 25), who served as the indispensable link between the unit in the field and air and artillery support.

REMF Shorthand for Rear Echelon Motherfucker.

Replacement The term used for a soldier who comes in to replace a veteran who has been killed, seriously wounded, or has rotated home.

River Assault Force The naval element of the Mobile Riverine Force, which in 1967 was made up of two River Assault Squadrons.

River Assault Squadron Together two River Assault Squadrons made up the River Assault Force, the naval element of the Mobile Riverine Force.

Rung Sat Special Zone A vast mangrove swamp that borders the Long Tau shipping channel, which connects Saigon to the sea. Was an important Viet Cong base area during 1966–67.

Sampan The common American term for most of the flat-bottomed Vietnamese boats that plied the waters of the Mekong Delta.

Tet Offensive Surprise attack on January 31, 1968, in which the Viet Cong struck most of the major urban areas of South Vietnam.

Toe popper A small anti-personnel mine designed to injure the foot.

United Service Organization (USO) Organization famous for putting on shows large and small to entertain the troops in Vietnam, most famous perhaps for its Christmas shows with Bob Hope.

Viet Cong (VC) The common term for any communist guerrilla forces in South Vietnam. Often made up of southerners, but commanded by the north. More properly the People's Liberation Armed Forces, the armed forces of the National Liberation Front (NLF). The main enemy faced by US forces in the Mekong Delta. Also commonly known as Charlie or Victor Charles.

Vung Tau Coastal town with beautiful beaches located southeast of Saigon. Was the port of arrival for many Americans in Vietnam and the location of many in country rest and relaxation (R and R) periods.

Webgear The military-issue harness on which troops organized their weapons, ammunition, and other gear.

WIA Abbreviation for wounded in action.

THE MEN OF CHARLIE COMPANY

Acevedo, Ben: One of ten children; brought up in the rural Yakima Valley of Washington where his father Benjamin worked as a farm laborer and his mother Berta was a housewife. Served as a team leader in 1st Platoon. Helped to rescue Charlie Nelson in the battle of May 15. After the war worked for Boeing for a short time, but then moved from job to job, especially as a truck driver. Loved to ride Harleys. He passed away in 2009.

Alldridge, Gale: Replacement who came to Charlie Company through infusion in September, 1967. Member of 3rd Platoon. Killed in action, October 6, 1967.

Bailey, Danny: Born in Hot Springs, Arkansas. Injured by a booby trap on April 8; threw away his crutches and returned to action in the fighting on June 19. Best friends with Cecil Bridges. Married after the war and had two daughters. Passed away in 2009.

Balch, Bobby: Member of 1st Platoon. Wounded in action on June 19, 1967.

Bauler, John: One of the California contingent of draftees. In Vietnam served in 1st Platoon and as RTO for squad leader John Young. Along with Doug Wilson retrieved the body of Don Peterson after the fighting on May 15. Passed away in 2002.

Benedick, Jack: From Omaha, Nebraska, graduate of Officer Candidates School. Married Nancy in 1965 and had a son, Jack Jr., in 1966. Platoon leader, 2nd Platoon, Charlie Company. Wounded in the fighting on June 19. Returned to Vietnam in 1969 as commander, Charlie Company, 3rd of the 60th Infantry. Wounded by a booby trap in April 1969 and lost both legs below the knee. Continued with military career and became a champion downhill skier.

Bertolino, Fred: West Point classmate of Lynn Hunt and John Hoskins. Platoon leader, 1st Platoon, Alpha Company, 4th of the 47th Infantry. Killed in action on June 19, 1967.

Black, Duffy: From Peoria, Illinois. Joined the military in 1962, and later attended Officer Candidates School. While at Fort Riley with Charlie Company met and wed Ida, the daughter of the postmaster of the 9th Infantry Division. Served as company executive officer in Vietnam. Wounded by a booby trap in the Rung Sat Special Zone on April 8, 1967, and died in the hospital three days later.

Blas, Pedro: Born in Guam, served as platoon sergeant for 4th Platoon, Charlie Company. Died in 1994.

Boetcher, Frank: Machine gunner in 1st Platoon who dueled with a VC machine gunner on June 19.

Bradfield, John: From Cleveland and was only eight when his father died in an industrial accident. Always managed to have a record player on hand to play Motown for his buddies. Member of 3rd Platoon. Wounded by a booby trap in August 1967. Returned home and worked for the post office and married Esther, his "angel and care giver."

Bridges, Cecil (Benny): From east Texas. Member of 1st Platoon. Served as John Young's RTO. Killed in action July 29, 1967.

Bryan, Ronnie: Member of 2nd Platoon. Wounded in action on June 19, 1967.

Burkhead, Danny: Replacement who came to Charlie Company through infusion in September 1967. Member of 3rd Platoon. Killed in action October 6, 1967.

Burleson, Henry: From rural Texas outside Abilene. Convincingly buried a cigarette butt at Fort Riley. Served in 2nd Platoon, where he was close friends with Mike Cramer, Phil Ferro, and Butch Eakins. After the war returned to Abilene, where he worked for a sign company for several years before going into business for himself.

Caliari, Tony: From an Italian family outside Pittsburgh. Family moved to California in 1959. Member of 3rd Platoon. Wounded in action May 15, 1967. Returned to California where he worked in construction for several years.

Cara, Robert: Member of 4th Platoon. Killed in action June 19, 1967.

Casares, Idoluis: From Brownsville, Texas, where he learned English in the local public schools. Served in the 2nd Platoon and was dubbed "Bear" by his friend Bill Geier. Wounded in action July 11, 1967. After returning from Vietnam, married Toni, his high school girlfriend, in January 1968. Graduated with BBA from University of Texas-Austin in summer of 1968. Licensed as a Certified Public Accountant since 1972. In 2007, went back in to Vietnam, with his three children and 13 others, to visit on the 40th Anniversary of the Ap Bac battle. Still resides and works as a CPA in Brownsville, Texas, a border town across from Mexico.

Cockerell, Stan: From North Hollywood, California. Though only 129lbs, was a star football player in high school. Volunteered for the draft, and served with 2nd Platoon. After the war he did, indeed, work up the gumption to ask Linda Walters for a date, and the couple married in 1969. Cockerell went to work as a propmaster for several major Hollywood movie studios and worked on a host of projects including *The Natural*, *Dead Poets Society*, and *We Were Soldiers*. Cockerell retired in 2008. He and Linda have three children, Scott, Jeffrey, and Mindy, and six grandchildren.

Conroy, Tom: Son of a meat cutter from Lancaster, California. Married Vivian after basic training. Member of 3rd Platoon. Served as RTO to platoon leader John Hoskins. Worked several jobs after the war, especially in construction. He and Vivian had three children. Tom retired in 1999 and now loves tinkering on cars.

Cortright, Carl: From Mission Hills, California. Came to 1st Platoon of Charlie Company as a replacement in April, 1967. Wounded in action and paralyzed on May 15, 1967. Became a champion athlete in the National Veterans Wheelchair Games.

Cramer, Mike: From Pacoima, California. Worked at Rocketdyne after high school. Served in 2nd Platoon as an RTO. Called in the first air strikes on June 19. Close friends with Phil Ferro, Butch Eakins, and Henry Burleson. After the war got married and graduated from college. Works as an insurance adjuster.

Crockett, Lynn: Born into a farming family near Cumberland, Kentucky. Entered the military at age 17. Served as first sergeant for Charlie Company and played a pivotal role in training at Fort Riley. Served a second tour with the 25th Division in 1969–70. Retired from the military in 1973.

Cusanelli, Jim: From Saint Louis, Missouri. Served in 3rd Platoon of Charlie Company. Was close friends with Jose Sauceda.

Deedrick, Don: Member of 1st Platoon. He and his wife Sue lived with Steve and Karen Huntsman and Don and Jacque Peterson while at Fort Riley.

Dennison, Jim: Son of an Irish pub owner from Chicago. Member of 1st Platoon. Once tackled a Viet Cong while on night ambush in July. After the war worked selling construction equipment and eventually moved to California, where he and John Bauler were instrumental in setting up the first Charlie Company reunions.

Eakins, Butch: From Cape Girardeau, Missouri, and later worked at Caterpillar in Peoria, Illinois. Close friends with Phil Ferro, Mike Cramer, and Henry Burleson. Member of 2nd Platoon. Killed in action on July 11, 1967.

Ehlert, Bob: Born on a ranch in Montana, but raised in Minnesota. Loved the outdoor life and horses. Worked as a machinist before being drafted. Served in 2nd Platoon of Charlie Company and was wounded by a sniper on June 5, 1967. After the war worked in construction and as a homebuilder in Minnesota, married the love of his life Linda, and raised four children. Foot and back problems stemming from his wounds in Vietnam led to a career change into real estate, in which he still works.

Eisenbaugh, Bob: From Philadelphia and Shamokin, Pennsylvania. One of Charlie Company's early replacements, arriving in April 1967. Wounded in action in November. After the war worked as a correctional officer and then a counselor with the prison system for 25 years. Married with one child.

Fadden, Paris: From Robbinsdale, Minnesota, where his father worked as a mechanic and his mother was a homemaker. Liked cars, drag racing, and girls. Drafted into 4th Division, but transferred into Charlie Company, where he served in the 4th Platoon. Wounded in action on June 26, 1967. After the war returned to Minnesota, went to trade school, and worked in sheet metal and air conditioning for 31 years.

Still enjoys working on cars and is married to a wonderful woman who understands him.

Ferro, Phil: From Northridge, California, where he won the Los Angeles city championship in high hurdles during high school. Was especially close to his sister Diane, and married Sandy in 1965. Close friends with Mike Cramer, Butch Eakins, and Henry Burleson. Member of 2nd Platoon. Killed in action on July 11, 1967.

Fink, Hubert: Member of 4th Platoon. Killed in action on June 19, 1967.

Fischer, Tim: From Cleveland, where he worked as a hod carrier on construction sites. Member of 3rd Platoon where he served as a squad leader. Close friends with Ron Vidovic. After the war worked in construction and then as a long-haul truck driver.

Frakes, Kenny: From Lancaster, California, where he was on the high school track and wrestling teams. Drafted with friends Larry Lilley and Tim Johnson. Member of 4th Platoon. Killed in action on June 19, 1967.

French, Bob: From Tampa, Florida, where he had quit college to work in the post office, which left him open to the draft. Married Kaye who accompanied him to Fort Riley. He did not find out that she was pregnant until he was in Vietnam. Served as an RTO in 2nd Platoon. His sister, Ginger, became a pen pal of Bill Geier. Wounded in action on June 19, 1967. After the war returned to Tampa and worked at the post office for 21 years.

Fulton, William: From Berkley, California. Graduated from the University of California as an ROTC honor graduate. Won a Distinguished Service Cross as a company commander in Italy during World War II. Served as a battalion commander in the 4th Infantry Division during the Korean War. In Vietnam served as Commander 2nd Brigade, 9th Infantry Division. Retired as lieutenant general in 1977 and then worked for the Association of the United States Army. Passed away in 2006.

Gann, Ronnie: From Los Angeles, where his father worked as a machinist for Lockheed. Member of 4th Platoon. Wounded in action on October 6, 1967. After the war, completed his college degree and worked as an accountant in a law firm. Married twice and has three children.

Geier, Bill: From the Chicago area, son of Jack and Bernice Geier. Medic with 2nd Platoon. Killed in action on June 19, 1967. Mother, brother, sister, and other family members still demonstrate love and support for Bill by attending Charlie Company reunions.

Gronseth, Gary: California native. Served with 1st Platoon. On May 15, 1967, hit a fleeing Viet Cong on the head with a shell from an M79 grenade launcher.

Hartman, Ernie: From Sugar Grove, Pennsylvania. After high school took a job as a precision grinder and married his sweetheart Jeannie. Arrived in Charlie Company as a replacement in 1st Platoon just after the battle of June 19, 1967. Wounded in action on July 29, 1967. Went back to work as a precision grinder for 37 years before the company was sold. Ernie and Jeannie have a child, Corey, and a grandchild, Dylan.

Harvey, Gene: From North Hollywood, where his father worked for Lockheed. After high school went to college, but dropped one too many classes leaving him open for the draft. Married sweetheart Deanna before departing for Vietnam. Member of 1st Platoon. In the fighting on May 15, 1967, volunteered to search for the downed squad. Re-enlisted after May 15, and was assigned to Transportation Command. Worked for United Parcel Service, rising to the rank of Human Resources Manager before his retirement in 2000. He and Deanna have been married 45 years and have two children and two grandchildren.

Hoffman, Edward*: Fictitious name for Dave Jarczewski's RTO in 1st Platoon who failed to give the order for the squad to fall back on May 15, 1967.

Hoover, Buford: From West Virginia. Platoon sergeant, 1st Platoon. Passed away in 2001.

Hopper, Steve: From the rural area near Greenfield, Illinois. After high school worked for Caterpillar in Peoria, Illinois. Member of 3rd Platoon. Wounded in action on July 1, 1967, and on October 6, 1967. After the war returned to Greenfield, married his sweetheart Jennifer, and worked for Caterpillar.

Hoskins, John: US Military Academy graduate, class of 1966. Platoon leader, 3rd Platoon, Charlie Company. Wounded in action on July 11, 1967. Later served as company commander, Echo Company, 3/60 Infantry. Killed in action May 6, 1968.

Howell, John: From Pismo Beach, California. Had a job that didn't take too much of his time, and loved surfing and girls. Member of 3rd Platoon. Wounded in action on July 12, 1967. Infused in August. After the war, returned to California, married four times and now has two children and five grandchildren. Owned his own company doing home remodeling and ceramic tile installation. For the last 12 years has lived in Florida.

Hubbard, Henry: Replacement to Charlie Company in June 1967. Served in 2nd Platoon. With Frank Schwan, narrowly avoided Viet Cong patrols following the fighting on July 11, 1967.

Hunt, Lynn: Grew up in the Miami area. Went to the US Military Academy on a swimming scholarship. Class of 1966. Platoon leader of 1st Platoon. Retired from the military as a lieutenant colonel in 1989. Next worked as manager of a computer war game simulation center for the military in Germany before moving back to the United States and working with Westinghouse in Aiken, South Carolina. In 1997 moved to Myrtle Beach and ran his own hurricane protection business until 2009. Now is semi-retired and enjoys playing tennis.

Huntsman, Steve: From Saint George, Utah. Attended Brigham Young University and married Karen before going to Fort Riley, where the couple lived with Don and Jacque Peterson. Served in 1st Platoon. Wounded in action May 15, 1967. Later re-enlisted. After the war worked as a truck driver for 27 years.

Irvin, Curtis: Grew up in Lutesville, Missouri. Member of 2nd Platoon of Charlie Company. After the war returned to Missouri, living in Farmington. Married and has two children and one grandchild. Owned and operated his own business in Farmington until his retirement in 2009.

Jarczewski, Dave: From Depew, New York. After high school worked in the Lackawanna, New York plant of Bethlehem Steel. Member of 1st Platoon. Squad leader of 2nd Squad, which was furthest from cover in Charlie Company's first major battle on May 15, 1967. Wounded in action May 15, 1967. After returning from Vietnam, went back to work for Bethlehem Steel until it closed and then worked in the US Post Office.

Jindra, Bobby: From Wickliffe, near Cleveland. Married to Dolly and had a daughter named Jacque, both of whom accompanied him to training at Fort Riley. Killed in action on June 19, 1967.

Johnson, Jim: Member of 3rd Platoon. Heavily involved in the fighting on July 11, 1967.

Johnson, Tim: From Lancaster, California. Worked for General Telephone after high school and was drafted along with Larry Lilley and Kenny Frakes. Member of 3rd Platoon. Killed in action on June 19, 1967.

Johnston, Jace: From the near north side of Chicago, father Jace was a military man and mother Bernadette a telephone operator. Turned down a draft deferment for his work in optical medical supplies. Served in 3rd Platoon. After the war moved to Arizona and first worked in construction and then as a real estate agent and broker.

Kayser, Evans (Sonny): First lieutenant and member of a Crusader Fire Team of Delta Troop, 3rd Squadron, 5th Armored Cavalry, which often provided fire support to troops of the Mobile Riverine Force, notably on the battle of June 19.

Kenney, Elmer (Fred): From Chatsworth, California. Married Barbara, who gave birth to their son, Freddie, while Kenney was on the troopship to Vietnam. Served in 3rd Platoon. Killed in action July 11, 1967. After the war Barbara worked for a title company, while she and Freddie did their best to honor Fred's memory.

Kerr, Daniel: From Indiana, Pennsylvania. Abandoned by his father in Beria, Ohio, and became a ward of the state. Joined the military in 1960, largely for survival. Married Karin while stationed in Germany, who accompanied him to Fort Riley. During his tour became platoon sergeant for 2nd Platoon. Retired from the military in 1980. Became a stock broker and moved to Tacoma, Washington.

King, Harold Wayne: From Copper Hill, Virginia. Arrived in Vietnam in February 1967 and became one of the early replacements in Charlie Company. Served in 2nd Platoon. Was close friends with Butch Eakins, Phil Ferro, and Mike Cramer. Killed in action on July 11, 1967.

Larson, Rollo: From Macon, Georgia. Joined the National Guard in 1952 as an enlisted man. Went to Officer Candidates School in 1963. Became first commander of Charlie Company in 1966. In June of 1967 rotated home. Retired from the military in 1975 and lived in North Carolina, where he worked for a building supply company. Moved to Atlanta to be near his parents and worked for the state of Georgia until he retired on his 65th birthday. Retired to Eatonton, Georgia, where he loves to play golf.

Layman, Ray: Born in Frostburg, Maryland, but raised in Mentor, Ohio. A Charlie Company original who served with 2nd Platoon. Wounded in action on April 23, 1967. After his service Layman returned to Ohio to his wife, June, and a family that came to include two sons, Raymond and Joseph. Worked at a major energy plant in northern Ohio 25 years before moving to a new job at Ameri-gas. Enjoyed bowling, golf, and billiards. Passed away in 2002.

Lerquin, William: Platoon sergeant, 1st Platoon.

Lethcoe, Mike: From Houston; survived polio at the age of eight and was abandoned by his father at 14. Served in 2nd Platoon, Alpha Company. Was walking point when the battle broke out on June 19, 1967. After the war worked as a truck driver before becoming a commercial deep sea diver.

Lilley, Larry: From Lancaster, California. Champion motorcycle rider in high school. Drafted with his friends Kenney Frakes and Tim Johnson. Served in 1st Platoon. After Vietnam took over the family group of motorcycle dealerships.

Lind, Herb: From St Paul, Nebraska. Got his draft notice as a senior in college in 1961 and went to Officer Candidates School. Married Becky during his initial assignments. Took over command of Charlie Company when Rollo Larson rotated home. Retired from the military in 1985. Settled in Manhattan, Kansas, and worked in auto parts before working part time for a local church as a step toward retirement.

Lopez, Mario: Born into a family of migrant workers in Calexico, California. Almost quit school before receiving a lesson in the true nature of hard work from his father. Served in 2nd Platoon. After the war worked for Owens Corning Fiberglass and then for Unocal agricultural products where he rose to the rank of Unit Coordinator, producing fertilizer for crops that provided agricultural workers with employment. Never talked about Vietnam until a 2010 camping trip with his son Mario Jr. Entranced by the stories, Lopez' grandson, Mario III, went looking for information on the internet, and located the 9th Infantry Division website. Lopez attended the 2010 reunion of Charlie Company – the first time he had seen his brothers since 1968.

Lovell, Wayne: First lieutenant and member of the "Long Knives" lift platoon of Delta Troop, helicopters that often ferried the men of Charlie Company into battle. Pilot of the first medevac helicopter that was shot down on June 19.

Lukes, Larry: From Sioux Falls, South Dakota. After high school moved to Fairmont, Nebraska, and worked on farms. Married Kay in December 1966. Served in 3rd Platoon. After the war returned to Nebraska and worked in a factory before taking a position as a truck driver. Now retired and owns 9 acres in the country where his grandchildren can come and play.

McBride, Terry: From Greenfield, California. Had a rural upbringing and loved boxing. Served in 3rd Platoon. In June 1967 wore the ponytail of a VC on his helmet. After the war Greenfield just didn't seem quite the same, so McBride picked up and moved to Alaska. Worked in several "tough" jobs including as a bouncer at a topless bar. McBride married Patti, and enjoys riding motorcycles and fishing, even though he has serious Vietnam-related health problems.

McMillan, Fred: A Charlie Company replacement universally known as Moon Mullins. Served in 1st Platoon. Wounded in action May 15, 1967.

McTear, Willie: From Newellton, Louisiana. Was drafted out of Las Vegas, while also attending school part-time at Southern University. Served in 2nd Platoon. Close friends with Ron Schworer. After Vietnam returned to Las Vegas, got married and had two children. Spent a few years homeless and addicted to drugs, before getting clean and working in California hospitals aiding those with chemical and alcohol dependencies. Now lives in Las Vegas and helps veterans with PTSD.

Maibach, Gary: From Sterling, Ohio. Worked for the local family store and was a member of the Apostolic Christian Church. Married Mary and had one child before departing for Vietnam. Was a conscientious objector, and joined 1st Platoon of Charlie Company as a medic. After returning home eventually took over the family business, helped to raise a family of four children, and became a minister in the Apostolic Christian Church of America. Is especially involved in veteran outreach.

Marr, Joe: From Warrensburg, Missouri. After high school did not find a job to his liking and chose to join the military along with three of his friends in 1958. Married Edna and had one son before departing for Vietnam. Platoon sergeant, 3rd Platoon, Charlie Company. Wounded in action on June 1, 1967. Got out of the military shortly after returning from Vietnam. Eventually went into the trucking business with his brother, and is still working in the same job.

Miller, Jimmy: From the hill country of Tennessee. Served in 1st Platoon. Wounded in action on June 19, 1967.

Moede, Steve: From Encino, California. Sent off the infamous "letter" during training at Fort Riley. Served as a squad leader in 2nd Platoon. After the war worked in the Los Angeles Police Department, rising to the rank of captain. Passed away in 2006.

Morgan, Lance*: Fictitious name for the soldier who served in 1st Platoon who froze up during the battle on May 15, 1967.

Morgan, Larry: Member of 1st Platoon. Wounded in action on June 19, 1967.

Nall, James: From Fairfield, Alabama, where he wanted to be the next Willie Mays. Moved to Los Angeles to live with his sister and worked for the US Post Office before being drafted. Served in 1st Platoon. Wounded in action after being infused to the 5th Battalion, 60th Infantry. After returning from Vietnam went back to work for the post office in Los Angeles where he worked for another 34 years.

Nelson, Charlie: From the Navajo reservation in Arizona and later moved to Los Angeles with his parents. Served in 1st Platoon, often as a mailman due to the fear that he could be mistaken for a Viet Cong. Talked his way into serving in the field with his brothers. Wounded in action on May 15, 1967. After the war tried living in Los Angeles, but returned to the reservation to deal with issues arising from the war. Now lives the simple life of a farmer.

Northcott, Richard: From Encino, California, where he loved to surf and race hotrods. Served in 4th Platoon. After the war worked with Lockheed for 41 years, working with Bill Reynolds and not even knowing it until the two reconnected as part of the Charlie Company reunion process.

O'Gara, Mike: Had grown up a typical Midwestern kid and gave college a try while figuring out what was next. Went to school only part time because he also needed to hold down a job, resulting in draft eligibility. Served in 2nd Platoon. After the war finished college, held down a good job, got married and raised a family. Today enjoys time in his cabin and with his grandchildren.

Peterson, Don: From Arroyo Grande, California. After high school worked with his father painting houses before marrying Jacque, who followed him to Fort Riley. Son Jimmy was born just before Peterson shipped out to Vietnam. Killed in action on May 15, 1967. Jacque remarried and separated from the Peterson family. All were reunited when Jimmy was a teenager and learned of his real father. Jacque works as a Licensed Vocational Nurse. Jimmy first tried a stint in the US Navy before working in the music business.

Rademacher, Jim: From Fowler, Michigan. Kept up a steady stream of letters to his sweetheart, Mary Ann, after his departure for Vietnam.

Charlie Company replacement, arriving in June 1967. Served in 2nd Platoon. Wounded in action on June 19, 1967. Returned home to marry Mary Ann.

Radowenchuk, Walter: From Lakewood, Ohio, near Cleveland. Son of Ukrainian immigrants. Had a short stint in junior college before being drafted. Served in 2nd Platoon. Wounded in action on June 19, 1967. After Vietnam returned home and worked for the phone company until his retirement in 2003. Married Carol and had two children.

Ramos, Forrest: From Wapato, Washington, where he often worked in the fields with his father as a hop thrower. Served in 3rd Platoon, where he was known as one of Charlie Company's top pranksters. Killed in action on June 19, 1967. His younger brother, Jesse, followed Forrest to Vietnam and served in the 101st Airborne Division.

Reed, Bill: Second son of a family of four from Lancaster, California. After high school enrolled part time at a junior college and worked several part time jobs. A Charlie Company original who served with 1st Platoon. After three months in Vietnam doctors removed him from the field for medical reasons. Reed kept trying to return to the field to be with his Charlie Company buddies, but doctors kept him from combat until he was infused to the 2nd Battalion, 60th Infantry. After the war went to college and received a Masters Degree in business and had a successful career with Lockheed Martin, retiring at age 55.

Reeves, Robert: Commander of Alpha Company, 4th of the 47th. Lost much of his command in the battle of June 19, 1967. Later took over command of Alpha Company, 2nd Battalion, 60th Infantry. Killed in action on February 21, 1968.

Renert, Marty: Raised in Fairlawn, New Jersey and was a varsity wrestler in high school. Went to college at Rutgers, but transferred to UCLA, which necessitated sitting out for a year. With deferment gone, volunteered for the draft. Served in 1st Platoon in Vietnam. In May 1967 was reassigned to a postal unit and remained in the military until 1970. Later was readmitted to UCLA, where he studied economics, while also working part time and helping to raise two children, John and Joey. Went to work for the City of Los Angeles where he rose to the position of Director of Administrative Services for the Los Angeles Water System. After retirement in 1998, worked as a volunteer for the Court Appointed Special Advocates of Orange County, California.

Reynolds, Bill: Lived in Texas and Australia before settling in the San Fernando Valley of California. Worked at General Motors and went to community college before being drafted. Served as a squad leader in 2nd Platoon. Wounded in action on June 19, 1967. After the war worked at Lockheed and has been instrumental in setting up the website of the 9th Infantry Division and in the development of Charlie Company reunions.

Reynolds, Ronnie: From Malvern, Arkansas, where his father worked for a local shoe company. Served in 2nd Platoon. Wounded in action on August 16, 1967. Returned home on 80 percent disability due to his wounds. Married in 1969 and had two children. Worked for Alcoa on mining equipment. Since the war has had an additional 150 small pieces of shrapnel removed from his body.

Rhodes, Dusty: US Navy commander who took his monitor gunship up a tiny stream to aid Charlie Company in the battle of June 19, 1967.

Rice, Cameron: Member of 4th Platoon. Killed in action on June 19, 1967.

Richards, Alan: From Mequon, Wisconsin. Raised as part of a family of nine, his father passed away when he was too young to remember. Served in 4th Platoon. Wounded in action on June 1, 1967, and on October 6, 1967. After the war worked in management in a machine shop in Wisconsin prior to opening his own business, from which he retired in 2007. Serves as state commander for the American Legion.

Riley, Bill: From Tell City, Indiana. Worked on farms but wanted to be a welder. Moved to North Hollywood before being drafted. Served in 3rd Platoon. Wounded in action on June 19, 1967. After the war returned to Indiana where he first worked in mining and then as a road crew boss in the prison system. Retired in 2006 and now enjoys fishing and golf.

Robin, David: Member of 4th Platoon. Killed in action on June 19, 1967.

Rubio, Richard: From Canoga Park, California, where his father worked as a foreman on a local ranch. Was a high school classmate of Fred Kenney. Served in 3rd Platoon, where he was especially close to Forrest Ramos. Returned home to California and worked for Schlitz Brewing Company, got married and had three children. Retired and teaching golf at the El Caballero Country Club.

Sachs, Robert: Served in 3rd Platoon. Wounded in action on June 1, 1967.

Salazar, Jimmie: From Austin, Texas. Married Aurora before departing for Vietnam. Served in 2nd Platoon. After the war returned to Texas where he worked for the Lower Colorado River Authority. Suffered from PTSD and heart disease, but he and Aurora fought through the hard times and reconnected with Charlie Company.

Sauceda, Jose: Son of Mexican immigrants, raised in Mercedes, Texas. Was a migrant worker growing up and later took a job at a General Motors plant in Michigan. Before departing for Vietnam married his sweetheart Noemi, who gave birth to the couple's first child, Belinda, early during Charlie Company's tour in Vietnam. Served in 3rd Platoon. After Vietnam went to college first in Texas and then in Michigan before becoming a teacher in migrant camps. Worked his way through various jobs before becoming the head of housekeeping for 83 Lord and Taylor stores, working out of New York. He and Noemi had two more children, Jose Junior and Omar, both of whom sadly passed away. Retired back to Mercedes, and Vietnam remains a major part of his life.

Schulman, Sheldon: From Chicago, Illinois where he graduated from South Shore High School. Married Fern Davidson before enlisting in the Army and attending Officer Candidate School. Remained behind when Charlie Company deployed to deal with complications from the birth of his son, Michael. Served as platoon leader of 4th Platoon in Charlie Company and was killed in battle on June 19, 1967. After Schulman's death, Fern moved to Florida to work as a travel agent. She married twice more and had another child, Marnie. In a 2004 ceremony Fern received the military decorations awarded to her late husband. The family gave the medals to Fred Rosenberg to display in his home, where they hang to this day. Fern passed away in 2011 after a battle with cancer.

Schwan, Frank: From a Hungarian neighborhood in Cleveland. After high school worked in a factory and loved to hang around in pool halls. Served in 2nd Platoon. Wounded in action on July 11, 1967, with he and Henry Hubbard having to evade Viet Cong patrols at night. After the war worked for Ohio Bell until his retirement in 2000. Now enjoys hunting and fishing, though his wounds sustained in Vietnam still bother him from time to time.

Schworer, Ron: Born in 1946; grew up in Lancaster, California and Las Vegas, Nevada. With a strained family life leading to a great sense of self reliance, Ron was an exceptional intellect, excelling in mathematics and the study of computers. Had formed a computer programming company with two of his friends before being drafted. Served in 2nd Platoon and was especially close to Willie McTear. Was declared missing in action on April 8, 1967 and later presumed dead. Ronald Schworer's remains were never recovered.

Sclimenti, John: From the San Fernando Valley of California. Excelled in gymnastics in high school, where he also served as class vice president. Served in 1st Platoon. Rescued Charlie Nelson from the battlefield on May 15, 1967. After the war worked for L-3 Communications, married, and had three children.

Scott, Enoch: From Texas. Served in 1st Platoon. Wounded in action on May 15, 1967.

Searcy, Ted: From Portland, Tennessee. Dropped out of school in the 9th grade, and enlisted in the army in 1959 to avoid trouble with the law. Out of the service from 1962 to 1964. Served as a sergeant in 2nd Platoon. Wounded in action on June 19, 1967. Retired from the military in 1972. Got heavily involved with drugs and alcohol. In 1978 found religion, got clean, and turned his life around. Has been preaching and working as a carpenter ever since.

Segaster, Joel: A Charlie Company replacement in July 1967. Served in 1st Platoon. Wounded in action on July 29, 1967.

Shires, Clarence: From Chesapeake, Virginia. Got married in 1962 and had a child, but a divorce changed his draft status. Took Charlie the Cat to Vietnam. Served in 1st Platoon, wounded in action on July 11, 1967. Returned home and married Loretta in 1970. Worked as a management analyst for the Department of the Navy for 34 years.

Slaughter, Sam: Leader of a Crusader Fire Team of Delta Troop, 3rd Squadron, 5th Armored Cavalry, which often provided fire support to troops of the Mobile Riverine Force, notably on the battle of June 19.

Smith, George: Squad leader in 2nd Platoon. Led the squad that first made contact in the battle of July 11, 1967. Killed in action on July 11, 1967.

Smith, James (Smitty): From Shaker Heights, Ohio, where he lettered in three high school sports. Attended college in business administration, but his grades didn't hold out and he was drafted. Served in 3rd Platoon. Wounded in action on May 15, 1967, and by a booby trap in August. After the war returned to Ohio, got married in 1973 and worked in many jobs, including working at Southwest

Airlines. Is heavily involved in the Veterans of Foreign Wars (VFW) and volunteers at hospitals.

Smith, Robert (Smitty): From North Carolina. Mess sergeant for Charlie Company, who also ran a perpetual poker game. Served in the military for nearly 30 years. Married with four children. Passed away in 2008.

Spain, Kirby: From Danville, Arkansas, where he was brought up on a farm. After his father passed away when he was 18, Kirby worked for International Harvester in East Moline, Illinois. Served in 1st Platoon. Wounded in action on April 8, 1967. Later re-enlists. After the war had several jobs, including as a crop duster before becoming a long-haul trucker.

Stancil, Wayne: From rural eastern North Carolina, Stancil had turned down a draft deferment and became one of the first replacements to join Charlie Company. Served in 1st Platoon and was wounded in battle on April 18, 1967. After recuperation Stancil was reassigned to an artillery unit where he had a run in with an officer who demanded that he not wear his Combat Infantryman Badge. After his service, Stancil worked for Orkin Pest Control, got divorced and remarried, and helped to raise a "flock of young 'uns and a house full of grand young 'uns." Now retired, Stancil works to help veterans who suffer from PTSD.

Stephens, Jim: From Morro Bay, California. After his mother left the family in 1958, his father was left to raise five children alone, resulting in some of the Stephens siblings being taken into foster care. After graduation from high school in 1965, Jim went to work for a local Sunland Gas Station to try to get a grip on what he wanted to do in life. Was drafted and served with 1st Platoon of Charlie Company. In October 1967 Stephens was transferred to the 3rd of the 39th within the 9th Infantry Division, after which he was badly wounded by a mortar round. After recuperation went to work for the California Department of Corrections and later into business with is brother. Vietnam remains a constant presence in his life; not a day goes by without him thinking back on the war.

Stephenson, Jim: From rural Marceline, Missouri. Worked for the Santa Fe Railroad and for Ozark Airlines before being drafted. Got married while on leave from training. Served in 1st Platoon. Located Don Peterson's body on May 15, 1967. Wounded in action on May 15, 1967. Infused after June 19, 1967. Went back to work for Ozark Air, which was later bought out by TWA and then American Airlines. Retired in 2002 after suffering a heart attack.

Taylor, Elijah: From Highbank, Texas, where he worked on cotton fields until his family moved to Dallas. Worked at the US Post Office before being drafted. Served as a medic with 3rd Platoon. Infused in August 1967. Returned to work in the Dallas post office from which he retired in 2004. Married with three daughters, one of whom served in the Persian Gulf War.

Thomas, Ray: From the rural Choctaw reservation in Newton County, Mississippi. One of seven children; father drove the bus for the local tribal school, where they were not allowed to speak their native language. Went to junior college before being drafted. An early Charlie Company replacement, arriving in May 1967 to serve in 1st Platoon. Wounded in action on March 8, 1968. After the war worked for the tribe and later in a government post. Married Ruby and had three daughters and one son.

Thompson, Sam*: Fictitious name for the lieutenant who took temporary command of 1st Platoon, leading it into battle on May 15, 1967. Also led 3rd Platoon into a minefield while on temporary command of that unit during August 1967. By happenstance turned up at one of Charlie Company's first postwar reunions.

Trcka, Don: From League City, Texas. Was the only student in high school to letter in all four major sports for all four years. Served in 3rd Platoon. Wounded in action on May 15, 1967. Dropped over 100 pounds while recuperating in the hospital. Married his sweetheart Beverly after getting out of the military. Moved to Houston where he worked as a director with a major auto sales firm from which he retired in 2006. He and Beverly now boast six children and 11 grandchildren.

Tutwiler, Guy: From Birmingham, Alabama. Drafted into the military in 1943 and went to Officer Candidates School. Served as a platoon leader in the 41st Infantry Division in the Philippines during World War II. Served as a company commander in the 2nd Infantry Division during the Korean War. Was a lieutenant colonel and served as commander of the 4th Battalion of the 47th Infantry (the parent unit of Charlie Company) during 1967. Retired from the military in 1976 and lived in Auburn, Alabama. Passed away in 2006.

Varskafsky, Bill: From Bremerton, Washington. Worked in a shipyard and got married before being drafted. His daughter was born the day that Charlie Company landed in Vietnam. Served in 2nd Platoon. After the war, returned to shipbuilding for the navy and retired in 2001 as Assistant Business Manager. Divorced his first wife three years after returning home, and two years later began a second marriage. He and his new wife, Cindy, now have seven grandchildren and one great-grandchild.

Vidovic, Ron: From Tacoma, Washington. Dropped out of school in the tenth grade and worked in a gas station. Got married at age 19, had two children, and worked in a cabinet making factory before getting divorced. Served in 3rd Platoon. Was close friends with Tim Fischer. Wounded in action in August 1967, losing a leg. Returned to Tacoma and worked for 20 years with a company that manufactures school furniture, until the job became too physically demanding. Then worked for the Tacoma School District in custodial services. Married Rosemary in 1982.

West, David*: Fictitious name for a squad leader in 3rd Platoon who broke down in battle on May 15, 1967.

Wilson, Doug: From Huntington Beach, California. Went to community college, but surfed too much and dropped out, resulting in being drafted. Served in 1st Platoon. Kept a diary while in Vietnam. Along with John Bauler carried Don Peterson's body from the battlefield on May 15, 1967. Was infused at the end of May 1967. After the war spent some time in the California redwoods before going to college and receiving a plant science degree. Managed a ranch for one of the biggest Kiwi planters in the country before becoming a grower-packer-shipper in his own right. Married Linda and still runs his very successful business.

Wilson, Ralph: From Andover Township, New Jersey where he lived on Lake Iliff and dreamed of growing up to own a bait and tackle shop. Came to 1st Platoon of Charlie Company as a replacement in May 1967. Wounded in battle on June 19, 1967. After the war went back to work in construction while dealing with issues stemming from his combat experience. Had two children, both boys, and moved to Williston, Florida. Retired in 2006.

Windmiller, Bernie: From Gary, Indiana. Was drafted in 1954 and served his hitch in the military before going to seminary and becoming a minister in the Evangelical Covenant Church of America. Married Esther and served as a chaplain in 2nd Brigade of the 9th Infantry

Division. Helped care for the wounded in the battle of June 19, 1967. Rose to the rank of colonel before his retirement from the military in 1992. Worked in various interim positions in the Evangelical Covenant Church and became Executive Director of the Board of the International Association of Evangelical Chaplains, working to train chaplains all over the world.

Winters, John: Member of 4th Platoon. Killed in action on June 19, 1967.

Young, John: From Saint Paul, Minnesota. Went to college, but felt John F. Kennedy's call to generational service and enlisted in the military. Served as a squad leader in 1st Platoon. Wounded in action on June 19, 1967. After the war held down many jobs before re-enlisting in the military. Was discharged in 1982 for PTSD. Got off alcohol in 1985 and received treatment for PTSD for the first time in 1993. John now resides in Picayune, Mississippi. In 1996 agreed to meet with a group of college students to discuss Vietnam, and this book was born.

BIBLIOGRAPHY

ORAL INTERVIEWS

Extensive oral interviews with veterans of Charlie Company and their family members form the bedrock source for this work. The recordings of the interviews are now open to use by researchers and are housed in the Center for Oral History and Cultural Heritage at the University of Southern Mississippi. Written interviews are also open for research purposes and, along with copies of other relevant primary source material, are housed in the McCain Library and Archives at the University of Southern Mississippi.

Interviews

Charlie Company Headquarters: Crockett, Company First Sergeant Lynn; Larson, Captain Rollo; Lind, Captain Herb; Lind, Becky (spouse); Windmiller, Chaplain Bernard.

1st Platoon: Acevedo, Benjamin; Bomann, Jacque (Don Peterson's wife); Cortright, Carl; Dennison, James; Eisenbaugh, Bob; Hartman, Ernie; Hartman, Jeannie (spouse); Hunt, Lynn (platoon leader); Huntsman, Karen (spouse); Huntsman, Steve; Inada, Ron; Jarczewski, Dave; Lilley, Larry; Maibach, Gary; Nall, James; Nelson, Charlie; Peterson, Jimmy (Don Peterson's son); Peterson, Rich (Don Peterson's brother); Reed, Bill; Renert, Marty; Sclimenti, John; Shires, Clarence;

Spain, Kirby; Stancil, Wayne; Stephens, Jim; Stephenson, Jim; Thomas, Ray; Wilson, Doug; Wilson, Ralph; Young, John.

2nd Platoon: Benedick, Jack (platoon leader); Burleson, Henry; Casares, Idoluis; Cockerell, Stan; Cramer, Mike; Ehlet, Bob; Emmerson, Jeanne (Ron Schworer's sister); French, Kaye (spouse); French, Robert; Geier, Bernice (Bill Geier's mother); Geier, Bob (Bill Geier's brother); Harvey, Gene; Hawley, Diane (Phil Ferro's sister); Kerr, Daniel; Lopez, Mario; McTear, Willie; O'Gara, Mike, Rademacher, James; Radowenchuk, Walter; Reynolds, Bill; Reynolds, Ronnie; Salazar, Aurora (spouse); Salazar, Jimmie; Schwan, Frank; Schworer, Dan (Ron Schworer's brother); Searcy, Ted; Varskafsky, Bill.

3rd Platoon: Bradfield, John; Caliari, Tony; Conroy, Tom; Conroy, Vivian (spouse); Fischer, Tim; Hill, Barbara (Fred Kenney's wife); Hopper, Steve; Howell, John; Johnston, Jace; Kenney, Susan (Fred Kenney's sister); Lukes, Larry; Marr, Edna (spouse); Marr, Joe; McBride, Terry; Ramos, Jesse (Forrest Ramos' brother); Riley, Bill; Rubio, Richard; Sauceda, Jose; Smith, James; Stone, Joanne (Tim Johnson's sister); Taylor, Elijah; Trcka, Don; Vidovic, Ron; Vidovic, Rosemary (spouse).

4th Platoon: Fadden, Paris; Gann, Ronnie; Northcott, Richard; Richards, Alan; Rosenberg, Fred (friend of Sheldon Schulman).

Alpha Company: Lethcoe, Mike.

Delta Troop (Air Cavalry), 3rd Squadron, 5th Armored Cavalry: Kayser, Evans; Lovell, Wayne.

PERSONAL PAPERS

Several Charlie Company veterans have been kind enough to share their personal papers (including letters, diaries, pictures, notebooks, and writings) with the author, a collection that forms a major source for this work. The papers (some of which are restricted by agreement with the donor) are now housed in the McCain Library and Archives at the University of Southern Mississippi.

Personal Paper Collections
Benedick; James; Dennison, James; Fischer, Tim; Geier, Bob (a collection of his brother Bill Geier's papers); Harvey, Gene; Hopper, Steve; Nelson, Charlie; Rademacher, James; Reynolds, Bill; Shires, Clarence; Wilson, Doug; Windmiller, Bernard; Young, John.

Other Collections

In the digital age, several important websites have become repositories for documents of all types. Of the most importance to this work was the website founded and administered by Bill Reynolds, one of the Charlie Company originals, located at http://www.9thinfantrydivision. com. The site is dedicated to the 4th Battalion, 47th Infantry, and contains a myriad of documents ranging from pictures, to personal accounts of battles, to reports from hometown newspapers. The website is a goldmine for researchers. Also of value were the websites of the 9th Infantry Division at http://9thinfdivsociety.org, an organization for riverine veterans at http://www.rivervet.com, and the Mobile Riverine Force association at http://www.mrfa.org.

PRIMARY SOURCE MATERIAL

3rd Battalion, 47th Infantry, 2nd Brigade, 9th Infantry Division, After Action Reports, February–December 1967. RG 472, United States Army in Vietnam. National Archives and Record Center, College Park.

4th Battalion, 47th Infantry, 2nd Brigade, 9th Infantry Division, After Action Reports, February–December 1967. RG 472, United States Army in Vietnam. National Archives and Record Center, College Park.

4th Battalion, 47th Infantry, 2nd Brigade, 9th Infantry Division, Operations Orders, February–December 1967. RG 472, United States Army in Vietnam. National Archives and Record Center, College Park.

9th Infantry Division, Asst Chief of Staff G-2, Operations Planning Files, 1967. RG 472, United States Army in Vietnam, Box 1. National Archives and Record Center, College Park.

9th Infantry Division, Asst Chief of Staff S-3, Daily Journal, 1967. RG 472, United States Army in Vietnam, Box 2–6. National Archives and Record Center, College Park.

9th Infantry Division, Asst Chief of Staff S-3, Operations Report, Lessons Learned, 1966–1967. RG 472, United States Army in Vietnam, Box 1. National Archives and Record Center, College Park.

9th Infantry Division, 2nd Brigade, Asst Chief of Staff S-3, Operations Report, Lessons Learned, 1968–1969. RG 472, United States Army in Vietnam, Box 1. National Archives and Record Center, College Park.

9th Infantry Division, 2nd Brigade, Organizational History, 1966–1969, RG 472, United States Army in Vietnam, Box 1.

BIBLIOGRAPHY

National Archives and Record Center, College Park.

9th Infantry Division, 2nd Brigade, Asst Chief of Staff S-3, After Action Reports, 1967–1968. RG 472, United States Army in Vietnam, Box 1. National Archives and Record Center, College Park.

"Base in the Swamps," 1967, Douglas Pike Collection, Unit 02, Military Operations. The Vietnam Archive, Texas Tech University.

"Benewah Bulletin," Joy Wilkerson Collection. The Vietnam Archive, Texas Tech University.

Charlie Company, 4th Battalion, 47th Infantry, Morning Reports, 1967. Author's Collection.

Clark, Paul W. "Riverine Operations in the Delta." CHECO Report 67, US Air Force, 1968. The Vietnam Archive, Texas Tech University.

Headquarters, United States Army in Vietnam Command Historian, After Action Reports. RG 472, United States Army in Vietnam, Box 23. National Archives and Record Center, College Park.

Ninth Infantry Division. The Old Reliable. (Divisional newspaper). Author's Collection.

Octofoil. A quarterly magazine published by the 9th Infantry Division. January–December, 1967. Author's Collection.

Order of Battle Study 66–44, VC Tactical Use of Inland Waterways in South Vietnam, 1965–1966. The Vietnam Archive, Texas Tech University.

Professional Knowledge Gained from Amphibious Experience in South Vietnam, 1968. Arthur Price Collection. The Vietnam Archive, Texas Tech University.

Riverine Warfare – Field Manual, 1971. Glenn Helm Collection. The Vietnam Archive, Texas Tech University.

Rung Sat Special Zone Intelligence Study, 1966. The Vietnam Archive, Texas Tech University.

US Naval Forces in Vietnam, Monthly Historical Summaries, February–December 1967. The Vietnam Archive, Texas Tech University.

SECONDARY SOURCES

9th Infantry Division: "Old Reliables," (Paducah, KY: Turner Publishing, 2000).

Appy, Christian, *Working-Class War: American Combat Soldiers and Vietnam* (Chapel Hill: University of North Carolina Press, 1993).

Atkinson, Rick, *The Long Gray Line: The American Journey of West Point's Class of 1966* (Boston: Houghton Mifflin Company, 1989).

Christopher, Ralph, *Duty, Honor, Sacrifice: Brown Water Sailors and Army River Raiders* (Bloomington, IN: AuthorHouse, 2007).

Clarke, Jeffrey J., *Advice and Support: The Final Years* (Washington: Center of Military History, 1988).

Croizat, Victor, *The Brown Water Navy: The River and Coastal War in Indo-China and Vietnam, 1948–1972* (Poole, UK: Blandford Press, 1984).

Cutler, Thomas, *Brown Water, Black Berets: Coastal and Riverine Warfare in Vietnam* (Annapolis: Naval Institute Press, 1988).

Dunnavent, R. Blake, *Brown Water Warfare: The U.S. Navy in Riverine Warfare and the Emergence of a Tactical Doctrine, 1775–1970* (Gainesville: University Press of Florida, 2003).

Elliott, David, *The Vietnamese War: Revolution and Social Change in the Mekong Delta, 1930–1975* (Armonk, NY: M.E. Sharpe, 2003).

Fitzgerald, Frances, *Fire in the Lake: The Vietnamese and the Americans in Vietnam* (New York: Random House, 1972).

Forbes, John and Robert Williams, *The Illustrated History of the Vietnam War: Riverine Force* (New York: Bantam, 1987).

Fulton, Major General William, *Vietnam Studies: Riverine Operations, 1966–1969* (Washington, D.C.: Department of the Army, 1985).

Gargan, Edward, *The River's Tale: A Year on the Mekong* (New York: Alfred A. Knopf, 2002).

Gregory, Barry, *Vietnam Coastal and Riverine Forces* (Wellingborough, UK: Patrick Stevens, 1988).

Hackworth, Colonel David, Steel My Soldiers' Hearts (New York: Simon & Schuster, 2002).

Hunt, Major General Ira, *The 9th Infantry Division in Vietnam: Unparalleled and Unequaled* (Lexington: University Press of Kentucky, 2010).

Jenkins, E. H., *A History of the French Navy: From its Beginnings to the Present Day* (London: Macdonald and Jane's, 1973).

Karnow, Stanley, *Vietnam: A History* (New York: Viking, 1983).

Kinard, Douglas, *The Certain Trumpet: Maxwell Taylor and the American Experience in Vietnam* (London: Brassey's, 1991).

Koburger, Charles, *The French Navy in Indochina: Riverine and Coastal Forces, 1945–1954* (New York: Praeger, 1991).

Kolko, Gabriel, *Anatomy of a War: Vietnam, the United States, and the Modern Historical Experience* (New York: Pantheon Books, 1985).

Krepinevich, Andrew, Jr, *The Army in Vietnam* (Baltimore: Johns Hopkins University Press, 1986).

BIBLIOGRAPHY

McAbee, Ronald, *River Rats: Brown Water Navy, U.S. Naval Mobile Riverine Operations, Vietnam* (Honoribus Press, 2001).

MacGarrigle, George, *Combat Operations. Taking the Offensive: October 1966 to October 1967* (Washington, D.C.: Center of Military History, 1998).

Maraniss, David, *They Marched Into Sunlight: War and Peace, Vietnam and America, October 1967* (New York: Simon & Schuster, 2003).

Marolda, Edward and Oscar Fitzgerald, *The United States Navy and the Vietnam Conflict, Vol. 2, From Military Assistance to Combat, 1959–1965* (Washington: Naval Historical Center, 1986).

Military History Institute of Vietnam, *Victory in Vietnam: The Official History of the People's Army of Vietnam, 1954–1975*, Translated by Merle L. Pribbenow (Lawrence: University Press of Kansas, 2002).

Mobile Riverine Force. America's Mobile Riverine Force in Vietnam (Paducah, KY: Turner Publishing, 2005).

Moore, Harold and Joseph Galloway, *We Were Soldiers Once ... and Young: Ia Drang, the Battle that Changed the War in Vietnam* (New York: Random House, 1992).

Moyar, Mark, *Triumph Forsaken: The Vietnam War, 1954–1965* (New York: Cambridge University Press, 2006).

Nguyen Thi Dieu, *The Mekong River and the Struggle for Indochina: Water, War, and Peace* (Westport, CT: Praeger, 1999).

Prados, John, *Vietnam: The History of an Unwinnable War, 1945–1975* (Lawrence: University Press of Kansas, 2009).

Race, Jeffrey, *War Comes to Long An* (Berkeley: University of California Press, 1972).

Schreadley, R.L., *From the Rivers to the Sea: The U.S. Navy in Vietnam* (Annapolis: Naval Institute Press, 1992).

Sharp, Admiral U.S.G., *Strategy for Defeat: Vietnam in Retrospect* (Novato, CA: Presidio, 1978).

Sheehan, Neil, *A Bright Shining Lie: John Paul Vann and America in Vietnam* (New York: Random House, 1988).

Sorley, Lewis, *The Vietnam War: An Assessment by South Vietnam's Generals* (Lubbock: Texas Tech University Press, 2010).

Stanton, Shelby, *The Rise and Fall of an American Army: U.S. Ground Forces in Vietnam, 1965–1973* (Novato, CA: Presidio, 1985).

Uhlig, Frank, ed., *Vietnam: The Naval Story* (Annapolis: Naval Institute Press, 1986).

Westmoreland, William, *A Soldier Reports* (New York: Doubleday, 1976).

Wiest, Andrew, *The Vietnam War, 1956–1975* (Oxford: Osprey Publishing, 2002).

Wiest, Andrew, Vietnam: *A View from the Front Lines* (Oxford: Osprey Publishing, 2013).

Wiest, Andrew, *Vietnam's Forgotten Army: Heroism and Betrayal in the ARVN* (New York: NYU Press, 2008).

Articles
Baker, John and Lee C. Dickson, "Army Forces in Riverine Operations," *Military Review* 47 (August 1967), 64–74.

Dagle, Dan, "The Mobile Riverine Force, Vietnam," *U.S. Naval Institute Proceedings* 95 (January 1969), 126–128.

House, Jonathan, "Into Indian Country," *Vietnam* (April, 1990), 39–44.

Naval History Division, "Riverine Warfare: The U.S. Navy's Operations on Inland Waters," Navy Department, 1969.

Smith, Albert C., Jr, "Rung Sat Special Zone, Vietnam's Mekong Delta," *U.S. Naval Institute Proceedings* 94 (April 1968), 116–121.

Unpublished Secondary Sources
Grau, Reagan, "Waging Brown Water Warfare: The Mobile Riverine Force in the Mekong Delta, 1966–1969," Master of Arts Thesis, Texas Tech University.

ACKNOWLEDGMENTS

Several people have provided me with invaluable help and inspiration over the years of work on this project, and I am forever in their debt. First and foremost I would like to thank the veterans of Charlie Company and their families. These brave men and women welcomed me into their tightly knit group and entrusted me with the stories of their lives, for which I am profoundly grateful. I must, though, single out two members of the Charlie Company family for special thanks. For years Bill Reynolds has served as something of Charlie Company's unofficial historian. The information he has amassed, much of which is available on his 9th Infantry Division website, has been invaluable to my research. Bill also went to great lengths to gather the photos for the book and served as an important sounding board for the entire project. My greatest thanks, though, go to John Young. It was in the tiny VA meeting room all those years ago where John Young, braving his own personal demons, introduced me to Charlie Company. Since that day he has been a constant presence in my classroom at the University of Southern Mississippi – making the hour-long drive to campus from Picayune, Mississippi, at his own expense to tell today's university students about his generation at war in Vietnam. From the beginning of our time together, I realized that I needed to write a book about Charlie

Company, but I didn't quite know how. Through it all, John was there. From going to Vietnam to learn more about the story, to going to Charlie Company reunions, to helping me with the research itself – he was there. John has been my guide through the many twists and turns that led me to and through this project, and I am proud to call him my friend.

I also owe a debt of gratitude to many people for their aid in the archival research for this project. Thanks first to Steve Maxner and his staff at the Vietnam Center and Vietnam Archive at Texas Tech for their help in researching their wonderful collections. I would also like to offer my thanks to Mitchell Yockelson and Richard Boylan for their indispensable aid in navigating the Vietnam records at the National Archives in College Park. During my time at the National Archives, Tim Frank, of Military Research Associates, also provided me with tremendous help and advice. Finally, I would like to thank Albert Moore and Roy Moseman of the Mobile Riverine Force Association, which serves as an important repository for nearly everything having to do with the riverine war in Vietnam.

During my time working on this project, I have been the fortunate recipient of funding from the University of Southern Mississippi, without which this book would not have been possible. In 2008 I received an Aubrey and Ella Ginn Lucas Endowment for Faculty Excellence research award, and in 2009 I was named Charles W. Moorman Distinguished Alumni Professor. The funding associated with these two important honors allowed me to make necessary research trips and to conduct the myriad interviews that form the backbone of this work.

Much of the inspiration for my work on this project came from my initial trip to the battlefield of June 19, 1967, with John Young and a stellar group of students and veterans during the summer of 2000. Courtney and Trang My Frobenius of Vietnam Indochina Tours did so much to make that first trip possible, and Courtney, a veteran of the 9th Infantry Division, has aided my Vietnam education for years. At the University of Southern Mississippi, Tim Hudson (then Dean of International and Continuing Education), Susan Steen, and Frances Sudduth were instrumental in providing the institutional support needed to make the trip happen. Two other veterans accompanied us to

Vietnam that summer, Charles Brown and the late Roy Ainsworth, who also served as real inspirations not only to me but also to my entire class. Also accompanying us on that trip were two PTSD experts who not only were integral to the success of that trip but also to my education concerning the reality of war: Raymond Scurfield, himself a Vietnam veteran, and Leslie Root. I owe Leslie a special debt of gratitude for taking that gamble with my phone call so long ago and for working so closely with me and John Young. Most of all, though, I would like to thank the students who made the Vietnam 2000 trip possible: Alice Archer, Danielle Bishop, Cheri Bolton, Trista Boudreaux, Patricia Buzard Boyett, Scott Catino, Janet Graham, Yaron Kaplan, John Littlejohn, Lana Lohrer, Martin Loicano, Shane Jones, Erin McNeely, Adam Ray, and Terry Whittington.

One of the wonderful things about working at the University of Southern Mississippi is the congenial atmosphere. I am indeed lucky to work with so many good friends who are so encouraging and free with their time. Several of my colleagues took time out of their busy schedules to read and offer comments on my manuscript, including Heather Stur, Susannah Ural, and Kyle Zelner. It was our department chair, Phyllis Jestice, though, who read the manuscript down to the final misplaced comma, adorning my text with a sea of pink ink along the way, providing invaluable comments that added significantly to the final product. I also owe my thanks to Steven Moser and Lashonda Thompson in the dean's office in the College of Arts and Letters for all of their help. I would also like to thank the students of my Vietnam War Historiography seminar, all of whom read the manuscript in one of its earlier incarnations and offered valuable advice: Colin Colbourn, Jason Engle, Matthew McGrew, Nancy Nicholls, and Robert Thompson.

A wide range of scholars and friends have helped me in rather more general ways through the life of this project, providing help and encouragement in settings that ranged from London pubs to internet chats. For their help in this regard I would like to thank (in no particular order): Glenn Robins, Jeff Bowersox, Ruth Percy, Geoff Jensen, Brian O'Neil, Ralph Ashby, Gary Sheffield, Sean McKnight, Michael Neiberg, Richard McCarthy, Pete Edwards, Mike Roberts, Kim Herzinger, Wayde Benson, Sean and Mary Beth

Farrell, Lewis Sorley, Jim Willbanks, Dennis Showalter, Kathy Barbier, Tom Ward, Jason Stewart, Michael Doidge, John Csaszar, Paul Harris, John Van Sant, Ron Milam, Andrew Haley, William Scarborough, Doug Mackaman, and John Kuehn.

As always I would like to thank the indispensable administrative assistant of the History Department of the University of Southern Mississippi, Shelia Smith, for her help and friendship over the years. I would also like to thank Deborah Gershenowitz for helping me to become a much better author and my agent Tom Wallace for his invaluable work in helping this project find the right publishing home.

Finally I offer my thanks to all of the wonderful folks at Osprey Publishing who took a gamble on this project and have done so much to help me make it better, especially Kate Moore and Marcus Cowper (publishers), Emily Holmes (project editor), Julie Frederick (copyeditor), and John Tintera.

My greatest thanks, though, are reserved for my wonderful wife Jill and our beautiful children Abigail, Luke, and Wyatt. They make every day a blessing.

DEDICATION

This book is dedicated to the Boys of '67 who lost their lives in Vietnam.

If you ever find yourself at the Vietnam Veterans Memorial, pause to remember these young men as they once were.

Name	Panel	Line	KIA Date
Alaniz, Benito	16	109	March 19, 1967
Schworer, Ronald	49	015	April 10, 1967
Black, Charles	18	021	April 13, 1967
Peterson, Donald	20	003	May 15, 1967
Cara, Robert	22	010	June 19, 1967
Geier, William	22	012	June 19, 1967
Fink, Hubert	22	012	June 19, 1967
Frakes, Kenneth	22	012	June 19, 1967
Jindra, Robert	22	014	June 19, 1967
Johnson, Timothy	22	014	June 19, 1967
Ramos, Forrest	22	027	June 19, 1967
Rice, Cameron	22	018	June 19, 1967
Robin, David	22	018	June 19, 1967
Schulman, Sheldon	22	019	June 19, 1967
Winters, John	22	022	June 19, 1967
Eakins, Marion	23	050	July 11, 1967

Name	Panel	Line	KIA Date
Ferro, Phillip	23	051	July 11, 1967
Kenney, Elmer	23	052	July 11, 1967
King, Harold	23	052	July 11, 1967
Smith, George	23	053	July 11, 1967
Bridges, Cecil	24	016	July 29, 1967
Sunday, James	27	032	September 29, 1967
Alldridge, Gale	27	056	October 6, 1967
Burkhead, Danny	27	057	October 6, 1967
Davis, Charles	27	058	October 6, 1967
Grizzle, Charles	29	066	November 10, 1967
Hoskins, John	56	009	May 6, 1968

INDEX

INDEX

INDEX

INDEX